# Customer-Driven Marketing

John Frazer-Robinson

# Customer-Driven Marketing

The Ideal Way to Increased Profits through Marketing, Sales and Service Improvement

KOGAN PAGE

## YOURS TO HAVE AND TO HOLD
## BUT NOT TO COPY

The publication you are reading is protected by copyright law. This means that the publisher could take you and your employer to court and claim heavy legal damages if you make unauthorised photocopies from these pages. Photocopying copyright material without permission is no different from stealing a magazine from a newsagent, only it doesn't seem like theft.

The Copyright Licensing Agency (CLA) is an organisation which issues licences to bring photocopying within the law. It has designed licensing services to cover all kinds of special needs in business, education and government.

If you take photocopies from books, magazines and periodicals at work your employer should be licensed with CLA. Make sure you are protected by a photocopying licence.

The Copyright Licensing Agency Limited, 90 Tottenham Court Road, London W1P 0LP. Tel: 0171 436 5931. Fax: 0171 436 3986.

First published in 1997
Reprinted 1998

Apart from any fair dealing for the purposes of research or private study, or criticism or review, as permitted under the Copyright, Designs and Patents Act, 1988, this publication may only be reproduced, stored or transmitted, in any form or by any means, with the prior permission in writing of the publishers, or in the case of reprographic reproduction in accordance with the terms and licences issued by the CLA. Enquiries concerning reproduction outside those terms should be sent to the publishers at the undermentioned address:

Kogan Page Limited
120 Pentonville Road
London N1 9JN

© John Frazer-Robinson, 1997

The right of John Frazer-Robinson to be identified as author of this work has been asserted by him in accordance with the Copyright, Designs and Patents Act 1988.

**British Library Cataloguing in Publication Data**
A CIP record for this book is available from the British Library.
ISBN 0 7494 2418 4

Typeset by Saxon Graphics Ltd, Derby
Printed and bound in Great Britain by Biddles Ltd, Guildford and King's Lynn

# Contents

| | |
|---|---|
| *List of Figures* | 7 |
| *List of Tables* | 9 |
| *Dedication* | 11 |
| *Acknowledgements* | 13 |
| *Prologue* | 15 |

**Part One:**
**Dear Customer...**

| | | |
|---|---|---|
| 1 | The false premise of excellence and quality | 25 |

**Part Two:**
**Backwards to the future**

| | | |
|---|---|---|
| 2 | On your marks | 41 |
| 3 | The marketing environment | 57 |
| 4 | Technology and marketing | 70 |
| 5 | The communications traffic jam | 87 |
| 6 | The media inferno | 98 |
| 7 | Selling has passed its sell-by date | 116 |
| 8 | 'New' marketing is coming | 122 |
| 9 | What will Customers want next? | 143 |
| 10 | Change is upon us | 154 |
| 11 | What will it be like at work? | 170 |
| 12 | Looking back to what's next | 180 |

**Part Three:**
**What's new, what's different?**

| | | |
|---|---|---|
| 13 | The trends that take us to tomorrow | 191 |
| 14 | There's a new kind of client looking for a new kind of agency | 198 |
| 15 | Marketing: the new objectives | 213 |

| 16 | The shepherd? He works in sales | 221 |
| 17 | Listen to me. I'm the buyer! | 231 |
| 18 | I hear you. I'm from sales! | 238 |
| 19 | The concept of granular structures | 243 |

**Part Four:**
**Relationship and integrated marketing**

| 20 | Change: nobody likes it, everybody's doing it | 261 |
| 21 | Getting the right rewards | 276 |
| 22 | The relationship to structure | 290 |
| 23 | How to develop integrated marketing | 298 |
| 24 | The facts and fallacies of customer loyalty | 310 |
| 25 | Here's an instant marketing miracle for you to start now | 326 |

**Part Five:**
**Making your own miracles**

| 26 | Checklists for success | 335 |
| 27 | The should you, shouldn't you bit | 349 |

*Bibliography*   *359*

*Index*   *361*

# List of figures

| | | |
|---|---|---|
| 2.1 | Growth in the CD-ROM market | 45 |
| 2.2 | The spread of ISDN subscribers in Europe | 46 |
| 2.3 | The four-way marketing model | 53 |
| 4.1 | The size of IT team dedicated to marketing (1989) | 72 |
| 4.2 | The size of IT team dedicated to marketing (1995) | 73 |
| 4.3 | The view of IT management on communication skills by internal departments (1995) | 73 |
| 4.4 | IT staff have a poor grasp of the marketing process | 74 |
| 6.1 | Consumer households in the European Union | 99 |
| 6.2 | Net 'reach' of daily newspapers in Europe | 99 |
| 6.3 | Net 'reach' of television (all channels) | 100 |
| 6.4 | European television watching times (all channels) | 100 |
| 6.5 | Average daily newspaper circulation to the mid 1990s | 101 |
| 6.6 | The age structure of Internet users in Europe and the US | 101 |
| 6.7 | Households with cable access to Interactive TV (000) | 102 |
| 6.8 | Western Europe – PCs installed in homes and homes with PCs as a percentage of total homes | 111 |
| 6.9 | Western Europe – PC density in EU countries (1994) | 112 |
| 6.10 | Decreasing local telephone charges – average cost per line (residential) in pounds | 112 |
| 6.11 | Decreasing PC components prices | 113 |
| 6.12 | The estimated numbers of Internet users | 113 |
| 6.13 | Predictions for Internet IP host addresses | 114 |
| 6.14 | PCs with Internet IP addresses in the European Union | 114 |
| 6.15 | Predicted growth of Internet subscribers worldwide | 115 |
| 9.1 | Word of mouth outscores advertising in creating name awareness for motor insurance – and probably most else as well | 146 |
| 9.2 | Internal and external marketing as vehicles for customer service | 152 |
| 11.1 | Gender values and the dominant business culture | 177 |
| 12.1 | Education at work. This figure shows where Britain stood against | |

|      | its competitors in relation to managers with degrees and young people in further education | 185 |
|------|---|---|
| 14.1 | Vertical or horizontal slicing? | 204 |
| 14.2 | The modified hierarchy – the micro-hierarchy within a hierarchy | 207 |
| 14.3 | A common division of labour within a Customer service micro-hierarchy | 207 |
| 19.1 | Customer service units: hierarchies within hierarchies? | 247 |
| 19.2 | Communications decision making must be devolved to the front line | 249 |
| 19.3 | Granular marketing | 252 |
| 19.4 | The marketer and commissioner groups: a total of three teams | 253 |
| 19.5 | The granular marketing banking process | 253 |
| 19.6 | A broadside granular structure | 255 |
| 19.7 | A network granular structure | 256 |
| 20.1 | Developing the organisation through people | 270 |
| 20.2 | Organisational design and performance measures | 270 |
| 20.3 | What makes people tick? | 271 |
| 20.4 | Managerial style and values | 272 |
| 20.5 | The organisation for change requires four groups | 273 |
| 21.1 | The Remuneration Map: different organisational styles have different remuneration systems | 278 |
| 21.2 | An outline job description | 286 |
| 21.3 | Career risk and change are linked to pay | 288 |
| 23.1 | The pyramid of expectation. As customer value increases so does their expectation of service | 303 |
| 23.2 | Actual corporate delivery level (of promise) should be pitched to exceed customers' expectations which vary up and down | 304 |
| 23.3 | Failure! As transactions take place, corporate delivery rises and falls but all below customer expectations | 305 |
| 24.1 | JFR's customer-driven marketing model – a myriad miracles for your business | 315 |
| 24.2 | Customer superformance guarantees repeat sales | 321 |
| 24.3 | Resolving Customers' problems is vital for future business | 321 |
| 24.4 | Effective problem recovery is powerfully good for sales (as well as relationships) | 321 |
| 25.1 | The Focus Game – Part One | 328 |
| 25.2 | The Focus Game – Part Two | 330 |

# List of tables

| | | |
|---|---|---|
| 8.1 | Product/market strategies | 124 |
| 8.2 | Marketing mix strategies | 125 |
| 8.3 | Corporate strategies | 125 |
| 13.1 | The synergy of strategies | 196 |
| 14.1 | Relationship styles and objectives | 208 |
| 16.1 | The three generations of selling | 227 |

# Dedication

This book is dedicated to two personal miracles: first, as they came into my life, my late wife, Julie, who delivered into our cruelly shortened, but wonderful time together, the most exceptional quality in such extraordinary quantity. Julie provided much inspiration and guidance with the work from which this book evolved.

Secondly, it transpired I was to be blessed with another miracle – Elaine. We both share a very real passion for ethical business practices, sound management methods and a belief in change, growth and personal development as a way of business and personal life. We both love our personal achievements to come through helping others to achieve.

Lastly, I would like to include three important younger people, each of whom is a miracle in their own right: my two children, Tracy and Kerry, who have shared the best and worst of me; and Chris, my stepson, completing a magnificent threesome of whom I am infinitely proud and caring, and all of whom I love and appreciate very much.

Elaine, Julie, Tracy, Kerry and Chris, I thank and treasure you all for your greatly valued love, support and understanding.

# Acknowledgements

*Pip Mosscrop:* Pip, many thanks for your thoughts, help and guidance. And it's good to have you there to work with, to talk to and to debate what's going on – and to put the world to rights! Indeed, my further thanks to Collinson Grant Ltd for sharing its market leader knowledge and skills yet again and, especially, to Hugh Dayton for his updated input on remuneration.

*Andy Macmillan and Saadia Asis*: Andy proved a brilliant researcher for much of the early part of my work and considerably facilitated my path and direction. Saadia, whom we found at Exeter Business School, helped with the more recent research and provided me not only with an extra pair of eyes to catch up on the reading, but also an astute sense in her synopsis writing. I pay tribute to you both. I am sure you will do well in your respective careers. I shall cheer you on!

*Trevor Phillips*: following my early presentations in South Africa, Trev took the concept of Total Communications Management to heart, so much so that he has actually named his business after it! Trev – thanks for your support and friendship.

To IBM's Communications Library, Rank Xerox, Olivetti, Royal Insurance; to London & Manchester Assurance – particularly Lawrence Smith and Derek Hall; to Karsten Wijk and other friends at Mölnlycke in Sweden and throughout Europe; to my many long-held and valued friends at Royal Mail; and to all those others who have shared their stories with me (or Andy); to Clive and Edwina at DunnHumby Associates; to Professors Phil Kotler and Lou Stern at Northwestern (again!); to my long-standing dear, dear friends and bottle-sharers, the multi-skilled and intellectually attuned David Pinder (whose reading and reviewing assistance was also very gratefully received) and the outrageously talented Jeremy Shearing in recognition of friendship that is so much more; to my son Kerry who fairly regularly sorts out my computer 'difficulties'; to all those other valued Clients, colleagues and friends who have given me the opportunity to assist with their problems (and learn some more about the

### ■ Customer-Driven Marketing

meaning of life). To the ever-patient Pauline Goodwin and her team at Kogan Page who waited while my life fell apart; then waited some more while it came together again; and then waited even more while I recovered from surgery.

And to all those kind people who let me use, abuse or mess with their material ... yes, to each and every one of you...

*THANK YOU.*

# Prologue

I feel you, the reader, might benefit from some explanation, thoughts and experiences that have occurred since *Total Quality Marketing* (from which this book evolved) first landed on the publisher's desk in 1990. In fact I would like to start by sharing with you the most frequent criticism that was levelled at the earlier book. This criticism was given by academics (not surprisingly); by fellow marketing and management consultants (disappointingly); by Clients and other marketers (infrequently); and by some of those personal friends and mentors whom I most respect and admire (well, they would, wouldn't they!). The criticism, over which I lament, but with which I must sadly concur, was that the book was years ahead of its time. The reason you have *Customer-Driven Marketing* in front of you now is because many of those same critics now agree – the time is fast upon us.

They may be right – you can decide. For me it feels as if some of those marketing issues which are technically and historically considered to be outside marketing – Customer aligned corporate restructuring, for example – may still be a little ahead, but for much of the rest of the work we are beginning to see some practices actually being adopted and some others still at the experimentation stage.

But I can tell you, since *Total Quality Marketing* first came out, I have seen some absolute miracles come to pass. Let's call them marketing miracles. And I am beginning to see these miracles with more and more regularity. They happen around people who are prepared to think big, accept that the past was yesterday and realise that what worked then will not work today because it is no longer suitable, no longer effective, no longer valid. These are people who would well understand why I wrote and pinned this legend to my office wall – if it ain't broke, fix it!

And that's where I believe today's business world has currently settled down. We've seen and survived the days of 'if it ain't broke, don't fix it'; we've seen and endured the slightly scary days of 'if it ain't broke, break it'; now here we are trying to cope with the relentless, unpredictable change-crazy world where we have to be ready with the solution after next just before we have diagnosed the problem before last. So, if it ain't broke, fix it!

## Assess your chances of survival

What we are talking about here is corporate survival. In fact you can easily rate yourself and the business you are in. Run down the following list scoring five as 'excellent' and zero as 'may not last the year'! Take a look at your business, the people around you and your present workload, then tot up your score. You really can determine whether your business will be in business in five, ten or even 15 years' time when you ask yourself these questions.

- Do I feel as if I am constructing the future of my business (5); or merely tinkering with the present (0)?
- Are my team and I more worried about what we can make happen this time next year – or even the year after (5); or about our present problems (0)?
- Are we truly giving our competitors something to think about (5); or just another business following along with the crowd (0)?
- Are we dedicated to redesigning our business to have a strategy which leaves our competitors on the starting blocks (5); or are we simply trying to fix the old problems, breakdowns and failures (0)?
- Are we perceived by Customers and competitors as groundbreakers (5); or followers (0)?
- How much of your personal work time is concerned with discovering tomorrow's opportunities (5); how much with resolving yesterday's hangovers (0)?
- Among all the employees in your business does there exist commitment, energy, belief and excitement (5); or stress, anxiety, uncertainty and a sense of being out of control of their own destiny (0)?
- Is the future of your business being fashioned by the directors' unique perception, dream or vision (5); or are you being driven to create new products and services, new methods and new standards and turn-rounds by your competitors (0)?
- Do you face most days with a smile and look forward to the years ahead, staying with the company (5); or is work quite often a drudge and you are thinking of moving on to somewhere where you are more appreciated (0)?

If you score less than 35 out of the 45 possible, you are at risk. To be specific, you are at risk because the future of your business is at risk. Businesses whose employees answer those questions and score less than

35 are destined only ever to reach the heady heights of mediocrity. Those businesses are content to let their people wallow, their position be less than highly competitive; those businesses don't realise or don't care that you can outsmart and out-think a good deal of change; in effect, those businesses are leaving their future to chance. If you are any good at all, get out of there! If you own it, sell it. And quick.

All of this serves to endorse the hard lesson that really should not be a surprise to any of us. It explains exactly why yesterday's solutions won't work any more. Even today's solutions are struggling! Technology is moving so fast; competitive edges and product life cycles have become so short; the business climate and environment is changing so rapidly; Customer expectations have reached such sophistication.

I often explain to people that what the Customer wants has changed from pies to pasta. Those who sit around trying to get their pie machine (that's their existing sales, advertising, marketing and Customer service processes in this analogy) to make pasta will waste a lot of corporate time, effort, resource and money. They will not experience any marketing miracles. Those who have, or who will soon begin to create pasta machines, they get to go for the breakthroughs and miracles. But there's no getting away from the fact that pie machines can't make pasta any more than the old style marketing and sales organisations, cultures and processes can cope with new style marketing.

To continue the analogy, the next question, of course, is which shapes the pasta from your new machine should be! Well, the answer depends on what your Customers tell you they want. And the answers from your own Customers will be different, sometimes subtly, sometimes not so subtly, from those of your competitors' Customers. But they will always be different – which is why the days when we could take other people's business solutions and use them to solve our own problems have gone. Nowadays we have to find our own solutions. If you hang around waiting to see what the others do, you get overtaken and often at the speed of light. It's getting harder out there – not easier. This is a point with which we will keep coming face to face!

## Breakthroughs are *big!* But they don't always bring miracles

Breakthroughs are big and to qualify as breakthroughs they should make big differences. I can't tell you the number of times I sit around with pleasant, well-meaning people who want to discuss things which will make tiny differences to sales volumes and tiny differences to market share. There is no chance of a breakthrough; no miracles will happen for them.

Yet, I vividly remember a story which an American friend and fellow conference speaker, Murray Raphel, once told me. It so affected me that I went out and tried the idea his story contained with another friend at the very next opportunity. I won't tell you Murray's original story, I'll share the personal experience.

I had a friend some years ago who was in a retail business. We were having lunch on my birthday which happens to be a few days after New Year. We sat in a Sussex pub chatting. Being the season it was, I asked him what he felt his business prospects were for the year ahead. Britain was in the grips of recession. His answer was gloomy. 'Well,' he mused, 'I figure I'll do well just to hit this year's figures again.' No breakthroughs here – not a miracle in sight!

Then the magic question (thank you, Murray). I asked him 'Can I ask you, if it were possible to lift your business by, say, 20 per cent – what do you think you'd have to do?'

Within ten minutes we had potential breakthroughs all around us. At least eight were viable and, it seemed, achievable ideas. Real potential miracles. His whole spirit lifted and he couldn't wait to finish lunch and get started. Weeks later when I visited his store, the buzz, the energy, was vividly at work. This was a business that was going somewhere.

I can tell you what happened. Business went up around 16 per cent. Sales productivity improved about the same again by realigning his staffing and changing his opening hours. Costs dropped by 8 per cent in a time when inflation was high. Of the eight potential miracles, five failed or made no discernible difference. Three initiatives succeeded. Three real breakthroughs occurred, three miracles took place.

### Are there some breakthroughs and miracles promised to you in this book?

I am privileged to work at the leading edge of what's happening. It's risky. It's fun. It's scary. It's exciting. It's where the breakthroughs and the miracles happen. However, I should explain, for this book it has a cost. Often, as a speaker, people ask you for results, facts and, most of all, case histories. They want to know what's happening to people that is new. They want me to tell them what is happening that is exciting and working. They want me to say, in effect, 'It's OK. Others have been here before you. It's quite safe.' The truth is, if others have been here before you, you've been overtaken. It's too late.

The problem is that most of my Clients are experimenting. Each time we seem to move nearer and nearer a solution, the question changes. Case histories are just that – history. If you want a book, like so many others, abounding in revealing details of the inner machinations of huge companies, by all means buy one – but know this: it will be a history book.

### This is no apology!

I'm not apologising! The fact is I'd rather feel free to tell you an anonymous story or share an anonymous experience than not tell or share it at all. Indeed, I sometimes take the view that if it's old enough to be openly told, it's too late to learn something *vitally* new from it. That's not strictly true. But it does tell you which bits to watch out for ... and, often, of which bits I'm most proud!

I know you would love to know! However, the people who pay me seem not to mind me sharing with you the things I do with them, but they naturally and reasonably fear their competitors – and that's possibly you – knowing too much about what they are doing. Competitive edges are getting harder to create and sustain, not easier! This means that, often for good and very valid contractual reasons, they are reluctant to set me free to tell you who, or in which country, they are. They will probably, however, recognise themselves!

Even if we – you, my reader, and I – should meet, I will still not reveal the 'who and where' information to you. A deal is a deal, after all! However, I respect and understand your thirst for information. What I can share with you, I will. I'll still tell the stories and I promise you, wherever I can, give you the names and places. Frustratingly, with the really interesting stuff, that's rare. But it happened or it is happening. It's out there – a breakthrough together with its accompanying miracle – to challenge, stimulate, motivate and excite you.

## Making your breakthroughs and miracles

You may be wondering what constitutes a breakthrough – or, for that matter, a miracle? Miracles to me are huge uplifts in sales productivity: one of my Clients is going for 300 per cent in three years. Miracles to me are massive shifts in the ROI (Return on Investment) offered by marketing. I have several Clients experiencing 30 to 40 per cent improvements. Some are spending less now with the same volume results. Some are redeploying the money elsewhere and going for increased growth. Some are using the savings to improve Customer communications and create long-term Customer loyalty strategies and activities. Each one of these I would consider a real miracle. The breakthroughs behind these are nearly always changes in thinking and attitude; often, later, of course, they lead to changes in method or process.

In this book we can find breakthroughs together. We can make miracles. This is not idle bragging. My role as a consultant is not to impose my solutions on people but to facilitate them creating and owning their own miracles. They, my Clients, carry the accolades as far as I'm concerned. Otherwise neither the breakthroughs nor miracles actually happen. However, things that are so big may not always come easily.

Indeed, few breakthroughs and miracles and the consequent accolades come easily. As with process or management re-engineering, inevitably there is often a human toll which I always bitterly regret. However, when you rescue or bring stability to, or create a future for, a business by boosting its performance or profitability, you effectively assure the future employment of others. This usually means the majority. And that comforts me and cheers me on.

## Will you really find your own breakthroughs and miracles in this book?

Hopefully you will, for this book contains the information that will enable you to create miracles. It tells how others have achieved miracles. But it does not provide you with ready-made solutions. The future does not recognise those words – 'ready-made solutions' – any more. This is a book about the future of sales, advertising and marketing. This is a book which explains how those three functions or activities are now one, with the additional dimension of Customer service. This is a book which preaches that 'thinking Customer' reaches into every nook and cranny of your organisation as well as deep into the hearts, minds and souls of every individual who works in it. This is, above all, a book about thinking quality before quantity. This is a book about why and how and what happens if you really do go for a miracle.

What happens if you don't create your own breakthroughs and miracles? This is not a pleasant thought. But at least the words 'long, lingering death' are not seen very often in the business community these days. Corporate deaths are much quicker now and often far more spectacular too!

Make no mistake, I say again, the future is harder not easier. It is fraught with problems – but most of all, in my view, for the sales, advertising and marketing people and processes. Sadly, they've been the slowest off the blocks. Sales, marketing and advertising people need all the miracles they can get. I hope such people will feel, by the end of this book, that they can see where the breakthroughs will come for them – and how to achieve them.

However, this is not just a book for marketing, sales and advertising managers and directors. It is for MDs and CEOs too. It is for management of all levels and every specialisation. For it is about survival and success in the Age of the Customer. When your business (or the business you are in) wins, you win. No business can win unless everyone in it is working for the Customer and understanding why this has to be so, from the accounts department, to the shop floor, to buying, to the front line. Every single company person must be, in part or in whole, a marketing person. Every single company person must be a Customer person.

I would like to end this prologue by wishing you, dear reader, as the French say, 'Bon courage'. As for luck, use this book to make your own.

*The object of a business is not to make money.
The object of a business is to serve its Customers.
The result is to make money.*

Part One: Dear Customer...

# 1

# The false premise of excellence and quality

Do you work in a quality business? Or a quantity business? Is it possible to work for a business that is both?

Since Peters and Waterman first wrote *In Search of Excellence* in 1982, the business world is alleged to have been heading towards a quality age. The fact is, back in 1990 when *Total Quality Marketing* was written, there was little evidence to show that quality standards overall were really improving. Now, I am privileged to work as a consultant with a number of firms that have made the link that quality matters and is the path to survival, if not for the future, at least for a good decade or two. Yet the number of companies throughout the world which are deeply committed to quality as a marketing issue, who see it as a vital strand to delivering beyond Customer expectations, are still small. For most it seems they are simply managing to regain lost ground rather than to improve quality. This has made me somewhat suspicious of the claims for the power of Total Quality Management.

You see, I come from the jaundiced school that says 'If man does not have a great enough perception of what quality is, then no amount of training can teach those who are deficient in appreciation of such standards, to deliver them'. More, if you examine the Excellence and Quality movements in detail you will see that what they really offer is to turn back the clock, applying the standards of bygone days to today's profit-based material age.

The premise is that if you get back to product supremacy through quality, you cannot fail. Sadly it is an undeniably noble, but entirely false premise. No marketing miracles there. For it would only work well if we were indeed living in a truly quality business age, but sadly, despite it being fashionable for almost a decade or so, we are not. We are living – today – in a transitional age, the crossover time between quantity and quality. It's not that they are absolutely mutually exclusive. But, I fear, they are a lot more so than the likes of the Excellence or the Total Quality brigades would have had us believe.

Some, possibly even you, may think these views extreme. Then take off your business hat and ask yourself, as a Consumer, how many genuine quality businesses do you know? If you can think of one, perhaps even two or three, where you are constantly and consistently super-impressed, not just with what they do but *how* they do it, you are doing well. You may have glimpsed a marketing miracle. And my guess is that you will be thinking of a business that puts its relationship building substantially in front of its business building.

These are the kind of businesses that share one of my philosophies about Customers. Namely, that it's far better to concentrate on what you do *for* Customers than what you do *to* Customers.

These businesses are often one-man bands, relics of the age of craftsmen. They do a job for you at home, they are a pleasure to deal with, leave no mess, make a skilled and exemplary job of the task, charge a fair price ... a miracle! But have you noticed how it nearly always takes you weeks or even months to get hold of them because they truly find it difficult to meet the demand. Of course! There is only the one of them. Yet if they should want to grow ... and oddly few of them do! ... how could they do it? Indeed, could they do it at all?

At the other end of the scale multi-national corporations, those who, basically driven by greed as opposed to growth, first abandoned these quality ethics for quantity, scale and size (and set us fair and square along 30 to 40 years of exploitation selling to deliver almost entirely to quantity based objectives) are now seeking to go into reverse thrust. Except, of course, many are still being run by quantity-minded materialists, men and women who have climbed the corporate tree during the last 20 years or so; they find it difficult to shake off the old ways. This is where the gurus of Excellence and the dragomans of Total Quality come in. These are businesses waiting for marketing miracles to come along. But they don't just happen like that.

## One to the power of the people

I well remember a greetings card I received from a friend, a management consultant whom I respect greatly. A few days after I left the corporate world to become a self-employed, one-man-band consultant, his message dropped on my mat. It said: 'Congratulations! You are now the perfect size for a business.'

## The false premise of excellence and quality ■

And he was absolutely right. Again my views here might be considered somewhat extreme, but I maintain that a business with 4000 staff will find it quite literally 4000 times harder to be Customer responsive, Customer focused and Customer caring. Indeed, the moment a business grows from one to two, the rot sets in.

The fact is that the business with 4000 people, to achieve and maintain a competitive stance as a Customer focused, Customer responsive business, has to cultivate and grow that Customer mentality and attitude in each and every employee. *Every* staff member has to make Customer first decisions *all* the time: down to when they take their lunch, how they answer the phone, how late they work and when they take their holidays. Getting a business of hundreds or thousands of people all to be Customer people, all making Customer first decisions, all 100 per cent on side, is incredibly, mind-blowingly, difficult – which is why it is equally rare!

As a result of all this, many people have now examined how a Total Quality ethic should affect their business. They are looking to see whether and how their business will improve from ideas such as Total Quality Management. Some started earlier and have made good progress. Others started earlier and have seen little difference. Indeed the latter group talk about Total Quality as a bit of a waste of time. The difference generally lies in the commitment and persistence of senior management and the ability of the business to recognise that Total Quality Management needs other things to go along with it, just like meat needs vegetables or salad. But we need to consider more the link between quality and marketing. And despite all the new technology, the improvement in databases, the incredible and laudable rise of call centres and some of those other magic Customer service enhancing devices, companies still frequently fail their Customers. And the reason is not so often that the system has gone down (which is frequent enough!), it is mostly because the culture or philosophy or ideal has gone down. And all of these are people issues, human issues.

Lately my wife, Elaine, and I have had a couple of perfect insurance company examples of these.

## When is your car not a car?

Answer – when it's under contract hire! Elaine loves her car. With her final promotion at the insurance business for which she worked until our marriage, her gleaming red sporty number had been part of her new remuneration package. When she left, she negotiated a deal to be able to buy the car and take it with her. Shortly after she decided to work alongside me and we created the Frazer-Robinson Partnership, she realised it would be more sensible to lease the car and so obtained quotes. She then

# ■ Customer-Driven Marketing

signed to sell the car to the finance company and lease it back. All was quite normal until she realised she had to advise her insurer.

The broker who arranged the policy contacted the insurer and called back to advise her that they were very sorry that they couldn't insure leased vehicles. Somewhat surprised, and after a further telephone call to double check that they really were so eager to lose a policyholder with an absolutely perfect and claim-free driving record, Elaine set about getting a new quote. She tried a different broker who assured her that it would be no problem and within minutes they gave her a quotation which was just slightly higher.

Elaine decided to accept the new quote. When she rang she asked who the insurer was. You've guessed! It was exactly the same company that she was already with – the one who 'didn't insure' leased vehicles!

It gets worse. She was just about to put her signature to the new documentation when the first broker rang back and said the insurers had changed their minds. Apparently now the company was prepared to keep her on at no extra premium other than an 'administration fee' for making the change. The figure quoted brought both prices to within pennies of each other. Now Elaine had a real dilemma on her hands. She had to decide whether she should insure with exactly the same cover for exactly the same risk with exactly the same insurer for exactly the same price with a new policy and move to the new broker who had really impressed her; or she could save herself the paperwork but stay with the outfit which caused all this wasted time and effort!

I've no doubt insurance companies can cheerfully laugh all this away. And, as people who work extensively for financial and insurance businesses, we both knew exactly what was happening. However, what on earth is a 'lay' Customer supposed to make of all this? It is patent nonsense. And, frankly, it was a small miracle in itself that someone at the first brokerage had the good sense to bring it up with the supervisor and deal with Elaine's case as an exception.

Even though there had been no single real circumstantial change that would have genuinely changed the risk as far as the insurer was concerned, they deeply, and in truth unnecessarily, aggravated a good Customer. Moreover, the first broker had now left a Customer feeling very disgruntled and unsettled, whereas, even though they didn't get the motor insurance, I know who Elaine will approach the next time she needs a quote for virtually anything – broker 2. They displayed great willingness to help, and were gracious and courteous when, after really putting themselves out, they still didn't get the business.

Incidentally, broker 1 tried to levy an additional 'policy adjustment' handling charge representing about 5 per cent more, when they confirmed the amendment. Elaine complained and didn't pay.

## Oh, please let me go on being your Customer!

There were just two hours before Elaine and I were due to set off for a week away on speaking assignments in Spain and the Philippines. We'd been back from South Africa less than two days, just long enough to clear some faxes and messages, pick up our slides and equipment, grab some sleep and unpack and re-pack. Then we were off. Our housekeeper, Lin, had kindly offered to run us up to the airport in my car. Suddenly, I realised, since I had changed my car a few months earlier, I had not included Lin as a named driver on the motor policy. Panic!

I rang the broker; got through to the call centre; gave the telephone operator my policy number. She paused a few seconds, waiting for her screen to load up with my record, and then advised me 'Your policy was terminated 17 days ago'.

No! Sorry, it can't have been. Otherwise I would have been driving round illegally, uninsured, for the last 17 days. 'Yes, Sir, that's correct. You have.'

I needed this like a hole in the head. I explained the situation in full, somewhat testily, but she kept her cool. 'Don't worry, Sir,' she reassured me. 'I'll transfer you to the quotations team and we'll have a new policy in force within minutes.'

'No you won't!', I told her, 'Because I don't fit your system.'

Let me tell you what had happened. When I first bought my present car, I rang to advise the broker of the vehicle change. They replied that my new vehicle was over the value covered by their contract with the insurer so they would have to get me a new quote. They did. The best they could find was four times the premium I had been paying.

As luck would have it, not only had I helped to launch this brokerage when it was founded many years before by a leading motoring organisation, but the general manager at the time, an old friend, had gone on to become managing director, and had, coincidentally, moved on to become chairman of the insurer. I decided to call him. The result was, as I had thought it might be, that of course they didn't want to lose my increased business. A call was made to the broker instructing them that, for a reasonably increased premium of about 20 per cent, they should accept the business. You would think, from the tone of the call that I received from the broker, that I had done something truly underhand, disgusting and possibly even criminal. All I had said to the insurer was – 'I've been with you nine years, I really, really want to go on being insured by you. Please, please will you go on taking my money!'

Back to the hectic morning – there are now less than 90 minutes until we're due to head off to Heathrow airport. I still have three to four hours' work to do. What little hair I have left is in severe danger of being torn out! Another person is now accessing the computer system to get me

29

■ Customer-Driven Marketing

a quote. 'You're wasting your time!' I tell her, 'My car is valued in excess of the amount covered by your agreement with the insurer.'

'I have now put your details into the system, Sir. I have to advise you that your car is in excess of the value covered by our agreement with the insurer.'

Growl.

'But don't worry. I'll put you through to our special underwriting department...' I could finish this one for her. It goes like this – '... who will come up with a quote which is four times higher than you presently have!' I was in 'the system' loop! Now I was boiling. And only then did it occur to me to go back to find out why they had terminated the policy in the first place. This was, after all, not a problem of my making. I asked to speak to a supervisor. The policy had been terminated because I hadn't paid the extra premium that had been asked for when I changed vehicles. But I hadn't been asked for any. They had failed to notify me of, and ask me for, the amount due. And, to be quite candid, I had totally forgotten too. 'However, Sir,' a quite curt voice informed me, 'we sent you a recorded delivery letter before we terminated the policy and you still failed to respond.'

Now we go into the letter saga. I had not received such a recorded delivery: and even though I travel and am away from home a great deal, being in a 400-year-old house, we don't have a letterbox, but we do have an 'arrangement' with the local post office 30m away. Betty, the postmistress, gathers our mail and, if needs be, signs for it too. There was no way a recorded delivery letter could have arrived without it being signed for. Richard, our postman, quickly cottoned on to the amount of mail I get from Royal Mail Strategic Headquarters, and 'looks after' me (which, actually, in this rural village community, he would have anyway). I explained all that. The call centre supervisor was at last lost for words. And I was speechless myself!

Thinks! How to get around this one? Fifty-five minutes left. At least 15 of which were needed to pack the hours of work into my briefcase to handle in the airport lounge! Eureka again! My old friend at the insurer.

He had retired. However, full marks go to his successor who had someone ring the broker. With 20 minutes to spare, my policy was reinstated and the outstanding premium was paid using a credit card. It is so damned hard to give people your business and your money sometimes! But why?

## Why should a Customer lose when the system wins?

I would be very surprised if you, or anyone else who picks up this book for that matter, hadn't had a similar, if different, experience. Believe me, everyone who attends my sessions of 'Customer-Driven Marketing' always has at least one nightmare tale to tell. Often they would like to tell two or three. They range from tales about banks to airlines to holiday companies to mail order businesses to the inevitable insurance companies. Everyone has such stories. And it seems that the more 'technologised' we become, the more woeful tales there are to tell.

This may not be true. It may simply be that the more used to the increasingly improving service we get, the more the apparently insane anomalies stand out. So here's the point for me. In each of these three cases the system was working just fine. What was failing was the human element – that unique ability we have as human beings to say 'that doesn't make any sense', to exercise our right still to be more intelligent than the artificial intelligence, even if it's not for much longer now! And, in a sense, here we have a truly ironic incompatibility; one of those glorious paradoxes life so tantalisingly and constantly dangles before us!

The very technology that is supposed to be helping us deal with Customers on a genuine one-to-one basis functions best when there is the maximum homogeneity between those Customers. Believe me, until this one is resolved, there will be an increasing role for the human touch and for sense to be made of things. We consumers are being told that we are allowed to be more and more different. We can have more and more choices and preferences which widen further and further our differences and support our feelings of individuality. Meanwhile 'systems' constantly try to deny it all, shove us back into the drab box of uniformity and close the lid on us.

Later, you will read that I place much emphasis on these emotional and human aspects of the business – the soft issues of marketing, as I call them. If we believe that Customer relationships are important, we must increasingly understand, respect and pay tribute to our Customers' feelings.

## Quick, quick, slow down!

Let's return to quality. When people crow about BS5750 or DIN9000, what are they saying? Are they saying that, despite the absurd bureaucracy, they are committed to the very highest levels of performance? Why do so many ads and commercials and letterheads celebrate these certifications? There are no marketing miracles here, I assure you. Aren't they, after all, simply a set of basic minimum standards? Frankly, any business which doesn't qualify for them doesn't deserve to be in business these days.

Yes, we are now finally beginning the headlong dash into the Age of Quality: but what a pity! Because if ever a directional change needed deep, reflective thought and time, this is the one.

■ Customer-Driven Marketing

Many people will say – 'Wake up to reality. Our business doesn't have time to stand still and think'. Who mentioned standing still? Let's think on our feet. Let's by all means act 'quality' now – but let's also recognise what this means.

For those involved in selling – and I cast the net as wide as it can be flung – this is a mammoth task. Selling has, it seems, been quantity driven since time began; but, in the last 40 years, it has become quantity obsessed. This obsession has, in my view, led to practices and standards which can barely be justified. There is no mitigation. We are all to blame.

The judge and jury will, over the next few years, pronounce sentence. Our Customers are our judge and jury, and, following a period of relative peace and affluence in much of the civilised world, they have come to realise that they have the money. Therefore they call the tune.

Now that we have a 'global village' created by the media, there are no little comfortable corners to hide. What a shopper in Brisbane, Australia gets today, Americans and Europeans see tomorrow and want the day after. The emerging world just wants to fast-track it to the front right away, but can't afford it.

These days, for Customers who have the money or who can access the credit, the world is theirs. Now the Customer can really be king, not like that limp attempt a few made at it the last time. This time it's for real. We've already seen, in the last five years, the 'ante' rising; first we had Customer satisfaction, then Customer delight (or other similar names) and now we're striving for what you will read about later as Customer 'Superformance', which is a permanent, dynamic, unceasing desire to exceed Customer expectations with every transaction or contact. There is a veritable field of marketing miracles waiting to be harvested.

## How can you change the way you sell?

Given the choice – and they will be – no Customer in his or her right mind would want to deal with a salesperson driven by quantity objectives. Customers already know that so often quantity objectives work against quality objectives. It is only those who sell to them who fail to do anything positive about this dichotomy.

Look at the classic high commission businesses and the reputation they have; double glazing or replacement windows, timeshare, perhaps even office equipment, and there are many more including, sadly, and despite a maze of absurd but entirely necessary self-regulation, some of the financial services. I so often listen to insurance people bemoaning the tight corset that bureaucratic legislation in Europe and Australasia – for example they are called Compliance and Disclosure in Britain – has forced upon them. 'No other business has so explicitly to tell Customers how

## The false premise of excellence and quality

much their charges are and how much commission the salespeople are getting', they say.

Don't they realise they brought it on themselves by failing to respond to the Consumers' demands? Didn't they constantly respond only to their own greed? Insurance, it seems to me, is about protection. The psychology that believes that I would want to deal with or, more importantly, to remain long and spend more with, someone who is aggressive (ie threatening) is preposterous and forces Customers to review their choice at the very next purchase, precisely because Mr Hard Sell managed to intimidate them into it the first time. No marketing miracles there.

The basic premise of this book has two dimensions. The first is that, for businesses, quantity objectives generally work against quality objectives. The second dimension is that the reverse is not true. Quality objectives can most definitely work for quantity objectives. This is why, when you get the quality right for Customers, you sell your wares and make profits in far greater quantity.

A great deal of this book is spent proving, exploring and explaining the second dimension of the premise. However, let us stay with the first dimension: quantity objectives generally work against quality. This notion is going to cause complete upheaval in selling and advertising, let alone the whole spectrum of marketing and marketing services for the quality driven age – the age not just of product excellence, not just of cost excellence, but mostly of service excellence. In other words, delivery of the corporate promise.

Consider it. For 40 years the once noble art of selling tarnished itself by responding to the mindless call for more orders. It has become obsessed with 'pile it high, sell it cheap'. You may remember those words as the immortal utterings of Jack Cohen, founder of the British supermarket chain, Tesco; a company now proud to boast that it is the greenest, cleanest, most Customer-attentive supermarket chain in the UK. Now they sell quality. Or at least they think they do.

Tesco were one of Europe's first to embark upon what I would call a Customer fidelity programme, but which most of the marketing fraternity would call a Customer loyalty programme – although sadly it seems to rely largely on a discount platform. My experience is that bribery does not build loyalty for long. Others can peel people away with bigger, better bribes. Those succeeding with tangible, sustainable loyalty programmes are looking to work in the 'soft issues' of marketing as well as the traditional old hard issues. They have realised that real loyalty is built in the emotions, even if it is expressed physically by the act of shopping or buying.

### Shock! Horror! It's the future

The future will cause many deep shocks. The pressure put upon business people by quantity objectives has caused many heart attacks. The pres-

■ Customer-Driven Marketing

sure put upon businesses by quality objectives will cause a new phenomenon, the 'corporate coronary'. It happens as a result of a business trying hard to keep up with the global levels of Customer demand; often they will quite literally fall to the ground dead – out of funds, out of time, out of energy, exhausted and exasperated. You will see the evidence unwind as this book progresses.

You will equally learn how to avoid such a corporate heart attack yourself – or perhaps how to avoid being the trapped and tragic victim, an employee of a stricken company.

Everyone is talking about change; indeed everyone is writing about change. I am going to be no exception. For the quite remarkable fact is that few have yet started to explain or describe the changes that will take place in selling, advertising and marketing. There are a few ex-direct marketers or information and database manipulators, who have picked up the flag and talk of one-to-one marketing or, as I call it, 'Individualisation'. However, I haven't found anyone yet who has taken a real look at how this affects the whole business. Most still discuss these so-called new concepts as if they are going to take place only in a marketing or a sales department.

No one, to my knowledge, has produced any serious evidence or advice as to how those changes which have already been predicted will affect the people involved. Yet, I maintain, that now even the companies must themselves change to deliver quality in all aspects of marketing – advertising, selling, promotions, public relations and all the other facets of their communications and their processes of persuasion. When one sees the need to change, then one has to ask these questions – how can you change the way you sell? How can we create our own marketing miracles?

## Is it back to the drawing board?

Yes and no. For many sales people, in the way that they operate, it is indeed back to the drawing board. But like so many other facts of business life, it is first of all a question of back to the board. Quality, as has already been demonstrated by the other founding fathers of the movement, is a board matter. Perhaps, now that it has reached into and beyond the marketing zone, it has actually become a matter even for shareholders. For it often requires mountains of courage and a massive financial investment – and often an enormous leap of faith. As I write that, I am aware of just how many project teams I have been a member of or with whom I have acted as a consultant, who have found themselves lacking numbers. Yes, an outcome feels right, appeals intensely to the gut, but has little by way of hard numbers upon which a board can make a decision. This is one of the reasons why since *Total Quality Marketing*, where marketing was described as a three-dimensional process, you will see now that I am suggesting it is a four-dimensional process – the shareholders being the fourth dimension.

One particular project comes to mind with an insurance business where the likely costs of their set of marketing miracles looked to be around £19 million. It involved a total restructure, fairly massive re-engineering, a complete new corporate culture and management style and, later, was to involve a 'Customer delight' programme which then added a further £12.5 million's worth of marketing miracles to the total cost. All this was finally accepted both by the board and the group board without any real end game numbers as to the success of the projects.

We shall look at this aspect – the numbers, or lack of them, and the leap of faith – in more detail again. My point is that it cannot be some short campaign. It's no good putting it on the topics for training for a month or two. There are no marketing miracles there.

This is not merely a question of how well you survive the next 40 years, it is *whether* you will survive to see the next 40. It has taken 40 years for the pendulum to swing in the quantity direction. In my view it is quite likely that the quality direction swing could last almost as long. I will show you my evidence. It is fascinating, convincing and points the way to your future.

## So who has to change? And how?

The kind of changes we are talking about – the future of selling, advertising and marketing – will be looked at in this book from many standpoints. Take the salesman. (Incidentally, I use the term salesman and other similar words throughout this book in a non-sexist, genderless sense, as a generic term. You may also note that the words 'Customer' or 'Client' are always spelt with a capital 'C'. This is not to confound the typesetters, it is a personal quirk! I always try to get my Clients to adopt the same discipline throughout their business – this simple idiosyncrasy constantly serves, every time the words are used, to remind us that, commercially, there is nobody to be held in higher esteem.) How should he or she, the salesman, actually sell in the future? How will management change the environment, conditions and terms that sales employees work under to engender, measure and reward quality? How will the company restructure its sales and marketing teams to deliver quality, if restructure they must?

We will even take a fairly frank look at where quality wants to be sold – and where it wants to be bought. We'll look at why quality and good Customer relationships are still considered a luxury at the moment, and how quality changes the Customer's basic needs and desires. We'll consider where, perhaps, a partnership approach might be more appropriate.

■ Customer-Driven Marketing

We will examine the view that selling is not about a single sale. Nor even is it about a series of sales. Marketing miracles are born of 'Success through Excess'. It is about success through exceeding expectations – Customer Superformance; the achievement of sales success through delivery of active, as opposed to passive, satisfaction to the Customer. We will look at the Customer loyalty issue and see why so many are missing the point settling for fidelity rather than loyalty.

There is to some degree also a matter of perspective. When the seller and the buyer have different perspectives, their starting point in negotiation is the opposite side of the fence. When they are both on the same side, trust grows, loyalty abounds and success is a natural result. A miracle has taken place.

## New methods for you, new directions for your business

We are about to embark along an exciting and provocative journey together. If you sit back and observe and do the thinking, I'll drive and show you around. I'm perfectly sure you'll find great comfort in all you read, although a great deal of the contents may challenge you, your thinking and your practices. If this is the case, I will have had my say and you will have had value. For this is the true purpose of this book: to change things for the better, for the Customer, in other words, for you.

How much you agree, how much you accept, how much you think about, how much you change is ultimately, of course, and remains eternally, your decision. You may not entirely enjoy what you read. Several times after presentations of *Total Quality Marketing* or, in its subsequent form as *Customer-Driven Marketing*, I have sat chatting to, in fact comforting is a better word, participants who have spent one or two days working on what I call their Customer gap. That's to say they were examining the way they want to be treated as Customers and the way they choose or are instructed to treat Customers. Such gaps are often wide. In a sense, what Customer-driven marketing does is to look at how that gap can be closed. Frequently there is fallout!

On the positive side, we get the Eureka types – people who leave feeling that they have seen the light. They know what they want to do, know how they want to go about it and can't wait to get back to work the next day and get started. On the negative side we get the trapped or the powerless. Some of these feel incredibly frustrated. Some feel downright angry. They know what they should do; understand the deep sense and 'rightness' of it; but know also that there is no way their company or their bosses will even think about it.

This is yet another area of business where enormous transition is taking place. All around the world, we come face to face with front line teams or team members and their immediate managers sensing and embracing their new ability to think and make a difference. However, these people still come up with enormous opposition from senior managers who are saying all the right things but who are having terrible problems letting go of their power and their old ways of command and control.

Today – and when I describe this I always picture the biblical waters coming back together after Moses and the children of Israel had passed through – the old energy flow from senior management is still coming from one direction while from the other comes this enormous rush of excitement, commitment and fulfilment. The result is a mind-numbing clash of cultures and methods – the waters coming together – which is causing upset and anger, like an incredibly disruptive backwash.

As you move your business forward to becoming Customer-driven these matters must command your attention. For, to be successful and to untap so much of their future potential, Customer focused organisations need these new structures, styles and cultures. It is precisely these which release the treasure chest of human talent that will enable them to compete more and more effectively. I see this as just more evidence that the silo-style boundaries of the past are tumbling all around us with increasing speed. We cannot and must not see marketing or selling or advertising in those old-fashioned boundaries of the past. They are integrating and embedding themselves deep into the heart of every aspect, every function, every activity of business.

Lastly, just before we come to the end of this first chapter, I'd like to point something out. It might seem obvious, but I'll say it none the less. Don't look for the switch. There isn't one. You can't turn a marketing miracle on. There is nothing anybody can or will flick to change the environment from quantity to quality. It is truly a pendulum; possibly even a 40-year pendulum. Some people will do some of the things you are going to read about. Some will not. Some will do all. Some will do none. Some will do them tomorrow. Some in five years' time. The only thing you need to know about this pendulum is that it is relentless, in fact, unstoppable.

A revolution is under way. Sales, advertising, marketing and service people cannot escape this revolution. The Customer has taken control. They can take their business anywhere. The survivors, the winners, will be those who master the new techniques and learn the ways of Customer-driven marketing and, therefore, what has to come next for selling, advertising and marketing. Let's call them the marketing miracle makers.

## Part Two: Backwards to the future

## 2

## On your marks

When this book's predecessor – *Total Quality Marketing* – was published in Swedish and Norwegian I remember being puzzled. In Swedish – *Total Kvalitet i Marknads Foringen* – it made sense. It was a direct translation. However, in Norwegian, it didn't feel the same as *Tilbake til Fremtiden*. On a visit, I tackled Universitets Forlaget, the publishers. 'Ah!', they told me, 'it means backwards to the future.' I wish I had thought of that. So thanks to Norway for the new section title!

The business of prediction gets harder as the rapidity of change increases (more on this later). Thus when you are dealing with a medium like television which gives you instant live access to your audience, you have the benefit of talking in 'real time'. A book, of course, affords neither reader nor writer such a luxury. For both of us, therefore, the task is harder. And of necessity we must limit ourselves to the major trends.

Certainly by the time you are reading this, some of the predictions I make will have started to happen; some of the stories I tell will have long past happened; and some of the events I report will no longer be happenings of such great significance. This is of no matter. They will serve to show you the route and path of the trend. You can use your more up-to-date knowledge, or the ability to avail yourself of such, to enhance or modify the situation that exists as I write.

Indeed, as I write, what is the situation in marketing, selling, advertising and their allied areas? And what model shall we take to position ourselves for the off? Where will we most likely uncover room for a marketing miracle to happen?

Let's start with where I position myself against the classic arguments that still mystify or mislead some; particularly US and European companies.

## Classic and traditional

Despite what follows in this book, I have to own up right away and position myself with the more classic and traditional marketers. Hence I will quite happily align myself with the school of thought that says marketing should control sales; sales is, indeed, a function of marketing. Having had the benefit of so extensively researching the future, and being able to set that in the context of the past, I feel strongly that, even if you are sceptical of such a view now, you will come to agree with it very shortly.

For me, marketing describes the total corporate Customer process. Sales represents a function of that process, the interaction between the business and the Customer, where the individual needs are identified and translated in product or service terms and then met, in the sense that the value balance for the Customer is fashioned into an offer or series of offers. This process – selling – takes place against the knowledge that this is where the importance of the Customer relationship has its roots: here the basis of trust must begin; here the 'bonding' procedure must begin; here the promises are forged and committed.

You will not be alone whichever 'camp' you are in – whether you see sales as separate from marketing or whether, like me, you see it as a part of the marketing process. There exist many companies who see marketing and selling as separate, if associated tasks. In such companies you often observe that a sales/marketing equivalent of the sales/production 'battle' exists – sometimes as boyish playfulness (whatever sexes are involved!) and sometimes as outright war. Occasionally a sort of strained professional coexistence prevails and very, very occasionally a complete, mutually accepting, respectful partnership.

Equally, as another example, there are still some people who regard advertising as above or below 'the line'.

## Above, below or across?

Such views are neither classic nor traditional. They are as antiquated as those wonderful old socio-economic groupings that are still evident in Britain and which should have been abandoned years ago – A, B, C1, C2, D and E. Happily, as the creators and protagonists of this invisible line rode into the peaceful sunset of their sheltered retirement housing, we no longer need to grapple with the intriguing notion that sales promotion or direct marketing is 'below the line' or, for that matter, that television and press are above it. My position, as you may have guessed, is that I believe there should never have been a line.

Certainly, again I use this word advisedly; there will be no line, nor evidence that there was one, in the future. This may be just as well, for I suspect that many of the inventors of new media would have greatly resented a below-the-line position.

In the late 1980s, I introduced readers and audiences to the California-based SoftAd Corporation. SoftAd were typical of the enterprising new media of which we shall see many, many more opening up in the next decade. The SoftAd product, when I first came across it, was one of a kind. It was certain to spawn lookalikes, it was such a great concept. The idea – novel at the time – was to give or mail a computer disk to prospects instead of the conventional letters, brochures and flyers. SoftAd developed special interactive software so that the recipient could play with or interrogate the featured products or services. The result was something of a television commercial, brochure, mailing and direct sales call all in one. People often spent 20 or 30 minutes with an ad – so you can imagine the recall, the depth of product knowledge and the potential relationship that could be established through such an idea. To some extent, of course, the growth of this kind of product depended on the growth of the personal computer market. And SoftAd certainly hoped so, since the figures they were working on in the late 1980s showed worldwide PC growth of: in 1989 – 40 million; in 1992 – 125 million. Actually those figures were to be something of an underestimate.

In fact, by 1994 Microsoft were claiming 50 million licensed users of Windows and sales running at a further two million a month. Windows 95 sold 40 million copies in its first year. If Moore's Law – that the capacity of a computer chip will double every 18 months – holds true, then in 20 years a computation which currently takes a day will take just ten seconds.

It was forecast that by 1998 European spending on PCs would overhaul spending on televisions: at the time of writing, 35 per cent of US households already own a PC. A survey by SBT Accounting Systems in the US suggested that the 25 million PC users at work spend 5.1 hours a week of unproductive time tinkering with computer software. They calculated this was costing the nation $100 billion or 2 per cent of gross domestic product (GDP)!

Let's not forget just how much data we are all storing these days. And how commonplace and cheap data storage and usage has become, and will doubtless go on becoming. Certainly the power and speed of the machine I am using to type this, receive and handle my faxes, and provide my globally accessible E-mail address was considered as unnecessary as it was unthinkable just a few years ago.

To finish the SoftAd story, when I first came across them, SoftAd believed that the companies who distributed high quality information to buyers to help them make an intelligent, informed decision would be the ones who would prosper in the future. Direct marketers who have been able to use database techniques to make their messages more appropriate and relevant to their readers must agree with this.

The people at SoftAd, I decided back then, would all be rich and famous by the end of the 1990s. They seemed to have one of those 'right product, right time' opportunities which should have yielded them a long and healthy future. However, at that time we were talking disks only, CD-ROM and the whole notion of interactive media being still a twinkle in the eye of the Pacific rim factories. The Internet was still unheard of by, and inaccessible to, the public at large. Some years after my introduction to SoftAd, I met and worked a few times with Andy Bereza of Digital Postcards in London who, in Europe, is probably considered among the most advanced at creating interactive advertising on disk and CD. At the time of writing Andy is sceptical of the Internet – mainly because of no currently (which probably means in the next few weeks!) foreseeable improvement in data transmission speeds.

As mail order companies around the world grapple with the relatively easy tasks of putting their catalogues on to CD, Andy, rather than simply transfer them on to a disk or CD, transforms them and brings them alive. Products can be demonstrated, different colours appear before your eyes, full motion video can be included, and games and puzzles can be used to engage the catalogue-holder. And Andy makes the creation of all these compelling ideas look so easy!

He created the most wonderful interactive ad for BMW when they introduced their new model – the seven series Chameleon – with the infinitely changeable exterior body colour. As the ad explained, just as sunglasses can be made to react to sunlight and temperature, the BMW technicians had perfected a paint which changed colour in response to the electric charge which was applied to it. It defies me to write about the brilliant interactive diskette that Andy created for BMW. It demonstrated how the car could be programmed to change colour in tune with the music you were playing, your mood or what was happening in the traffic that day. It could be made less reflective in times of bright sunlight; could change to a pacifying shade of green to calm you when road rage was building inside you; and would change to a sludgy old brown colour when you parked because research showed that sludgy old brown cars got broken into and stolen less than any other colour.

You may have realised, as you read, that this whole thing was complete nonsense. There is no such car. Andy used this spoof ad to demonstrate the compelling power of interactive advertising. And I should tell you that with several audiences around the world, I used his diskette, showed people the car, demonstrated its remarkable colour-changing capability and then asked, 'If money wasn't a problem, if you could afford the car, how many would actually want one?' Typically, well over 50 per cent of the audiences I asked, and in total we must be talking a few tens of thousands of people here, would have bought a car whose colour they could change at whim.

The power of advertising! And power it certainly had. Imagine my surprise and wonder when, some months after Andy had given me the diskette, I read in my morning newspaper that just such a car was actually being worked on by US car manufacturers! They should be greatly encouraged by my research.

As I write, the Internet is being heralded as one of the ways of the future. Large and small businesses alike are charging headlong to join – myself among them – you can e-mail me on jfr@jfr.co.uk. I wonder whether CD-ROM isn't also set to conquer the business world and, before long, our homes. The factories of the world are certainly geared to it and the prices are low (Figure 2.1). Already my 16-year-old stepson, Chris, and I agree, as a communications opportunity and as a reference bank, the Internet is wonderful and indispensable!

Recent research showed that, in Britain, by the millennium well in excess of three million people will be working from home. It also showed that one in three workers expects to work from home within the next ten years and a startling 60 per cent would prefer to do so. Indeed, it has

CD-ROM market

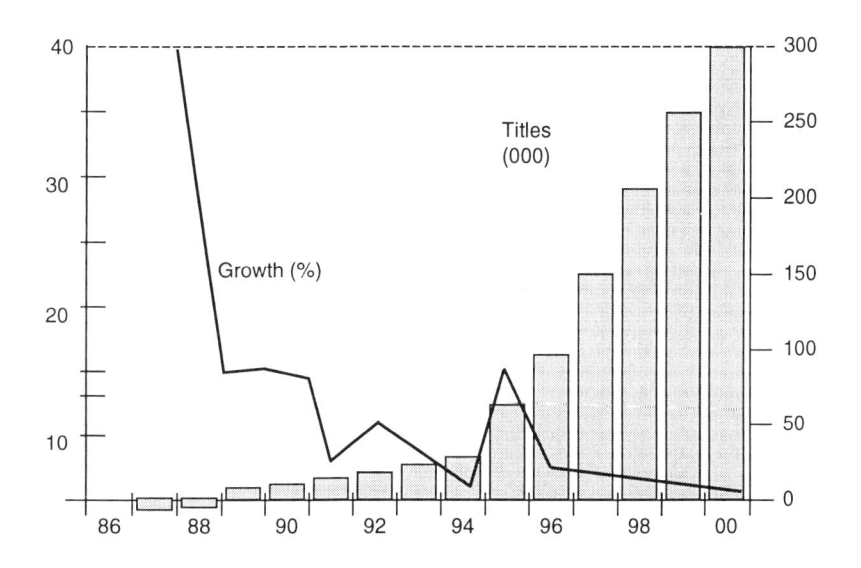

**Figure 2.1** *Growth in the CD-ROM market*

■ Customer-Driven Marketing

ISDN subscribers (basic rate access lines)

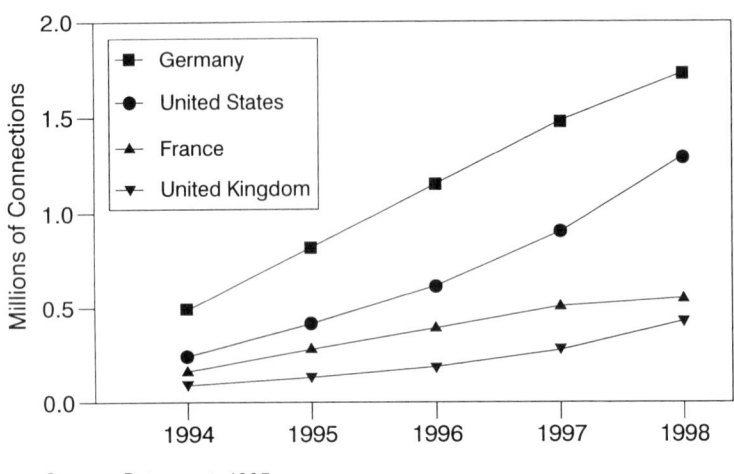

*Source: Dataquest, 1995*

**Figure 2.2** *The spread of ISDN subscribers in Europe*

been calculated that a typical British city centre firm employing 100 people could save itself upwards of £2 million in office and transport cost by adopting 'teleworking'. With video-conferencing improving, hardware and software costs reducing and falling telecommunications costs as well, the idea of working from home, using the 'Net', and the most computer literate generations now well into their adulthood and careers, our homes are just as likely to become high-tech communications centres as our offices (Figure 2.2). My newspaper this morning carries a half-page ad for British Telecom with a headline proclaiming '**Go home** and get 40 per cent more done today'.

Recently I spoke at a conference where the technical director of one of the global players in the telecommunications business informed his audience that the 'phone was dead'. They saw the medium-term future market as being several million households where the domestic communications medium connected the PC, the telephone and the television to one processor of which the screens were a series of walls around the house. Voice technology was used to 'instruct' the machine and you could use your 'wall' whether you wanted to e-mail someone, video call or conference with them, or to call down any of a vast range and assortment of entertainments. The speaker left the rostrum after informing his audience that, whereas at the moment we boot our computers in the morning and, effectively, we take our dog for a walk, in the very near future, as the next generation of computing arrives, we will boot up in the morning and our dog will take us for a walk! We are but relative moments away from the time when artificial intelligence will out-perform human intelligence.

Yet, surely, the biggest problem we all have to face in marketing is the number of people who want merely to fiddle with the status quo. This is another notion devoid of marketing miracles. And when you look at technology, where you would think innovation would be rampant, it really isn't.

## Forget the future, where are we now?

As we shall see later, you can be sure of very little these days.

Let's just put the future on one side for a moment and consider where exactly we are now. What stage have communications reached – whether for advertising, selling, Customer recruitment, retention or repair?

Having spent some time specialising in the direct marketing field, I have found a convenient 'yardstick' there. Because direct marketing relies so much on other aspects – computers, machinery, printing processes, all the creative tasks of photography, typesetting and so forth – it's probably quite an interesting and valid example to consider.

Back in the 1950s, soap coupons worth just a few pence were distributed the length and breadth of Britain by direct mail. These days, no one would even think about it. They would use house-to-house distribution for that task. And probably they would harness one of the increasingly sophisticated targeting systems to select the audience which most carefully matches the known profiles of their Customers. Using addressed, stamped direct mail would no longer be considered viable, effective or worth while simply to disseminate low value soap coupons.

In the 1950s, advertisers would happily send out a mailing of 250,000 where each and every mailing package was identical, distinguished only by the name on the outside of the little brown envelope which carried it to market. Such users still exist but they are few. And there are not many left in brown envelopes! By the 1960s, that same organiser of the 250,000 mailing was looking at new capabilities. Increased knowledge about the market, increased mechanisation of mailing lists, increased recognition of the importance of market sectors and – I think – increased postage, had combined to make greater cost-effectiveness both necessary and possible. One way to achieve such was to break down the market into groups, and for the sake of the rest of this example, let us quite hypothetically imagine they are all the same size.

So our friend would now mail perhaps 250 different mailings of 1000 within the total of 250,000. As that decade passed by, so the next held equal new opportunities. By the 1970s, we were drawing well into the age of computerisation. People across the world were being exhorted to put their lists on to computer.

I remember how we used to balance out the number of times the list would be used, against its size, and the likelihood and number of selections that might be required to help a Client decide between staying on a manual system, choosing the mechanical addressing systems or the infant but capable computer complete with all its teething problems. (Oddly enough the manual system remains the only method still remaining outside the British and, I believe, some other European Data Protection Acts.) Problems or not, the benefits far outweighed them and so we had moved into the next phase.

Now our friend's 250,000 mailing could consist of 1000 different mailings of just 250 like packages. This was the beginning of the Age of Personalisation – an age which was only finally to be unseated and replaced towards the end of the 1980s. During the 1980s we saw the blossoming of the laser printer. In those few years it changed from the rather unreliable $500,000 10m box, to a desktop at less than $5000 with many much cheaper still. Moreover as the direct marketing industry grew, aligning itself alongside the computer industry, so the software market grew more sophisticated; together they provided extremely capable multi-disciplined marketing databases for everyone, from the large companies with millions of Customers to the one-man band with only a few hundred or even less.

The growth in direct mail also warranted research and development in other production technologies; thus there is mailing enclosing machinery which will take a whole range of different leaflets, brochures and other enclosures, and, based on the letter being sent, enclose the relevant materials with each letter. New technology equipment is thus used in conjunction with high capability software, mailing programmes and accurate databases.

You can understand why I explain to audiences that we have transcended the Age of Personalisation and arrived at the Age of Individualisation. This is the age when we need to make miracles happen! For there is no reason why each person in the mailing should not today receive an offer, proposition, message or whatever, which is entirely individual to them, cognisant of their own individual circumstances, recognising all the multiple facets of their particular relationship with the advertiser.

Now we truly can see how that mailing in fact comprises 250,000 completely individual mailings. But this is not the only evidence of the Age of Individualisation.

For this is also the time when, while the motor trade in Germany still asks for three months to take the order for your precise specification of car and then deliver it to you, in Japan, you can have it in just a few days; your own individualised car. It's a miracle! For the moment.

In the US, one refrigerator manufacturer, I'm told, asks you these questions before supplying you with your equipment. After all, who else would want it?

- How big is the gap you wish to fill?
- Describe your family's eating and drinking habits. Particularly tell us about:
  — cooled drinks
  — salads and fresh foods
  — frozen foods.
- Please send examples of your kitchen decor. Any exterior colour can be matched, toning shelf and interior materials will be offered before building.
- Please advise which of the following you would like built in to your unit:
  — stereo radio/cassette/CD player
  — black and white or colour television
  — video.

At the last question you might decide they've gone too far. After all, designing a unit which reflects the family's consumption and actual storage needs is one thing; trying to turn the fridge into an entertainment centre is something else. Not so, says the company, as their research shows that almost 70 per cent of free-standing equipment ends up with a radio, CD, television or tape player on the top. All they do is organise your kitchen for you as an individual or individual family. Miraculous stuff, huh?

As time passes you will see the phenomenon of individualisation grow larger. It's inspired not just by the producer's ability to harness design and manufacturing technology, and to deliver such products, but also by the Consumers' need to differentiate themselves and their belongings from an increasingly uniform and dehumanised world.

## The future's here, let's get started!

I suppose, with all the research and star-gazing that goes on, to write a book like this you can't help becoming a bit of a futurologist. However, like all futurologists, I find I want the world to go a little faster than it does. I want marketing miracles today, by this afternoon, please!

Consequently, when something you predict accurately takes ten years to happen instead of five, you get a little irritated. And I do find that I get more than a little irritated with the marketing world and how long, as a profession, we take to adapt to new ways and methods. Actually, viewed

■ Customer-Driven Marketing

against other business disciplines, we are not very good at all at practising what we preach.

Most of my work these days is really pure management consultancy specialising in helping businesses to identify and then handle the issues of becoming a truly Customer focused organisation. And it is interesting how my direct marketing heritage is standing me in incredibly good stead; my strategic understanding of database capability is proving invaluable; but my work staying at the forefront of marketing technology makes me very impatient!

Anniversary! It must be now almost exactly ten years ago that I first suggested that 'within ten years 90 per cent of all marketing will be direct marketing'. Well, to be accurate, I also said that it probably would not still be called direct marketing but repositioned within an integrated marketing mix. On reflection, I feel the first part of that could still almost happen given a few extra years and the second part, ie the integrated marketing bit, will arrive too, but even later!

Well, to be a good futurologist, I'm told, you need to be proclaiming that 'This is the Age of Whatever', at least five to ten years before the world really wants it to happen. I managed to work out where the marketing process needed to go, but failed abysmally to calculate how long it would need to do it. Since Professors Kotler and Levitt's various predictions of the 1970s are only just coming to pass, I guess I should have known better.

However, when you look at the rate and pace of change in marketing, it is painfully, mournfully slow. In fact, direct marketing is a good example. The fact is that the direct marketing business is still growing rapidly. The front-runners may be struggling hard to improve and adopt new technology, but all the time newcomers are entering the business at a basic level and the learning curve may be getting shorter, but it is still there none the less.

Indeed, you only have to look, as I frequently do, at the prize-winners at the annual awards events around the world to see just how slowly progress is really happening out there where marketing truly touches the Customer. We seem to be able to do the same faster, more accurately or with modest service improvements but, as yet, the communications revolution which could have happened, has not. I was chatting to another of the grey panthers of the global direct marketing scene a while back. He had sold his shareholding in his agency and retired with a very nice sum. The vast majority of his money had been wisely invested but he, for some personal reason, had decided to keep about £100,000 on deposit at his bank where he kept his normal banking facility– the self-same bank which had seen these happy sums of money go through on their way to being invested. The morning of our call, he had received a heavily personalised mailing offering him a £5000 unsecured loan!

The fact is that many people are talking about individualisation of their marketing, but few have actually got anywhere near it. Many are still satisfied with the relatively prehistoric ways of 30 years ago. The most rudimentary targeting and segmentation is still not taking place. But why not? I have two theories to offer as to why progress is so slow.

**THEORY 1:** it's more difficult than we realised. Individualised marketing does not really work well in the IT environment we have today. Customer communications need to operate in real time before they can truly become individualised or fully respect a Customer relationship. This means that management of communications is critical to success and this needs experimentation to get right. I guess what I am saying here is very obvious: the technology may be there, but it is the use we make of it which is failing. It's a people, not necessarily a technology, failure.

Just as responsibility for Customer issues succeeds better when devolved to the front line, so too do Customer communications of most sorts. There are marketing miracles galore wrapped around getting this right! However, it means that the fundamental task of the marketing department changes – at least for Customers anyway – from one of implementation to one of cultivating excellence, transferring skills and knowledge and maintaining guardianship of brand and corporate values. Apart from those, strategic planning and market intelligence are the other key roles.

In a nutshell, devolving responsibility for the timing and activation of Customer communications as near as possible to the frontline is a tricky, but potentially miraculous, business. It requires a 'core to Customer' database (a state few have arrived at yet!), a 'letting go' culture from the marketing department and fast learning about the value and importance of marketing issues by teams who are used, in the main, to sales issues. These are tough nuts to crack and, without doubt, much experimentation is needed before the many potential marketing miracles emerge.

Yet there are some out there trying it with varying degrees of success. No one said integration was easy. No one said relationship marketing was a piece of cake. No one said marketing miracles come right first time. And, whoever no one is, they are right!

**THEORY 2:** technology is holding us back! I mean it! I get to attend more than my share of fairs (of the trade variety, that is). And exhibitions. I see the latest stuff. I hear the latest stories. I hoard the latest samples and examples. Next time you go to one, I bet you'll find two kinds of technology on display.

The first kind is genuinely new kit and new ideas. And, sure, it helps us to achieve new things. It is in the minority and the stands will be busy – but they won't sell much. Why? Because only the risk-takers and the pioneers will buy from them. In themselves, they are another minority group. However, there is a higher percentage of miracle makers in this minority.

The vast majority of technology you will see offers us the chance to modify slightly something we already do or to make current practice cheaper, easier, faster or more accurate. This means that what we really need to achieve, the significant leaps forward which your average guru or futurologist, or whatever, bangs on about – *innovation* – is actually hampered with our obsession safely to tinker with, improve or re-engineer the cosy old status quo. No miracles there!

Yet whether we like it or not, here we are at the Age of Individualisation. And that is, in many ways, the starting point for our time together. Glance around you now. Find out where you and your business are. Remember it well, because the future holds some difficult and frightening times in store, times of uncertainty and high risk.

You will remember these times for the ease with which you could do business, the ease with which you could make money ... and the ease with which you could satisfy your Customers. Times will change beyond all recognition.

Far be it from me to put the fear of God into you about the future, but that's exactly what I think might need to happen. I have pointed, as indeed have many others before me, to *change* being the cause of this fear – not just change itself, but the rate and frequency and scope of change.

A definition of change might be 'making or becoming different', but this is not quite what I mean. I would like to build in far greater emphasis on the future inconsistency and unreliability of the status quo. The status quo should no longer be seen as cosy. It will be the status quo for a decreasing amount of time. You're going to need one miracle after another.

This means in turn that things you used to rely on – product life cycles, a competitive edge, Customer satisfaction, material sources, prices and suppliers and so on – many of these will become unreliable and untrustworthy in the next decade.

In such circumstances you must look to make yourself stronger, more resilient. I have two suggestions for this. The first lies in your marketing process; the second in the quality of what you use your marketing to create. Specifically, I am referring to the quality objectives of your marketing. For an aspect of the quantity/quality discussion we have not considered is this: quantity only builds immediate sales; quality builds friends; friends, in the long term, build greater quantity which yields the marketing miracles.

## Marketing is a four-way process

I have a confession! When I wrote *Total Quality Marketing,* marketing was a three-way process! Now it's up to four. And the fourth one has some contention wrapped round it because I have no doubt many people will suggest I was wrong to leave it out – or ignore it – in the first place. They would have been right!

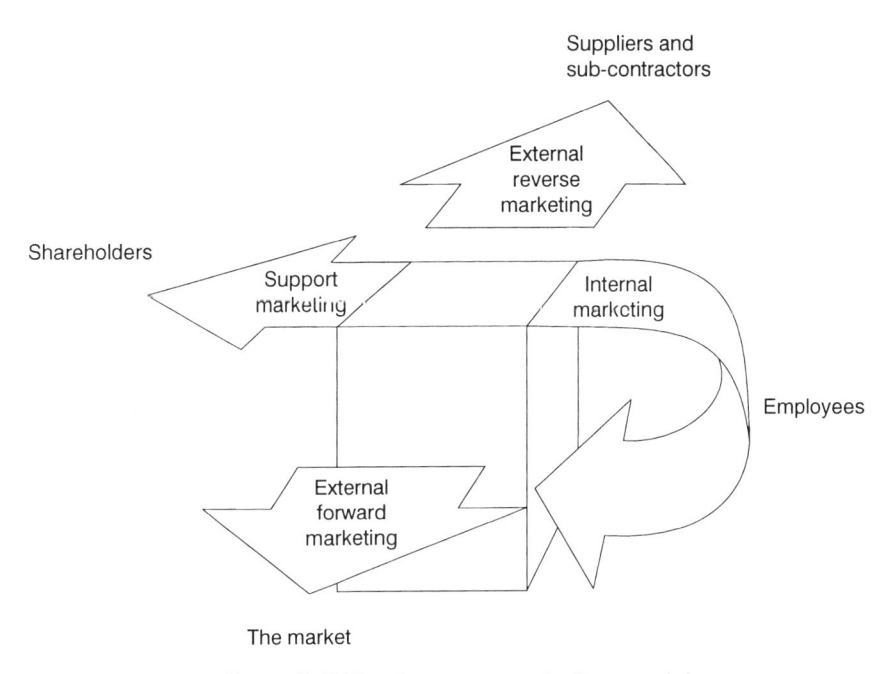

**Figure 2.3** *The four-way marketing model*

For marketing to achieve its full effective power and to provide you with its full benefit, I now believe it must be a four-way process. Your marketing should stretch forward to your market, inside to your employees and behind you to your suppliers and sub-contractors and alongside to your shareholders.

Let's examine this notion a little further.

Although I believe the needs for marketing towards our Customers and prospects – the marketplace – are well accepted, I'm not sure the other three directions are. These are marketing to our own colleagues (Internal Marketing) and to our suppliers and sub-contractors (Reverse External Marketing), and then to our shareholders (Support Marketing).

In relation to Internal Marketing, we are really considering the role, involvement and influence of marketing, training, and even some personnel and recruitment matters. These are areas which have a bearing on, or direct contact with, the market and therefore in effect become part of the product or service. It is within our internal marketing that we address the building of motivation, confidence and commitment to our corporate direction.

Reverse External Marketing is sadly still born of, and generally reserved for, times of scarce or limited resources when it is used to ensure continuity of supply and, as far as possible, maintenance of price. I remember first seeing this technique used tactically during the three-day weeks and power rationing caused by the industrial disputes which hit

■ Customer-Driven Marketing

Britain in the 1970s. A major heating and ventilating equipment manufacturer simply switched its whole marketing effort into reverse thrust and as a result surprised both its market and its competitors by making optimum use of its own limited production times. Not only was their resource planning careful, but somehow they always seemed to have the wherewithal to manufacture while the others were making more excuses than equipment. It was an early marketing miracle.

In another time altogether, while carrying out a consultancy project for a supplier of office, factory and warehouse equipment, I uncovered a company who, by tradition, seemed to care more for its suppliers than its Customers. At the time, as if defying gravity, this company was one of the most successful, solid and profitable I have ever encountered! It was also on a precipice. But that's another story.

In complete contrast, I was whisked off to Västerås in Sweden one day to address an audience of about 800 for ABB. It was the second convention they had held for a fascinating group of people. They were putting their suppliers together with their own teams and their Clients – a genuine partnership approach where they had been able to overcome the conventional fear about 'giving away' their sources and secrets. Instead, ABB had stood the whole thing on its head and, in a spirit of complete openness and partnership, were encouraging a full team mentality to brainstorming and problem solving. I wish I saw more genuine, trusting, 'everyone wins' approaches to building lasting Customer relationships. I also greatly admire the confidence this shows in the value of their own skills and the trust it builds in both their Clients and suppliers.

The moral of these three examples is that supplier relations are crucial to delivery of the Customer promise and, as such, in my view, merit planned strategic marketing. You may feel that to run this kind of marketing continuously, when I have referred to it as being excellent in times of resource shortage or threat, may be a little extreme. That depends on your resources and your suppliers – and I would propose that the ABB experience suggests otherwise. But the fact that I am suggesting *all* corporations should provide for external reverse marketing in their total marketing effort, serves to underline the seriousness of my warning in relation to change and the extent and suddenness with which it will strike.

Lastly, we come to the market of shareholders or what I often refer to as the insiders outside. I know that many corporations have been offering fidelity 'bonuses' and other perks to shareholders for many years. And this is not quite what I am referring to by 'support marketing'. I have no proof, but I suspect that these kinds of loyalty or fidelity schemes suffer the same inherent flaws as Customer loyalty schemes which ultimately rely on bribery. They don't build anything like as much loyalty as businesses hope because the only human appeal is basically to greed.

I am cognisant here of the increasing number of institutional shareholders, such as US mutual funds and what the British call unit trusts. These shareholders are basically there to provide a return of capital growth or dividends for their own Customers or investors. 'Long term' is not the watchword of such people and when businesses are seeking to undergo a period of change or transformation, which many will associate with risk, these kinds of shareholder need managing carefully and communicating with sensitively.

## What factors will most affect marketing in the new millennium?

When we examine the factors which will most affect marketing in the early decades of the new millennium, we discover some rather predictable old friends – such as the economy – and some new ones. Indeed, the whole thing is a bit of a jigsaw. And it may only be when all but the very last few pieces are in place that you will start to resolve your own uncertainties and make decisions about your future.

I intend to spend some time looking at these, because without this background you will not understand all the reasons for the change in marketing, and the extent to which all its facets, not just selling and advertising, will change.

The major points of this chapter relating to the marketing environment and how it affects the marketer for the run up to 2000 and beyond are as follows:

- We have arrived at the Age of Individualisation. This relates to products and services, not just the media used to sell them.
- Quantity builds immediate sales. Quality builds friends for your business. Those friends build the long-term quantity which yields the marketing miracles.
- To be at its most effective, marketing should become a four-way activity aimed at:
  — the external market (prospects, Customers and lapsed Customers)
  — the internal market (employees)
  — the external reverse market (suppliers)
  — the support market (the insiders outside – shareholders).

# 3

# The marketing environment

Prediction – the art, science or skill of foretelling the future – is a notoriously insane activity in which to become involved. And one can understand why: apparently people have developed as much in the last ten years as we did in the previous 5000. Looking back over those ten years, I do find myself wondering about the definition of 'develop' in this context! I am informed that every three years, the amount of information on this planet actually doubles. It's no wonder that prediction is increasingly difficult and less reliable. It was bad enough in earlier times: most memorable perhaps are the examples of Charles Duell who was commissioner of the US Patents Office in 1899 and predicted 'everything that can be invented has been invented'; and the spokesperson for Decca Recording Company who, when explaining their rejection of the Beatles, said 'we don't like their sound and guitar music is on the way out.'

## The answer is: there is no answer

You don't have to be an optimist to look at economic predictions for the future, but as the saying almost goes, it certainly helps. In fact there are some well-informed gloom and doom merchants who would try the strength of even the most optimistic optimist. I think it was the South African, Clem Sunter, who said, 'The global economy will go up. Or down. But not necessarily in that order.' One can feel the economist's problem. The world is now a seething mass of micro and macro economies.

Electronic systems and information technology have accelerated reaction times to the point at which one hot word in the US can wipe billions off the British or other stock exchanges around the world while ordinary people sleep the night peacefully away. In my view, you'd have to be a complete lunatic actually to want to make cast iron predictions for the economy during what I believe will be one of the most (if not the most) economically turbulent decades in history. Some predict, following the turn of the millennium, a global spirit of rejuvenation and enterprise will lift the human race on a euphoric tide and that this will have massive impetus and stimulus on trade. Whether this is either true or sustainable if it happens, you don't have to be the wise man of the world to know that the world and its resources are ultimately finite and will probably remain so for the life of this book. I will eat the original manuscript if this increases predictability, decreases risk and slows down the pace of change for businesses wherever they are.

## Being economical with the future

Perhaps that is the only predictable fact about the global, continental and national economies of the future. They will become more turbulent; and then more turbulent still. It is an irony that it should be so, but history shows that 'progress' in itself does not generally improve economic stability; just the reverse. Particular situations, government policies, crop successes etc may provide stability on a national or regional level – but one negative situation which causes reverberation on a global or continental basis will nearly always overshadow or overpower them.

One conventional analysis of our global economic future suggests low growth or no growth; yet several international forecasters dismiss this. Some valuable new markets are opening up, they point out, suggesting that the increasing number of countries with market orientated policies will provide vigorous growth.

An economist at a major bank in Los Angeles nailed his flag firmly to the mast saying, 'the 1990s could be the most prosperous decade of the century'. Unlike almost everyone else this renegade contended that stability would be one of the strengths of the 1990s and that we would not see 'the sharp ups and downs of the earlier cycles'. Much as I envy someone who can make up his mind and come out with a positive statement for the future, I found this one to be somewhat reckless and lacking in regard for the evidence, although I would have loved to have been proven wrong, preferably by an optimist.

The truth is that these days one cannot foretell the future with any reliable degree of accuracy. There are far too many factors which muddy up the pool. Some forecasters say that the greenhouse effect may wreak havoc through even the most informed and reliable forecasts. Others say the Greens were finished by the beginning of the 1990s. If so, I predict they'll be back and in force! Our children want a planet, please.

I do believe, for example, that global warming may wreak havoc through even the most informed and reliable forecasts. The tragic devastation and crop failures it has caused already in some areas of the US, such as the mid-West, could be just a beginning. If it continues the way it has started, we could see huge shifts of economic structures built around agricultural traditions that have stood the test of hundreds of years. Will the French vineyards continue to produce wine which they consider the best in the world? At the moment, as well as increased heat and drought in the summer, some producers are having to fly helicopters over their vineyards during the winter nights to stop the damage caused by frosts such as they have never experienced before. Meanwhile, enterprising wine merchants are discovering that other wine producing climates are improving rapidly. They may not yet be stealing the crown, but they are certainly stealing sales. You only have to look at the climb of Californian and the so-called New World wine exports to find the evidence. The world is beginning to compare Californian, South African, Australian and New Zealand wines with the very best it can find, even from France. In the US, the domestic market already appreciates its home-grown wines to the full. But what might happen if the Californian vineyards were to suffer the same kind of climate changes that the French have had to deal with? Or, worse, suppose what happened in the mid-West happened on the slopes of the Californian vineyards?

That's only wine. Add all the other thousands of climate-related products or services into this picture and you have a potential upheaval of a massive amount of business. It could be chaos. Yes, the fact is, when you examine scenarios for the future economy, the honest conclusion must be – 'Who can tell!'

But it doesn't stop them trying. The Deutsche Bank, prior to the rejoining of the two Germanies, was prophesying that the economies of nearly all the advanced industrial countries would be forced to accept a huge influx of immigrants from the developing world – they said 'By the mid 1990s we're going to see the strongest surge in migration ever witnessed on this planet'. Oddly enough, whereas they based their notion on entirely different factors, again it is the global warming changes which many said would award their prediction the accolade of being correct. Being right for the wrong reasons may be the best that our unpredictable future will allow us. As it transpired they were more right for Germany than they were for more or less anywhere else except the African continent.

## The shrinking world is growing

Does going international represent an answer to economic uncertainty? After all, if you choose your countries carefully, at worst and at least it spreads the risk. Again – right answer, wrong reason. There can be little

■ Customer-Driven Marketing

doubt that more and more companies will want to be international. For as business development speeds up, staying on top of a market or keeping in front of a business will require strong presences across worldwide markets.

## The global economy

In his book *The Borderless World: Power and Strategy in the Interlinked Economy* (Collins), Kenichi Ohmae suggested that the developed world has become 'an isle, an interlinked economy'. He points out, absolutely correctly, that the costs of marketing and technology have turned most advanced and contemporary companies into high fixed cost businesses. This means they must seek out global markets to justify those costs. This proves, he asserts, globalisation is, ironically, the direct result of internal corporate economics. Yet the cost of internationalisation is great. So we have a paradox. Small to medium size businesses, those who are not yet international, may need to develop internationally to gain, regain or maintain their commercial high ground. Yet at the same time large multinational corporations are unbundling because they have found that the hierarchy-laden 'big is beautiful' approach doesn't work; they become over-managed, over-costly, distant from and inflexible to Customers and their needs.

## How can failure signpost success?

If you're smart, you too can only fail at predicting a precise economic picture for the future. But how can we turn such failure into a successful consideration of the economy in relation to your marketing for the future? The answer is simple. We must predict for unpredictability – plan not to have a plan – construct ourselves to be re-constructed; possibly continuously. Be flexible.

Flexibility is my answer to the problem. And we'll look at how to implement that shortly. Although this book is not really limited to Europe, from whichever viewpoint you stand, Europe impacts on both the marketer and the economy. I'd like therefore to pull in at this stage some thoughts which are relevant. Both items relate specifically to Europe: the Blossoming East and the Brand and Europe.

For corporations considering the possibilities of Eastern or Western Europe, these will be important issues; those involved already appreciate the relevance. For those who have only a domestic scene to consider, stay with us.

It is fascinating that many Europeans believe that the US has had much more experience in dealing with the kind of market which Europeans now have to learn about: they draw a comparison that where

Europe has countries, the US has States. Although of course there are many States with an ethnic spread or bias, Europe may find it easier that most of their 'ethnic spreads' are packaged neatly into countries. However, there are other problems for US companies in Europe. Few Americans know that, tiny but significant as it is, Switzerland has four indigenous languages to cope with.

## Eastern Europe – new markets for old?

New markets have the benefit of hindsight. They may not be able to look back at their own experiences, but they can look back on ours. New markets also have new problems. Old or mature markets solved their own problems along the way. Thus the new markets should not make the most of these mistakes again. Of course, this does not mean that they won't have problems. It means they should have different problems. One of these will be the effect of 'fast forwarding' developments which have taken 30, 40 or 50 years to take place. The same process happens successfully but it is condensed within a time frame of five to ten years. It's risky, but irresistible. South Africa will tell you all about it.

Eastern Europe is a new, developing market. A market which requires patience from the most impatient animal after property developers - the marketing man. The biggest product that can be sold to Eastern Europe is not cans of food, motor cycles, cars, clothing or computers. It is know-how.

Selling know-how – in effect training managers and providing knowledge – is also the method which leaves East European national dignities and pride intact and creates a consumer for the hardware which is required. Japan, for example, is very familiar with this notion.

## Who's got the cheque book?

To have a new market with a fat wallet would be ideal, but Eastern Europe does not have a fat wallet. A few may be created in the process of development, but not yet. What's more, the Eastern Bloc internal credit line is poor to non-existent. The citizens don't have funds, the corporations don't have funds and the countries don't have funds. With almost half the leading banks in the world being Japanese, unless we see some substantial change in Japan's position, it could be well placed to score.

I am no particular supporter of the Japanese. Indeed, in my view they, more than any other nation, fuelled the quantity spiral of the 1960s, 1970s and 1980s. But I guess that's like asking 'Who's to blame, the pusher or the junkie?' Ironically, of course, quality is a notion embedded into Japanese culture, and Japanese business and industry would be anxious to claim that they have played as much a part as any other nation to

■ Customer-Driven Marketing

forward the cause of quality. However, the effect of the Japanese industrial might and its need to mass produce and to export globally to sustain its economy and feed its factories, was a major factor influencing what happened to sales and marketing throughout most of the world in the period 1965 to 1990.

These comments are made for the assistance of those looking at Eastern Europe as a potential. Without any disrespect to its citizens, one has to realise that in market and marketing terms, it is primitive. When Eastern Europeans first were shown US and European advertising they were shocked. They could not understand lifestyle advertising at all. All those people singing and grooving in the street – why? People lazing on tropical beaches – seemingly because they prefer certain drinks, cigarettes, fastfoods or banks? It doesn't make any sense. They want to know about the product: what it tastes like; what flavours it comes in; how much it costs; where it is stocked.

Many conventional or traditional marketing approaches and activities will remain difficult, impossible or unnecessary in Eastern Europe for many years. It is a market which needs help and partnership first. I fear that just as we are beginning to see the end of exploitation-based, quantity-driven marketing here, some nations or some corporations will prefer to take their old ideas to the new territory rather than change and adapt themselves. Many international brand names have rushed to set up – particularly in Moscow. Two people told me the following two stories on the same day.

A Russian goes into a dealership to buy a new car. He tells the manager what he would like and the manager says that he will check to see if this is possible. After about an hour, he returns to advise the would-be buyer that 'Yes. It is possible. Your car can be collected on Thursday the 14th of June in just four years' time.'

The buyer is beside himself with delight but requests that the delivery must be in the morning. 'Why in the morning?' asks the manager. 'I have the plumber booked for that afternoon,' he replies.

When McDonald's opened up in Moscow, a Customer waited in line for hours to get to the counter. Finally he got there and ordered over a hundred items. They were all for his family. Apparently, Muscovites were not used to retailers having any stock for more than a day and the Customer was taking them home to freeze!

The second story is, apparently, true!

I truly wonder whether the impact of Eastern Europe as a market for the rest of the world may for a while yet be significantly less than many expect. Certainly I expect the process to have a slow lift off and for the eventual build up of cash or suitable borrowing means to provide the fuel which will drive Eastern Europe's current desire to 'catch up' with the West. Following on from that, therefore, I also wonder whether the effect on the global economy may prove unpredictable and almost impossible to quantify in the long term. Don't hold your breath!

## The non-European will survive

In *European Business Strategies* (Kogan Page), author and management consultant Richard Lynch looks at the costs and resources of building a Euro-brand. He rightly acknowledges the vast profits that can accrue to those who can pull it off. However, we are also seeing it happen. Quoting directly from the book, 'it can be seen that Euro-brands do not guarantee profits and require, as one might expect, substantial and costly brand-building activity'.

Will the Germans still get to the beach loungers first in the year 2000? Will the British still cook the worst food? Will we still crack Irish or Belgian jokes? Who can tell! But I expect so.

Inside each of us living in the European Community there is both a European and a non-European. I suspect it will remain so for quite some time and no more so than in paranoid Britain. The point here is that you may be able to change more legislation and rationalise more regulations with each new parliament, but to change people, it takes whole new people. In other words, it takes generations. So far as Europe goes, we are about one and a bit generations in.

The marketer who wishes to succeed in Europe must understand his own brands as well as the markets he serves. We may well be developing a 'Euro-consumer' but we are not there yet despite multi-lingual packaging and shameful attempts at dubbing voice-overs on to standard visual imagery. However, creating a Eurobrand does not need a Euro-consumer. Nestlé markets about 20 different blends of coffee in 20 different countries, each meeting what Nestlé have determined as the preferred taste of that marketplace, yet they all sell under the same label.

It is true that in the US, the East Coast and the West are quite different – not just in geography and climate, but in marketing matters too. However, at the end of the day, the US is one nation. You may notice a gradual change of the consumer as you head from East to West, as indeed you will from North to South, but when you cross from France to Spain, the difference is remarkable and, in sociographic terms, instant: it all happens in 20 km or less.

I believe the converging European consumer to be still quite a novelty – an invention of the EuroAd agency who would like an easy life or the EuroClient who wants a cheap one! It may happen – it is happening – but, for the majority, it will take time to have major impact on anything other than long-term planning.

■ Customer-Driven Marketing

## Understand your brand

You must understand your brand. If you are Rolex or Coca-Cola, you have a brand which crosses national frontiers. If not, you may still need to market first to the non-European inside us. What's more, if you are looking to your fellow marketing colleagues to sit beside you and help you create a EuroConsumer, then you may be bitterly disappointed. For many of those colleagues have sales strategies aimed at ever-narrowing market tastes and specialities. They have moved down the steps from mass marketing to segmented marketing and have just got to grips with niche marketing.

The 1980s ended on the trend of database marketing; this gave the ability to target, the information to understand and the tools to cultivate the individuality of Customers; as distinct from the desire or need to weld them together into bigger groups.

Moreover, as you travel around Europe, or if you see EuroAds such as I referred to earlier, you will become aware that the different nationalities approach advertising differently. Nobody uses more plays on words than the British; few use sex more than the French; the Germans have a very laid-back, matter-of-fact style and so on.

## So where are the EuroConsumers?

Where one can pull Europe back together with the economy is in conjecture about whether we are dealing with a Euro-economy or a gathering of several different economies. For a while yet, despite whatever eventually happens with a common currency, each country will remain better or worse at managing itself, deciding how much it wants to tax its citizens and what the tax should pay for. Each country will have its own problems and dilemmas, and for the foreseeable future so it will continue. Indeed, as the likes of McDonald's, Benetton and Coke rampage across Europe, West and East, this may be one of the major differences they must recognise. Some differences, I suspect, will remain for ever.

Only in France will Crocodile Dundee's famous expression ever ring true – 'It tastes like Pschitt [that's the unfortunately pronounced name of a quite pleasant soft drink there] but you can live on it'. Only in Spain will a Bum biscuit be a good one. And why shouldn't the Austrians drink twice as much milk as the Belgians; the Germans own three times more dishwashers than the Dutch, who own twice as many video cameras as the Belgians? Across the border the French are busy consuming almost twice as much butter as the Italians. Meanwhile things are even more affluent outside the EC where, even by the beginning of the 1990s, the Swiss had installed an amazing 1.3 telephones per person – twice as many as the British. No one has yet successfully explained to me why dull, dismal and wet as it always is when I visit, Belgium has a remarkable nine times more freezers than Spain which, by contrast, roasts me alive whenever I'm there!

Actually, Europe is a seething mass of anomalies trying not to get out. And long may it stay so. Yet I fear it won't, because we're just growing our EuroConsumers right now. They're our youngsters. They seem much more relaxed about sharing their cultural values and quite happy to purchase the same things.

Despite this, there will nevertheless be a growing use of pan-European media – if only because it's easier to get a pan-European message across to the Consumer and there are an increasing number of pan-European media, just as there are a fewer but still increasing number of global media, thanks to satellite broadcast media and the Internet. Few pan-European trade media yet exist so, despite the wastage, specialist pan-European consumer media will be attractive for reaching the other category who are among the front runners to becoming EuroConsumers: the business market.

Another interesting use for pan-European media is emphasised by one enterprising ad agency who overlaid what they call 'Golden Circles' over Europe. Prosperity it seems does not conform to national boundaries, although interestingly they found that Europe's wealthiest consumers live mainly within a 400 km radius of Cologne, Germany. This may have something to do with the fact that the area includes the whole of Luxembourg! My own years of direct marketing experience, however, would remind me of the value of targeting and targeting criteria. I must pose the question: do the affluent French buy the same as the affluent Germans? Do affluent British and Belgians buy the same brands, fly the same airlines or drink the same wines? I think not. I think maybe never! The British may seem the ultimate ditherers of Europe but they are seemingly and perhaps ironically a lot less nationalistic in their purchasing than most of the other nations.

## One language, one culture, one market? I don't think so!

Some time ago I was asked to help out by a leading European tour operator – actually American owned – who had suffered a major problem with the marketing of canal boating holidays in France. He had printed some leaflets and, as a classic low-cost solution to the language problem, had remembered to keep all the copy to the black, enabling language changes to be made with a single, simple plate change, leaving the other three of the four-colour set common. Having paid handsomely for an English copywriter to come up with terrific copy, he had various translations made and sat back and waited for the business to come in. Except for the British, they stayed away in their thousands!

After some research we were able to establish why. The copy approached these boating holidays as if they were a luxury item for luxury-minded people; for in Britain to the British, that is what they were. Yet to the French domestic market they were not luxury at all, just a good middle class, middle of the road product. Its big appeal to the French was that it was an activity holiday. Once sold as such, sales lifted off nicely.

The same was true of his German market where, far from being a luxury holiday, it was an economy package for those who couldn't afford the grand financial splash of the Côte d'Azur in high season. Of course the copy to a bemused, be-sandaled, rucksacked Rhineman was totally wrong. Once adjusted to point out the fantastic quality despite the low price, the package sold well to Germany too.

I was more than a little delighted, shortly after I had written this section, to hear Professor Louis Stern at the 1995 Global Conference on Marketing telling his audience, 'One Europe, one market? You must be off your rocks!' We concur.

I think we will see several types of product. Some will flourish with a Eurobrand headlining their marketing; others will benefit from retained national branding. Equally some countries will more readily accept Eurobrands (or brands perceived to be foreign). It seems quite plausible that children will suck Eurobranded, Eurotasting confectionery, yet equally plausible that, in an adult market, Nescafé will have success with one brand and many tastes. Other products have one taste and many brands.

If you look at the US for an example you will see many different courses being followed. Yet strong brands such as Coke and Marlboro may not tailor their products like Nescafé, but they certainly tailor their advertising. One quite often sees a kind of ethnic advertising with a particular approach to the Hispanic market, another for the Chinese or Italian or even Irish-descendant communities. Europe too has sophisticated advertising and marketing professionals who are increasingly capable of tightly targeting the message as well as the medium.

### Why should you be big; how can you be beautiful?

In many ways, the argument for size is dwindling if you are a national, European, US, African, Australasian, Asian or, even, global company. Many now prefer to be beautiful than to be big. Because often to be beautiful you need to make yourself more attractive to a greater number of smaller groups. This leads one to the false conclusion that to meet the likely economic profile of the future, you need to be small to medium size, manageable, adept and fast reacting to Customer needs. Yes, you need to be all of these things. But the pressures on the managers of small

## The marketing environment

to medium size companies will increase cruelly: more money for research; more money for technology; more money for developing long-term Customer care programmes; more money for breaking and funding new markets.

What all this demonstrates is the need to do away with mass production of product and replace it with massive production of know-how. This is where the miracles lie. Thus small to medium size companies wishing to compete will need to look for partners or become available for acquisition. We may sadly see a rapid decline in the number of small, independent companies, as we continue to grapple with 'Europeanisation' and globalisation. They may look to save themselves through networks. And they might find a miracle there.

Yet, on the Internet, we are already experiencing the complete contradiction of this phenomenon. The Internet provides a global business with the ideal medium through which to market services.

## So how will marketers and marketing cope with unpredictable economies?

The root cause of the unpredictability is uncertainty. To cope with uncertainty, one must stay alert, fast and responsive. But above all else one must understand that the key quality will be flexibility. This quality will repeat itself significantly throughout our thinking.

The resilience lent by flexibility will be crucial to successful marketing in the future – many a marketing miracle will be found here. The marketing director has to learn to live by a new creed:

> **It is better to control a big budget
> than it is to control a big department.**

Inevitably this means the use of more consultants, specialists and outside contractors and the reduction of the marketing payroll.

Although I do not believe we can predict very far ahead the vagaries of the economy, I do believe we can predict, or rather look back through history to see, how marketing reacts to different economic climates or different economic corporate situations.

## When the going gets tough, the tough get fired. Or do they?

What normally happens to marketing spend and marketing departments when times are good, bad or indifferent? In my experience, the indifferent is the worst of all, but it varies across the disciplines. For example, a lot of direct marketers and sales promotion people see increases in spend on their disciplines in lean times, when advertisers want either to main-

■ Customer-Driven Marketing

tain sale-related activity because it's at the 'sharp end' or, in the case of direct marketing, because it is so measurable in terms of its cost effectiveness that you see exactly what works and how well. This is a great comfort when money is tight.

However, with only those odd exceptions, the reaction to unfavourable economic change is fairly predictable. The better the times, the more is spent. The harder the times, the less is spent. It's only when a real storm hits that the actual marketing force is affected and heads start to roll.

In order, the trimming seems to go as follows:

1. PR activities, sponsorship etc
2. Advertising and mass media spend
3. Direct marketing, sales promotion etc.

When at last the hatchet starts to hover, PR seems to smooth-talk itself out of the number one slot and into a fairly safe, dark corner, leaving a usually quite flabby marketing department to be attacked and slimmed down first of all. The sales department tends to be threatened while the others get fired. When the salesforce start getting fired, it's generally either a time to panic or a sign of bad sales management being flushed out and replaced.

However, I suppose quite understandably, we marketers are, as a breed, reluctant to fire ourselves! The point is that this rather cosy attitude will not help us to attend to the changes with which we will have to cope in the future, and to react as swiftly and decisively as we must.

By outsourcing – using sub-contractors, specialists and consultants to a greater degree – we are left with control but without the greater part of the workload. In the later section, covering the advertising agency of the future, you will see how this in time will work hand in glove with the Client of the future, for ad agencies must undergo some radical changes before they can satisfy the Client of the future. They too need marketing miracles, not just their Clients! More, they must develop – and Clients must encourage them to provide – far better, far wider ranging strategic marketing skills.

## You have been warned!

As I warned at the beginning of this chapter, making reliable predictions is not only increasingly difficult, but when you should chance to get it right, it may not be for very long. It may be a salutary thought that occasionally it is those most regarded for forecasting or prediction who can get it wrong. In 1984, *The Economist* asked people from a range of different occupations to make predictions for the next decade. Ten years later, when the magazine reviewed the results, it discovered dustmen had scored 'an easy victory' over the trained economists. A leading City analyst commented that, 'nearly all the main turning points have been missed by forecasters'.

To summarise, then, the economy in which you will have to operate, whether you are affected locally, nationally, across your whole continent or even globally, is equally difficult to predict because of the number of 'wild cards' in play at the moment. However, critically, we have established the following points:

- Economies will become more volatile and turbulent.
- One method of spreading risk is internationalisation – but it's pricey as well as risky. Partnership could be a better answer.
- Planning must include less rigid parameters.
- Eastern Europe may, for a while yet, prove less of an opportunity than forecast.
- Brand strength will remain significant, although greater understanding of markets and their individual relationships with brands will become more important.
- EuroConsumers will come for some brands later than others, for some never at all.
- Marketing departments will need to implement flexibility as the principal strategic quality for the future enabling them to react decisively, rapidly and effectively. In other words:

**It is better to control a big budget
than it is to control a big department.**

- Advertising agencies must provide wider ranging, more intelligent strategic marketing counsel for their Clients.

# 4

# Technology and marketing

In my 'Customer-Driven Marketing' workshops and seminars I call the technology review 'The Technology Holocaust'. I've a simple enough reason for this. My experience suggests that each new generation of technology actually puts the previous generation to death, for nobody seems to want old software or hardware when there's new available. And there nearly always is. This is not merely the impatience of the users. The market – competitors in some cases, Clients in others – can exert an enormous pressure on you to invest in the very latest technology. I have already referred to the impending squeeze on margins. Undoubtedly, the galloping desire to adopt new technology will cause more than its fair share of this.

As I took the Royal Mail's roadshow version of Marketing 2000 around Britain, one managing director told the assembled few how his company was in the throes of installing its third complete computer system inside a two-year period. As he told the story, his fellow delegates groaned in sympathy with him. They associated immediately with his pain at the disruption, the frustration, the time failures, the chaos that he must surely have endured.

'Bugger that!' he cried. 'Think of what it's cost and then tell me how I recover the costs.' He went on to reassure us that one only embarks on such drastic repetitive installation of new technology if you absolutely have to. And he absolutely had to. His market, his competitors' capabilities and the demands of his Clients forced his hand.

So I do see it as something of a holocaust. And perhaps until we find the miracle of a technocrat who can resist new products, innovation and the latest capability in favour of the old kit that has been in for two or three years, then I feel inclined to let the title rest.

## Marketing and information technology: two crazy, mixed-up kids!

Why has marketing (and it might surprise some that I include direct marketing in this) taken so long to make friends with computers? It must have held everyone back immeasurably. Somehow or other, the world seems to be full of companies and organisations which have marketing people (especially at the top) who don't speak IT language. And, equally, it must be said, IT people who do not understand, nor want to understand, marketing.

A fascinating research exercise was carried out in Britain by the DunnHumby consultancy. They specialise in pulling together the IT and marketing disciplines and functions of a business, and have developed some interesting methods of helping marketing to understand and make sense of its numbers. Their surveys were carried out in 1989, 1992 and 1995. Predominantly here we shall consider the 1989 and 1995 survey results to give us the widest span.

The reports highlight two critical gaps which have not significantly improved over the years: first, a gap between the peoples of technology and marketing; secondly, a gap between the acceptance that technology must assist marketing and the knowledge of how it should help and what it can do.

I was grateful in 1990 to Clive Humby and Edwina Dunn for permission to use their findings in *Total Quality Marketing*; I am doubly grateful that they have kindly obliged again with access to their 1995 findings. The following extract was taken from the original survey in 1989. After this we'll take a look how much some things have changed and, disappointingly, how some haven't at all!

> IT and marketing management both recognise that computer technology will play an increasingly important role in the marketing department in the next five years.
>
> Computers in marketing or database marketing is not just about direct marketing and communication with Customers. Quite the opposite. These applications are considered fairly low priority in the grand corporate scheme. Management feel that database marketing needs to encompass most of the business functions for which marketing is responsible, from product development to market research and selecting channels of distribution.
>
> The survey revealed that the number one priority of the company is 'Improved Customer Care and Knowledge' and that marketing have an important role in helping to achieve this objective.

■ Customer-Driven Marketing

Sales management and product measurement are vital to company success and technology has already made a significant contribution to these disciplines. Sales management normally falls outside the remit of the marketing department. Product management technology, whilst invaluable, has without doubt held any number of companies hostage. In some cases it has become a barrier to Customer-driven systems. The product and Customer views of data represent important but conflicting decision-support systems.

The sales management function, which is not generally within the marketing department's remit, saw the greatest support from technology. According to marketing managers, most of this support is provided internally by the IT function.

There are only two activities which are both marketing's responsibility in the majority of cases and use technology to any reasonable extent. These are 'Management and Measurement of Products' and 'Market Research'.

The survey showed that manufacturers appreciate that they have the greatest distance to travel in order to accomplish these objectives by 1995 and most fear the consequences if they fail to achieve them. Financial Services are so convinced of the major benefits of database marketing that they believe a discrete budget should be allocated to help build them.

The picture of marketing and technology today is not rosy. Barely one company in three has a full-time IT team dedicated to marketing. Managers trying to develop marketing systems do not always know at the outset what data is relevant and what is not.

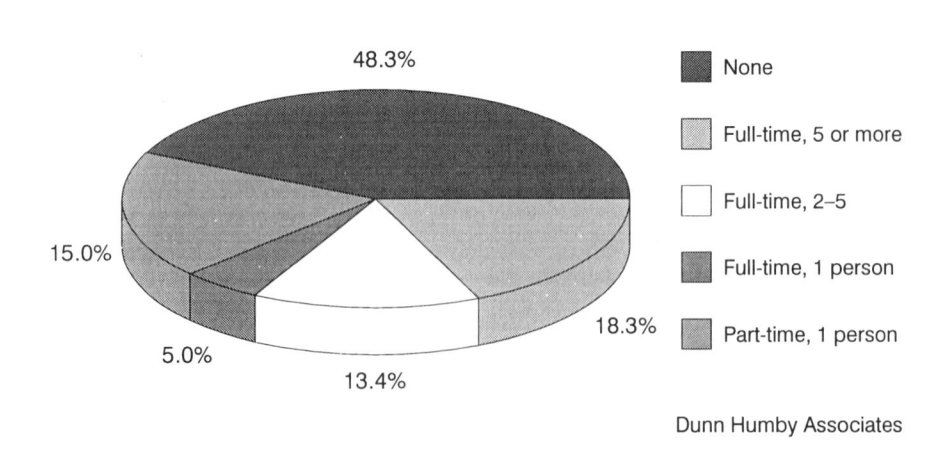

- 48.3% None
- 18.3% Full-time, 5 or more
- 13.4% Full-time, 2–5
- 5.0% Full-time, 1 person
- 15.0% Part-time, 1 person

Dunn Humby Associates

**Figure 4.1** *The size of IT team dedicated to marketing (1989)*

**Technology and marketing** ■

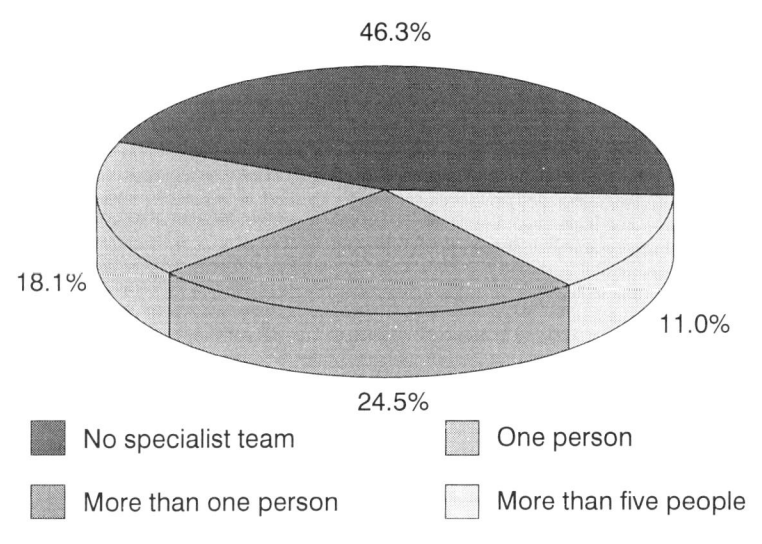

46.3%

18.1%

11.0%

24.5%

■ No specialist team     □ One person
■ More than one person   □ More than five people

**Figure 4.2** *The size of IT team dedicated to marketing (1995)*

Marketing managers feel that new skills are needed in the department. IT managers recognise the need for more training, particularly in helping them to understand the marketing process.

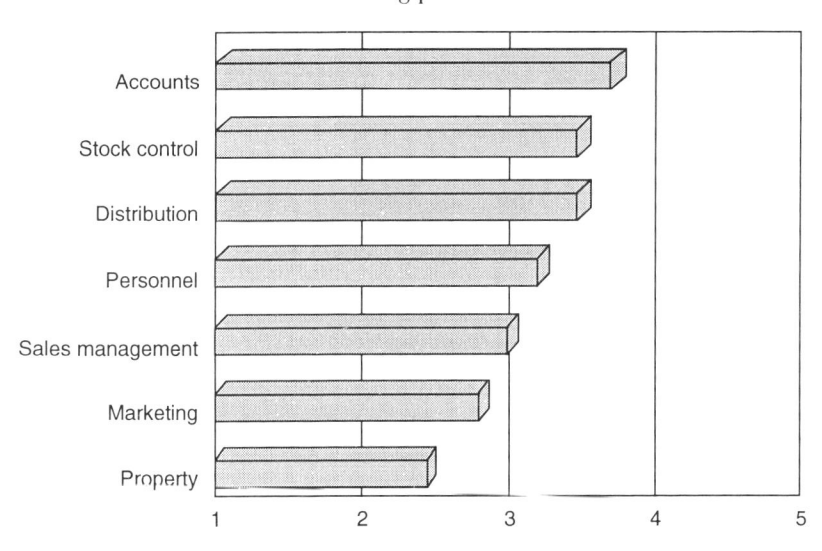

Accounts
Stock control
Distribution
Personnel
Sales management
Marketing
Property

1  2  3  4  5

**Figure 4.3** *The view of IT management on communication skills by internal departments (1995)*

The budgetary spend and limited number of marketing staff are features of a department highly dependent on third party suppliers, particularly advertising agencies, market research companies and sales promotion agencies. And yet, clearly no one is under the illusion that any of these third par-

■ Customer-Driven Marketing

ties have any real knowledge or expertise in the field of marketing technology. Mainstream advertising agencies are seen as particularly naive – unaware of even the business benefits database marketing, or a marketing database, has to offer.

By contrast, direct marketing to Customers and prospects is much more technology orientated (62 per cent and 51 per cent of companies respectively). More than half rely on a third party.

Clearly, marketing people need to communicate their technology requirements more effectively. It is not just about having a dedicated IT team.

Marketing is dependent upon information which is external to the business (market research, media costs, competitor intelligence, etc). Unlike most other data within the company, this marketing information does not tend to be transaction based, it's more likely to be statistical summaries (a collection of Customers sharing common characteristics).

For this reason, and because the development of marketing systems is very new, the IT department finds it difficult to understand the needs of the marketing department.

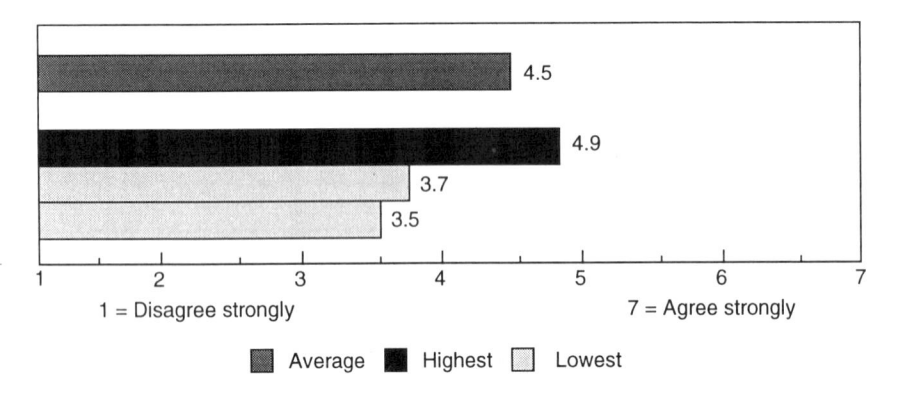

[Bar chart: values 4.5 (Average), 4.9 (Highest), 3.7, 3.5 (Lowest); scale 1 = Disagree strongly to 7 = Agree strongly]

**Figure 4.4** *IT staff have a poor grasp of the marketing process*

The survey quite clearly demonstrated that marketing managers expect the IT department to fulfil the role of adviser and provide the main focus of technology and systems development. Second choice are the specialist systems consultants.

Today the IT manager has a fairly poor opinion of the marketing department's use of technology. Even those departments rated 'above average' are still seen as the worst communicators amongst a number of other departments, including the sales department.

The IT manager is aware of the potential problems they face in 'getting to grips' with marketing. They have few concerns in terms of the available hardware or even software, although advanced software tools, such as CASE tools, do appear to help. The missing link is training and education and, in particular, knowledge of what makes marketing data different.

## Technology and marketing

There is little doubt in the minds of respondents that database marketing and the use of computers in the marketing department is set to increase dramatically. Indeed many expect their company to have realised the full potential of such technology by 1995 – most notably retailers.

The two statements attracting the highest level of agreement overall were:

'The marketing department must have user friendly access to computer systems'; and

'Marketing will see an increase in the use of computer technology over the next five years'.

## How had things changed by 1995?

Over 46 per cent of companies surveyed still did not provide a full-time IT team to look at the marketing department's needs. Also, marketing management expect the internal data processing (DP) department to be their main ally in the development of such systems. External suppliers came a very poor second.

After the six years had passed, the third survey results were equally disappointing in many ways. For example, Figure 4.3 still shows that marketing and sales management are viewed by IT as the worst communicators in the company and there has been negligible improvement in the results. I shall have to bang my drum harder!

There was an apparent paradox in that the shift in media spend suggests that media which use computers such as those employed for direct marketing are sharply on the increase, however there appears to have been a decline, from 18.3 per cent to only 11 per cent in the companies with five or more full-time IT staff dedicated to marketing. In the middle range, however, companies with one to five full-time IT staff dedicated to marketing show startling growth – from 18.4 per cent to 42.5 per cent. Discussing the decline of dedicated five or more teams with Clive Humby and Edwina Dunn, we came to the conclusion that outside consultancies and suppliers were more highly favoured and were probably being used much more these days. DunnHumby's own corporate growth and success would certainly endorse this. It seems most likely, therefore, that the middle range now standing at 42.5 per cent is being fattened both by fallout from above as well as genuine growth from below.

Today, the marketing department's main use of technology is in relation to media selection and market research and this is generally provided by third parties.

The marketing department do not see any of their current suppliers as major partners in technology. The top three suppliers are advertising agencies, PR consultants and market research companies. I was pleased that marketing managers gave a firm thumbs-down to each of these as allies in technology. I say that I was pleased; I would not have been if there was any evidence whatsoever that agencies, PR consultants or market researchers had anything significant themselves to offer their Clients as partners in technology. Alas, however, even if there may be one or two minor but welcome exceptions, in general, they do not.

Marketing managers actually rated the advertising agency's understanding of 'the potential business benefits of technology in marketing' as very poor. This must be a serious issue, since advertising agencies are in constant or frequent use by the marketing department. Certainly, they must at least understand the potential of computers in marketing to stay as central as they now are to the marketing function.

Conversely, the IT manager is aware that he does not fully understand the marketing function; the answer evidently is education and training. All management recognise is that there is a long way still to go. They are mindful that they need to show results and pay-back as early as possible from corporate investment in technology and software systems.

The overwhelming conclusion of the research is, frustratingly, just as it was in 1989: it proclaims the need for better communication between marketing and IT departments, and relevant education and training. These two factors will undoubtedly lead to a new breed of business analyst, literate in both the marketing and IT disciplines.

The survey clearly proved that getting IT and marketing together is a task which is not made any easier by the fact that, while both sides clearly accept the need, they are reluctant to get started mainly because of ignorance of each other's methods and work. DunnHumby's excellent and pioneering work will no doubt help many to solve this and related problems. For it is crystal clear that those who will be the successful businesses of the 1990s, those who will be leaps and bounds ahead as we cross to the new millennium, will be those organisations who can effectively marry their marketing and IT teams, in fact, those who create a culture within their marketing department for IT to thrive and grow.

This must come from the top. I have not yet seen a successful company where the tone of the organisation's IT activities, and its whole attitude to IT generally, is not set at the very top. Although this doesn't mean that everybody from the top down needs to be at the leading edge of IT – it does mean that those without sufficient strategic and tactical knowledge of hardware and software will be likely to see the price of their ignorance in reduced profits later.

This goes far deeper than merely understanding the media opportunities for which we can thank new technology. It is about understanding how – in all its widest aspects – technology can assist in the marketing function. In tactical terms we are already seeing major advances; despite the fact that I have always found the consumer – with some notable specialist areas of exception – to be a lot less enamoured of technology. For a while, when the first automatic teller machines (ATMs) arrived enabling us to dispense cash from 'holes in the wall', it looked as if nobody would use them. Not only is the majority of cash now withdrawn through ATMs in the developed world, but new models are on the streets which enable you to transact your whole banking service that way. This is a possible alternative to the so-called Yuppie Bank, First Direct, who introduced twenty-four hour telephone banking to Britain.

With less than one in four companies having IT represented at board level, progress may slow a little, but never in my view to the speed preferred by the consumer. If you ask a consumer or buyer if they would like something faster or earlier, the answer is invariably affirmative – and often they will pay a premium for it. If we go back to the introduction of same-day, then four-hour, then two-hour and finally one-hour photo processing, we have a graphic example of technology bringing speed to the consumer. Of course, with this kind of progress the premium you charge for speed does not last long, for that is the bit a competitor will 'give' away to grab the business and you are back to where you started!

In Europe, the French consumer seems to lead the way in the acceptance of technology. Not only is their market alive to technology but their consumers also seem to delight in each new innovation. One wonders sometimes whether it has reached a level of technology for technology's sake.

It's not in France, I know, but I read the delightful story recently about a busy branch office of the Client of a friend of mine. They employ about 70 people and have a wages department of one woman. She works two to three days a week and uses a mechanical device with a cranking handle to calculate the wages, bonuses, tax and other payroll deductions. She keeps ledgers in the most wonderful copperplate script and her accounts are always the first to arrive at head office. She is never absent or late and has been employed at the same branch continuously since the mid-1940s, when she was 14 years old. She shows no signs of flagging and no one can recall a mistake. Tell this to any computer enthusiast and they grin broadly – mainly because they are human too. But they always maintain a wise silence.

## Technology, too, should have a clear Customer purpose

At the beginning of the 1990s, Britain's National Westminster Bank announced plans to spend over £1 billion on its computing and telecommunications in the first five years of the decade. Displaying his vested interest to the full, their IT director proclaimed the bank's Computing Centre to be 'the most important part of the bank's business'. While accepting his enthusiasm, it is worth everyone, whether in marketing or not, reminding themselves that the most important part of any business does not actually lie within the business at all.

■ Customer-Driven Marketing

Those who will have marketing miracles happen to them are those who know the Customers of the business are by far the most important part. This is not some glib cliché. It is a fact, which despite decades of training and education, too many businesses still fail to recognise – especially banks. With massive profits returning in the mid-1990s and overpaid, greedy senior directors milking their profit at great cost to both shareholders and Customers alike, these businesses are likely to receive their penalty within the next decade. For one of their competitors, probably foreign, will make a marketing miracle happen.

Putting the Customer first is something that many people find extremely difficult. Cast your mind back. Have you ever been engaged in conversation with a so-called Customer representative when their phone rang? Who won – you or the phone? Usually, it's the phone. But why? The answer is because the notion of Customer is so often a veneer – and a veneer that is coated around the outside of a business rather than seeping and infusing itself into every facet of the business, and every level and every aspect of its decision making. Nowhere is this more so than where technology has been used to bring about service, product or communication improvements which have the major task or priority to improve the Customer's value and delivery.

## IT has the power to transform marketing

You will find examples around, some in this book indeed, where IT has already demonstrated the power to transform marketing and Customer service. It will not do so while kept to base pragmatic tasks such as segmentation and data manipulation both of which, while valuable, are also trivial when set against the bigger picture.

For the Marketer, harnessing computer technology at this level – particularly with the versatility offered by Local Area Network (LAN) linked PCs – would seem quite adequate. One reliable source estimated that the early years of the 1990s showed:

- 33 per cent compound growth in PCs and
- 61 per cent compound growth in those which were inter-connected.

In the latter part of the 1990s it is anticipated that we will see the arrival of a computer a hundred times more powerful than those in common use at the beginning of the decade (and probably a hundred times smaller!). Machines already respond to voice and touch and soon, probably, gestures too.

All of these features will serve to enhance the acceleration of the computer's acceptance at every business level. This is important, since one of the benefits we should look to from computers, especially in times of uncertainty and risk, is their assistance in speedily analysing market data which can then be used as a strategic tool for creating insight, making discoveries and assisting forward planning.

In 1980 there were as few as 10,000 desk-top systems. A decade later, in 1990, that had risen to 90 million and by the year 2000 you can expect that to double up to (estimates vary) 180 million to 250 million. It may be unbelievable, but you'd better believe it! These already incorporate, as does my laptop, DVI (Digital Video Interactive) technology, full motion video, mobility using cellular telephone technology and three-dimensional quality graphics through imaging and rendering technologies. This enables, for example:

- Architects to show your new building on screen, with 3D 'feel' to the images.
- Scientists, engineers and designers to use similar visualisation to alter designs or ideas at will.
- Travel, hotel and tour operators to show you full motion videos, and use computerised booking through the same screens and terminals.

And, of course, most of this can be transmitted or exchanged at will via the Internet and its graphical user interface, the World Wide Web. Intranets will also have a huge part to play. As you read on, you will be introduced to the major role that self-managed units have to play in the future of marketing. These are small, highly autonomous Customer focused teams. Information technologies will undoubtedly form the backbone of these decentralised, project orientated workplaces. Bill Gates at Microsoft declared:

> The direction we are heading is to shift much of the disk space on the PC to a server. PCs will continue to have hard disks which can caché information effectively and will allow users to be mobile. But with this approach, if your PC breaks, you plug in a new one. If you want to upgrade applications in your office, you do so on the server and everyone is upgraded at the same time. What we are doing is taking PC technology, combining it with an intranet and using it to attack the cost of ownership and ease of use issues.

## The longer marketing waits, the harder it gets

Partnership ventures were mentioned in the last chapter as an aid to helping small to medium size companies cope with staying in front of their competitors. The whole concept of partnership as it affects both business-to-business and consumer marketing will arise again later in the book. As more and more organisations get together to work on collaborative ventures, so we will see networks increase. IBM predicted networked PCs will top 90 per cent of all PCs in the workplace before the millen-

■ Customer-Driven Marketing

nium. Networks undoubtedly offer faster communications, wider access to information. Along with these benefits and crucial to collaborative ventures, they also support shared and decentralised decision making.

In *Total Quality Marketing* I predicted that the marketing world would become obsessed with speed: speed of delivery; speed of response and reaction; speed of innovation. This is because I felt that speed, for a while, would become an increasingly fashionable management technique. The computer can be used to assist this primarily to find product design and manufacturing solutions. Strapped to Computer Integrated Manufacturing (CIM), computers facilitate the product cycle and enhance individualisation techniques. We will see robots employed in increasingly sophisticated applications requiring perhaps vision, navigation and manipulation; and all aspects of business will make wider use of artificial intelligence.

The pressure on marketers will increase from the manufacturing units enthused with their new capabilities. For in CIM plants, the computers not only run the plant on a day-to-day basis, they will also use their experimental analyses to develop new software and product design: all the while, they will manage and monitor the supplies resourcing, housekeeping, and all the logistics relating to materials and product shipment.

As you can imagine, it is quite possible that the largest inhibiting factor in all this will be education and training, for the technology is, in most cases, already well beyond prototype.

## A quick look at speed and re-engineering

I said that speed, as a management technique, has become an obsession and might stay so for a while. It has also become a marketing obsession. Let's consider the reasons.

There is still a belief among some – predominantly American – management advisers that speed is a factor which can enhance, or rather in some way turbo-charge, an organisation. Kaiser Associates, who operate from Vienna, Virginia (US) surveyed 50 major US companies which had adopted speed strategies. Their belief was that it was a competitor-killer. I don't doubt that Customers love it; although I hold a firm belief that obsession with speed is fine from time to time but detrimental as a way of life. I have found that used periodically it blows away cobwebs and is a great shock treatment for corporate lethargy; as an obsession that becomes a way of life, human nature obliges the cutting of corners and failure of quality standards. It seems to me that speed eventually loses its perceived added-value with a Customer as soon as each burst is added. Almost as if, in perception, the Customer sees each speed improvement as a step up, and is content to rest a while at the new level before feeling the need to move on again. Again, I would cite film processing as a good example. Technology is already providing speed increases at every level of business.

I think it was Domino's who offered the pizza free if it was delivered later than 30 minutes from your call. This was a terrific speed promise! They could hardly believe their eyes when in one isolated community an independent operator advertised, 'Why wait so long?' He guaranteed a 15-minute pizza. Apparently Mr Enterprise had loaded an oven on to a truck; the driver had a cellular phone and as soon as you called he started driving and the man in the back started baking!

At the other end of the scale the facts are less amusing but more startling. Prior to the 1990s General Electric had reduced to three days the order fulfilment system that used to take three weeks to provide the box for an industrial circuit-breaker. Motorola, according to a report in *Fortune*, used to take three weeks from order to manufacture their pagers: by the early 1990s it was down to just two hours. The design of a telephone at giant AT+T was once a two-year task; now it's halved to one year.

In 1989 IBM were deposed from their apparently unassailable position at the top of *Fortune* magazine's 'Most Admired Company in its Industry'. The culprit was none other than Hewlett-Packard, headed by one of the Speed School's greatest advocates, their chief executive, John Young. Young was quoted as saying 'Doing it fast forces you to do it right the first time'. At the same time, the Boston Consulting Group uncompromisingly suggested 'If you come up against one of these fast corporations and you're not prepared, you're history'. Despite this Ramboesque rhetoric, the case histories in favour of the Speed School build to an impressive list of graduates and masters. So it seems, as I feel obliged to point out, that not everyone shares my disenchantment with the 'way of life' prognosis for speed.

There are two sides to this coin. Let's appraise them. Is speed something you should align with periodically to maintain your rate of acceleration; or is it a notion you should view as a permanent obsession? Ultimately, of course, it's going to depend what business you're in and what kind of business you want to run – not to mention the quality regime you wish to prevail.

## If you're thinking of the speed technique...

If you are thinking about the speed technique, here's some advice that may help you to decide whether to investigate it further in your search for a miracle. Some have found one there.

■ Customer-Driven Marketing

### Think first. And think new

It's unlikely that you are going to make significant speed improvements by chipping away at existing processes, controls and systems. Radical improvements will come from radical thinking. Be sure to set yourself radical objectives. But be warned, if you simply wind up the existing resources to go faster, they'll just burn out.

So think first. Take a long, hard look at your business. Question long held traditions; examine your sourcing; put each and every step under the microscope. Make a flow chart – look particularly at the administration and bureaucracy. Approvals are a particular and well-recognised source of delay and procrastination. Often they do more for the ego than they do for the end-product.

### Look at the whole operation

There's no point in cranking yourself up to a new speed, and then letting your suppliers at the back end, and your distribution at the other, let you down. What's good for you is good for them.

### Look for ways to worship speed

If you want your people to live speed, maybe there are things you can do to help them give it enough thought. Breed a speed culture – from the design of your offices to the look of your trucks, to the out-of-work activities you encourage; or, maybe, even the sports that you sponsor.

### Build in responsibility

The only way to ensure you don't lose quality as you turn the heat up is to make it abundantly clear to those responsible for it – and that's everyone. If you're in manufacturing, and haven't already explored the 'Right First Time' and 'Just In Time' concepts, do it now.

Many people would recommend that a team cultured business is best geared to cope with speed techniques with least risk to quality. All the evidence suggests that you can give teams difficult objectives; you can make teams responsible for the maintenance of their quality standards; but you must also give them the authority to make their own decisions. Being in control of one's own destiny is a true motivator.

### Make a shrine of the schedule

Time is infectious. Taking a little more is tempting. Holding something over until tomorrow or just hanging on until the weekend's out of the way are mentalities with which 'speed' businesses cannot live. Speed requires commitment – nothing short of a serious Act of God should put the schedule out!

Lastly, remember what Carnegie used to say in the last century – 'The Pioneers get scalped'!

The speed technique is, for me anyway, rather an over-rated idea. It is one of those management fads which will come and mostly go. There will be those for whose business it may perform a miracle; but in my view the biggest miracles would be likely to be performed in highly predictable places. Would Motorola be so delighted with their two-hour pager if they hadn't been happy before with a three-week pager? The answer could be that they were simply too bloated, flabby, bureaucratic and sleepy. Other forms of good management would have provided prevention, whereas speed provided a cure.

## And what of re-engineering?

Leading international management consultant, Pip Mosscrop – whom you shall meet again later – told me that he felt business process re-engineering (BPR) now had a well-documented lack of success. He suggests that 'it worked well for those who were about to fall off a cliff (Xerox, IBM, DEC etc). It was, however, an impossible task for those who were already highly profitable and had a lot to lose.'

Many consultants would agree with this. It's certainly true that BPR demanded that usually massive investments were made with consultants on redesigning 'core' processes through participation of large numbers of senior managers. This required much of their time and that of consultant 'facilitators'. However, many discovered that a consensus decision on a process or structure is often not the best or even a viable solution. This reminds me of the old expression about a camel being a horse designed by committee!

The original message of BPR had its roots in the academic world and was propagated by a series of books and articles. Influential gurus like Peter Drucker claimed 're-engineering is new and it has to be done'. The idea of improving efficiency and profit levels by redesigning work structures seemed to be the way that organisations would survive in the increasingly competitive global market. Despite often excellent profits, companies began to cut costs, making large numbers of employees redundant and reorganising to maintain the basic level of service. Shareholders and investors alike perceived this as the right approach to maintain future profitability.

The message that was received was not one of improving productivity by reorganisation but reducing costs by cutting the workforce. The move into re-engineering eclipsed the school of thought which advocated con-

■ Customer-Driven Marketing

cern for people, rather than axing jobs. Human nature took its course, greed and the rot set in as partners in crime. And, again, consultancies who should have known better made a fortune from Clients on the back of the latest fad. Companies in the 1990s were keen to be a part of the new wave and, although it started in the US, it moved rapidly across the Western world.

The re-engineering message originally began by stating that the process should not be initiated simply as a cost cutting exercise, as excessive cost cutting is likely to destroy value. It is important to care for the human dimension of change and this may be one of the primary reasons why re-engineering has delivered inconsistent results. Poor implementation and badly defined needs have meant that many organisations have ended up with processes which are more difficult to manage than the ones in place before. Re-engineering should be considered, not as an exercise in cost reduction by eliminating jobs, but as rethinking work. There is presently considerable criticism of BPR, while in the past it was hailed as the latest in a long line of corporate saviours. The companies who have made a success of BPR are those who have adopted a more realistic view of the process rather than trying to adopt it wholesale.

The biggest obstacle to the success of BPR was people, primarily because it treated employees inside the organisations as interchangeable objects. According to Davenport, one of the early architects of re-engineering, massive layoffs were not a part of the original vocabulary. However, since the initial architects did not lay out a specific strategy for implementing the process, consultants adopted strategies which suited them, often to the detriment of the companies they were there to serve.

I have introduced the topics of speed and re-engineering for two reasons. First, because speed is often used to give a quick fix – if you'll excuse the unintentional pun. BPR has been sold as the answer to everything and it plainly isn't. Otherwise we wouldn't still have problems! However, in both cases, technology is often used to provide an essential plank to such initiatives. And the rationale for embarking is often the Customer promise. To become a Customer-driven business you will need to look at a broader horizon and avoid being tempted by the speed or re-engineering routes in their own right. In few cases do they really have their own right!

## Changing shape for the future

There is massive evidence to demonstrate that restructuring and re-engineering of companies (as distinct from processes) for the future is both necessary and beneficial. We will consider this in more detail separately, since even if a company in total does not restructure, marketing departments and sales departments will have to, for the market already has.

Technology will both help and hinder this process. Ultimately the take up of new technology will depend as much on the consumer as anyone else. Very few consumers would welcome new technology simply because it is new. They seek only the benefits it brings – a less direct demand upon the marketers of tomorrow, but a demand none the less.

## Back to the survey

Returning to DunnHumby's survey, there was one aspect which was quite promising if, as Edwina Dunn pointed out, a little puzzling. The latest survey showed a major shift in policy from winning new Customers to keeping existing Customers satisfied – the message was clear. When asked how important Customer care was to their organisation, marketing directors ranked it a poor eighteenth in the previous survey, but a much healthier third position in the latest survey. While more importance is attached to Customer care, Customer communication techniques such as direct mail and telemarketing are still not perceived as very important methods of achieving these goals. Edwina asks 'How are companies communicating with their Customers if not through these two important channels? They seem to have accepted a strategy of improved Customer care without some of the most important tools'. Perhaps the heart is finally in the right place but the head and the hands are not ready to follow yet.

## Technology is here to stay!

Every time you turn round some new device is being launched upon us. Interactive advertising messages sent on disk or CD, supercomputers, global corporate teleports, the Internet and World Wide Web, robots that feel, and software upgrades seem to be issued weekly – on the Internet, it's daily!

If it is true that there are more scientists actually alive today than the sum total of those that have already retired to that great Silicone Valley in the sky, then I do not yet see the pace of invention and innovation slowing down to the pace of implementation.

In Chapter 4, regarding technology's influence on future marketing, we noted the following major points.

- Marketing and IT must work more closely together and both sides must have a clear understanding of each other's objectives.
- Marketing is still using technology mainly for media selection and market research supplied by outside sources. Marketing managers correctly rate their agencies as technologically backward. This must change if agencies wish to remain so influential.

■ Customer-Driven Marketing

- Technology should have a clear Customer purpose for IT has the power to transform marketing.
- Marketers will most likely favour LAN linked PCs for day-to-day working. Major databases will be handled on higher machinery but the flexibility and access of the PC is vital to successful marketing.
- Computers will be adopted to speed up CIM techniques. This in turn will put pressure on marketing departments to move more products and faster.
- Intranets will have a major role as many marketing departments fragment to become autonomous self-managed units – highly Customer focused teams.
- Speed will remain a fashionable management technique in Europe and on other continents – it will need thoughtful application to maintain quality. In essence, the essentials are:
  — think first and think new
  — look at the whole operation
  — look for ways to worship speed
  — build in responsibility and autonomy.
- Business process re-engineering should be used selectively and with caution whereas corporate restructuring may be vital.

# 5

# The communications traffic jam

With all the new technology multiplying with all the new media, we are inevitably heading for a potential communications traffic jam. There are so many people trying to say so many things, so many different ways, so many times, to increasingly *fewer*, in other words more closely targeted, individuals.

The people I buy from want to communicate with me; the people I used to buy from are ringing and writing and knocking on my door. My fax machine responds to a caller who is trying to get me to be a Customer of theirs. The cellphone interrupts the commercials on the radio, which distract me from the posters telling me which paper I should buy to decide which television channel I should watch. I think I'm getting media phobia!

But who cares anyway – I can zap the lot of them! Figures published in France show that technologically advanced homes (definition: they have a remote control channel changer) will switch channels while the ads are on. Thirty-one per cent will go and look around the other channels while 29 per cent just kill the sound. The birth of the Silent TV Ad is only around the corner. When you've got it you simply show it on all channels simultaneously. It's easy!

Seriously, I am convinced that this 'traffic jam' will become one of the most critical factors for marketers of the future. Why? Because it is the crossroads for so many of the other factors: communications; the media explosion; the techno-splosion; the desire to improve Customer service; and so on and ever on. The Romans were quite prophetic when they came up with the word 'trivia'. Apparently, it is derived from the Latin for 'three roads'. In Roman times, they decided that wherever three

# ■ Customer-Driven Marketing

roads met, there was likely to be enough traffic to merit a bulletin board. Hence the word. So even the communications traffic jam is not new! And poster site contractors already know this.

Figures from the US demonstrate this point quite well and are supported by Europe: consider the implications of these assorted facts.

- US supermarkets typically have 17,901 items on the shelf and they deal with 123 new items per day.
- US cable television in 1980 offered 27 channels, by 1992 offered 150 channels and the capability exists now via fibre optic cable to pump up to 500 channels into a household - the difference being that these channels will handle anything from computers to television to telephony. If you're thinking that it must be very expensive to re-cable the globe, that's not a problem either, as apparently scientists have now worked out how to bring multi-channel facilities to the old 'twisted pair' cabling which covers 70 per cent of global telephone interfaces!
- The US automobile buyer, by the mid-1990s faced or enjoyed, depending which view you take, a remarkable 656 choices of vehicle. Typically, they would look at six, get serious about three and end up buying one – even if it was their second one! However, car buying is comparatively easier than choosing a US mutual fund to invest in: they have increased in number by 850 per cent in a decade, standing at around 3000 funds.
- The US citizen who was out hunting for a new automobile or weeding through all those investment funds might also have noticed this: a typical US citizen sees a veritable myriad of advertising. Each day, they are exposed to no less than 560 ads, of which they notice 76 and remember 12. Of those 12, sadly for the marketing profession and those who pay them, they remember three negatively! In Europe, life is so much more relaxed! By the age of 35, a European will have been exposed to a mere 150,000 different advertisements. Nobody has worked out what that number would be when you think of the number of times you see some of them!
- According to the figures I could find, there were 3244 new products launched in the US in 1994.

To fan the flames of this burning issue, there is a common fallacy among marketers that more communication equals better service and, equally, better service means more communication. It may be true in some cases, but one is not a prerequisite of the other. I will, however, concede that very often more communication *feels* like better service.

Although I am no friend of the phrase 'junk mail', many people who are Customers of some of the more old-fashioned direct marketing or

## The communications traffic jam

mail order houses may still suffer from the seemingly endless bombardment of apparently untargeted mail that invades their letterbox. I doubt for a moment that any one of these Customers would agree that more communications equals better service.

Indeed, for one large mailer, I carried out a fascinating exercise just recently. It was a large insurance company well and truly locked in to the old way of direct marketing. They still saw it as a numbers game – hammer the house file without any thought as to profiling, segmentation or any real targeting and no consideration of the damage that over-mailing or irrelevant mailing might do to business. There was simply an obsession with the old notion that the bigger the run, the lower the unit cost and, therefore, the lower the breakeven. With this product and this highly aggressive and incentivised mailing pack the breakeven was a tiny 0.4 per cent. Easy! Chuck it in the mail!

I started working on the difference in lifetime values of business brought in by mailings like this versus other, more sensitively prepared and targeted, approaches which projected clear corporate and brand values; but, most of all, which were in harmony with the Customer or prospect information.

Instead of measuring business written at the front end, I started examining damage down the back end in terms of Customer opinions, attitudes, satisfaction, performance and loyalty. I was able to demonstrate quite conclusively that the huge, untargeted, over-promotional mailings were actually doing more damage than they were making in low profit, low persistency business at the front end. For certain this is completely off-track for marketing miracle seekers.

In fact the kind of direct mail I am describing was born and grew up in America. It has been cloned around the world. On a recent trip to Asia, Manila Bankers Life brought along just such a mailing to a seminar I was doing there. I think these mailings must have been invented long before the phrase 'brand equity' was born! These were workhorse mailings: they cost little, pulled low, but were unassailably cost effective. They were – are – junk mail, just as throwing leaflets out of a plane is principally litter!

There are still a few of them around in the US and this may be a contributing factor to the way that the reputation and reception for direct marketing is nose-diving compared with Europe, where it seems to be predominantly either on a level or slightly improving. For example, the US, which has historically enjoyed a reputation of being one of the more 'friendly' countries towards direct mail, has seen figures for that friendliness reduce over recent years as follows: 1987 – 68 per cent; 1990 – 57 per cent; 1993 – 46 per cent. In 1994, it was calculated that 44 per cent of US direct mail was thrown away unread or unopened. In the UK the figures for direct mail opened were: 1989 – 80 per cent; 1991 – 80 per cent; 1993 – 83 per cent. The UK figures for direct mail which was read (presumably after it was opened!) are: 1989 – 61 per cent; 1991 – 63 per cent; 1993 – 68 per cent. What's more, 77 per cent of direct mail users claimed that the quality of direct mail was improving. I agree with this and believe it to be because of the increasing recognition that direct marketing techniques can be powerful brand builders as well as powerful business builders. We will return to this topic later.

However, you can turn this issue the other way round and know you are on safe ground. That's to say we can be quite sure that bad or lower quality communications will damage (or be perceived by the Customer to threaten) Customer satisfaction. The need therefore is to focus on, assess and prioritise the quality, method and validity of the communications. To over-communicate or to mis-communicate generally will actually harm Customer relationships. Nothing gives a Customer a more telling idea of just how much a company cares for them than the organisation of their communications.

You may have experienced the appalling frustration of ringing someone with an enquiry or complaint and being passed around a building from extension to extension; each time relating your story yet again to someone who doesn't know you from any other of 2,000,000 Customers. This is not a question of bad company organisation or structure. It is not a question necessarily of poorly trained or motivated staff. It is usually the sign of a company that doesn't appreciate that Customer service starts with having someone you know there. You know they know you. You know they will sort things out. You know they know what's going on in relation to you. *They* care about *you*. A miracle in itself!

Why is this so difficult – or apparently so?

## Customers – consumer or business – need to be someone

Like the majority of people in the UK, I bank with one of the major high street banks who tell their Customers that they have a personal banker. But my personal banker doesn't know me and is strangely absent when things go wrong. To him I am a number rather than a name. When things go wrong, the manager signs a standard letter which was written either by a manager at the same branch in 1956 and it has served well ever since, or possibly which was written by the corporate form letterwriting officer.

It seems to me that this simple basic human financial need – a banking service – cries out to be made more human, not less so; to require more recognition, knowledge and understanding; and made to be of optimum benefit to the Customer whether delivered at a distance or not. None of this defies automation, rather it requires it. Surely there must be a miracle or two waiting to be discovered here?

It is the use to which the automation is put that must change. Why was it possible in the 1950s, but with all the technology and communications at our disposal in the 1990s, apparently neither available, achievable or cost effective?

I had an extraordinary conversation with one branch manager one day. I asked him how many staff he employed. Having explained to me, at first, that this was highly confidential information, he finally agreed to let me in on the fact he had, say, 25.

Next question. How many individual banking Customers did he have? Well, he couldn't possibly let me know that. Finally, after the most extraordinary game playing, I was allowed to come to a conclusion which he felt would not 'mislead' me. For the sake of the story and round figures, let's say this was 5000.

Thanking him for this help I asked him whether – in theory only, just as a hypothesis, mind – it would be possible to distribute the 5000 Customers among the 25 staff so that each had 200 to look after. The man was outraged. Who would answer the phones and take care of 'housekeeping'? Was I, with respect, completely mad?

I tried again. OK, what if we put five people on one side to do all those non-Customer things, was it possible then to divide the Customers among the staff so that each of the 20 remaining staff had 250 Customers? He checked again. This was a hypothesis? Yes. He was only answering theoretically speaking – because I did understand there would be enormous problems of technical competence etc? Yes, I did understand. Then, reluctantly he admitted, yes, it was possible. But why was I asking?

Because, as I explained, this would feel to me like personal banking. I would get to know the banker, and they would get to know me. I could begin to feel 'looked after' because they would indeed be looking after me – personally. It would, indeed, merit the word personal. A marketing miracle if ever there was!

Now he understood. Why hadn't I explained in the first place? More, some of their branches did have some places where this actually already happened, where genuine personal banking was really given. I was surprised. Where? How? For whom?

It transpired that you needed a minimum of £100,000 with the bank to merit the service. Some months later I moved my business elsewhere.

## Yes, why do more Customers mean less service?

It is another fallacy to believe that Customer service has to decline with the number of Customers being dealt with. Yet, in banking and many other services, automation and technology should have provided these suppliers with the means to maintain quality while profitably delivering service. It appears not to have done so.

■ Customer-Driven Marketing

So here is a classic Customer service dilemma, one that many organisations would set about solving, just as my bank did, by providing someone (or two!) who will speak to you personally, who can call up your information on their screen, who can pretend to know you. Your personal banker. And so they are. Just as soon as you tell them your number!

## My Customer Number should be Number 1 – and so should all the others

Oddly enough the bank example is only a fraction away from the right answer. It's just that they should provide the service not the lip service. I have dwelt on this example not because I have the answer but because marketers all need to consider how the problem is solved. To their credit, the bank has managed to avoid the obvious mistake – the campaign answer.

One of marketing's favourite solutions is to hit the problem head on with a campaign to prove to the Customer that no problem really exists. Thus a campaign is mounted to make personalities of the various service managers at the bank, to hold 'open evenings' so you can meet all your 'friends' at the branch (they're the ones who still need to give *you* a name badge!). And so on. Psychologists maintain that people often say the exact opposite of what they feel, want or believe – this campaign is a classic example of the syndrome. Now you are encouraged to communicate with each individual 'expert' for each service. And, of course, they will do the same. You'll get letters from the insurance experts, phone calls from their investment experts – and the mandatory quarterly newsletter or magazine. You now have a standard Customer service campaign formula at work on you. No miracles there!

## How does it feel to be just another Customer, Mr Whatsyername?

You're about to enjoy the communications traffic jam with junk mail from head office, more from the branch, telephone calls when you least want them. And that's happening with almost every business you use, from your bank, your insurance company, your travel agent or holiday company, all your credit card companies to the department store, catalogue, and so on.

Hang on to your hats. In the next ten years, you'll see these messages come from your personal fax, your E-mail system, your video phone (tellyphone) or wall, not to mention the PC link you have and, of course, the interactive television. Super-clean, hi-tech, fibre optic lines will bring all this to your home complete with cable networks – all of which will offer you virtual and tele-shopping and the latest in video mail order catalogues.

## Who loves you, baby?

So who loves you? Is it the people who communicate the most or the people who manage their communications best to build a satisfying relationship with you? The difference will be that the latter has a Total Communications Management (TCM) policy and therefore one person (or one small team of people) looks after you, understands your dealings and knows you. It happened in the 1950s and now, thanks to our technology revolutions and particularly the capabilities of sophisticated marketing databases and intelligent *internal* company communications, it can happen again. We can definitely find marketing miracles here.

There's one small family bank I have worked with where we have adapted their entry security system to help deliver better Customer service! This is one of those in a country where it is quite usual to swipe your account or credit card to open the doors on entry. That's the security bit. Now the Customer service bit. We hooked the door entry technology up to the bank's computers. Then we placed a large electronic noticeboard at the lobby entry. This advised Customers which teller to visit.

Each time you came it would channel you to the same teller, let's call her Joanna. If Joanna was away, it would direct you to Terry. Indeed, whenever Joanna was not there, it would always propose Terry. And if Terry wasn't there? Then, you'd consistently be recommended to Lynne. Always the same three. If you decided to use the cash machine in the lobby on the way to the teller, then that transaction was included in the information which was pumped through to the teller's PC ready for your arrival. Your information was in, as near as possible, real time. Terrific! But here's what happened ... it was a definite marketing miracle.

What we were trying to do with this project was push the bank back, just as the chairman had asked me to, to the days he remembered when, as a child, he used to go there with his father and they were always greeted by name. That bit was easy. Interestingly, we found that within months, the technology was, with regular visitors, almost unnecessary. The tellers and the Customers got to know each other, and many were back to the good old days without any of our fancy kit!

Technology, when used for the right end result is quite wonderful at knocking the clock back and getting us back to those times when individual, personal, caring service was what everybody got. There'll be more on this and I'd like you to help me find someone I met a few years ago and lost touch with. I'll tell you about him soon. His story is quite brilliant! It is a great miracle. I wish it had been one of mine.

## TCM brings order out of chaos and someone who recognises you

The TCM strategy is as effective for the individual consumer, the family unit or any scale of business. The fundamental realisation is that the communications are not there to sell in their own right (the second biggest cause after poor targeting of junk mail!), they are the means through which the interaction – the dialogue – of the relationship will take place. There is absolutely no reason why they cannot be made to sell for you, but to do so effectively, one must recognise that selling or repeat or cross-selling to a Customer within the privileged, trusted position of a Customer care or Customer service programme, is a very different activity with a very different tone and a very different style.

Did you notice that word trust? What impact did it make on you? Does selling to an existing Customer feel like selling from a position of trust? This trust is perhaps most openly and obviously displayed, as I hinted earlier, in the way that you organise your communications with the Customer. How is it possible to trust, or give any semblance of credibility to, a 'personal banker' who doesn't know me, doesn't know my name, doesn't know my financial position, nor even understand the background of my relationship with the bank? Plainly, one can't. The title exaggerates.

Let's get back to your marketing miracle hunting ground. So, what do I mean when I suggest and repeat that the organisation of the communications is the shaft of realisation through which the Customer will most quickly assess the true level of caring that goes on for them within any organisation? The answer is simply this.

For a start I mean they won't be sending you mailings for unsecured loans if you're a Customer with stacks in the bank! Those businesses which recognise you as an individual stand out from the crowd. They know that the most successful way to deal with you as an individual is to appoint an individual on their side to be guardian of their relationship with you. Furthermore, and this is the truly distinctive aspect, in that single individual they invest finite control over all their communications with you. He or she can make the Customer miracles happen.

Old-fashioned sales people the world over will greet this comment with much ribald laughter and great 'I told you so's'. Well they should quieten down. They may have been right, but it is not possible that the businesses they worked for, employing them and rewarding them the way they did, could possibly have vested this power in them. For, to be truly effective, the controller of communications must also be the controller of the relationship generally. Few business practices of the last 30 years would permit this to happen because their structure, employee standards and the resulting regulations and safeguards would preclude it.

Just as manufacturing went into mass production to achieve greater efficiency and reduced costs, so too Customer service went into mass communications and mass handling methods for the same reasons. All the trends are now in complete reverse; the methods of quality are to do with individualisation, not only in terms of the product or service as discussed earlier, but also in terms of the relationship and recognition which is developed with the Customer.

TCM requires that communications are all ordered and enacted (or triggered) by the guardian of the relationship, since only this person knows at any given moment what the precise status quo is with any individual Customer. Thus the Customer perceives that the right hand knows what the left is doing all the time. One is never passed on to a different unknown or unnamed individual; one never leaves the caring hands of one's guardian. Never!

For those involved in mass mailings to Customers, however personalised those should be, this does not rule out anything that you are doing. It does make two important differences. First, large bulk mailings to Customers must become a thing of the past. There are no marketing miracles there. The wherewithal for those mailings is now placed at the disposal of the guardians. They in turn feed them in to the Customer communications programme at the optimum time. Secondly, the communications must be seen to emanate from the guardian, not from some central point.

Many who have discovered the exceptional cost effectiveness of direct marketing programmes to their existing Customers may worry that the cost will increase as bulk mailing postal savings and other savings disappear. However, they can be reassured that the benefits from improved timing generally far outweigh any increased costs. After all, no one can be in a better position to know when the timing is right than the guardian. Timing is a great provider of miracles.

For those who have a logical product/service line extension there is another valuable advantage. By logical product/service line extension, I mean a range of products for which it would be possible to build a logical and progressive path of relationship building. In many cases such ideas are not even conceivable at the moment, but they become possible with the added closeness and intimacy of the relationships that result from TCM. Financial services are ideal for this approach; so are any kind of products where the taste and style of the Customer are an issue; or even those where such apparently unlikely activities may seem foreign to relationship building such as in professional fundraising. The ultimate product there is your last will and testament! Incidentally, my own experience in charity fundraising suggests that legacy income will increase beyond all bounds when the kind of techniques we have discussed here are in operation.

■ Customer-Driven Marketing

So let's close this chapter on the story of a mail order business for whom I adapted the same concept as the bank entry system but to their telemarketing team. First, we channelled Customer groups around operator teams to get people to know each other. Next we graded the Customers and set service standards for the grades. Then we sat back and watched these – predominantly women – get to know each other. Abundant marketing miracles!

Indeed, it went so well that we introduced a Phase Two, encouraging the telemarketers to make outbound 'social' calls to the higher priority Customers. As I explained at the beginning of this book, some of my best stories have to stay anonymous. So I can't say more – other than that sales have gone through the roof! I mean through the roof! This was one of my best schemes. Don't ask my Client. Ask her Customers who will tell you that they have never experienced anything like it in their lives.

However, we must watch the dangers as technology provides more and more ways for us to communicate with each other. It will mean, if we do not take these communications seriously, that 'junk' communications could proliferate – 'spamming' could come to many of them. This will force the consumer or Customer to build defence mechanisms and rightly so.

With portable faxes, cell phones, phones in planes and almost everywhere else, global universal telephone numbers, E-mail, voice mail and computer contact from almost anywhere, in any hotel – or, indeed from any phone socket – readily available for years, we are potentially on the verge of a traffic jam for the Customer. The very best way to show that you wish to distance yourself from that whole game is to bring integrity to your Customer relationships. That means letting the Customer decide how they would prefer to hear from you, using TCM, bringing your communications into real time and making them as relevant as possible to the individual who is receiving them.

Let's take a run through the major topics of this chapter – as harmless as they might seem at the moment, they will prove to be among the most pivotal in your marketing of the future.

- We are in danger of witnessing (or becoming involved in) a Communications Traffic Jam of global proportions. This will be caused by an increasing number of people wishing to communicate with the Customer and the rapidly increasing communications media and opportunities they will have at their disposal. This jam will alienate Customers and prospects alike.
- Customer service levels should not decrease as the quantity of Customers increase. Indeed the reverse should be true.
- Total Communications Management (TCM) provides an effective method of organising and controlling *all* communications with the

## The communications traffic jam

Customer to maximum effect for the building, maintenance and growth of broad-based, successful and satisfying Customer relationships.
- TCM delivers improvements to marketing effectiveness by maximising all the elements of the Client relationship and thereby adding significant timing benefits to repeat or cross-selling activities.
- Mass or bulk Customer communications (most especially mailings) will generally become a thing of the past. The materials or resources for them will be deployed to the guardians of the Customer relationship.
- Products or services which have a logical growth or progress path will show special benefits from TCM methodology.

# 6

# The media inferno

Throughout the world, as we have already discussed, we are seeing massive explosions in growth of the media through which we marketing people can transmit our messages; from the growth of radio in Africa to the massive increases in television in Europe, not to mention the additional media which technology places before us.

There is plenty of conjecture about what will happen to prices; to jobs in the industry; to quality; to effectiveness. The media winners and losers of the future will depend on two pivotal issues. The balls are in the air at the moment. The future depends on where they land.

In Europe, against a backdrop of fairly consistent populations (Figure 6.1), the 'classic' media are still slugging it out. Newspapers, unlike televisions, can be shared and in low newspaper density markets, such as Spain and Greece, this is exactly what happens. It is interesting to note, however, that high newspaper 'reach' countries (Figure 6.2) tend to be the low television 'reach' countries (Figure 6.3). There are exceptions; Britain for example seems to like reading newspapers and watching television. In Portugal, they obviously have far more distractions (such as a family life!) because both are in the low sector.

And television is obviously catching – Spain not only has the second highest television 'reach', it also has the second highest viewing hours. Austria, on the other hand, has the equal lowest 'reach' and the lowest viewing hours (Figure 6.4).

The European printed media are in decline at the expense of the growth in television. Nowhere in the European Union has any print medium experienced more than 5 per cent growth in real terms since 1990, whereas television has gone from relative strength to strength. The

■ The media inferno

Source: NTC

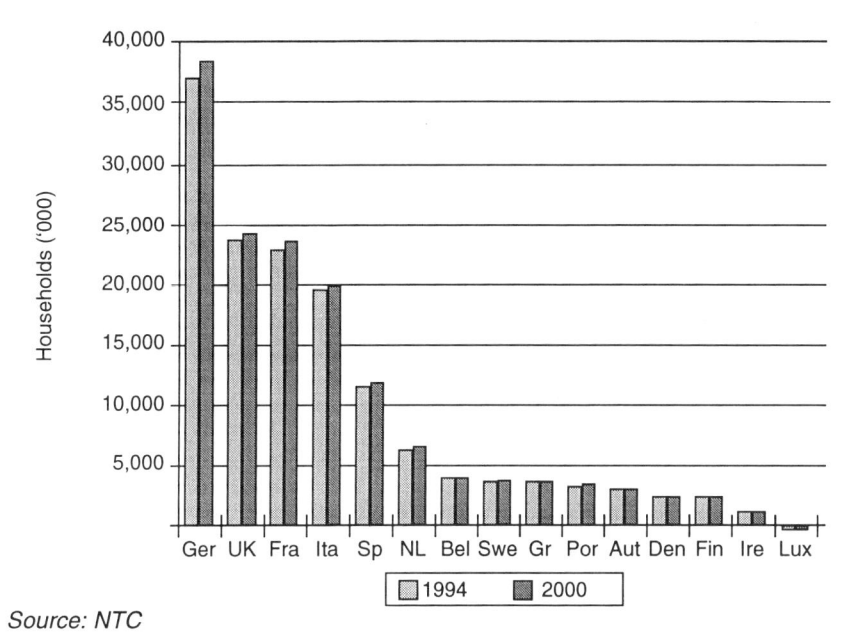

**Figure 6.1** Consumer households in the European Union

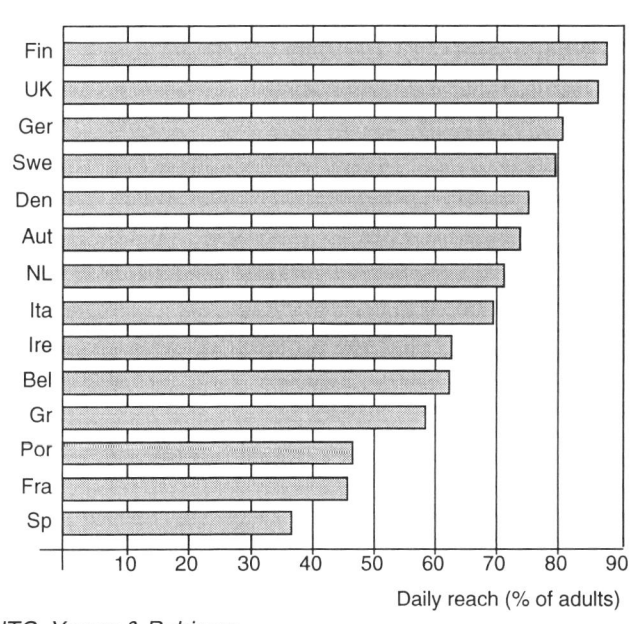

Source: NTC, Young & Rubicam

**Figure 6.2** Net 'reach' of daily newspapers in Europe

99

■ Customer-Driven Marketing

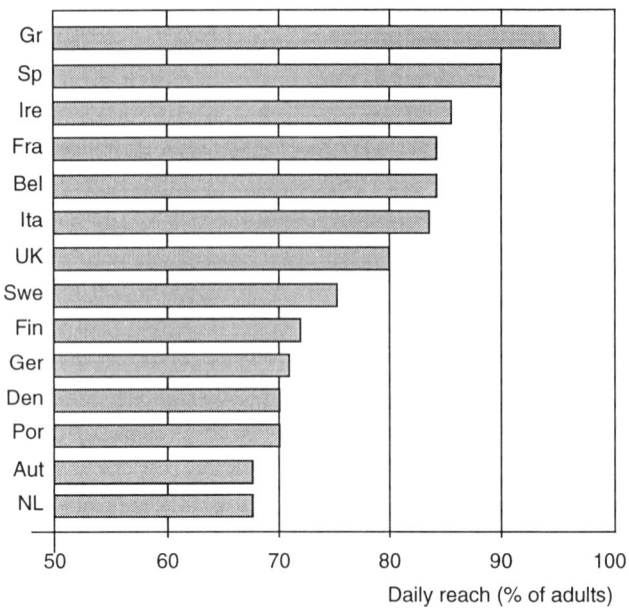

*Source: NTC, Young & Rubicam*

**Figure: 6.3** *Net 'reach' of television (all channels)*

press still hung on to the majority of mass advertising expenditure at 51 per cent in 1995 but with a decline running from 63 per cent in 1985 to 51 per cent in 1995, there is much conjecture about where this will bottom out. Indeed, there is as much conjecture about what will happen in the longer term as electronic publishers take advantage of a market offering 145 million homes, of which it is predicted by 2000 that 50 million (in

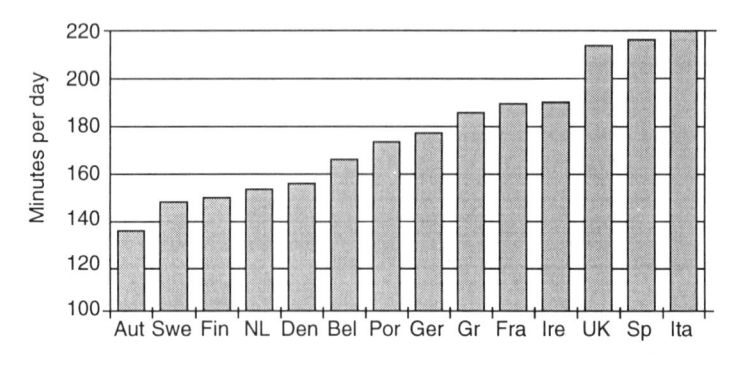

*Source: IPAplus*

**Figure 6.4** *European television watching times (all channels)*

## The media inferno

Europe) will have PCs and 90 per cent of those will have modems. The small office/home office (SoHo) market will by the same year offer a further 20 million sites with virtually 100 per cent modem ownership and then there are a further 650,000 professional sites, again all with modems.

The market volume in ECUs by the year 2002 for the dominant mass media are: magazines – 27,500 million; newspapers – 36,800 million; and television up from 33,300 million in 1995 to 46,600 million. The fact is that, within the Western industrialised markets, newspaper sales are either stagnating or dwindling (Figure 6.5). As circulations rest dormant or slipping, so advertising expenditure and even the classified ads are expecting a fall. It is the infamous Internet from which the classified sections are expecting real competition.

|  | 1987 | 1990 | 1993 | 1994 |
|---|---|---|---|---|
| EU (15)* | 81.9 m | 83.0 m | 84.8 m | 83.2 m |
| USA | 62.8 m | 62.3 m | 59.8 m | 59.0 m |
| Japan | 70.2 m | 72.5 m | 72.0 m | 71.9 m |

* including Austria, Finland and Sweden (although not being EU members in 1990/93 and early 1994); 1990: West Germany only

*Source: FIEJ*

**Figure 6.5** *Average daily newspaper circulations to the mid 1990s*

With the added attraction of interactivity for those connected by cable, when the technical problems are finally resolved, the pressure will really be on the printed media: especially when you consider the younger computer literate consumers maturing through the marketplace (Figure 6.6). Thus I feel inclined to accept the predictions for the cable networks (Figure 6.7) which suggest by 2002 something in the region of 13 million

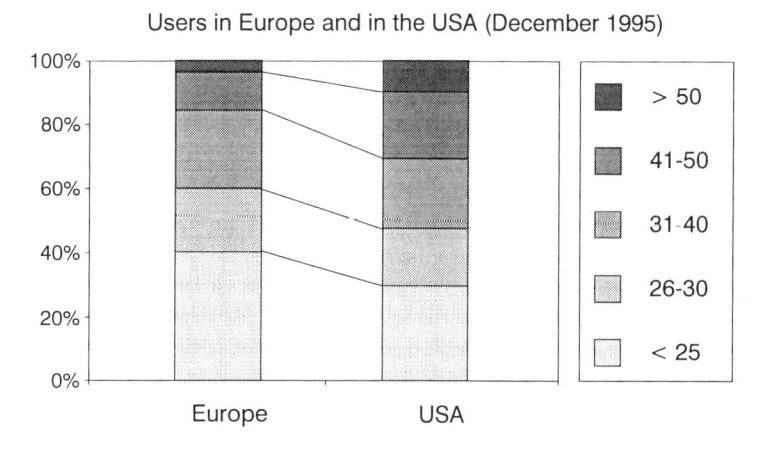

**Figure 6.6** *The age structure of Internet users in Europe and the US*

■ Customer-Driven Marketing

homes in the US and approximately 11 million in Europe. These still represent very small fractions of the number of people who have the cable passing right by their door, but who find cable prices to be much higher than they are used to. Pay per view (PPV) might offer these viewers a better answer, however, and when combined with interactive television (I-television), it is only predicted to reach penetration levels of 3 to 4 per cent throughout Europe by 2000.

Interestingly, market research in the US supports the belief that television and the electronic media are set to repeat the printed media/television clash. Since 1984 television viewing among children aged between two years and 11 years has dropped by about 18 per cent while in other age groups it has either remained the same or increased. The kids are on-line and PC literate at frighteningly younger ages!

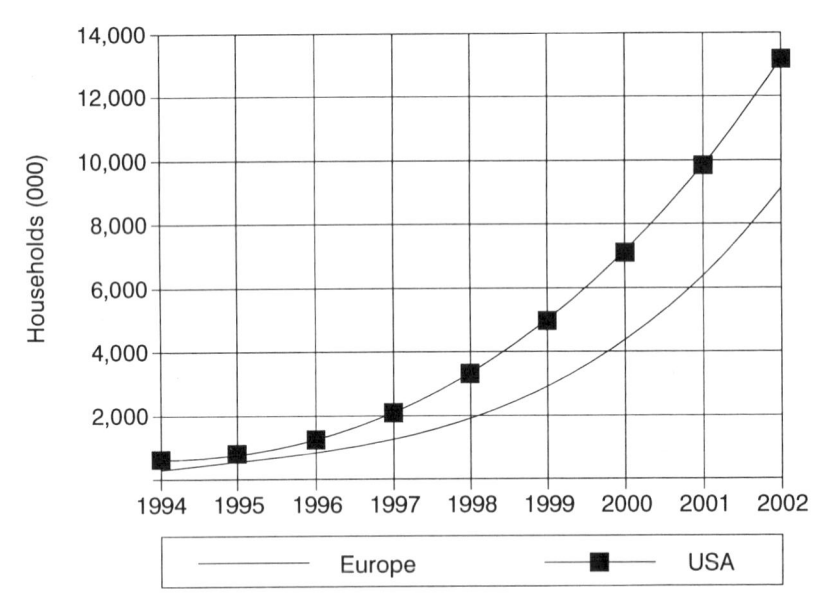

*Source: Ovum*

**Figure 6.7** *Households with cable access to Interactive TV (000)*

### The future role of mass media

In many ways the attributes of media will be measured differently in the future. Some of this has to do with the changing objectives of the marketers, as we will see in Chapter 15. A lot has to do with the fact that we have left the era of mass marketing, passed through the era of segmented marketing and arrived breathless and slightly perplexed in the era of the niche market, and are gazing at the arrival of individualised marketing with some apprehension. It's easy to say the words one-to-one: but much more difficult to achieve. And, let's be honest, it makes great stuff for speakers to speak about and authors to write about: but for many, in the real world, not only is one-to-one a laughable target, it's an impossible one.

Relationship marketing is about using an integrated marketing approach to enable you to deal with as many Customers as possible on as personal and individual basis as is sensible, in harmony with Customers' expectations, while still profitable for you.

It would be a strange irony indeed if, just as the television invasion climaxes, the advertising world were to decide it didn't need it any more. I don't think that will happen. I suspect we are not discussing whether the media are used, but for what they are used and what proportion of spend they will command.

Many of the so-called below-the-line media have come to realise that they too can play a much greater role in both the brand and corporate building process. Thus, whereas once they concentrated solely on their tactical objectives; they now spread across both planes – tactics and strategy. This duality of role makes good economic sense. And it makes powerful advertising too.

## The Marie Curie Story

I learned this lesson from my late father. Thomas Bernard Robinson OBE founded the Marie Curie Memorial Foundation, more popularly recognised these days as Marie Curie Cancer Care. It's a somewhat romantic story, starting with the influence of Sir Winston Churchill to whom my father directly reported towards the end of the Second World War, and an old lady who, when hearing his intention to start a cancer charity, took off her engagement ring and offered it to him. He sold it, as she had suggested, for about £75, in those days a reasonable sum for a first donation.

However, my father decided to devote all of it to raising more money. So he carried out a mailing (although I suspect his early efforts of hand-picked, hand-signed missives didn't seem like direct mail to him!) to raise funds. It was successful. The amassed funds financed another mailing and so on until he had built a base of regular subscribers and enough surplus to start on the serious work of fighting cancer and caring for the stricken.

As the years passed, the professional marketing skills increased and my father learned, as all charities do, that the donorbase becomes the high response, high donation centre of activity and the prospecting element the low response, low donation part. Indeed, it is often only the lifetime value of a donor which makes the prospecting effort worth while. I wonder why people expect marketing a charity to be any different to life!

■ Customer-Driven Marketing

Many have found that one acquires a donor at a loss, turned into profit later through re-approaches and perhaps trading in some way.

As more years passed my father got more creative. He introduced a mailing shot that covered ten houses at once (and effectively blackmailed each house into giving more than the last!); a way to personalise mailings before personalisation was economically viable, thus for many years turning the telephone books into his top-pulling list; and – may we all forgive him – the charity Christmas seal to stick on gifts and cards.

By now the Marie Curie was mailing its donor list (the word database of course was not invented for years to come!) twice a year and 'cold' prospect mailings were dispatched in millions, literally. At one point, I believe, he had the rate well in excess of 12 million a year; for one extensive period, more than any other charity, and certainly for almost two decades he mailed more than any other cancer charity.

There were two side-effects, both of which were extremely valuable. Both, all these years later, hold a moral for all advertisers, especially those who use direct marketing.

- *Moral One:* He accrued extraordinary loyalty from his regular donors, to the point where massive levels of legacy income were attributable to the long-term donors. Indeed, in the fundraising world the correlation between loyalty building long-term donor mailings and legacy income is now well and widely recognised.

- *Moral Two:* Marie Curie achieved the No 1 slot in brand awareness. Their unprompted figures left the others light years behind! The learning point here is that he achieved this coveted position without spending any significant sums on advertising. The 'advertising effect' was achieved as a by-product of the massive mailings. It cost him nothing.

This example clearly demonstrates what many advertising traditionalists have been reluctant to admit. Direct mail, like many of the other marketing disciplines, can have a powerful effect on brand building and brand equity and make an equally strong contribution to the process of loyalty building, which, as the marketing world refocuses on relationships, will be thrown under a greatly increased spotlight. Indeed, as I will come to tell you later, since writing *Total Quality Marketing*, I have come to believe this to be the single most important success leverage factor for marketing in the years ahead. Hence you will find later in this book a chapter to enable you to understand and manage loyalty building. It's truly wonderful marketing miracle territory out there, I promise you.

It can be seen that the media of targeted marketing can reach and address the niches, but can achieve their own objectives as well as some of those usually reserved for the mass media. I anticipate the demand for hitherto mass media objectives to increase through those media that have not been used to delivering them in the past.

## So what of television, the press and radio?

While there may be a decrease in some areas for the mass media, some consolation might be drawn from the increasing prominence of the corporate position behind the brand. For undoubtedly as the 'Western' consumer sophisticates and reappraises their buying criteria, so we will see them look behind the brand to the corporation that owns it. The policies and practices of that corporation will be watched more closely, discussed more intelligently and be acted up more aggressively. The Green movement is a perfect example – woe betide those who are tempted to pay mere lip service to Green. When Dupont makes a declared aim to be a 'zero-pollution' company the Greens, who thankfully suffer no fools gladly, will look for the pledge to be honoured.

I hold the sincere conviction that for the future such criteria will prove to be of major significance to corporate survival. The world's population is selfish enough to consider its own longevity of far greater importance than any corporation or, for that matter, any industry.

The mass media do seem to be demassifying themselves to some extent and the term narrowcasting will soon be used nearly as frequently as broadcasting. And, as I remarked earlier, the major conjecture lies around what will happen to the media as they fragment. Europeans may look to the US for a model but should take note of the different position in relation to cable and also the fact that Europe is running behind. Therefore it is nearer the precipice of new technology.

In Britain, towards the end of the 1980s, television costs rose at twice the rate of inflation and the cost of production rose three times faster still. It is therefore reasonable to expect that prices will moderate as new channels get up and running. At first glance, certainly, if my career had been in selling for a television channel, I think I'd have looked to the mid-1990s for a good long holiday, probably paid for by the previous three decades! Ultimately, as we read at the beginning of the chapter, in Europe, the population sizes will remain roughly the same for the immediate future, the number of hours in a day will undoubtedly still be 24 for a while, so saturation will probably come when the proliferation of audiences is so diverse that their numbers will no longer profitably support a channel or station.

However, if you look beyond that basic supply and demand conclusion which suggests falling prices, Britain did follow the US model in the latter part of the 1980s, when available airtime effectively trebled with the advent of Channel 4 (the second nationally networked commercial channel), all night television and TV-AM, the breakfast-time contractor. With

■ Customer-Driven Marketing

this experience it became clear that advertisers were not so much interested in commercial minutes as the right audience for their ads. With the further proliferation of commercial radio in Britain, following the pattern of France and the US amongst the principal 'radio' nations, it is likely that the delivery of the right audience to the advertisers' expectation – either geographically or demographically – will assure the future of at least some of the new names on the airwaves.

Much the same view could be drawn of what is happening to the consumer press throughout Europe where, in 1994 amid recession in many countries, some 400 new magazine titles were launched (but no one could tell me how many of them survived!), although it could be argued that many European nations, particularly in terms of their magazines, have been prolific in these respects for some years. Britain reads less, but watches more. Indeed, the national average viewing hours per week is a staggering figure – in excess of 24 hours!

## Broadcast television – the big threat

Reverting to television, it is likely that the biggest threat to broadcast television – terrestrial or satellite – will not come from other media. While the amount of television increased in Britain the total audience for commercial television did not. This simply meant advertisers found it both more difficult and more expensive to achieve coverage which only large audiences provide. And there are currently still plenty of advertisers needing such opportunities.

The biggest threat to broadcast television undoubtedly looked as if it would come from cable, certainly in the UK and, I suspect, over a decade span, throughout most of Western and what is currently described as 'Eastern' Europe. I spent some time working on the strategic and creative elements of a US cable corporation laying down its tentacles in the UK. For a creative, there is no greater delight than becoming 'sold' on the proposition oneself before having to sit down and get to work on the serious job of converting the rest of the world. A number of times in my life this has been quite hard. However, as a consumer, subject to the price and mix of programming, I was in no doubt that the superior option was cable, especially when you add, as they already have, the telephone and computer link options – plus the inevitable home shopping tele-logues. Television has in the past enjoyed much of its success not from its ability to deliver, but from agencies' inability to use their imagination. In the 1960s and 1970s their answer to almost any problem you handed them was either 'Let's do television' or 'Let's do more television'.

This was not the professional unbiased strategic counsel that Clients thought it to be. It was sheer, unadulterated greed. The criteria were the agency's bottom line, and the way they were remunerated, as a percentage of the media rates. During that same ten-year span, the rates climbed through the roof, yielding even greater profits. Who, among those agency ranks, would tell the Client to reduce or come off television?

Ironically, despite this, television advertising spend has moved from approximately two-thirds of total advertising spend to less than one-third. Television hoisted itself on its own petard. For, as the rates increased, so Clients started to look for other, better value options. Winking seductively at them were the sales forces and account teams of those so-called 'below-the-line' marketing service companies.

## The future for television

After 20 years of nearly unabated growth, US basic cable television is experiencing its first real competition, apparently from itself! Emerging cable networks are fighting established channels for access and share of viewers' minds, while veteran networks are facing cannibalisation from within as the newer niche services threaten to fragment the audience even further. However, cable's growth comes in part from new channels, many of which do not account for a significant share individually but, in aggregate, boost cable's audience. Currently, Nielsen requires a channel to be available in about 3.3 per cent of US television households to qualify for its national television ratings report. Even then, Nielsen cannot guarantee the report will show any ratings. If an emerging cable network offers a focused enough niche to deliver hard-to-reach target audiences, advertisers might suspend their need for quantitative ratings documentation.

In Europe the situation is slightly different; in terms of the total number of subscribing households, Germany is Europe's largest cable television market, with 12 million connected homes by the end of 1993. Yet, only 60 per cent of the homes passed by cable actually take up subscription. Aside from the fact that cable television in Europe is expensive, there is also a lack of worthwhile programming. Cable would be more popular in Europe if more US programming were made available, but European Union quotas restrict made-in-America programmes to under 50 per cent of each European channel's output. In France, 60 per cent of all programming must be European in origin and 40 per cent of that must be French. In Italy, there is no cable television whatsoever.

In the US the other major area of growth is pay per view (PPV). Distributors like Request Television predict double-digit growth in PPV households through 1996 and onwards. The number of addressable PPV households will increase by 14 per cent from 26.5 million to 30.2 million homes.

One view of the future can be made by taking the example of Hughes Communications Inc's investments in a direct broadcast satellite (DBS) service. The first two DirecTV satellites enabled Hughes to offer 150

■ Customer-Driven Marketing

channels of digital programming across the continental US. Their third satellite will enable the system to add another 30 channels. The number of subscribers – each of whom has paid $700 for a DirecTV receiver dish and decoder box – is targeted at 1.5 million by 1997. Significantly, the venture has signed several major programming agreements, including its purchase of rights to broadcast hundreds of professional football, basketball and hockey games that often cannot be seen on cable or broadcast television. A similar agreement with major league baseball is anticipated.

Infinitely more programming choices for television viewers in the year 2000 were predicted by a panel of US television industry executives. Consumers will choose from a menu of more than a half-dozen types of programme providers by 2000, according to Josh Sapan of Rainbow Programming, including as many as five companies and one, two or three different cable wires.

In Europe, thanks to the advent of digital compression and the ambitions of Europe's media companies, it is likely that Europe's television viewers will be deluged with an unprecedented choice of new channels. Most of these newcomers want viewers to pay to watch.

The hot money at the time of writing is on satellite now that broadcasting has 'gone digital'. And this is all shortly after they finally cracked the problem of pumping dozens of channels down the old 'twisted pairs' of copper wires.

## Let your radio turn you on

Ninety-nine per cent of US households have a radio. In fact, the average home has 5.6 radios. Radio has the ability to adapt to changes in popular tastes and to mould itself to listeners' lifestyles. Radio listening has grown in step with population increases because its immediate, portable nature meshes well with a fast-paced lifestyle. Radio listeners tend to listen habitually, at predictable times, to stations with narrowly targeted formats. They are loyal, identifiable and cheaper to reach than television audiences. US radio advertising nearly tripled between 1980 and 1992, from $3.5 billion to $8.7 billion.

In the UK by 1995 commercial radio stations notched up £270 million in ad revenue. In the previous five years, they had rocketed by 88 per cent. A milestone was reached in 1995 when commercial radio's listening share overtook that of the British Broadcasting Corporation's (BBC) for the first time. Advertisers had begun to treat commercial radio as a serious mass market medium and were no longer regarding it as a parochial and cheap alternative to television.

Another enterprising hybrid is Netcast, an on-line network of live audio and multimedia entertainment designed to attract radio listeners at work. It is scheduled to roll out across the US by 1997 over the Internet and via commercial on-line services. Netcast offers 12 channels, seven of which contain music formats and five with live sports coverage, talk shows and news. Through Netcast, on-line browsers can access music channels featuring live broadcasts of songs in various formats as well as tour information for bands featured on the channel. Netcast have formed a strategic partnership with AT&T to license The Sound of AT&T audio compression technology. By 2005, the Internet's World Wide Web is expected to become a $5 billion industry and radio is positioned to reap some of that revenue according to broadcasters and technology experts.

Establishing a Web site on the Internet enables individual stations to interact with listeners, measure exactly the number of site users who saw a particular advertisement and poll listeners easily.

In the mid 1990s listeners in London have at least 27 licensed radio stations to choose from. The niche commercial stations seemed to be finding a market although some of them had very shaky beginnings, one closing down in little more than its first week. The problem for such stations is that they offer limited reach of a desirable demographic. Maybe London is reaching media overload?

## New media – where will the growth be?

Although we have spent most of this chapter looking at advertising media it would be far more realistic to look at communications media in general since almost any medium can be put to an advertising or marketing use. Perhaps the one which instils least confidence for me was the enterprising farmer whose fields bounded the railway line north of Brighton in southeast England; he sold cow-sides, promising the target market of the travellers on the passing trains on the rail tracks which were alongside his grazing fields. I suspect the page-space value of the PR he generated as a result was greatly in excess of his eventual sales.

A good example of a medium that has been overlooked as an advertising medium is the telephone. Yet many claim this to be a selling medium rather than an advertising medium. This is not a semantic discussion. As the future unfolds this is a discussion that you must join in.

Believe me, the telephone can perform marketing miracles with ease. According to direct marketers, the telephone is now enjoying extraordinary growth, similar to that of direct mail 20 years ago. As long as the telephone business does not shoot itself in the foot by letting it all get out of hand and becoming another consumer gripe, I cannot see what can stop the telephone becoming the primary medium of what we still perceive to be the 'direct' basket of media.

However, new media will arrive in profusion as technology and communications capabilities grow. It is the use to which those media are put that will define their value to the advertiser; together, of course, with

■ Customer-Driven Marketing

their success at capturing the hearts and minds of the particular segment or niche they call their own. For example CD and other interactive media now combine the opportunity for incredible individualisation. Indeed, as the user or consumer spends time with the message, so the message itself 'learns' more about its user and, therefore, knows which of the masses of information it holds will be most relevant. And, equally, it knows which will not. When you think that much of this was possible with a conventional floppy disk anyway, remember that the original CD-ROM can hold so much more, and that the version about to be released around the time this book is published has four times more again and, I am told, we will shortly have a ten times capacity version readily and cheaply available.

## Let's go surfing!

The Internet started out as a loose confederation of interconnected networks which were the domain of computer scientists and academics. It was a mode of electronic conversation that no one else would understand anyway. Its phenomenal growth could be attributed to the fact that it met a need which had not been recognised by anyone else and its requirements were simple. When the Internet linked up to the public and commercial networks in the 1980s its growth accelerated, but most of the telephone companies whose lines were being used continued to think of it as the equivalent of 'nerd heaven' but little more. In mid-1993 the addition of multimedia made the Internet a place where pictures, sounds and video could all travel: cyberspace combined aspects of broadcasting and publishing with interactivity. The commercial world dominates the Internet and, by 1997, over 80,000 companies were connected to 1,400,000 host computers.

In 1983 the Internet consisted only of 500 host computers; it now reaches over 5 million each of which in turn is connected to several users. It has doubled in size every year since 1988, while at the same time the Web has grown 20-fold, with an estimated 68 million users by 1996. No technology, whether fax or PC, has seen comparable growth. The Internet offers services today which most telephone and cable companies are still a decade away from delivering. It is now a permanent feature of life, allowing people to exercise their most basic need to communicate with those around them.

With home PC ownership predicted to hit 50 per cent of European and US households by the early part of the first decade of the new millennium (Figures 6.8 and 6.9), if the whole thing doesn't go into overload, which I see as a genuine fear, the likely continuing decrease in the cost of line-time (Figure 6.10) and the well-documented trend of price improvements for the future (Figure 6.11), Internet expansion appears guaranteed. It is only possible to make estimates of the total number of Internet

## The media inferno

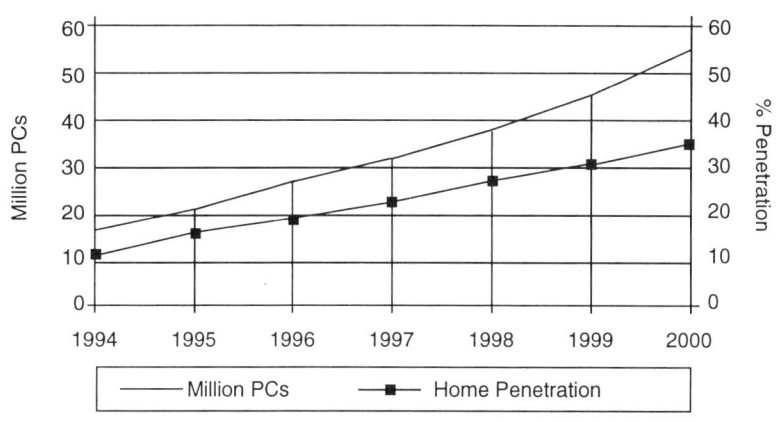

*Sources: AC/IENM (based on data by EITO and Datamonitor)*

**Figure 6.8** *Western Europe – PCs installed in homes and homes with PCs as % of total homes*

users (Figure 6.12), but even by 1996 this totalled some 68 million. However, with those who have an Internet Provider (IP) address, there are much more reliable statistics. They are equally staggering (Figure 6.13), showing almost 125 million predicted by 2000. The 1996 figures for Europe (Figure 6.14) positioned Sweden well ahead of the race with over three times the European Union average. Yet, by 2002, in terms of growth in subscribers, unless something currently unseeable happens, it will be over (Figure 6.15) – the Electric Bazaar will have peaked!

As this book is written, the Internet is commercially still really in its infancy. Its impact is being researched and prophesied by many. For example, as more and more publishers turn to the electronic media to distribute their wares, they go virtual. Who needs a magazine on a news stand when you can have it delivered to your home or office? Equally this impacts on content and editorial. Magazines are already being produced which are tailored to individual readers so the idea of a virtual distribution channel is a natural fit. But it radically changes the face of publishing since there is no need for any physical presence of the end product.

## Decreasing value, decreasing cost effectiveness

The most important point to note for the future is that the vast majority of media – particularly the mass media – will follow the fragmenting market and endeavour to reach tighter targets. For this they will expect to chase a premium – in other words, rates per thousand (or whatever quantity) will undoubtedly increase. For marketers and advertisers among them, this means, by and large, markets will become more tightly definable, but more expensively available: the classic advertising media generally will become

■ Customer-Driven Marketing

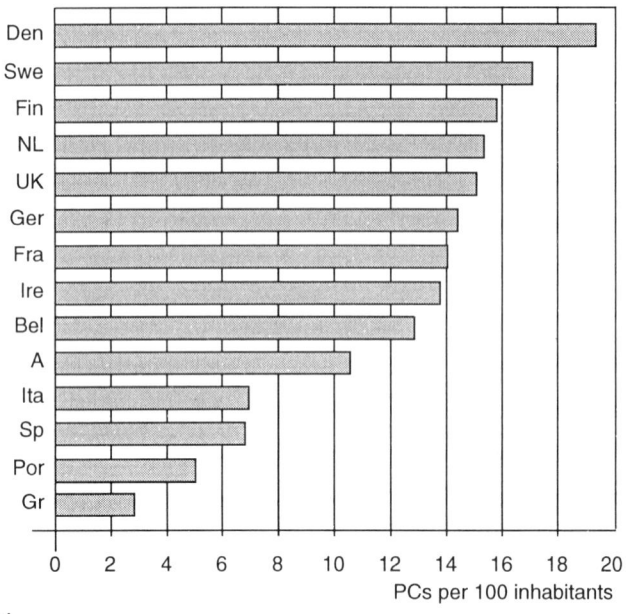

*Source: ITU*

**Figure 6.9** Western Europe – PC density in EU countries (1994)

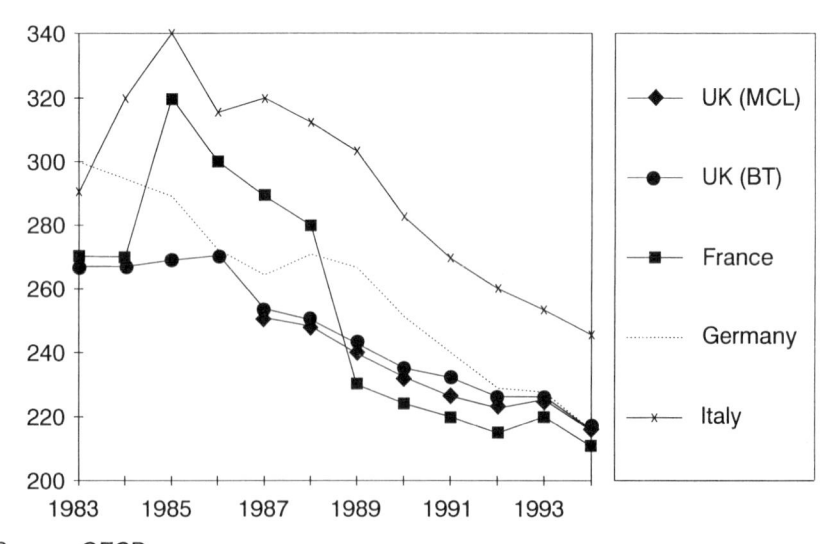

*Source: OECD*

**Figure 6.10** Decreasing local telephone charges – average cost per line (residential) in pounds

The media inferno ■

| Component | Price improvement per year |
|---|---|
| Microprocessor | 50% |
| Memory (RAM) | 50% |
| Disk | 25% |
| Modem | 25% |
| Display | 15% |
| Printer | 5% |

*Source: Price Waterhouse*

**Figure 6.11** *Decreasing PC components prices*

less cost effective and I anticipate they will attract less spending. The only possible area increasing its use of mass media against the general trend is the area of corporate image and positioning, which may at last come out of the airport corridor display case and into the mass media.

In this chapter we thought about these factors and how they would affect us tomorrow and beyond.

- Media profusion is set to continue at explosion level for many years – particularly outside the conventional mass media areas.
- Media will tend to follow the fragmenting markets to offer tighter geographic, demographic and sociographic definition, for a tighter economic price!
- Brand objectives can be successfully delivered by all media – as long as their strategic objectives are recognised along with the tactical. This is a realisation sadly much overlooked until the last few years – mostly by the marketing services community who controlled them.
- The 'brand behind the brand' – the corporation – will take on an

|  | 1994 | 1995 | 1996 |
|---|---|---|---|
| EC | 5.118 | 8.189 | 13.102 |
| Other Europe | 824 | 1.318 | 2.109 |
| USA | 17.485 | 27.976 | 44.762 |
| Asia | 909 | 1.454 | 2.327 |
| Africa | 150 | 240 | 384 |
| Oceania | 1.058 | 1.693 | 2.708 |
| Other | 1.114 | 1.782 | 2.852 |
|  |  |  |  |
| World | 26.658 | 42.653 | 68.244 |

*Sources: ITU, Internet Society, IENM/AC*

**Figure 6.12** *The estimated numbers of Internet users*

■ Customer-Driven Marketing

|      | Europe | USA    | World   |
|------|--------|--------|---------|
| 1990 | 80     | 250    | 376     |
| 1991 | 158    | 440    | 727     |
| 1992 | 322    | 730    | 1.313   |
| 1993 | 625    | 1.250  | 2.217   |
| 1994 | 1.195  | 2.450  | 4.582   |
| 1995 | 2.382  | 4.308  | 9.251   |
| 1996 | 4.590  | 7.205  | 17.681  |
| 1997 | 8.358  | 11.000 | 32.699  |
| 1998 | 13.872 | 15.000 | 56.831  |
| 1999 | 20.254 | 18.300 | 89.729  |
| 2000 | 25.800 | 20.400 | 124.256 |

Sources: Internet Society, MGM

**Figure 6.13** Predictions for Internet IP host addresses

increasing prominence as the consumer becomes more sophisticated and informed. Expect the Greens to take full advantage of this as they, and other consumer groups, gain in strength and influence at all levels of society.
- The 'right audience for your ad' will become more influential on the price an advertiser is prepared to pay. Quantity will be less influential.
- Cable television, because of its aesthetic values (everything on the set and nothing on the roof) and its ability to offer computer and tele-

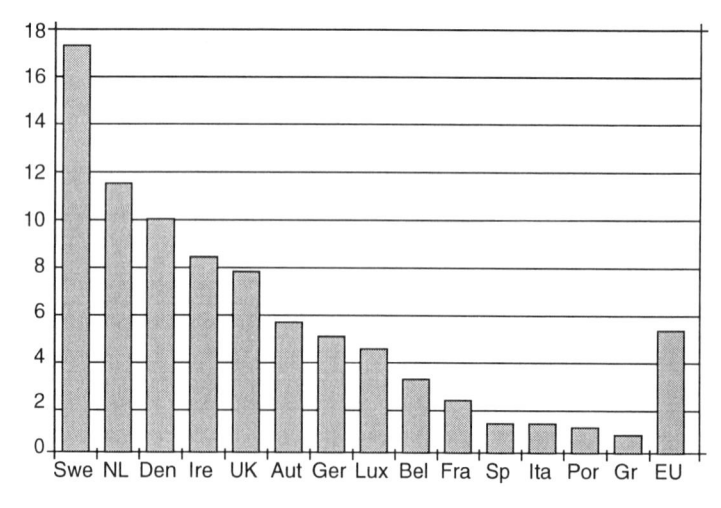

Source: RIPE, AC/IENM

**Figure 6.14** PCs with Internet IP addresses in the European Union

## The media inferno

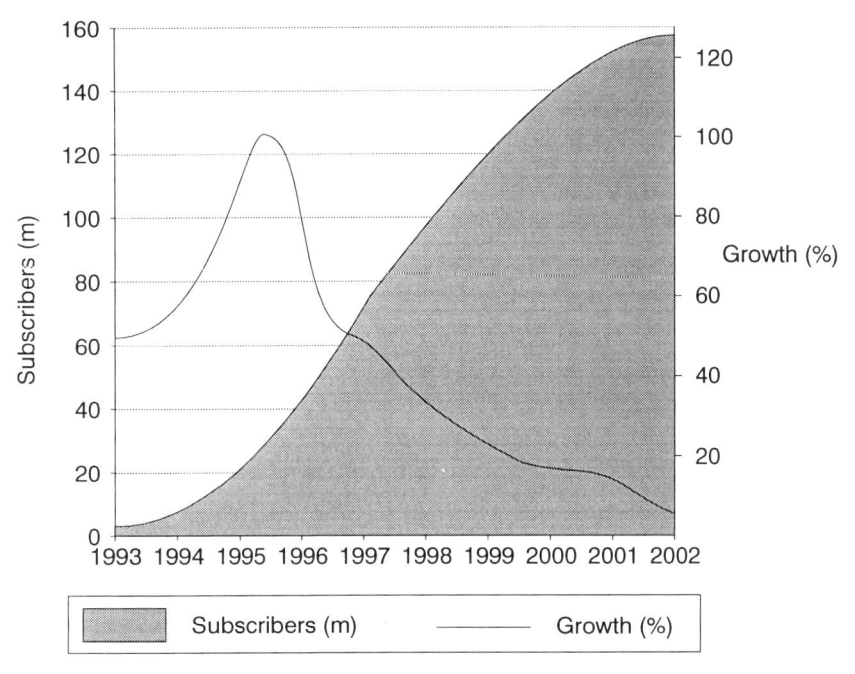

*Sources: Durlacher Ltd., ITU, Internet Society, AC/IENM*

**Figure 6.15** *Predicted growth of Internet subscribers worldwide*

phone services – all three at optimum quality digital standards and without interference – once looked to become the predominant carrier, at least in urban and suburban areas throughout the developed world. Satellite, thanks to digital broadcasting, is now back in the running. However, now that technology has found a way to use the old copper wire twisted pairs in much the same way as cable, the costs may be greatly reduced in return for a compromise of quality and data transmission speeds.

- As more advertisers seek unbiased strategic marketing counsel, television will have a difficult job to retain favour and will probably lose out to those media who can deliver 'double duty advertising', direct marketing and sales promotion for example. Corporate advertising, at this stage, would appear to contradict this trend and increase in its priority.
- The Internet will prove a formidable medium for marketers. Small businesses will suddenly have global reach. Data transmission speeds and overload appear the only inhibitors.
- It will generally get more expensive and need more organisation to reach audiences on a mass basis (although mass audience products will remain in quantity) – thus many methods of advertising will become less cost effective.

# 7

# Selling has passed its sell-by date

A short but telling article appeared in the British newspaper *The Sunday Times* a few years back. It commented as follows:

> Criticism of sales methods employed by photocopier distributors has prompted Southern Business Group to introduce a code of conduct for its salesforce. Central to the code will be a 14 day 'cooling-off' period similar to that in the life insurance sector allowing Customers the chance to consider the implications of any service or leasing agreement. It is a reform other distributors would do well to follow.

Fantastic! This simply says, 'We're going to go on cheating and lying. But if you're smart enough to spot that we ripped you off within 14 days, we'll work something out. If you spot it after 14 days you can go to hell just like you did before!'

For the life of me, I could not work out why *The Sunday Times*, which had previously led a witchhunt against these types of malpractice, was not asking the obvious question. The obvious question was: 'Why don't you fire the cheating, lying no-goods who are bringing the company into disrepute and running round conning Customers simply so they can pocket the commission?'

This chapter covers ground that may be difficult for many to accept. This is not because its thesis is complex or hard to absorb, but because of the challenge it makes and the investment it requires.

Indeed the next chapter – 'New' Marketing is Coming – will seem to exacerbate what certain people may choose to see as a prejudice against selling and sales ideas. It is of course difficult to point out weaknesses, suggest modifications or demonstrate new methods without some implicit criticism of the past or even the status quo. Thus, traditional sales people could look at my career in marketing and claim that the grudge has tumbled out of my head and on to the page. I feel at least that if I make my personal position clear then those who feel they have spotted prejudice will at least have the measure of it.

I have always considered that I hold the strategic views of a marketer and the tactical skills of a sales person. In relation to the art of selling, I have, when appropriate (and that was often), energetically and enthusiastically worked to bring a high level of professionalism to both of these. In my view, you can only be a professional sales person when you have an understanding of both the value and process of marketing. Equally, marketers can only fully appreciate the sales person when they understand that it is the sales person, generally, who achieves the successful results which are the testimony to the marketer's ability. When it's working well, it's truly teamwork. Despite what I feel to be this rather balanced disposition, it has never been difficult for me to accept that selling is a function of marketing.

I suppose that, from these views, you can clearly understand my long-standing interest and preoccupation with direct marketing; it requires the two in absolute harmony. However, you may also appreciate my disenchantment in recent years when so many direct marketing practitioners failed to understand the need for quality with quantity and chased the Holy Grail of the Cost per Sale. You may also understand how the most recent years have led me to work for the re-establishment of quality as a primary marketing requirement!

## What has selling been all about?

Let's not beat about the bush. Let's leap in with both feet and alienate a whole group of people! Here goes...

Selling for decades has *not* been about the Customer. Selling has been about the product or service. This is neither new nor prejudiced thinking. In the *Harvard Business Review* in the late 1970s the eminent Professor Philip Kotler of Northwestern University (at Evanston, Illinois) in his paper 'From Sales Obsession to Marketing Effectiveness' suggested 'Selling focuses on the needs of the seller. It is preoccupied with the seller's need to convert his product to cash.'

I own a factory. It makes widgets. My factory makes widgets five days a week. By Friday the warehouse is full, I have nowhere to put next week's widgets. I'd better get a sales force.

'OK, Sales people, get out there and sell these widgets. The more you sell, the more you earn.' They cleared the warehouse. But the factory goes on manufacturing, and the staff and the overheads need paying, and the suppliers too. Better get the sales force back, the

■ Customer-Driven Marketing

warehouse is full again and I need to collect the money they've raised from the first lot. In comes the sales force. It leaves the money and clears the warehouse again! This cycle goes on all very nicely for a few weeks, except soon the sales force seem to be having some trouble clearing the whole warehouse. 'We're selling as many widgets as we can, but it's getting harder to find new Customers and we need something extra to tempt the existing Customers to buy more.'

'OK, Sales force, give them a discount.' The warehouse is empty again, but only for a day or so; soon the relentless production at the factory has filled it up again. 'Get back here sales people – my warehouse is full again.'

'But it's only Thursday – and we've still got problems getting rid of last week's production.'

'Give 'em a BOGOF.'

'What's that?'

'Buy One, Get One Free! Now BOGOF out of here and get going. And don't forget to leave the money!'

As the sales force clear the warehouse yet again, their eyes boggle. The warehouse is bursting at the seams and the next week's production is filling up the shelves one end as they're clearing the other. What can they do next to make the Customer buy more?

## Selling had to manipulate to succeed

I have taken you through the simple example above to illustrate my point. Excuse its microcosmic simplicity, please. But you can see from this that Kotler is right. Selling is, or has certainly become, a manipulative and exploitative process. As I said in the introduction, it is obsessed with quantity. It sets its objectives by quantity. It rewards by quantity. It is an aggressive, offensive action.

I remind you that this is not a criticism. It is a statement of fact. The transition to this posture took place over the mid 1950s and early to mid 1960s. It was the beginning of the end for Customer care as a way of life; and to a very large extent, for the kind of sales person who put first and foremost the relationship they created with the Customer, the selling second.

Kotler went on to point out that the selling mentality requires that:

- you think in terms of sales volume
- you think in the short term (next sale)
- you think in terms of individual Customers rather than the market as a whole
- you think field work is more important than desk work.

118

(On hearing the last one, one weary, worldly-wise sales director called out from an audience – 'Not on expenses day!' We know how he feels!)

Whether Professor Kotler had an academic crystal-ball-like mentality, or whether the US got there first we can speculate. Certainly, to many nations, American methods became the role models of the quantity selling age. Or were they just a little more extreme than others?

Now the time has come for sales people to look at the new challenge: to examine the ways of the past 30 years and to decide how they can maintain the quantity but develop methods that do not leave devastation and a trail of bodies behind them. This is not as hard as it seems. There are improved communications, databases, software and all manner of aids becoming available to assist. But the old-fashioned sales director or vice-president, that John Wayne-like charismatic super-hero who led his sales force like some cavalier hit squad, is well on his way out. These days, he looks like something from an old black and white 'B' movie!

I recently completed the manuscript of a book about sales management in the new culture. In fact this book was commissioned by a financial services Client company. In it I wrote the following.

*The Future is Different. It's better ... but harder*

> The fact is that teams can be run democratically or autocratically. The culture which your sales team was run by for many years was autocratic. And, to be fair, so were almost all the others. Businesses used to be run like armies. The centre of control and command was at the top. The managing director effectively dictated the direction of the business and charged his fellow directors with implementing his plan. The MD's job was to get the maximum return for the shareholders by screwing as much out of Customers as they could. The directors interpreted the bosses' plan and handed it down to their managers who worked out the detail and created the implementation plans. These plans they passed on to the lower levels of management who figured out what to do and issued instructions to the staff. The staff then did as they were told or they got fired.
>
> In those days, Customers got what they were given, which was what the company had decided to sell or offer. Or, as it came to be with financial services for many years, the Customer was cajoled – even tricked in the worst cases – into buying anything which made a fast buck for the sales team and seemed to make a good sale for the business. Everyone was chasing new business. What happened to the Customer after the sale only mattered if they had more money to spend. It's a sorry tale and no wonder, really, that regulation was to be the end result. Frankly it is a miracle that it is still self regulation. The whole thing was driven by greed. Of course, it couldn't last. Customers rebelled. No Customers, it became clear, meant no return for shareholders. MDs and CEOs globally went in to a quick huddle in their changing room and came out 'new men' and 'new women'.
>
> So, now, and quite rightly, we are seeing the pendulum swing the other way. Indeed I am proud to be a vocal crusader and campaigner in the

■ Customer-Driven Marketing

cause of bringing the old ways to an end. More, I am totally committed to helping businesses turn round, become Customer facing, and learn how to deliver the new (or should that be old?) standards and practices.

The reason for this little history lesson is to explain, to some extent, why salespeople must spend so much time and concentrate so much effort in coming to terms with so many new practices and an almost totally new culture. Senior management is now looking for enterprise and initiative from its stars. In the days of the old culture, the one who did as he or she was told the best, or the most, became the star. The new culture appreciates that you and your team are out there with the Customer. You see, hear and feel their needs. It is in assisting you to meet those needs that your management can best achieve the aims of the business.

In simple terms, the energies and dynamics of many businesses have turned, or are turning, completely about face. So as well as learning to take on these new cultures, restructure to deliver improved service, re-engineer processes to be faster, lower cost and more accurate and put back a quality ethos into sales and marketing, the whole life assurance business has been handed a double whammy of the worst kind. An already flat market has had to cope with enormous self regulation and disclosure too...

... Now you may have been a sales manager for some years and it would be very easy for you to sit back and say 'I'm OK. I've been a manager quite a while. I know how to do it. I don't need this book.' Take that risk at your peril. For in the 'new' Customer focused ethos the task and role of the sales manager has changed radically. You are no longer an officer on HMS Command and Control. It's no longer about flogging stuff as hard as you can and the sales manager standing behind the lads with a whip keeping them at it, hyping them up. Now the company has explicit objectives to deliver a quality-based service-orientated method of gaining sales which is arrived at by making the vehicle for sales achievement a strong, caring and satisfying relationship. It's a whole new way of getting business. Today's sales manager is predominantly a coach, a counsellor and trainer. There's an emotional and psychological content to your work which just wasn't there before.

This is all going to have enormous effects on the skills that are required by sales people. In a sense they have to come to terms with the difference between the power to profit versus the power to please! And particularly this will put greatest pressure on the sales manger as they get to grips with their new role.

The shift in selling style warrants much greater attention and it shall have it: in the whole of Chapter 16 where we look at the concept of Three Generations of Selling and identify just how the style has to change and what influences have brought all this about. There are definite marketing miracles to be found in this area.

Meanwhile, this short introductory chapter has served to identify the changes going on in selling as one of the key factors in the next decade and to show the following:

• Selling has not been a Customer-driven process for decades. It has

been a production driven process.
- Selling has required that the market is manipulated and exploited to achieve its aims.
- Selling has sadly become a process which is over-influenced by the quantity obsession and thus shorter term objectives have won out over longer term objectives; the sale has taken precedence over the Customer relationship. In effect this means the second sale has lost out to the first!
- Sales people, especially those who lead sales teams, have to learn a whole host of new team leadership skills.

# 8

# 'New' marketing is coming

At Northwestern University they have a distinguished record in leading edge thinking and teaching in marketing; and two distinguished professors who have played a huge part in creating that reputation. One of those professors is Phil Kotler, a man whose work some 20 years ago is now beginning to look almost prophetic (he shares this distinction with another prophet, Ted Levett). The second professor is Louis Stern. You will hear more of Stern in a moment, but in the mean time let's look at Kotler's 'From Sales Obsession to Marketing Effectiveness' as published in the *Harvard Business Review* and see what he suggests is the object of marketing. He wrote 'Marketing focuses on the needs of the buyer. It is preoccupied with how to generate Customer satisfaction at a profit.' This is theoretically correct. However, sadly, since Kotler wrote that in the late 1970s many years have passed, and the pendulum I believe he was trying to stop swaying even further towards its quantity climax continued, regardless, for a further 20 years. Now, in retirement I believe, he will see it on the way back and thus like someone with a broken watch will have the pleasure of being right twice.

Kotler further explained the tasks of the marketer to be very different from those of the seller. He proposed that they:

- think in terms of long-term trends, threats and opportunities
- think in terms of Customer types and market segment differences
- think in terms of developing good systems for market analysis, planning and control.

## The route and path of the changes

Yet marketing has as much change to make as selling. I mentioned at the beginning of this chapter Professor Louis W Stern, a colleague of Professor Kotler, also 'carrying on the Northwestern tradition' as he once described it to me. I have twice listened to Lou Stern make a similar presentation – once in Cannes, France, at a strategic symposium there, and once much, much further afield when we found ourselves grappling with our consciences (and most pleasantly surprised at least by the marketing community) some years before the black and coloured population were given the vote in 1994 in pre-election Johannesburg, South Africa. Lou and I had been booked for the same conference, and he had the honour of the keynote opener. And this 1990 work remains, in my view, as I told him when we met again in London at Management Centre Europe's Global Marketing Conference recently, just as valid.

## The last 30 years predicts the next ... how many?

Lou Stern presented an analysis of marketing over the last 30 years which he and Phil Kotler had worked on together and their resulting predictions, based on this, for 'at least the next ten'.

When you look at the tables Lou kindly sent to me for Marketing 2000, you can see clearly where marketing is coming from and, to some extent, where it's going. The charts themselves are largely self-explanatory, but there is some background to set the perspective.

You will quickly notice a missing decade from the analysis, namely the 1970s. Professors Kotler and Stern discerned that there were so many distorting factors in the 1970s that it skewed the picture further. See if you agree. Certainly some of the factors they list hold fairly painful memories for me. In Britain, along with their list, we had three-day working weeks, crippling power strikes, and terrible political and union unrest undermining our commercial scene and playing havoc with our export performance.

What happened in the 1970s:

- unexpected cost inflation
- shortages of needed materials
- new technological breakthroughs
- unwanted government regulations
- high interest costs
- aggressive internal competition
- the end of the Baby Boom
- unemployment.

■ Customer-Driven Marketing

Phil Kotler and Lou Stern's look at the decades of marketing fell under three main headings which are tabulated here as Tables 8.1, 8.2 and 8.3, and cover the three decades of the 1960s, 1980s and 1990s.

Let me show you what I mean by a clear route and path. Take a look at line 1 of Table 8.1. Mass Marketing evolves to Segmented Marketing evolves to Niche and Customised Marketing. Take that back to Chapter 2 and you'll see how this progression relates to what marketing services and technology were delivering: mass mailings through to the almost individualised mailings that current techno-creativity facilitates.

## Setting the scene for the future

A prerequisite of customer-driven marketing is that it establishes relationships before or during the sales process and then continues to recognise that, given the level of product quality, of course, on-going sales will prosper so long as the relationship is satisfactory – poor sales often being one of the more obvious results of a poor relationship.

I had to smile a while back when one major travel business was forced into liquidation owing just under £100 million and the public administrator assigned to act for the creditors explained that it would be 'a long slow business' since, before they could start settling matters and seeing who

**Table 8.1** Product/market strategies

| 1960s | 1980s | 1990s |
| --- | --- | --- |
| Mass marketing & product differentiation | Segmented marketing & product proliferation | Niche and customised marketing & product positioning |
| Product orientation | Market orientation | Customer/ competitor/channel orientation |
| Random product lines and products | Full product lines | Product line rationalisation |
| Growth mission for all products | Differentiated mission for each product | Strategic mission for each product |
| Random market coverage | Maximum market coverage | Selective market coverage |
| Domestic marketing | Multinational marketing | Global marketing |
| Standardised marketing | Regional marketing | Local marketing |

## 'New' marketing is coming

Table 8.2 *Marketing mix strategies*

| 1960s | 1980s | 1990s |
|---|---|---|
| Survey research | Qualitative research | Decision support system research |
| Competing on product features | Competing on price lines and price | Competing on quality, design, and service |
| Pricing based on cost | Pricing based on competition | Pricing based on Customer perceived value |
| Suppliers/distributors as adversaries | Suppliers/distributors as cost-centres | Suppliers/distributors as partners |
| Generalised sales force | Differentiated sales force | Multiplexed sales force |
| Hard selling and heavy advertising | Heavy sales promotion | Targeted and coordinated communications |

Table 8.3 *Corporate strategies*

| 1960s | 1980s | 1990s |
|---|---|---|
| Core business development | Conglomerate diversification | Synergistic diversification |
| Cost excellence | Strategic excellence | Implementation excellence |
| Scale economies | Experience economies | Economies of scope |
| Hierarchies | Markets | Governance structures |
| Autonomous corporation | Mergers and acquisitions | Strategic alliances |
| Independent marketing functions | Coordinated marketing functions | Coordinated business functions |

would get how much, they had first to decide how many of those Customers who had complaints about the company's holidays were due some money back and, therefore, who would have a rightful place among the creditors. One frustrated creditor – a bank trying to salvage a loss of about $120 million – enquired as to the number of complaints this involved. 'We have a little over 50,000', replied a poker-faced administrator.

■ Customer-Driven Marketing

Now I cannot conceive that any business which tolerates 50,000 complaints at any given time should or would stay in business. It is perhaps about time that those looking to invest in businesses should pay a little less attention to the projected numbers and a little more to the Customer dynamics. I am certain that if any banker – or for that matter any marketer or even holidaymaker! – had looked into the level of satisfaction among the customers of this business, they would not have made the loan in the first place since they would have been able to predict precisely what would happen well in advance. This was plainly a business which was incapable of building good customer relationships because product quality and service – or rather lack of it – inhibited it from so doing. The team which sanctioned the $140 million loan at the bank have probably since been promoted to better things! I wonder if they have learned anything more about what makes a business a good risk yet?

Getting back to the point, what we need to look at, to enjoy the true predictive value of both Stern's and Kotler's conclusions, is a correlation of some of the factors and their value and contribution to the building of relationships. So, assuming that you have absorbed the left to right lines of the three tables, let us now piece together some of the items from the top to bottom of the right-hand column, the 1990s.

From this you can see just how many of the items from the 1990s column endorse, facilitate or suggest the building of relationships and an individualised approach to marketing. From this the direction of marketing progress is quite clear. We are going backwards to the future. The quality elements that have been driven out over time by the quantity merchants are about to be put back again. The marketer's biggest problem will be to find the tenacity and perseverance to hold out for the long-term benefits that will surely accrue, and to find the funding to pay for it all. In fact, let's take each of the contributory points and look at them briefly here.

## Niche and customised marketing and product positioning

Marketing is lining itself up to deal with smaller and smaller units. Much of the business-to-business market has accepted individualisation for some time now. Plainly this is a posture aimed at the long-term relationship to make all that customisation worth while and profitable. It has arrived on corporate missions now and is fast becoming an obsession for the wise in the consumer markets, although, whatever the pundits say, individualised treatment for the consumer markets is damned hard – and, frankly, not all Customers deserve it, as we shall see.

## Customer/Competitor/Channel orientation

Look how specific your marketing has to become; no longer satisfied with what the consumer wants and thinks, now you must react to Customer types, relate each of those to the relevant competitors and channels and act accordingly. This makes strategy much more complex and tactics quite diffuse.

## Product line rationalisation

The product line is being rationalised so that it makes more sense to the Customer. This enables more and more marketers to plan the way the relationship should develop, and to encourage Customers along that path by more readily being able to offer the right product at the right time. Again this is clearly a relationship facilitator since it enables the marketer to match the product or service to the real lives of the individual Customers. And the nearer we get this to real time in real lives the better.

## Strategic mission for each product

This takes forward the cause of the last point, that a clear path is laid down – not the same path for all, but a clear path for each – and that each product within the rationalised line has a mission in the growth and cultivation of the Customer relationship. Instead of the old Henry Ford attitude – 'the Customer can have any colour they want as long as it's black' – we have now arrived at the time when the Customer can have any colour they like as long as they like it!

## Selective market coverage

We've already looked at the ways many of the media are beginning to address this new highly targeted objective of the marketer. As the media rates increase in terms of the numbers they deliver for the cost, so the need to fine tune and cut wastage to a minimum increases proportionately.

## Global marketing/Local marketing

I have lumped the last two together. Although an apparent dichotomy, the riddle is solved by the saying that has become popular: 'Think global, act local'. It says it all in this context too! Indeed, I have two projects on hand, as I write, where Community Marketing is a priority, that is to say embedding the new decentralised, smaller, more autonomous business units we have created in the restructuring into the communities they serve. The principal here is that you contribute visibly and actively back to the communities from which you take, or perhaps make, a living. They nourish you, you nourish them. I'm trying to take an holistic approach, if you will, to make the relationship symbiotic as opposed to parasitic.

## Competing on quality, design and service

Notice the absence of price! Not an actual absence, of course, but recognition of an experience many have shared that the more individually tailored the product or service, the more value it has to the individual for whom it has been created and, therefore – all things being equal – the more it is worth to them. However this point holds the clue that Customers who have or are beginning a relationship will look more and more at the quality you deliver, since in so many cases they will have in prospect a longer term. They will look at the design capabilities you have; the promise that the next product will meet their needs further or deeper; and the service you give. Get these right and you're worth your weight in gold! And, importantly, you are far more difficult to compete with. Any fool can compete on price. In the past too many of them have.

## Pricing based on Customer perceived value

As the once proud owner from new some while ago of a completely priceless (to me) BMW with its mileage well over 150,000 and too attached to part with it, I asked a dealer, 'What's it worth?' He smiled rather condescendingly, left his price guide firmly in his pocket and said, 'What you can get for it!'

For the future marketing will find itself enjoying the same thought, but for the reasons we have already looked at. The more the quality, design and service aspects are addressed, and the more individually tailored the product, then also the higher the price perception – and the price obtained. Remember that refrigerator questionnaire earlier? Thus, happily we can see that as the Customer gets more demanding, so they are prepared to pay more for their improved goods and services. So here, then, the marketer will find some of the funding for his investments in the longer term using Customer-driven marketing. Much of the rest will come from switching to high focus marketing and away from high activity marketing. This switch alone is the one that has enabled me to make the drastic reductions in Clients' marketing budgets mentioned earlier; in one case as high as 40 per cent and quite frequently around the 30 per cent mark, usually without any significant dip in sales volumes.

One of the problems today is simply that CEOs have come to accept that marketing is a high cost business and they have been misled about the return on investment (ROI) it can bring. There are still plenty of miracles out there waiting to happen. Just as some people have pulled off time, cost or service miracles with re-engineering their processes and management, so too they can have now have marketing miracles.

## Suppliers/Distributors as partners

Over the next decade, there will be a major shift in the custody of the relationship. We will need to discuss this point and, although I would like to share my view and, to some extent, my advice with you, it is possible you may find it controversial. Thus it will follow on after this run-through.

Lou Stern's point is – particularly in the business arena and I guess the personal services consumer arena – the role of the distributor, dealer or intermediary (often almost an adversary in the past) will reposition to become much closer and more co-operative.

## Multiplexed sales force

The FMCG (fast moving consumer goods) companies popularised the use of brand or speciality sales forces. Thus one buyer might have two or three sales people dealing with him – one for each brand or group of brands. Each had a different view of him, each dealt with him differently. Not one of them looked at his total spend with the company. Some called personally, some dealt by phone, others were van sales. The buyer became confused and undervalued.

Cast your mind back to the notion of Total Communications Management. This proposes that one person controls the communications and therefore looks after and understands the situation with any given Customer at any given time. For this to work, clearly this individual must represent all the company brands and products or services. He or she may need the help of specialists to support them, but in essence they are multiplexed. Their mission is to understand and communicate how best the Customer can benefit from the full range of products or services on offer. You can see why, from this explanation, so many companies will relegate the brand almost to a recognition device and seek to transfer or extend the loyalty to the corporation. Hence my development of the phrase 'the brand behind the brand'.

## Targeted and co-ordinated communications

This joins together the need to target, thereby maximising spend and reducing wastage, and focusing the message with the co-ordination and understanding of total communications management. Can you see how this can operate successfully without being as near as possible in real time? I can't.

## Implementation excellence

No marketing can move inferior products. Many of the world's leading manufacturers have moved on from Excellence. Indeed I have been suggesting for some time that Peters and Waterman should get together again to write *In Search of Absolute Bloody Perfection*. IBM would buy a copy. Their famous quality improvement programme, 'Six Sigma', had the intention over a four-year span of improving their excellence level by a factor of 20,000 to accept no more than three to four defects per million units. Perfection has become the avowed goal of many forward thinking companies. Apart from the human interaction within the relationship there is nothing other than product and service perfection that can foster such close accord. However, with the new millennium, our expectation of product and service perfection will be so high that almost everything will actually focus on the relationship and the individuals that make it happen. This is more evidence that we're going backwards to the future!

## Strategic alliances

The shift in corporate strategies to encourage alliances is yet another sign that the real products of tomorrow are information and knowledge. The alliances are about knowing which to buy to a degree, but more, how to use it or what to use it for. I have already presented Marketing 2000 a number of times for software houses who have held symposia for their Clients and prospects which were co-sponsored either by other partner software houses or by computer manufacturers whose aim was to sell the boxes which processed the data using the software. This kind of ad hoc co-operation will become more formalised (as we discussed in Chapter 3) in relation to the need for smaller companies to compete on the international global markets. ABB of Sweden, a company truly committed globally to quality, have a greatly advanced partnership programme. I spoke to an audience of 800 Swedes there about the quality aspects of Marketing. The whole day was designed to get not just their people together with the Customers, but also with ABB's suppliers who were also invited. Now that's what I call sharing the vision!

## Co-ordinated business functions

I have often thought that marketers can be quite an insular-minded group. We are often quite ready to tell the world (or our market) what it thinks – or what it should think – and equally, quite arrogantly, to pass this information on to our colleagues in production or planning. After all, we know what's right, because we're in touch with the market. Ironically we have demonstrated over the last two decades at least that we are actually very bad at listening to the Customer. We seem often to hear but not necessarily to listen. The marketing world is full of marketing directors who take the views, strategies and policies of the company to the market or the Customer, but sadly devoid of marketing directors who accept the duality of their responsibility and fully represent the market to the company. And there are even fewer still who, as board members, can see that aspect of their task which is to be the voice of the Customer on the board.

Marketing people must take on much wider skills, or become, at least, much more aware of them. Marketing is not an insular or isolated function. And for the future it will be even less so. Marketing will become even more integrated into the very fabric of the business. Therefore, it is essential that marketing people become more rounded business people. This is a need which our academics and syllabus controllers must address, and quickly.

I hope you will see by now the valuable job Professors Kotler and Stern's analysis has made of defining the trends for marketing through the next decade and more. I have related some of their points to highlight the terrific, almost magnetic, pull of so many of them towards the relationship at the centre of all we do in marketing for the future. Fourteen out of the 17 strategic directions lead, unequivocally, to a quality approach: 14 out of 17 pointed categorically to relationship and integrated marketing. Not one of the remaining three strategies suggested otherwise. They just didn't agree or disagree. The quantity merchants are getting pushed back to where they belong: they are the barrow boys and bargain basement sellers of tomorrow. There is always a place for them. But they should never have taken over.

However, I have left two points which I want to look at – the first is the subject of the role of the intermediary – wholesaler, retailer, dealer, distributor etc; and the second is the increasing need to look behind the brand and increase activity to add power to corporate image and positioning.

## Whose brand is it anyway?

In Western Europe, I think we are going to have to see a regaining of control by a lot of brand owners. For in certain areas the strength of the brand has almost been hijacked or perhaps neutralised by some of the larger specialist retailers. This story was first told in an earlier book and the situation has worsened since I reported the story of my conversation with the marketing manager of a white goods manufacturer – in fact a refrigerator maker – who, as I was given to understand, effectively waited to be told by certain large retailers, first whether they would get any floor space at all, secondly how many units of what types they would take and thirdly what price they would pay for them. This particular retailer – and others like them – controlled sufficient outlets to be able to dictate terms this way.

This same problem reared its head again when I facilitated a small in-house strategy-building session for one of Europe's leading names in the small electrical goods field. The first problem we hit at the start of the day was that they had lost control of their margin and were now effectively dictated to by the majors in their market. Naturally, this power was used to squeeze the company (which had brand leadership in several areas) to cut its margin to the bone. The result, of course, was that the retail groups were now acting so greedily and so short-sightedly that the company was facing understandable difficulties in maintaining its investment in quality, Customer service and new product development.

## The short answer is there is no short answer

The next few lines are not a prediction, they are a hope – a hope that, as we move towards times of increased quality, we will see a resurgence of the time-honoured values in retailing. Let's think about these.

Essentially, it seems to me there are two types of brand with which retailers must deal. The first is the brand which the Customer will buy anyway – soapflakes in the supermarket are as good an example as any. Here the retailer has really only two major influences; whether to stock and, if so, whether and how to promote. I would call this latter the promotional influence. Such products are usually simple commodities essentially requiring, as far as the brand holder is concerned, the optimum shelf space; and as far as the Customer is concerned, a fair price and reasonable circumstances in which to buy. Simplistically, the market for such products is created by the product's performance at meeting the needs or expectations of its buyer and the efforts of the manufacturer in spreading the gospel through the usual marketing methods. The retailer in this example is, to coin a good old-fashioned word, a purveyor. The only real complication in this process is where the store owner, chain or buying group offer their own-branded alternative. The practice originated as a low price alternative, but has matured to a point where, to bring back Britain's Tesco for an encore, they have used their own brands to further their green moves by offering higher priced but greener or organic alternatives. Others have followed suit. Indeed, the marketing and packaging trade press often carry stories of the supermarkets 'copying' the brand leaders' packs so that the Customer is fooled. Coca-Cola took umbrage when Richard Branson's Virgin Cola was launched and even more so

## 'New' marketing is coming

when Tesco's main competitor, supermarket chain Sainsbury, launched their own brand in a Coke look-alike can.

By and large, despite the occasional squabbles and to differing degrees of sophistication, this process has a sense of equilibrium. The manufacturers provide the product and the demand (brand demand and loyalty), the retailers provide the arena – and often have a hand in providing their share of the demand. So that is the Promotional Brand.

Then there is the second type of brand which I shall refer to as the Broker Brand. Here the retailer provides more than just the arena. They provide (or should!) a range of choices, value for money and service. And, lastly, they provide two additional items; expertise and advice.

Here again the retailer is charged with providing what I described earlier as the arena and all that goes with it; but equally, here they become the honest broker as far as the Customer is concerned – providing advice to match the right product(s) or service(s) to the particular Customer. They also provide expertise, most frequently in terms of after-sales support to the Customer – and possibly further sales where supplies and consumables are involved. I call this retailer the honest broker since in my idealistic account here, they are deemed to be that by – significantly – both the brand owner and the buyer of the brand.

When this balance is distorted – the manufacturer interferes to the detriment of the retailer (or lets him down) – they both suffer. The Customer buys another brand from another retailer. Essentially here the retailer has to purvey the product and act as custodian of the goodwill that the brand owner has built up – often with the invaluable support of their retailers – in the brand.

In my view, a retailer who deals in 'honest broker' products should accept the limitations of their role and the responsibilities that go with it. Once they try to dictate as opposed to apply sensible negotiatory pressure for the Customer's best interest, they step beyond their remit and become an intolerable interference which has potentially drastically detrimental effects on the consumer's position in the long term. To those involved in marketing such products and who have lost control there is no short or easy answer. The only way to restore power is long, risky and expensive. In many cases the damage will have taken place over five or even ten years and to minimise risk could take as long to correct. It is my belief that you must do it to survive in a world of increasing quality and Customer service levels. Margins should increase over the following years as value perceptions increase and as Customers become more demanding. It is essential that the battle to control margins where they have been lost is started right now. Otherwise, as the cycle of product development increases and the life span of the new products developed decreases, so you will be sucked into a vortex of decline so strong you will not survive.

■ Customer-Driven Marketing

## The simple act of selling

The human race is extraordinarily good at taking the simple and making it enormously complex. Let's just consider some of the ways we 'distort' the perfect and make it harder! The following represents my ideal flow-chart for the sales process...

**SELLER**
↓
**BUYER**

This, to me, represents a perfectly balanced and satisfactory negotiating position for both parties. But let's compare it with some of the other distribution channels.

A familiar one is this...

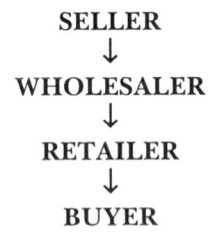

**SELLER**
↓
**WHOLESALER**
↓
**RETAILER**
↓
**BUYER**

It doesn't look too bad until you think about how it gets extended – each extension pushing the buyer and the seller further apart...

**MANUFACTURER**
↓
**IMPORTER**
↓
**SELLER (SOLE COUNTRY SUPPLIER)**
↓
**REGIONAL SALES OFFICE**
↓
**BRANCH SALES OFFICE**
↓
**WHOLESALER (HEAD OFFICE)**
↓
**RETAILER (CENTRAL BUYING)**
↓
**RETAILER (LOCAL STORE)**
↓
**BUYER**

Then there's the familiar business version of the earlier one...

**SELLER**
↓
**SOLE DISTRIBUTOR**
↓
**APPOINTED DEALER**
↓
**BUYER**

Or even the insurance and financial product system...

**CARRIER/REINSURER**
↓
**BROKER**
↓
**POLICY HOLDER**

And what confusion these corrupted systems, as I call them (meaning only that they are less than perfect!), cause. Take that insurance situation. Let's start with the policy holder. Who do they think they're dealing with?

Well, when everything is going well, most think they are dealing with the broker. Some realise that their contract is actually with the underwriting company. You can imagine how confused they get with a serious claim when into the picture comes a loss adjuster!

I can't recall how many dithering insurance companies I've sat down with. They've researched the enormous profit potential of using, particularly direct, marketing to their Customers; they've worked out that cross-selling products to their policy holders would be a great idea.

In this day and age I am amazed that there are still some insurance companies that will write a life policy and expect simply to take the premiums throughout the term of the policy. They do this without ever contacting the client – the buyer – during the whole length of the term, sometimes for as long as 25 years. Now, as a customer, how would you feel about somebody who took your money for 25 years and never bothered to get in touch with you? Unless you missed a payment, in which case you receive a terse administrative document that tells you to pay up or else you'll find your cover withdrawn. Arrogance rules! Whether you like it or not!

So back to the ditherers who want to tap the profit potential of marketing to their Customers. What's the problem? The brokers! We don't want to bite the hand that feeds us. You see, brokers are responsible for the

■ Customer-Driven Marketing

vast majority of our business. And well, they see the policy holders as their Clients.

There is an answer of course. And, those companies that are brave enough, forthright enough and fair enough to find it have taken the profit rewards that result. But all this paranoia and confusion develop because the relationship between the buyer and the seller – an equal balance of power and responsibility – becomes distorted and corrupted. A three-layer chain becomes an eternal triangle – as in the insurance example. A four-layer chain becomes a wrestler's tag match.

Let's go back to the refrigerator example I mentioned earlier. You will recall that the marketing manager said that, basically, they had to do as the retailers told them. In effect, therefore, the major multiples had achieved such high off-take levels that the company couldn't really afford to lose them. Thus, using this as a lever, the retail chains could threaten withdrawal of floorspace unless the manufacturer supplied at the price they demanded.

You can imagine how that little line works out! Brand owner advertises to persuade consumer to buy. Consumer visits large, well-known retailer:

'I'd like to buy a Chillo fridge.'

'We don't deal with Chillo any longer.'

'Why? What did they do wrong?'

'I don't know. But Head Office told us that they've been deleted from our list of authorised suppliers.'

Great. The situation described by this marketing manager seemed to my ethics to verge on commercial blackmail – a far cry from market forces.

Well, I said to her, posing a hypothetical question, 'Why don't you appoint another retailer and write to all the purchasers over the last, say, five years and tell them that henceforth you have withdrawn stocks from Nasties National, and your new official supplier will be Nicer National'.

I should have known better, of course. Here comes the marketing manager's question. 'How could I possibly reach those customers? It's a lovely thought, John. But there's just no way.'

'Then you must do something about it,' I said, 'because apart from anything else you are letting those customers down. They decided to buy your product. They wanted Chillo. You are obliged to accept that as a responsibility beyond supplying the cabinet. People don't buy "cabinets". They buy benefits, satisfaction and trust. They reward their brand choices with loyalty and with profit.'

Here's what lies behind these comments – retailers/brokers/agents with a clear conscience have nothing to fear. They add to the process of conventional marketing. The Customer benefits. And the retailer benefits. Everybody's happy.

These retailers accept that a manufacturer not only places his goods in their store. He vests an enormous responsibility in them – the responsibility for building a sound Customer relationship on their behalf. That relationship must include service, confidence, courtesy and trust.

This means they must train their staff in human relationships and, importantly, not just to sell the product, but to know it. They must learn to listen to the Customer, appreciate their needs, and with skill and experience match the right product to the right Customer.

For now there exists an alternative distribution channel for most – not by any means all, but for most – manufacturers and suppliers, and indeed, significantly, for most Customers. You only have to look at the enormous growth in 'direct' financial and other service businesses to get my point. It takes it back to:

**SELLER**
↓
**BUYER**

## The new power of corporate image

As the marketing mix reshuffles itself to cope with the future, so each of the voices of its disciplines is claiming that they have an increased role in the future. Sales promotion is a fine example, where the practitioners are making all manner of new claims for their trade and effectively digging themselves in to an entrenched position which has far more to do with the old ways of exploitation selling than it has to do with satisfaction marketing. However, I know there are some among their ranks who can and will make this change. And they will reap the rewards they deserve.

I think the only mistake in listening to the voices of the various marketing disciplines would be to take any strategic notice of them. Just who you should be listening to will be revealed in Chapter 14. In the mean time, one of those voices can be heard crying out that it shall have increasing prominence – and it is right. It is the voice of the corporate identity or, as I have referred to it several times, 'the brand behind the brand'.

Boston Consulting were called in by Royal Insurance in the UK. Royal's CEO at that time was Peter Duerden, who gave me one of my most often used and favourite quotes. The quote was that 'a key characteristic of successful businesses is their ability to respond to changes in their market place before there is any widely-held perception of the need to do so'.

Prior to its merger with Sun Alliance, Royal Insurance (UK) Ltd was a wholly owned subsidiary of Royal Insurance PLC, the parent holding company of one of the world's largest insurance groups operating in over

■ Customer-Driven Marketing

80 countries. Peter Duerden was to lead the company through a sustained strategy of change. Royal reviewed Clients' needs within each of its principle channels of business: the conclusion was that they had to change the organisation itself as well as many of its decision making processes. Dubbed 'Channel Focus', Royal had realised that if their different Clients across their different distribution channels (brokers, agents and financial service intermediaries) had different expectations of them, it was counter-productive to try to force them all into the same response, delivery and service mechanisms.

Furthermore, and sharing great courage and insight in an industry not overburdened with such qualities, Royal set about devolving the decision making authority in relation to the vast majority of its day-to-day business operations. This authority, passed down to the staff closest to its Clients – its branches – required a new structure with highly skilled insurance people at branch level.

These changes took some three years to complete and demonstrated that to deliver quality through to the market many changes must take place outside the true remit of marketing. As an observer, I found two factors interesting about the Royal case. In many ways it could be classified a text book example in changing direction: a prime example of a huge company doing its utmost to change from one of those faceless self-perpetuating, self-obsessed monsters which manipulate markets to their own ends, to a new leaner, keener, versatile and energetic group of Client-orientated units which live and breathe Customer needs. My first point is that although these benefits will all in time supposedly benefit the end-Customer – the policy holder, in all their reshaping and rethinking Royal seem to have started in the middle, centring all their changes on the intermediary Client. The assumption here is that the benefits will reach the policy holder in the end. I hope so.

Secondly, I found it strange that this 'revolution' took place in just the one Royal group company. If you are a Customer of Royal you may deal with Royal Insurance for your general business (such as household or motor insurance) and Royal Life for your life, savings and pensions products. I suspect that to most prospects and policy holders the name Royal is the name they remember. They will not appreciate that there is a difference between Royal Life and Royal Insurance. The brand name they will remember is one word – Royal.

Yet, if the change programme were to be in any way successful it would create a real difference between Royal Insurance and its sibling companies. This vast cultural difference could only serve to confuse Customers who may understandably expect some similarity in methods, systems and services. The more the changes at Royal Insurance became effective, the greater the problem could have become.

At chemical multinational ICI the brand behind the brand also became an issue. In a totally different market to Royal, ICI managers have had to consider the total needs of some of their Customers. This often stretches beyond the conventional product disciplines which are recognised by ICI. After all, a Customer who buys fertilisers on the one hand and plastics for packaging on the other sees itself not as two separate Customers of ICI, but as one. Only ICI separates its needs; and it does so to meet ICI structures.

This has led ICI to look at Customers' total industry requirements. Yet individual companies or operating divisions within groups can often be quite competitive and jealously guard their information and contacts. Such petty insecurities may not exist within ICI, but I have often seen the most outrageous non-cooperation between group members. ICI have said that they feel the answer might be in putting together its businesses in structures aligned to the marketplace; my view is that the design of corporate structure starts with Customers and works back. My guess is that the ICI analysis is correct provided that: the business groups can quickly assimilate sufficient expertise in its new specialisation and convince its market of the benefits; provision is made for the forwarding of the overall corporate strategy and culture; and a network for information and communication is created between the market-aligned fragments.

One tendency with market-aligned fragments is for, as it were, an overflow of commitment to its market sector. This in turn leads each to see its resource demands as the highest priority. When the correct communication, training and information networks are in place a much better balance between corporate direction and strategy and market sector obsession are achieved.

## Brand loyalty needs a strong corporate attachment too

The hard fact is that we face an epoch where there is a convergence of factors over which an organisation's failure to address its corporate image and position will seriously damage its health. To name some, they include parity products, both better and more similar; and a consumer that is more informed, more vocal, more sophisticated, more demanding and more willing to vote with their cash.

I remember Murray Raphel reminding me that people often bestow human qualities on the companies they deal with. 'Just listen to the way they describe them', he explained, 'they say they're a mean outfit. Or pretty generous types. Or friendly. Or stand-offish. These are not corporate qualities, these are the qualities or failings of another human being.' He's right! And so, in a way, it is fair to suggest that a corporate identity is an expression of corporate personality.

Everything a company does, the way it acts, the opinions it expresses, the people it hires as well as the way it treats its Customers, is seen, to a lesser or greater degree, to be an expression of that personality. Thus the identity can be used quite powerfully to join with, differentiate from or simply endorse a chosen position. I am suggesting for the future that as the products get more similar, so the corporate identity should support and enhance the role of the brands. It can help to provide further competitive differentiation. Naturally the methods used to do this will vary depending on which of the three classic identities the business had adopted. These are as follows:

- **The Monolith** – an organisation that revolves its whole style around one strong core name and visual presentation such as IBM and BMW.
- **The Patron** – this company operates through a series of brands, often with no logical relationship to each other or the organisation. Often, too, they have been added through acquisition or merger. Nestlé, and Procter and Gamble are examples.
- **The Umbrella** – a cluster organisation which endorses or sponsors multiple activities – such as General Motors.

Richard Branson, of course, takes it one step further. Is this a man or a brand? Perhaps his family dropped a 'd' somewhere along the way!

## Back to Stern

Before we close this chapter, I would like to bring you the latest from Professor Louis Stern. His predictions for the first decade of the millennium continue clearly on the path demonstrated by his earlier work. For example, he feels that whereas the 1990s proved to be a time of customising and repositioning products to fit the needs of niche markets, in the following decade this will transform to a time of streamlining by removing stress from the acquisition and consumption processes; retaining and defending Customers from competitors; and searching for innovations by studying lead Customers.

The market orientation of the 1990s will continue to show an increased concern about how companies take their products to market – particularly what channels to use and ease of availability.

By 2000, Stern is convinced that most companies will want to exceed Customers' expectations with every transaction and interaction; they will also concentrate on developing value propositions – this will continue the trend of moving away from price for price sake and take into account how the Customer feels as well as the way they act. The prediction is also that corporations will focus much more on sales growth but in a much more strategic fashion. That's to say, they will more clearly define the precise set of benefits they will deliver to specific target groups of Customers at a price which yields a profit. I think this is a significant point since a great number of the companies I visit fail to distinguish, in terms of level of service, who deserves it and who doesn't. I believe firmly that standards of service should be consistent and sacrosanct. Levels of service should vary, set broadly against the value of the Customer and a reasonable perception by that Customer of what service they should expect for their money. This means it is as important to know who not to target, sell and serve as it is to know who should be targeted. There is no point in paying out to get Customers who will not be profitable or whose expectations you are not able to meet or exceed.

Also beyond 2000, Louis Stern suggests that companies must concentrate on providing packages, bundled together into turnkey solutions. Using the databases developed in the 1990s, businesses will begin to focus on segments of one. I agree that this is a goal and that some companies may reach it. I also believe that for many, many marketers, it should be seen as a principle or a goal. In reality we may not yet have developed the technology, the service elements and the ability to create anything other than commodities out of certain simple and vital necessities of life. These may always be sold on price in certain arenas and on availability or convenience at other times or in other places.

Within a few years six-sigma standards, in other words, essentially perfection will be the norm and the Customer expectancy. Businesses will appreciate that they must invest in intellectual property (software more than hardware!); that to survive they must transform from being fixed cost businesses to variable cost businesses; and that they must develop into modular or sometimes virtual organisations.

Lou Stern's valuable insights for the next decade simply add even more fuel to the notion which this book proposes and endorse the view that you should already have started.

There is another point here too. It is this. What this book proposes, that you should turn your business into a Customer-driven business and grow it by embedding a quality culture into every aspect of your sales, advertising and marketing thoughts and activities, is not something you should do in part. Pick of any one of the suggestions of what you must do from this book and you will receive less than its proportion of value. Think of it as a jigsaw; when all the pieces are in place it could be a work of art. Until then it will always be an unfinished puzzle.

In this chapter we have covered a lot of ground, much of it difficult comprehensively to include in a short summary, but here is an attempt.

- Whereas the old-fashioned sales techniques are on the decline, marketing techniques are on the increase. Much of this softer, more professional style has to do with the longer term objectives that result.

■ Customer-Driven Marketing

- When you consider the prophetic qualities that Professor Louis Stern predicted for the 1990s, an incredible 14 out of 17 had to do with or would facilitate the growth of, long-term, broad based relationships; the same relationships that are the cornerstone of Customer-Driven Marketing.
- The correlation of these factors demonstrates clearly that the future lies in the past. The ways of quantity must now give way to those of quality.
- Many companies, in their conviction that the Customer and quality hold the future, have moved on from the pursuit of excellence to the pursuit of perfection.
- Marketing people must show far greater awareness of broader business skills and acquire broader knowledge in this respect.
- Marketing leaders must pay greater attention to their responsibility as the voice of the Customer to the board of their company.
- Brand owners would be well advised to stay in control of their brands, particularly in relation to margin from which so much else in the future will require investment. This means particularly customer service, product development and brand and corporate strengthening. Those who have lost control of such factors should start the battle to regain it now.
- Retail groups who step beyond their remit as the purveyor and/or honest broker and seek to exert undue influence on manufacturers' margins do so in the knowledge that, at the end of the day, it is against their Customers' best long-term interest.
- In the battle to differentiate choices in a market of increasingly similar products, corporate identity will play an increasing part, underlining the point made earlier.
- Professor Stern's latest predictions for the mix of strategies which corporations must adopt to survive and thrive in the next decade continue to support the whole notion of Customer-driven marketing and (I would venture) there is no sign of any swing or change in this or the path of quality as the engine of marketing issues.

# 9

# What will Customers want next?

There seem to be hordes of people who involve themselves in Customer care tactics but very few who are involved in the strategy. This is a great shame. And no marketing miracles there! For Customer care – to provide anything like the levels required for relationship-centred Customer-driven marketing – should not be thought of as a tactic. It has to be considered strategically and systematically. So many of the companies I meet talk passionately about Customer care (as they often do, incidentally, about quality) and then treat it as some kind of occasional or spasmodic campaign. Displaying a certificate in reception given to the person in the organisation who did something outstanding for a Customer last month is a campaign. Expecting *all* your employees to do something outstanding for a Customer every month, every week or every day suggests you've got a strategy in place.

## Where doesn't the arrogance come from?

Many poor organisations have a reputation for attracting commentary or criticism for their failures. You only have to talk to their Customers. Certain divisions of pre-Granada Forte, indeed certain units of the old Forte, for example; the well-known high street bank referred to earlier is in danger of becoming something of a running gag in this book; a few years back, Payless, the do-it-yourself chain (before they were taken over) were another. I have a Payless story which is entirely true and which I share with conference delegates from time to time. It's good for a smile and was originally told in a previous book. In fact there are two excerpts that I want to take out of that book for you and the first is the Payless

■ Customer-Driven Marketing

story so – with grateful acknowledgements to the publishers McGraw-Hill who published The John Frazer-Robinson Direct Marketing Series – let me take Payless first. Here's the original excerpt:

## Desire is not enough – you have to make it happen

There's a branch of a well-known DIY superstore near me. I personally wouldn't work for them – simply because their name suggests you're not going to get a very fat pay packet. In fact, judging by their checkout staff that may well be the case. My experience is that I intrude inexcusably into their day-long, apparently very important, conversations with each other. There's no contact whatsoever. However much I spend, whatever I've bought, I'm just another one in the line. And on the rare occasions they look up, they can never work out why I'm laughing. It's the sticker on their till that says, 'SMILE – and give your Customer a nice day'. Perhaps that promotion is over now.

Now there are two significant aspects about this story. The first is that it was obviously not just my local store that had the problem. I know this because I've experimented around Britain and found with some better and some worse experiences, it was a national phenomenon. Secondly, reassuring me that it's not me being picky, whenever I mention this topic at a conference or seminar in Britain, the audience relate to it generally almost as one. In fact I've even had them telling me of their own similar experiences. Obviously this is a widespread, commonly recognised problem; not me developing a sort of commercial version of the mother-in-law joke that relies on everyone identifying with or sharing the problem.

So if I know about it and nearly all those I talk to know and have experienced it, what on earth was going on inside Payless HQ? Without intimate knowledge of their particular company one can only hazard guesses. My guess is that the distance from the Boardroom to the Branch was about four times longer than it should be. They were acquired shortly after by another company who promised a difference. But in my experience, it didn't happen.

The second reprise from my earlier book is about 'My Businesses'. They're few and far between, but when you come across one it's love at first sight.

## Let me explain about 'My Businesses'

The philosophy of 'Customer is King' requires the virtues of something we all already know. We know because we like it when it happens to us. And it's never often enough. We all like to be remembered. We all like to be cared for. We all like recognition. We love good service and bask in personal attention.

And when you feel this happening, you have found a 'My Business'. Take My London Hotel for example.

A few years back, I took a suite in a hotel on Park Lane. I was attending the British Direct Marketing Awards. It wasn't a good night for me. It was a

## What will customers want next?

great night. Probably a once in a lifetime. I collected six or seven certificates, I think five trophies and the coveted Gold Award. For me, a real event, since it made me the only person to have received the 'Gold' twice in the entire history of the awards.

The odd bottle of champagne was seen to pass the table. But most of it stayed right there. Around 4am I staggered into my hotel. I was showered with greetings and congratulations. There and then it seemed that everyone on night duty was joining in.

When I checked out around lunch time I made a point of thanking the manager for his kind hand-written note which had been delivered on my breakfast tray.

Let a year pass. A year, I have to say, when I think I only used the hotel once between my 'Gold' night and today. How do you think I felt when the front desk clerk greeted me with this:

'Mr Frazer-Robinson. We are so pleased to have you back with us again. We checked with your secretary, and she said it was Awards night. So we've given you the same suite as last year. It seemed so lucky for you.'

And more along those lines. How did I feel? Wouldn't you make that 'My Hotel'? So what is this? Salesmanship? Professionalism? Excellence? Yes, it is undoubtedly all those things. It's also note-taking, record-keeping – and a great deal of belief in the very highest standards of relationships.

Have you noticed how people accolade professionals? You go to **the** grocer. You go to **the** supermarket. But you talk about '**my** accountant', '**my** solicitor'. Even the ones you don't like. '**My** bank manager'. You decide to 'own' these people because they are important to you. Or, rather, because they've made themselves important to you, or even influential in your life.

So I know I've made it when a client says, 'JFR is **my** strategy man!' – I still have a job to do when they say, 'I use JFR'. Personally, I 'use' a toilet. My advice is to go for a 'my' position in the lives of your Customers. No matter whether you're a (my) charity, a (my) jeweller or a (my) supermarket. They owe you when they own you. Because you've made yourself theirs.

There's nothing particularly new in this thought. Pendulums swing. And this one is on its way back.

In order to book a table, I rang a restaurant that used to be a haunt, but where I hadn't been for the best part of ten years. Paul, the owner, answered the phone and as soon as I announced myself ten years dissolved as if they had never been. We had some catching up time and then I told Paul that I would like a table for six the following Sunday. 'Sure,' he said, 'would you like your usual table?' Not bad after ten years!

Maybe you have a favourite good service story, or perhaps a place where you always feel special, or even welcome. Perhaps you have places you go where you're recognised and made a fuss of. If you're typical, you'll react by going there regularly, taking your friends and generally giving them a terrific 'word of mouth' testimonial whenever you get the opportunity. I have always described word of mouth as the cheapest, most effective kind of advertising you can buy: the trouble is, of course,

■ Customer-Driven Marketing

you can't buy it. You have to earn it. I maintain, and I know that I am among many who feel this way, that we are going to see all this change radically. In the same way that the bushfire of democracy was picked up in Eastern Europe, so the bushfire of 'I'm a Customer – and King is not good enough for me' is being picked up in the developed world.

Just before we move on, you might be interested by the following British research which was published by CMT Direct. They had the motor insurance market under their particular microscope and discovered that based on a sample of 65,000 motorists, 'word of mouth' provided the motor insurance business with more name awareness than television, press and direct mail put together (Figure 9.1). In fact, 'word of mouth' tops the list at a tad more than 27 per cent. Let this tell you something about what your Customers will do for you – if you get it right!

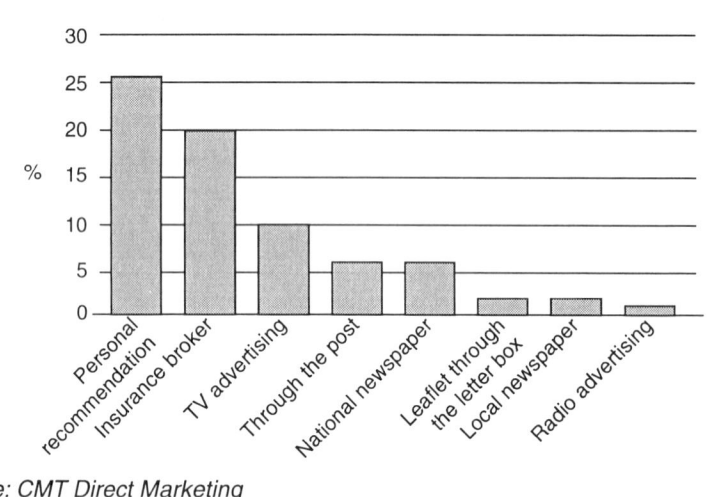

*Source: CMT Direct Marketing*

**Figure 9.1** *Word of Mouth outscores advertising in creating name awareness for motor insurance – and probably most else as well*

## Who enjoys their shopping these days?

To get a measure on how sales and marketing people feel about this I have made a point during all my Marketing 2000 conferences of asking audiences 'Hands up. Who enjoys going to the supermarket?' There are some that do. In fact, if I'm honest, I do! I enjoy watching the people and I enjoy casting a professional eye over the marketing and particularly sales promotion that is going on. But do we enjoy the shopping? My show-of-hands research tells me few people do. Back to that bank again! While writing parts of another book I spent some time in the English seaside town of Weymouth in Dorset. The branch there had 'streamlined' itself to have perhaps a dozen cashiers or tellers and, of course, two personal bankers! I decided to visit during a lunch hour and found myself among a queue of some 30 or more people, waiting like good citizens to have the honour of a cashier's attention for a short spell. It was well organised. If you visited during the lunch hour, of course, half the cashiers were at lunch. Thus, the management team there had thoughtfully installed a Q-matic. This ingenious device tells you, when you are lucky enough to get to the front, which of the cashiers not at lunch will pass the time of day with you. To celebrate this golden moment it chimes like a slightly damaged doorbell. Waiting with the other Customers, many of whom, like half the cashiers, were in their lunch break, it became obvious that the system the management had devised worked extremely well for the bank, but was the subject of some resentment and anger from their Customers. As I got to the front of the queue, I turned to face the long thin line of angry and frustrated people behind me. 'Excuse me,' I said just loudly enough to get most of their attention, 'but why do you put up with this atrocious service?' I thought I'd be a hero, chairlifted on to the shoulders of the two chaps behind me and taken on a tour of the premises while the rest of the queue followed chanting the magic plea 'We shall, we shall soon be served'. It was not to be. Most of them looked at me and prayed they wouldn't find me sitting next to them on the bus home. So to those nice Dorset folk and those members of my audiences who don't enjoy shopping I say to you again – 'Why do you put up with it?'

## The answer lies in the 1960s

What has all this to do with selling? The answer is not so much as it has to do with the mentality which took over the driving seat of selling. Banking, it seems, is not an experience you should enjoy, it is something you have to put up with in order to get the facility. Why is supermarketing, in Britain at least, such a joyless, impersonal experience? It is because we have been conditioned to accept it as such. Although I take Britain to task particularly, I am enough of a European to know that the problem is in no way peculiar to Britain, but it is certainly the worst in Europe. In fact it distresses me that there is much more interest in the quality aspects of marketing in continental Europe than in Britain.

But it wasn't always like that. I used to have a grocery fairy. Most children have a tooth fairy. Me – I had this grocery fairy! The tooth fairy visits in the middle of the night and generously exchanges money for your first teeth as they are shed. My grocery fairy didn't get any teeth, but nevertheless, generously donated a box of groceries to my mother every Friday. Miraculously, the grocery fairy always seemed to know exactly what we wanted and always called, as regular as clockwork, before my mother got me back from school each Friday.

■ Customer-Driven Marketing

Eventually, probably about the time my mean school friends pricked the bubble of illusion that stopped Father Christmas from conscientiously each year squeezing his corpulent frame, all red-faced and puffing down our chimney, I discovered the truth. It wasn't a fairy at all. You've guessed! It was a grocer – the nice man who patted my head whenever I went into his shop with my mother. The man to whom she always spent such a long time chatting about this and that. Our grocer. He definitely ran a 'my business'.

This would be the mid-1950s. Our grocer used to ring up on a Thursday evening to discuss the weather, exchange family news and ask my mother whether she wanted anything more than 'the usual'. Sometimes she had a list. Sometimes he prompted her. Sad to think it'll never happen like that again...

## The return of the grocery fairy (with slightly clipped wings)

Here comes one of my favourite marketing miracles. As you will read, it had nothing to do with me whatsoever. I just wish it had!

'What do you make of this?' said my fellow diner, waving a credit card sized piece of plastic under my nose with obvious pride.

'A credit card?', I ventured.

'Nothing so ordinary,' he laughed. 'It's your Customer visiting card for my supermarket. A Customer comes in, swipes it, now the store knows they're there.'

'Aha, security!' I tried again.

'Better than that. My store helps them to shop.'

The owner of this particular chain of stores went on to describe his pride and joy. As each Customer enters a store, they swipe in and the visit is logged. As they arrive at the checkout, a further swipe alerts the computer and as the checkout operator works through their purchases the machine logs them and checks them out against previous buying patterns. The computer then reminds them of any purchases they may have forgotten based on their previous purchasing patterns. The operator keys in the products they decide to take. Next it gives them a screen full of special offers based on what it knows they like, what it has in stock and on offer.

'My Customers love this service! It's just like they used to get in the old days. If they want any of the product prompts they tell the cashier, she adds it in. By the time we've packed for them and they're on the way out, their extra goods are waiting at the door, in a box, with their names on. On top of all that wizardry, they get a loyalty value bonus that builds every time they shop here, they get express priority at the checkouts and free coffee in the coffee shop. Is that good, or is that great?'

'That's great,' I agreed, my mind doing handstands at the information that his database could yield on purchase patterns, cross-brand selling and the opportunities for phone calls just like my mother used to get.

'What's more', he continued, pulling back my attention as his enthusiasm bubbled over, 'the database marketing opportunities are incredible. You know we ring up people who've missed a visit and offer to drop their goods round! What do you say about that?'

I looked at this happy, happy man. When you're on to a winner, it's a first, and you know you can license it round the world, it's a fabulous feeling. He looked at me, waiting for the mixture of envy, fascination and admiration which the story no doubt always provokes. His face took on a completely puzzled expression as I, without thinking, turned to him and replied, 'You remind me of a fairy I once had'.

Earlier in the book, I said I needed your help. It's because I've lost track of this man and I want more of the story and to know what he's up to now. I met him in South Africa, but I recall his name is Bob and the stores, of which he had three or four, are, I believe, in Australia or New Zealand. Naturally, I've had friends out there checking for me with no luck. But if you should hear anything, I'd be deeply obliged.

Back home in the UK, I have been a regular Customer of Tesco. In one town that I lived, I got to know Harry, the guy who ran the fish counter rather well. I didn't eat meat at that time, but I ate a lot of fish. Harry soon realised this and he also realised that there were many times when my wife and I didn't seem to frequent the store. Once he asked me about this and I explained that I, and often we, went overseas quite a lot. 'Hey,' asked Harry, 'how about I call you when we have specials? That way you can top up the freezer and save a lot of money. In fact, if you let me know your favourites, I'll keep some by for you even if you're away.' It sounded good to us and for two years, until we eventually moved, that is exactly what happened. Harry became my fish man. It was only when, the day we broke it to him that we were moving, he told us that he was 'actually quite relieved!' We were puzzled. It transpired that to call us up on the phone to tell us about the specials, Harry had to get permission to phone out. Harry went on to tell us that there was a new manager in and he was deeply suspicious of Harry's phone calls to us! Oh, Harry, you had it right, my friend, they were the short-sighted, crazy ones!

## There's no escape. We all have to deliver

The Customer's expectation of satisfactory service, both as a consumer and a business, is about to go through the roof. Smart businesses are already planning to adopt the kind of techniques I call 'Success through Excess'. Six-sigma comes to service! It is no longer adequate merely to meet the Customer's expectation. Customer Superformance is the name

■ Customer-Driven Marketing

of the game. That's where you'll find the marketing miracles on the trees waiting to be picked. Encourage your Harrys. Let them build the Customer relationships for you. It is well worth every penny or cent on every phone call. Tear down the barriers between you and your Customers. Don't be like the Swede who, when asked why he was attending one of my sessions in Stockholm, told me, 'I have to find a way to get my Customers to call in with their orders after 10am and before 4pm. Otherwise we'll never have time to run the business and take care of the administration!' It didn't take long for him to realise that fewer Customers equalled less administration and no Customers equalled no administration! Let them order when they want. Cope with the administration any other time.

During the 1960s the quantity drive brought the benefits of mass production, competitive pricing and wider availability. Consumers who were used to post-war austerity throughout the world revelled in being able to obtain a range of goods such as they had never experienced before. Credit became more readily available and the Age of Plenty was well under way. In relative terms, the Age of Plenty has now become the Age of Sufficiency. Household equipment in most Western European countries extends to television, refrigerator, telephone, washing machine, video, microwave and dishwasher with many other things considered basic necessities. And that's before you step outside the home. As the consumer becomes more experienced so, quite justly, they become more sophisticated, more aware and concerned about their rights, and much, much harder to please. Why? Because they've observed now several decades of the contortions sales and marketing people will go to in the process of obtaining their business and they know they hold the purse, so they call the tune. There is nothing wrong with this. It is right and proper they should feel this way.

Moreover, watching consumerist and pressure groups, most particularly in Europe, I am now convinced that suspicion, anger and resentment are surfacing for the processes of sales, advertising and marketing, and at the people who practise it. This is all caused by the abandoning of quality, the greed of quantity driven marketing and the years of being subjected to exploitation selling processes.

Now I know that in the US particularly, selling has a different image to that in Europe. In Australasia and South Africa, it is somewhere between the two. But where in the world do people implicitly trust, respect, and have total faith in sales and marketing people? Nowhere I've been. I mean we may all be jolly nice people, easy to get on with, fun to talk with ... but trust? Whose interest do our Customers think we put first; ours or theirs? It is strange really, because my mother trusted her grocer. When and why did Customers stop trusting the people who sold to them? And, the pivotal issue which determines the need for Customer-driven marketing is how we can regain that respect and trust. The solutions to these questions are easy to identify, but more difficult to implement, as we shall learn later. Regaining the respect and trust of the Customer is a magnificent and extremely profitable marketing miracle.

## Why have the new demands of the Customer become a global issue?

The first reason is the way the media network their programmes around the globe these days. Suppose you're watching CNN in a hotel in Copenhagen (or on cable in your sitting room at home); you're watching a news clip of some shopping innovation in Australia; you now want it and you know you can have it. Your assessment of your local shops is measured against the local shops from Helsinki to Vancouver to Auckland.

Secondly, as technology and design find similar answers to the same old questions, the parity products issue forces corporations to look at other ways of securing business. Customer service, Customer care and the added-value route will turn up the heat.

Thirdly, as I have pointed out, the Customer is becoming increasingly sophisticated and informed. They will, naturally, become more discerning and hold greater expectations. The only real dilemmas are not whether you should do it, whether it will do you good or whether your Customers will like it. The dilemmas are how you will fund these new service and care levels, and what will happen to you if you don't.

I am not going to delve greatly into the practical aspects of Customer service or Customer care programmes, for this is not a book about these subjects. However, it is a book about the need for them. And to practise the art of Customer-driven marketing one must become a master of Customer service and Customer care. For me the building of a Customer relationship is rather like the building of a strong brick wall. The bricks are the individual sales or units of sales. The cement is the loyalty created in that Customer. It holds the sales process together, bonding between the individual sales, creating strength and resilience. The water, sand and mortar from which that cement is made are Customer satisfaction, Customer service and Customer care. Customer-driven marketing is in effect a safe and secure place for your company to weather the storms of the business world. Now you know how the walls to that safe place must be built.

Another view which I was attracted to during the processes of my research for this book was the schematic reproduced on page 152. It is stolen (with permission and my thanks) from a short book called *Sold on Service* written by Phillip Forrest (Carlson Marketing Group, UK). Although I have some problems with the fine detail of the external mar-

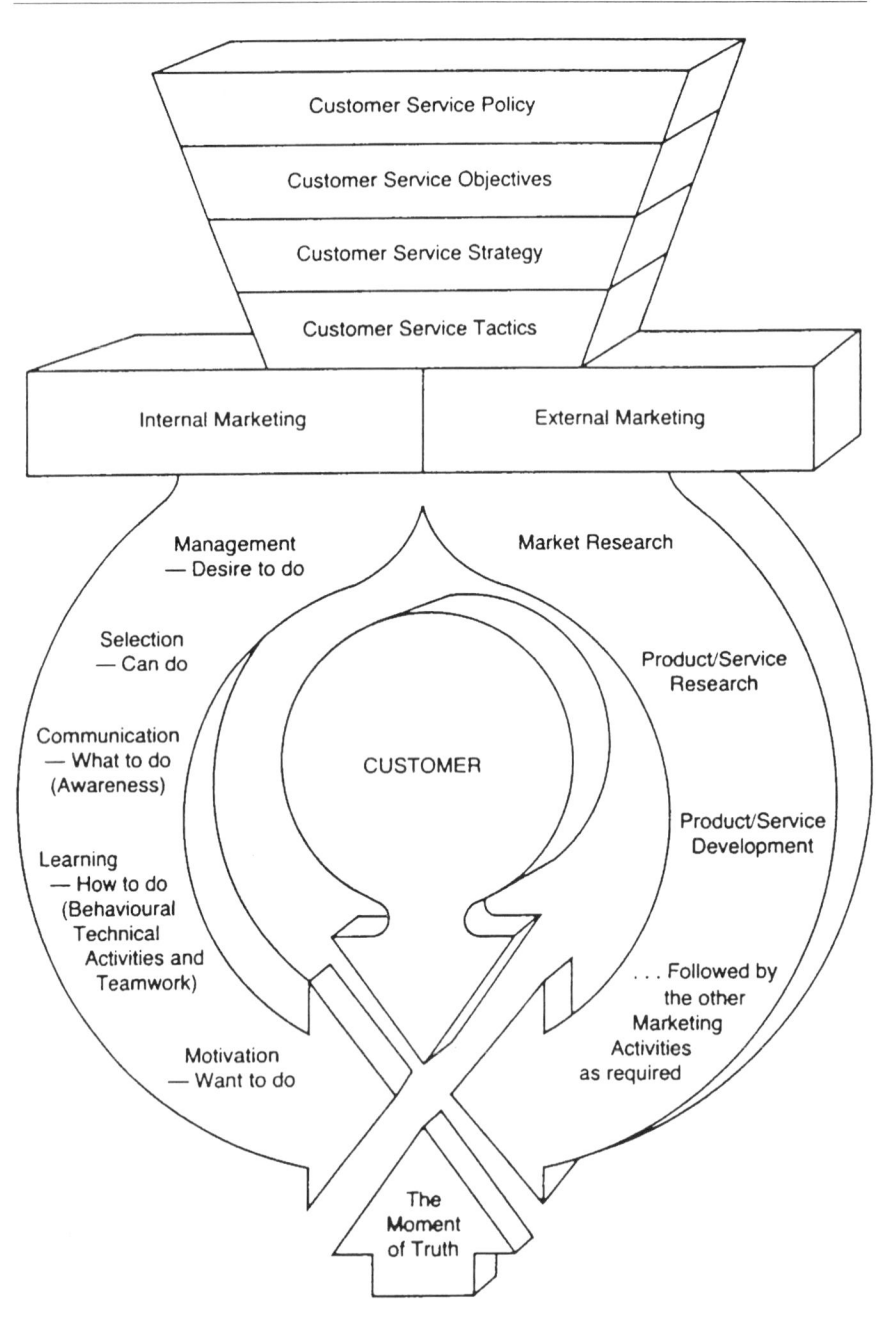

■ Customer-Driven Marketing

**Figure 9.2** *Internal and external marketing as vehicles for customer service*

## What will customers want next?

keting side I reproduce it here because the way it is designed suggests that the Customer will be almost enveloped in the two marketing processes and this has a very caring and attentive implication.

This chapter looked at the New Demands of The Customer. In it we considered the following:

- Customer-driven marketing requires the building of stable and rewarding Customer relationships. Customer service must have strategic integrity and be built into the system. It must be practised by all, from the top down, with no exceptions, no excuses.
- Companies that build relationships, not sales, stand out from the crowd. They attract and receive vastly increased levels of loyalty, affection, respect and trust.
- Customer service and quality standards went into rapid and severe decline during the 1960s and 1970s. Standards throughout Europe are poor, but in Britain they are markedly worse.
- An example was given where the harnessing of technology and marketing skills was able to return the quality and individual treatment to relationships to a great extent while maintaining the scale and quantities required today.
- By the end of the 1980s we had moved from the Age of Plenty to the Age of Sufficiency. The Customer has taken control of their spending. They have freedom, they have choice and they have legs. They will use all three increasingly.
- Consumers the world over view marketing and the marketing process with suspicion and distrust. This must change, but it must be a real change. It's no good polishing our smile and our armour. We have to learn to listen, to respect and to practise our handshake.
- The three major influences that will spread the word as far as what the Customer can get are:
  — the media – the global village is full of gossips
  — parity products – Customer service gives an attractive edge and it's difficult to withdraw it
  —- the Customer is more sophisticated and informed, and as a result more demanding and discerning.
- From a sound relationship, sales and loyalty are cultivated together. Customer-driven marketing uses Customer satisfaction, Customer service and Customer care for the bonding process.

# 10

# Change is upon us

Has it occurred to you that marketing is in a rut? Think about it! Look at how little has changed in the last 30 years. Don't look at the fine detail; the proliferation of television advertising, the arrival of the Internet, the proliferation of data, the transformation from corner store to hypermarket or the increase of wealth and the rise of the wasteful, materialistic society. Look at the fundamental process and structure of the Customer facet of your business–marketing.

Do you agree? It's in a rut. Nothing of any real consequence to the process has changed at all. Our information systems are better, the disciplines argue more aggressively with each other, making strategic planning increasingly more confusing. Yet the good old marketing department looks pretty much like it always did; nobody can quite decide where PR fits, much of the market information still comes in on hard copy, and the agency still over-rates creativity and charges too much for it. So, what's new?

As we get started with the next millennium, companies will have to deal with more change and faster than ever before. It is well forecast: the mass of companies involved at every stage of preparation are written about and talked about in almost every book, magazine and conference. Some are studying to decide what to do, some have decided and are setting off, some like ABB, IBM, British Airways, Marriott Hotels and many more, feel they are well down the road. Where are you? I don't mean your company, your marketing department or team – you! The fact is marketing will see as much, in fact more, change than all the other business functions. It's change cubed. The change within marketing and the change within the market would be change squared. When you multiply again by the change within your own company, then it's change to the power of three.

One rarely thinks of marketing people as a group without perception or vision, and yet (no doubt a version of the cobbler's own shoes syndrome) I find hundreds of people preoccupied and fiddling with the fine detail, yet very little concentration or obsession with the factors that really matter for the times ahead. Where are the people who care about the big picture? Let's deal with some of that now. In fact both this chapter and the following (on new workplaces) will look at areas that marketing, advertising and sales people have been somewhat negligent in exploring. So where will all this change come from? And what types of change should we expect?

## Identifying the pressures

I think we have already identified the first of the major pressures for change, the need to stay flexible. As I suggested earlier, this will mean a move away from the big bureaucratic marketing department of the 1970s and 1980s, to the new smaller department, bigger budget set-up of the future.

The second is also something we have already unearthed, the need for marketing and technology – more precisely information technology – to get their acts together.

The third area of pressure on marketing is its need to come to terms with new management styles and structures. Do not confuse this with corporate restructuring. Many companies have restructured their businesses and made the mistake of maintaining marketing as a separate specialist resource; a unit to which other departments can refer when they need or which can pass down marketing initiatives. This may function, but it is not the most effective answer for a company that wishes to become Customer-driven or Customer oriented. No marketing miracles to be found there! I see this as sending your army out to a distant battlefield and leaving the medical corps at home. If anyone gets sick or is wounded they have to fly home to be seen to, whatever the gravity of the problem. It plainly doesn't make sense. The frontline troops need medical specialists with them at both basic and intermediate levels. The brain surgeons get to stay home.

And the fourth pressure is for marketing and particularly the sales people, to understand the huge difference between marketing and 'new marketing' or even Customer-driven marketing. The old sales mentality people could look on Customer-driven marketing as enigmatic – a fuzzy, woolly sort of business, centred as it is on the building of relationships and, in business marketing especially, using the concept of alliances and partnerships to further its cause. The old ways are not team ways. The

■ Customer-Driven Marketing

old ways jealously guard one's contacts and knowledge, where possession is ten-tenths of the game. The future is more open in its perception of horizons and more open in its style. Cast your mind back to the ABB story where suppliers, the company people and their Clients all mingled together to share ideas and discuss ways to improve things for the future, where trust and openness were the order of the day.

The fifth and final pressure is the need for marketing to become more responsible and to increase its understanding of business generally. We considered earlier the need for marketing people to acquire broader based business skills. Marketing people should be business people with specialist marketing skills rather than as hitherto in an isolated skill area. I would like to see top level strategic marketing skills outside the company and most probably outside their agencies too.

These five factors, of course, are not self-contained. They impact on each other. For example, the need to stay flexible will require better information systems and more network controls rather than departmental controls. This will make great use of the new technology available, but will require the pulling together of IT and marketing. As marketing people acquire IT skills along with broader business skills, they may need increased specialist help, particularly on strategic matters. After all, one only has so much capacity!

## Getting together with IT

This problem is out of all proportion to its solution, the solution is simple, but as time passes the gap widens, thus making it harder to correct. And at the moment marketing and IT do seem to be heading in divergent directions. Thus the simple solution – get them together – has, over time, to cope with the greater distance between the two.

Marketing and IT seemed to part company in the 1970s, leaving probably only the then slightly frowned-on direct marketers to keep up with the latest developments. Rather than backtrack in time to the breakpoint and then start over, I prefer to build a bridge of some kind.

The most effective method so far available seems to consist of two simple steps. The first is to find and develop a common language – the 'pidgin' of your business – so the two can converse; the second, to find a common picture or vision. This usually benefits from outside specialist help and is achieved by constructing a process diagram or flowchart of your marketing process, similar to those used by the computer people. The marketing people naturally recognise it as their process and the computer people's eyes normally open wide with realisation of what is actually going on. This bridge-building has become very much one of the specialities of the DunnHumby Consultancy, whose research we had extracts of in Chapter 4 and which quantified the gap so clearly.

Hitherto, being used to the fixed process and variable inputs of, say, the accounts department (often the original reason for IT's existence), IT could not make any sense of the experimental, fluid and entrepreneurial variable processes with variable inputs that is marketing. Yet this is their part of the bargain; to bring their enormous 'what if', modelling, number-crunching, information-building skills with which the new marketers can bob and weave like young boxers on something suspect! Plenty of marketing techno-miracles here! Just let our younger computer compatible recruits have their head. Let them play games tapping away into the night as the emptied cola cans pile up.

So there is a short-term answer, a way to pull them back together; but, in their wedded bliss, will marketing and IT require a new kind of operative? In my view, the answer is yes. And the pioneering is already being done here in manufacturing and production businesses such as Esso, Norsk Data, British Airways and BMW. These companies are looking for, encouraging and taking their part in creating what has become known as a 'hybrid manager'. This is a person who is as accomplished in IT skills as they are in their discipline or function. Until now marketing has not taken IT seriously. It has only paid lip service to IT skills and done everything it could to ignore the gap rather than bridge it, yet Customer-driven marketing can make better use of hybrid managers than anyone else in the business.

## How do you breed a hybrid?

Basically, what we are looking to achieve to bring marketing forward is a new kind of executive and manager; someone who is literate in both IT and marketing. For IT can virtually reinvent marketing. And when you look at the task of turning so many aspects of the marketing process, again particularly selling, from quantity to quality, a capability to reinvent is precisely what is needed. Real re-engineering!

We're going to need people who can take the process, step by step, examine its logic, evaluate its contribution to the building of long-term, broad based, satisfying Customer relationships, and then reshape and remodel it to be more efficient using the new criteria we shall consider. We're going to need people who can bless and respect the past, and let it go. Encourage those people to turn and face the future with courage and initiative. Let them experiment and 'play' with their new ideas. Praise their failures as well as their successes – at least they tried!

It's interesting that in July 1989 *Pharmaceutical Executive* magazine reported that 'many companies have given each of their sales reps a laptop that can run applications such as electronic mail and territory management...'. And yet, nearly a decade later, I am aware of many businesses still wrangling over whether this idea is worth while; how to train the sales people to become computer literate; and what uses the hardware and software might be put to. Financial Services must surely qualify as one of the business sectors most likely to benefit from the use of computing at the front line, but which has been the slowest to get their teams to become hybrids. It seems to me that relative computer literacy must surely be a pre-requisite for a sales or marketing job these days at even the most basic level.

But let us also remember that the Customer may not want to be so technologically inclined – at least in the consumer markets. I have had some involvement with life insurance businesses who have seen the obvious use of the laptop at playing 'what if' games and of combining this ability with up-to-the-minute graphics to make stunning and powerful audio-visual sales presentations. However, it was noticed during experiments that the Customer or prospect displayed quite strong feelings of discomfort and unease at two points. First, often in order that they should be able to see the screen as well as the Customer, representatives would move into, and thereby invade, the Customer's personal space. It was only when a second screen or monitor was introduced, respecting the comfort zones of both parties that they relaxed and things improved. Secondly, as irrational as this seems to people who have everyday experience of computers, prospects (as distinct from Customers) did not like having their personal details input directly into a computer in front of them. If the same questions were asked and the answers hand-written, that was fine as long as the computer input – the actual keyboarding – took place elsewhere and at another time. Those familiar with British and other countries' financial services legislation, particularly in respect of life insurance sales, will probably have realised that I am referring to what is known colloquially in the business as the 'fact find'. This questionnaire asks that the prospect reveals almost their entire financial situation to someone they may never have met until ten minutes earlier. It's daunting enough without the thought that 'Big Brother' might be getting his teeth into it.

## Let's get back to the office!

A study by the British Computer Society came to the conclusion that by the end of the 1990s as many as 30 per cent of all managers should be hybrids. It recommended steps to create a minimum of 10,000 such managers by the middle of the decade. How many, I wonder, would be in marketing? Sadly the answer will almost certainly be 'not enough', for I assess marketing's need for this new manager to be between 40 to 45 per cent of their total. If the business of marketing does not forthwith start to make friends with IT, then it will not begin to equip itself for the future. And no hybrid manager of any consequence will waste his value or abilities working in an environment which is not good for him or equipped for him. IT has to become endemic to marketing before it can maximise the benefits. Moreover, it has to show a demonstrable start at this goal before it will convince the talent it requires to be recruited.

## How will the hybrid manager flourish in marketing?

Marketing departments will soon start to experience radical changes in their strategies and in their infrastructures. This new climate will be perfect for the hybrid manager. As the structure flattens out, so the administrative functions and self-support services will decrease substantially. The manager in the new environment will be able to concentrate on their new quality goals, attending to the Customer service aspects of the partnerships and allegiances which the company must form to grow and to tap new potential. And be sure, the role of marketing in the searching out, assessing and bonding with these new partnerships is crucial. Who else can represent the Customer?

We discussed in an earlier chapter the influence of internationalisation or globalisation as a method of large and small companies alike finding the resource for leading edge thinking and staying ahead with technology. A further task of the hybrid will be to support the integration of sales and distribution strategies across different time and language zones, and to manipulate the sophisticated information and communication systems this will require.

It is my experience, and this is not meant to sound patronising, that the most successful hybrids have so far resulted in line managers moving into IT rather than the other way round. IT seems to have a better reputation for performing the task than for management per se. However, it is still relatively uncommon to see senior IT people moving into other disciplines, just as, in the past, one was more used to seeing Clients moving to agencies rather than the other way. This latter is actually changing considerably. I suspect that being one of the 'new' management sciences, IT has yet to acquire sufficient general business, social and political skills that it can afford to lose its best leaders.

The two qualities required of marketing's hybrid managers will be no different to the hybrids at work elsewhere.

These are as follows:

1. **Experience** – current thinking suggests two to three years' IT experience is required in support of the conjoint business area. With such, the manager is able to recognise the business opportunities, make a convincing case for them and sufficiently anticipate the practical implementation issues.
2. **Skills** – hybrids need to make a feature of their interpersonal, social

and presentation skills. It is these which enable them to overcome the classic objections to IT projects. With accomplished social, political and organisational skills the hybrid can command green lights right down the block. Sadly, so many incredibly talented but rather introspective individuals have associated themselves with the 'nerd' mentality popular with young computer buffs. It is precisely the heightened interpersonal skills to which I refer that they lack, and which must be sharpened and encouraged.

Esso in the UK were one of the most rapid and successful at identifying the advantages of hybrids and then cultivating them. By the beginning of the decade, they had consciously placed some of their best IT managers in line positions, successfully bucking the directional trend. Equally, Esso looked to fill senior IT posts with business managers from other areas; effectively thereby it 'grew' its own hybrids. Esso believe this to be responsible for an increase from 60 to 90 per cent of projects being delivered both on time and within budget. Marketing would revel in such a rate. And this is surely an answer to one or more of the warnings which follow in the final chapter.

Common features that have been noted in companies where the hybrid programme is advanced, suggest that they develop a bias towards strategic rather than reactive management; this in turn leads to greater awareness of long-term issues. Such managers flourish in open management styles where experimentation and risk-taking are encouraged, observed and understood. For marketers who are thinking of 'crossing the line', it is not necessary to develop more than an empathy and understanding for the role of technology; deep technical skills are rarely required. However such individuals will need a strong sense of purpose, the ability to deal with high stress levels and the faith of a bridge-builder – not knowing just that you can get to the other side and back again. In the drive to build effectiveness with marketing departments, groups and teams, I believe the hybrid to be in a fine position to acquire leadership positions since they should be ideally skilled to provide a solid sense of direction, to create teamwork and engender the spirit required to encourage this, and lastly, to inspire, encourage and practise truly creative thinking.

## The new styles of management in marketing

Perhaps the first and most noticeable change will be the new broader vision of tomorrow's marketer. More the business person, less the obsessive marketer; also an even greater consciousness that to serve the Customer perfectly, the whole organisation needs to be fit and healthy. At times this need to balance the corporate good for the welfare of all

Customers against the specific service requirements of one or a group of Customers may prove something of a dilemma for this 'new' marketer. At the end of the day, however, it will prove that the corporate good serves all Customers.

But a word of warning goes with this. Some years ago as a director of three inter-trading companies within a group, I introduced a series of team meetings. However, in order to break down the formal structures and encourage cross-boundary dialogues, the teams were formed of the people who dealt with each other day to day, rather than those who worked in the same department as each other. Thus, for example, drivers got to talk to the people who prepared their loads and both of those to the people who took the phone calls that specified the load. It was difficult not to include the switchboard operators in every team! These were monthly meetings; they lasted as long as they lasted and the aim was that half the time would be in 'company time' and half would be 'personal time'.

The meetings started with a designated leader, but became democratic. This move sounded right, but in fact left me undecided about the better of the two. With sensitive and thoughtful designation, often a designated team leader worked better than the democrat type. Although there was no rank, it took courage for even the most lucid and articulate young secretary to face up to a director ... and you may judge from the comment, as much strength and personal security from the director to forget his or her rank altogether. It started well. The basic premise behind all meetings was that you could raise any topic you liked as long as there was a clear link that the Customer would benefit in the end. Thus, for example, staff welfare had a clear mandate – discontented staff don't work at their best! Gradually, however, at the team leaders' forum, where the actions were decided and judgements were taken, one found the items raised went from enthusiastic and outward thinking to enthusiastic and a great deal more inward thinking. At times, the approved link for getting your item on the agenda, the one that had to do with staff welfare being in the Customer's best long-term interest, was stretched to extraordinary new and ingeniously creative lengths. It was also interesting to watch the qualities and moods of one company cross the boundary and spread to another.

Overall the experience was beneficial, worth while and quite fascinating to observe. I certainly wouldn't hesitate to use it again in appropriate circumstances. The proviso is that one may need to monitor and assist until those who are not used to freedom and democracy learn to use it fully, and those who are used to power and command learn to control it and enjoy the sight of others exercising their freedom and opinion. The experience, I believe, did most to make me explore concepts of less hierarchical, more democratic management, and the use of teams which in themselves had formal recognition in the corporate structure and which benefited from strong, visionary and creative leadership; teams which learned to talk to each other all the time rather than at scheduled meetings.

Stafford Taylor, who headed mobile telephone service provider Cellnet when they had just 1.6 million Customers in the UK, tried a similar device with success. Until his arrival, the company had been engineering led and did not have the Customer as the principal focus. In a national newspaper interview Taylor explained, 'The whole company culture needed to be changed.' In the process, he brought in some new managers, but cleared out one whole level of the management structure, 'so I could be closer to the day-to-day running of the business'. Such comments are quite fashionable from industry leaders at this time, but Taylor knew he had to make genuine changes to attitudes in the business. Therefore, he started courses within the company to teach and spread the gospel of 'Customer First' and something he calls 'diagonal lunches' where a cross-section of the staff met together informally to air their views. Whether these suffered the same problems as I had with the team meetings or not, my point can be further illustrated by perhaps an unkind but factual observation.

In many countries we enjoy the existence of 'mutual' insurance companies. They often have some special status, having no shareholders and therefore existing (it is claimed) entirely for the mutual benefit of their policy holders. The added edge is that profits, instead of being distributed to the shareholders, are returned to the benefit of the policy holders, thereby increasing their returns, keeping prices to the minimum or adding value to their cover or ancillary services. It is noticeable that accommodation, staff facilities, conditions and terms of employment in such companies are generally well at the top end of their business! I guess balancing the welfare of the company against the welfare of the Customer works well as long as enthusiasm, motivation and commitment stay strong and pure, which has to do with leadership.

Certainly, our 'all-rounder' style of manager should have far better leadership credentials. Interestingly, it was published that at BMW managers are encouraged to enshrine the best attributes of each of the three different kinds of manager they had identified:

1. the specialist or expert
2. the leader who pulls his team together and
3. the skilled corporate game player who was capable of recognising and using power within the organisation.

No one single style of manager, they claim, was better than the other; however, it was noted that as you rose in rank so the latter, the game player, became more important. Some things may never change!

## And where would you like to do your work?

As we move into the next century, we have arrived at a point where, compared with the last century, we have a significant change. We used to have to move the people to the work. For a vast number of businesses, this will not be the case in the future. They can move the work to the people.

This may prove a huge temptation for many non-production based companies. Why, for example, should a finance house or insurance company pull workers in to do their work when so much of it could be done from home with the simple provision of some basic communications equipment? In percentage terms, this population, remember, is set to increase enormously.

To focus on this aspect solely from the marketing view, and to look at the right probability from your organisation's point, you must look at the element of team influence, and particularly bearing in mind the degree of social interchange in the marketing business, consider all aspects of this team mentality, not least team spirit. Further, you might consider the likelihood that teamwork will become more vital for successful Customer-driven marketing. The major question is, who will be in the team with the marketer – fellow marketers or, more likely I propose, mostly others from other areas? This brings us to two final challenges of change: the rise of the team and, therefore, the increased emphasis on leadership.

## The rise of the team

Teams have existed in marketing and sales for decades. What is a product group if not a team? Has the sales director not been welding his sales force together as a team for years (pity his reward system often turns them against each other!); hasn't the sales promotion unit been a good team? Yes, yes, yes. But it's the type of team they are: some, so built into the marketing hierarchy they're as essential as the leg of tripod, others clinging to the infrastructure like a benign parasite.

You could look at agencies and claim they have been organised into teams since they began. Is there not an account handling team, a creative team, a traffic team, a planning team and a media team?

Teams in marketing will change to show the two types in place: first, a formal multi-discipline team. This will be a part of, either a network structure, or a broadside structure, as discussed in Chapter 22. Depending on the complexity of their marketing task these teams will themselves fall into two categories: the autonomous business unit, where marketing is but one function of the team; or, where the problem is more complex, the specialist marketing team which includes a whole full capability marketing group. Where the formal team is not appropriate, marketing leaders will recruit special project task forces – superteams, if you will – to investigate, shape and manage the special tasks which occur or which are created.

Similarly agencies, themselves concerned about both the relationships they build and the relationship of which they are in effect guardians for their Clients, will choose to work in multi-discipline teams. Headed by a business controller, they will in effect become micro-agencies glorying in furthering the corporate cause, but as a self-run, self-sufficient, wholly free total business. They may look after just one or two or three Clients. Their location is open to their choice! Even central resources of which I suspect there may only be one – information – will be networked. This lean, lithe, super energy unit will come as a huge culture shock to the old timers of advertising. They seem to have been so brainwashed by their business as to view the size of their corporate edifice, the depth and thickness of their carpet pile, the length of the boardroom table, the style and design of their office to be some kind of show of their own corporate ability. You'd think it was a work-based comfort blanket that holds together their own senses of self-accomplishment and self-worth.

It is said that teams work best where a task or series of tasks depends on three or more people and or disciplines. Usually marketing does. And the more complex the work, often the more suited it is to teams. Customer-driven marketing will benefit without doubt from team methods. It will benefit from the cross-disciplined attitude that enables and encourages breakthrough style thinking and problem solving, and teams on both sides – agency and Client – that are strong enough to make their own decisions: the more autonomous the better. To embed quality into the marketing process requires cross-disciplinary thinking and working. It cannot succeed in the old tunnel function world where teams from each marketing discipline must be individually briefed, enthused and motivated and then controlled and supervised until all the different tasks come together as a successful initiative. It requires teams that care about, and whose motivation is centred upon, the whole initiative; thus breeding a group commitment to the business objective. Inevitably the spirit with which the team dedicates itself will turn the spotlight on the leader and his or her leadership skills.

## Lead from the middle

As marketing sheds or flattens its hierarchies and cultivates its new smaller micro-agencies within agencies, so too, its workers will have to come to terms with new styles and situations. I prefer to envision this as a series of circles with the centre 'bulls-eye' as the leader and variable size pie sections as the disciplines, the proportion of the pie slice being the proportion of influence of the discipline (not necessarily the number of people) as shown in Figure 19.3 on page 252. In this environment leaders will require managers and workers who can think beyond classic hierarchies to understand and enjoy a life where power, authority or influence may not necessarily come from above, but most likely from alongside or across the circle. More and more marketing people will learn that whereas the hierarchy manager has to accept responsibility, the manager inside the team – as it were a horizontal manager – gives out responsibility. This requires understanding of more than one discipline and adds weight to the cause of the hybrid. Just as the business of the future must learn to cope with risk and uncertainty, so must the manager who works for it. In Chapter 1 we looked at a view of this that proposed four-way marketing on the premise that, in times of risk, long-term satisfying relationships represented the most stable safe haven for the corporation. Realising this as the greatest stabilising factor for personal security and financial welfare, Customer-driven marketing will flourish with the clear focus and responsibility this gives to those who work throughout TQM organisations.

## The bond of friendship – the factor that makes sales a partnership

Should you be involved in consumer marketing, you might be tempted to skip this section on the reasonable assumption it is of sole use to your counterparts who work in business-to-business marketing. You would be partly correct. It may be of more use to them, but far from exclusively so; service, leisure and financial consumer markets or retailers enhancing their 'My Business' or 'honest broker' positions would be well advised to take the information and consider it.

Workers formed unions because they harness their power; they spoke as one, but louder and stronger. NATO and the United Nations were formed because nations learned eventually that in a difficult, complex and uncertain world the risks are great, but none so great as when you are alone. So too, in business, the forming of relationships on a long-term basis will breed new style partnerships and allegiances. This process is much heralded in the production and supply functions, probably because each supplier is in turn a Customer of another supplier! The proposal of partnership, of some kind of strategic alliance, is very often a natural goal or development of such relationships.

The most common concern about such bondings is control paranoia – the fear that some kind of pressure will be exerted which will drive the company off course or cause it to lose financial control. This fear forgets that two healthy partners make the best partnership, two content co-operators form the strongest allegiance. When the paranoia is put aside and the benefits to Customers examined, you will evaluate most alliances in their purest light. Certainly the forming of alliances takes courage, as

■ Customer-Driven Marketing

any relationship does. However, if you fear you may become Jonah and your partner a whale, or vice versa, neither will ever be content. The worst of all would be to enter the relationship with a victim or predator mentality. One is a dangerous psychological pre-condition, the other will destroy your credibility for ever. As with all relationships, an equal balance is best, but in corporate relationships there is every need to be faithful, but no need at all to be monogamous; three, four or five-way partnerships can work well too. If such complex inter-trading causes a problem with pricing, I urge all parties to play openly and come to terms on margins rather than prices.

## Change? What change?

Looking at the kinds of change we will have to deal with, this has elsewhere been identified as continuous change (one might call this the progressive development path upon which you and your business are embarked) or discontinuous change (the beyond-your-control kind of change that comes from nowhere and hits where it hurts most).

Broadly, these categories suffice with the exception that this neat pigeon-holing doesn't have any cautionary ring to it. Discontinuous change for certain should have the word 'caution' labelled to it. It's often vicious and uncompromising. Think about it. If you're Spanish, Portuguese, Dutch or British and you're in the holiday hotel or travel business, you'll have experienced discontinuous change. It happens when you walk into work one morning and your colleague tells you the French air traffic controllers (ATCs) have gone on strike again. The feeling hits your stomach like a stone. You're completely at the mercy of these ATCs. If their strike is short you only suffer a spate of cancellations, otherwise your whole season is in jeopardy. And if you look to next year to save you and pay off the bank loan, chances are they'll do it again.

Global warming is another discontinuous, unpredictable change. Having discussed this with many, many people at Marketing 2000 conferences I'm of a mind to promote this from discontinuous to continuous changes. Together with the greenhouse effect, it seems to have earned its place on the list of hazards, problems or opportunities which marketers need to put on their checklist of outside influences to monitor constantly. Even one charity selling limited edition collectibles to raise funds reported a major shift in consumer preferences to 'nature and natural subjects' over the last few years with their Customers expressing strong views about their packaging materials. I contentedly report this last influence and encourage it. My heart even warmed to the British tax collector who recently wrote to me requesting a contribution: noticing the reusable envelope was made of recycled paper as was the clumsily laser-printed yet outrageous demand, my resentment level dropped a whole 10 per cent!

## Change is upon us

The president's statement of one of the world's leading insurance corporations included the following statement. The second part was lamentably predictable: the first, just lamentable. He said, 'While the climatologists may argue over differing prognoses for the development of weather patterns, there can be no doubt there will have to be further premium increases in commercial, household and motor business. In the marine and aviation and in several liability classes, rates do not match the risks covered.'

While this may qualify as the most public and least subtle announcement of a rates increase, it is also an important recognition of the influence of discontinuous change on a business. We must not underestimate climatic change and its effect on us. In an unlikely alliance with the green lobby, 60 major global insurance companies have joined an initiative under the United Nations Environment Programme. These companies believe that governments must act to curb the growth of greenhouse gases which contribute so significantly to global warming. These companies have avowed to use their vast financial muscle to put pressure on so-called 'dirty' businesses by either refusing to invest in them or deinvesting themselves of present holdings. Perhaps they are remembering the 1987 hurricane which devastated the South-east corner of Britain, not previously a country over-run by hurricanes. This one storm cost more than $1billion: or even that Hurricane Andrew in 1992 not only uprooted almost everything in its path as it rampaged across Florida, it also cost $20 billion and wiped out seven US insurance companies in the process.

If you don't think these tales noteworthy, or you haven't yet felt the effects of such changes, why not reflect upon the plight of the American mid-Western farming communities over the drought-ridden period they have experienced in the 1990s? Or, think why it is that every stockmarket analyst around the world has an opinion about the fact that global warming is about to cause the biggest leap in temperatures for 10,000 years. The British government predicts that, for its territory, the real bite will not come for 20 to 30 years. However, their boffins can predict that the number of gales will increase by 30 per cent by 2050; there will be a 30 cm rise in sea levels within 50 years and that throughout that time drought and malaria will become major problems for the average Briton. While the life and health insurance businesses will be thinking about that one, no doubt the general business insurers will be pondering the fact that the Thames Barrier would be well and truly compromised by a rise of 30 cm in sea levels, as would many other parts of the country, notably East Anglia. The Thames Barrier alone protects up to $30 billion insured value. Lord didn't it rain!

Chapter 10 was about changes. And about challenges. Some will no doubt cause you problems; they may be hard to picture and hard to

## ■ Customer-Driven Marketing

believe. Others hopefully will excite, inspire or encourage you. Let's review the ground we covered in this chapter:

- Marketing, which has seen little change of process over the last decades, is set to develop more in the next 15 years than it has since the Second World War.
- Marketing and IT have to get their acts together, together.
- Demassifying the company infrastructure, and leaving the marketing function as a central resource, apart from distancing sales and marketing, is not the best solution for a Customer responsive company. Marketing needs to be simultaneously near the Customer and near its own decision centre.
- Customer-driven marketing is an inexact science. It is an experimental, risk taking, creative process. It deals primarily in the long term and is flexible in posture.
- Marketing people must take on new wider responsibilities for which they will need new skills.
- Hybrid managers, proving successful elsewhere, represent a sound and rapid method of entwining IT and marketing. However they must develop a mutual language and a mutual picture of the process of their business. IT must see past the individual transactions; marketing must understand the logistics of its groups of transactions; both must understand the influence of the transactions – single or grouped – on the Customer relationship.
- A successful hybrid manager, for Customer-driven marketing, will probably require two to three years' IT knowledge to complement their career marketing skills or the reverse.
- Hybrid managers elsewhere in business have cultivated environments which should prove beneficial to marketing in the future. They are more inclined to favour strategic rather than reactive management, they flourish in open management arenas which share an appreciation of risk taking and experimentation; they bring creative thinking – and, all in all, could represent the most likely leaders of the next decade.
- The marketer of tomorrow has a finely tuned perception of what is good for the corporation and what is good for the Customer. And what is both.
- The 1990s will see the influence of it becoming easier in some fields to ship work to people rather than people to work. Marketers, in evaluating this concept, must recall the amount to which a team style assists their tasks, and further the very likely increase in such teamwork in the future of Customer-driven marketing. The major resolution to be made is whether marketing is a member or members of multi-discipline teams or remains as teams of specialists. Many fields, including advertising agencies, should study the multi-discipline team approach.

- Structural changes will require attitude changes from marketers. Greater 'horizontal' responsibilities and reporting will be observed with a sharp decline in hierarchical behaviour and thinking.
- Trust and openness will need to be developed in many respects to encourage partnerships and allegiances. This attitude will be present in both forward and reverse marketing, both with clients and suppliers. Greater inter-trading will lead to more companies being involved in two-way traffic. Healthy partners build the best relationships so long-term, quality issues should be top of the mind in the negotiations prior to co-operation. There may be safety in numbers; partnerships can be multi-partnered as well as multi-faceted. If price is a hurdle to marriage, negotiate on margins.

## 11

# What will it be like at work?

It is at least a decade and a half, maybe more, since Professor Peter Drucker, when internationally lauded Professor of Social Services and Management at the Claremont Graduate School in California, predicted with unnerving accuracy the very demassification of corporate infrastructures which is now happening all around us. Professor Drucker then suggested that: 'The typical large business 20 years hence will have fewer than half the levels of management ... and no more than one third of the managers.' The prediction proved faulty only in that it started sooner than Professor Drucker suggested and is taking businesses far too long to complete. Demassification is under way on a national and international scale.

Back in 1990 British Telecom announced the shedding of several tens of thousands of staff as it reduced the levels of management, a process that IBM started in 1986. By the end of 1989 IBM had reduced its payroll from 243,000 to just 206,000, a reduction of 37,000, pulling it back to its 1981 total. It launched the largest retraining and redeployment programme in its history asking IBM staff worldwide to consider career changes and new work habits so that this massive logistical elephant could become gazelle-like in its response to Customer needs.

The much reiterated quote of CEO John Akers as the 1990s got under way was, 'We took our eye off the ball'. The IBM story, which was to become a near horror story around the time that Akers went, had resulted in much praise and acclaim for its remarkable achievements in turning round the company. And, in many ways, it was a fabulous achievement.

However I can never work out why nothing was said publicly about the lack of vision and bad management which let it get into such an outrageously flabby and grossly lethargic state in the first place. Taking one's eye off the ball is one thing, running a company with such extraordinary waste and underperformance is, to my mind, something altogether different; and Akers, as history records, was later to pay the same price as he had asked of so many of his middle managers and other staff. He was moved out.

## The death of the middle manager

Look out for your job! If you're a middle manager it could dissolve before your eyes; at least, it is in severe danger of doing so. That may not be so bad, since you may end up having much more fun, enjoying much more stimulation and getting far greater satisfaction in among the Customer facing jobs which are bound to increase. There you'll be involved with real live Customers, getting to grips with events and actualities that really matter. It feels great. And the most significant element is that more and more people are coming into marketing, more and more people are discovering the satisfaction, pleasure and fulfilment of attending Customers' needs and desires. It is actually what business is for. Yet there is a massive dilemma. This whole preoccupation with demassifying companies is further confused by the demassifying markets. Now to achieve our objectives in marketing we may have to look at fragments of fragments; niche marketing for niche markets.

Let's examine Professor Drucker's original premise and luxuriate in the benefit of hindsight. Further, let's look at the validity it holds for marketers. My confession is one of bias. In the mid-1980s I was correctly quoted as saying I would rather run a networked group of small agencies than one large one. The danger is that you set up an evolutionary continuum; no sooner have you unbundled the whole group than someone has the fabulous idea of creating a central resource for something. Then the overheads of all the different units are examined against the reduced costs of a bundled unit under one roof; the costs and facility of communications are reviewed and, surprise, yes – they too would be improved in one building. What people forget is that you lose speed and flexibility and, pretty soon, you too have taken your 'eye off the ball' as IBM's Akers so dismissively put it.

Think Customer. What's best for the Customer? For example in the case of an ad agency, there is nothing that a small agency can't do as well as a big agency. It's generally only big for its own sake. This is true of many businesses.

Look at your own business. Think Customer. Question why you are the size you are. Search for justifications. Generally there are plenty, but few are to do with the Customer.

■ Customer-Driven Marketing

Think Customer. Examine your processes. Your systems. Your structure. Your culture. Look at everything. Examine the real benefits of size. But when you look at each facet, evaluate it with those two words up front. Think Customer.

Examine the role of your people. How many touch Customers? How many exist for the benefit of the momentum of the business? How many come to work – and how many come to serve the Customers by serving the business? You'll find the more people you have who are involved with Customers, the more motivated they are. For in today's hi-tech, automatic, computerised, digital work society – every business has to become a people business. Otherwise the motivation goes. You can only play computer games for so long.

In a way it is this scenario which lies behind Drucker's thesis. So many businesses have become glorified data processing machines. I recall in this respect those cartoons that appeared in the 1960s. They wryly poked fun at the executive who had gone to lunch to return only to find that he'd been replaced by a computer. The marginal inaccuracy was that it is whole layers of the business that are being made redundant.

If you stand back and observe businesses, you can clearly see their data processing at work. The front line gather data like scurrying ants. Often, like ants, they gather more than their own weight! They return to base and pass the data to their managers. The managers sift and batch the data and pass it with a satisfied smile up to the next level. The next level devour the data hungrily. What is there here that can help the decision making process? Finally with decisions identified and the data processed and transformed into information it arrives at the top ready for the decision to be made. Once the information is considered and the decision made, the whole process starts up once more, but in reverse. The first level down takes the decision and forms an implementation plan. The departmental or divisional responsibilities are handed down and the news finally reaches the front line where our scurrying ant-like creatures dash frantically in and out of the market place excitedly going about their business. It is a very cumbersome, costly and time-consuming process.

So, when you analyse many a big corporation, and identify the tasks where being big or bigger is genuinely useful – in other words, it adds something for the Customer – you find they are few and far between. At least they are when you bear in mind that, as a networked group of autonomous business units, most of any benefits still exist. For example, nobody has done away with the range of experience; the diverse skills of the work force; the buying power; and so on. The result of such an analysis leads to the demassification process that Drucker predicted and which now many companies have found leaves them in far better shape. But, importantly, the flatter structure moves the heart of the company nearer the Customer and the unit far more responsive to their needs. However,

I maintain, for optimised marketing, reducing the hierarchy alone is not sufficient. For at the end of the day a hierarchy is only a mechanism to appease the fragility of mankind.

The essential accompaniments to restructuring also include a radical change in management style and culture. Leadership becomes a key issue, too. I know of a company with a multi-million pound change project on hand at the moment which I suspect will fail for one reason and one reason only. The CEO is a 'command and control' man. It's actually the way he is. And, sadly, that's no way to work in a 'flat' business. Time will tell. And I hope he has the strength to prove me wrong. If he doesn't, he'll either have to make way himself – which I can't see happening – or he, like Mr Akers, will be moved on. Otherwise all that money, all that time spent by a really talented core of people will go to waste.

Just today, as I write, I had a conversation with a senior manager of a company which is equally flabby and lethargic. This business is 'enjoying' a Customer life of about half its industry average. However, because the sales team are adding new business at a terrific rate, nobody is worrying about the quality of business. Of the total new sales, a little more than half is to replace lost Customers. This business could be a gold mine if somebody would take a hold of this 'bath' and put the 'plug' in. I hope it will be my pleasure. The fact is that possibly two-thirds of the orders the sales force is bringing in are not profitable anyway. Focus them on quality business, concentrate on building those Customers into a loyal group of satisfied people and this is a business which will have more than its share of miracles. The burning question is why has it been allowed to get into this state. The answer this prospective Client gave me was: 'We're profitable. We have new business coming in thick and fast and we're growing. So who cares?' I do. Let me at 'em!

## How does marketing relate to the demassified infrastructures?

Marketing's major problem is that not only are the businesses it serves fragmenting but so is its market. It is this added factor which makes the creation of marketing as a central resource less than satisfactory. The problems are as follows:

1. Marketing and sales become distanced (or further distanced) at a time when they need to become closer than ever. Not a miracle in sight.
2. Marketing as a central unit stays just as slow in response time as it always did, in contrast to the other areas which, as they speed up, will become increasingly frustrated with marketing slowness. No miracles here either!
3. Marketing becomes more distanced from the Customer, less in tune

■ Customer-Driven Marketing

with their needs and hence less capable of predicting the future with validity. A veritable miracle famine.
4. A central resource is less flexible and cannot be redeployed or refocused easily. Still no miracle potential.
5. The central resource is ill-equipped and ill-positioned to join in any partnerships, allegiances or relationship building and will therefore not be encouraged to involve itself when, in fact, it has a vital role if success is to be achieved. This is lean on miracles, too.

However, the largest reason why I do not recommend marketing as a central resource is that it does not suit its role for the future. The future is not simply about putting on single transaction sales, it is about creating and nurturing long, healthy and happy relationships with satisfied Customers. Marketing is therefore not to be seen or used as a resource. It is or must become, for true Customer-driven marketing, an integral part of your product or service. Nothing less. Now we're looking at a possible miracle or two!

## The argument in praise of hierarchies

Businesses – and particularly the large management consultancies – do have a habit of following trends, thus assuming that one solution suits all. Or, even worse, they come up with some wonderful new concept and run around selling it to anyone who'll listen.

There is a lucid case for maintaining hierarchies, not the least being that they have worked well for so long. Those in favour of the status quo argue quite noisily that, in IBM's case, if Mr Akers and his team had kept their eye on the ball they wouldn't have let the company become so lethargic, flabby, indolent and perhaps even a little arrogant. Structurally, it *was* just fine.

The most vocal of academics in favour of hierarchy is American Professor Elliot Jacques, whose book *Requisite Organisation: The CEO's Guide to Creative Structure and Leadership* (Casson Hall/Gower, 1989) lands firmly on the side of hierarchies for large companies. The only thing wrong with hierarchies, the professor suggests, is that after some 3000 years, we haven't got them right yet. The part of his argument which I believe is most valid falls into two areas which, even though I find my own sympathies lie elsewhere, serve to highlight the danger areas for the demassifiers.

These two danger points will be addressed in Part 4 when we look at implementation ideas for the future. They are as follows:

- **Danger Point 1** – Professor Jacques suggests, rather like my own view of communism, flat businesses (or we might call them non-hierarchies)

defy human nature. As individuals we want a pecking order and we want a ladder to climb. He argues that people feel more comfortable, work better and have more career motivation in this environment. My view is, that's fine, but people have to change to fit in the changing environment.
- **Danger Point 2** – Professor Jacques holds severe doubts about the way groups, as distinct from individuals, can be held accountable.

In an article published in the *Harvard Business Review* in 1990 under the title of 'In Praise of Hierarchy', Jacques wrote 'It [hierarchy] is the only form of organisation that can enable a company to employ large numbers of people and yet preserve unambiguous accountability for the work they do'. He later concludes the article ... 'hierarchy is the best structure for getting work done in big organisations'.

A flaw in this argument may lie in the thought that most users of the fragmentation concept are creating a network of small organisations out of the large one. In my own view, if there is evidence that hierarchies work well in your business, it may be better to break up the business into smaller units and create small hierarchies than to suffer the imperfections and burdens of a large one.

The concept of work groups or teams, a system about which Professor Jacques also has concerns, even ten years ago, was talked about as new and innovative. The notion, it is said, that a leader supported by multiplexed disciplined colleagues of equal or similar status is an unproven commodity, yet to me it sounds for all the world as the perfect description of a board of directors, a group which I think might want to claim a fairly well proven case.

## The prime resource of tomorrow's marketer

Whichever or whatever structure you choose, the single most important resource for the future is the marketing database (as distinct from database marketing). The ability to access information, especially Customer information (or indeed the ability to find the data to process and turn into information), will become the issue around which all other issues revolve in the future. Information is, in this context, power, in that it is the future commodity of marketing. As both sides fragment, communications and logistical problems increase, although bureaucracy and waste decrease.

So no great step can be taken towards Customer-driven marketing without the ability to move and process information around the network; or, indeed, to provide the built-in monitor, the finger on the pulse, the control systems. Customer-driven marketing focuses on improved human interaction. It takes time. It feeds on information. Organisations need to have a 'Core to Customer' database operating in real time or as near to it

■ Customer-Driven Marketing

as possible. Customer-driven marketing improves not only the nature of transactions and communications but the quantity of them, whether improves means up or down. That's where some of the marketing miracles will come from. The database will prove key to the effectiveness of your personal and corporate marketing effort.

## The increasing role of women in marketing

Marketing workplaces are enjoying another change which must be included in this chapter. You may already have noticed. And I have noticed that it is an almost global change.

There are many more women involved in sales, advertising and marketing and I have every belief that this will continue to rise. I used to wonder why. I now know. I used to think it was to do with the global thrust of emancipation. And it is, partly. However the increase of women involved in marketing, and their abundant success at it, is in greater proportion to many other sectors of business.

Yet, it's not just the number of women, it's what they're doing and the way they are changing thinking. I find it fascinating to observe how the scope of women in sales, advertising and marketing is expanding and changing too. In direct marketing in Western Europe, for example, women now seem almost to dominate the lower ranks (intellectually, at least, if not numerically!); in the middle ranks, it's nearing 50/50, and at the top it's a lot better than any other business I know. As a Fellow of the Institute of Direct Marketing in Great Britain, I couldn't help noticing how well women do on the Diploma Course to which I have been a contributing guest lecturer since it first started.

I have now realised that it is no coincidence whatsoever that, as we move into an era of 'relationship marketing', the role of women increases enormously. Also, later, you will read about the increase of high focus marketing, as distinct from the past decades' favourite – high activity marketing. Activity is a very male thing. And activity for activity's sake, which I suggest was the unspoken predominant marketing strategy of the 1970s and 1980s, is now decreasing quite rapidly.

On a recent trip to South Africa, a friend handed me some photocopies of a speech he had heard by Clem Sunter. Sunter is highly regarded in South Africa and his 'High Road, Low Road' scenario in pre-election times was, in my view, a milestone in South African transformation. In this case I was browsing through the notes and came across the following diagram. It clearly illustrates my point and endorses much of what I have written about the soft issues of marketing.

Psychologically, the way men and women give and receive love has always been one of the great learning points in making our personal relationships work. I know this to be a great generalisation, but one of the

## What will it be like at work?

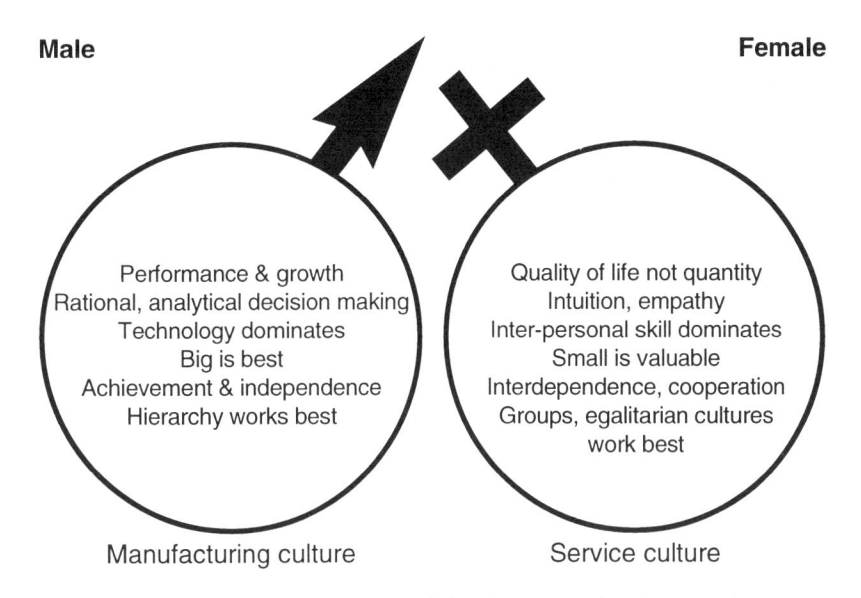

**Male**

- Performance & growth
- Rational, analytical decision making
- Technology dominates
- Big is best
- Achievement & independence
- Hierarchy works best

Manufacturing culture

**Female**

- Quality of life not quantity
- Intuition, empathy
- Inter-personal skill dominates
- Small is valuable
- Interdependence, cooperation
- Groups, egalitarian cultures work best

Service culture

**Figure 11.1** *Gender values and the dominant business culture*

distinguishing features between the two sexes is that men like to win approval and validity for themselves by doing things. Men are obsessed with action. Women on the other hand tend to give their love by way of caring and understanding.

I have observed that contemporary communications between couples seem to be most successful when they can break this pattern and develop something of a hybrid style together.

I'll dwell on this for a minute because I believe it raises several interesting issues, not the least of which is the extreme similarity between the *process*, as opposed to the *content*, of our Customer relationships and our personal ones. This is something which I often demonstrate in seminars and conferences by 'courting', 'marrying' and then breaking up and 'divorcing' a woman from the audience, a routine which first came to me spontaneously with a large group in Milan, Italy. What we explore together and, with the help of the audience (and usually much merriment!), is the nature and style of the relationship as it starts, develops, matures and eventually flounders and fails. Then we find there is a way to a happy ending!

A major bestseller at the moment is *Men are from Mars, Women are from Venus* by John Gray (HarperCollins). In the book Gray is endeavouring to help couples with 'improving communication and getting what you want in your relationships'.

■ Customer-Driven Marketing

Assessing the basic emotional needs of women, Gray lists caring, understanding, respect, devotion, validation and reassurance: and, for men, trust, acceptance, appreciation, admiration, approval and encouragement. Gray further suggests that one of the most common problems he sees in his work is that women and men give their love in the way they want to receive it. He suggests that, when they truly understand each other's needs, men and women relate better together if they can adapt the way they show their love to meet each other's needs and blend them together; to develop, as it were, a hybrid style which is both special and unique to them as a couple.

Men, explains Gray, are obsessed with objects and things. We like to achieve goals and offer solutions. A man's sense of self is somehow defined through his ability to achieve results, to make things happen. Women, however, find their sense of self defined through their feelings and the quality of their relationships. Thus women, suggests Gray, unlike men who are goal oriented, are fundamentally relationship oriented.

Relationship marketing (which, incidentally, goes hand in hand with integrated marketing since the two are quite useless and, I believe, doomed to failure without each other) adds new dimensions to marketing. I have referred to these new dimensions as 'the soft issues'. These issues call on the core skills of womanhood – not just as defined by John Gray, but by plenty of others before him. Of course this does not preclude men from marketing in the future, I'm pleased to say. Many of us have plenty of caring and understanding capacities and sensitivities which, happily, it is currently 'OK' for us to show and of which we can now make even greater use in our work as well as at home.

This link between the emphasis of marketing on to relationship skills and away from the frenetic high activity of the past with the increasing and welcome success of women in marketing is not a coincidence. It is progress.

In Chapter 11, we discovered that our new workplaces are likely to be quite different. Marketing as a function has as much reason to fragment as the organisations it takes to market. The points covered were as follows:

- Middle management now performs a large data processing function, much of which can be handled automatically or differently in the future.
- Many firms are finding that redeploying such skilled and literate people at the Customer end of the business makes better use of them and increases Customer satisfaction.
- To be most effective marketers may need to consider fragments of fragments, niche marketing for niche markets.
- In analysing and quantifying the problem – THINK CUSTOMER.

## What will it be like at work?

Look at yourself from the Customer's perception and appraise what real benefits will be lost when the structure breaks up.

- The aim of such fragmentation (as it refers to Customer-driven marketing) is that it enables marketers to involve themselves, and in some cases lead, the building and maintenance of Customer relationships. Marketing is therefore not a corporate resource, it is an integral part of the product or service.
- If you believe hierarchies work well and you are in a big corporation, an alternative to group or teamwork could be to restructure into smaller hierarchies.
- The two significant risk areas for groupwork are that it could be less than satisfactory in relation to human nature's historically preferred method, the hierarchy – and that it is unsuccessful in matters of accountability.
- A major and prerequisite central resource of Customer-driven marketing is the marketing database.
- Customer-driven marketing improves both the nature and number of Customer transactions and communications.
- The number of women in marketing has grown and will grow more still; indeed, there is a need for the 'core skills of womanhood' which bring extraordinary benefits to all aspects of relationship marketing.

# 12

# Looking back to what's next

For business, I'll say it again, the future gets harder. For marketing, it gets harder still. There is such a long way to go, so much lost time to recoup, such an appalling lack of quality standards to correct, so much happening all around us, so much to learn anew.

We've already looked at some of the major factors; but there exist many others, of course, not least of which are the three commodities required to take Customer-driven marketing into your organisation. These are money, time and courage.

## Pressure on the margin

As we progress into the next millennium, and the quality aspects start to recover, the added-value perceptions that we give the Customer will decrease price sensitivity. In a sense the only people locked into a price sensitive situation should be those shortsighted enough to get themselves into it in the first place; or those equally shortsighted enough not to have taken the opportunity to move out of it. The slackening of pressure on price will be gratefully received because elsewhere the margin will be at severe stretch. Consider the list of items queuing up for a greater share:

- Product development: can you afford not to keep up the pace as product life cycles get shorter?
- The increasing demands of the Customer: quality and design cost money, can you recover all of it?
- The decreasing cost effectiveness of the media: you'll need a bigger budget to have the same effect.

- Internationalisation: going international or global is an expensive business before it yields rewards – even if you're only looking for partners.
- Customer service and Customer care: both these aspects of Customer-driven marketing cost more money. The good news is that some things can self-liquidate and therefore at least spread the budget a little.
- The need to build corporate image and positioning: some of this work can be carried out along with advertising but the rest needs funding.
- Building and running the marketing database: any database is only as useful as it is accurate and up to date.
- Quality dedication means picking the best staff and then training them: training levels, if you have a good standard now, will increase by 50 per cent; if less than good, your budget will need to double or treble. If you're British you have another problem, details following.

So you see the margin will come under stress. How much of this is passed on and how much must be financed by improvement elsewhere is for you, your competitors and your market to establish.

While considering the pressures that will apply to margins in the future, it is possible that the 'Europeanisation' of companies (or even globalisation) might cause further stress. I have strong views about where retailers should exercise their strength – and particularly where they must show greater care. I am most concerned about so much pressure being applied that their manufacturers or suppliers are squeezed to a point where they can no longer control their margins and therefore, in effect, run their own businesses. One very real threat to margins could emerge from the arrival of Euro-Super-Group Retailers.

There is a great deal of activity – acquisitions, mergers and equity exchanges – taking place at the moment. Should this lead to a level of Europe-wide central buying where the needs of all the alliance or partnership are consolidated to increase the buying power, then the results will, I suspect, be quite negative for the consumer in the long run. Such organisations do not so far have a great track record at fostering the independence and profitability of their suppliers – they seem to favour control and margin squeezing. Furthermore, while such centralised mass negotiations may make sense from the retailer's position, they are often entirely against the interests of both the Customer and the original manufacturer. Such arrangements may succeed for a while with basic commodities but are generally contrary to the predicted direction for Customer requirements.

## The battle with time

Quality takes time to implement. It has to become woven into the fabric of the company; so, for that matter, does putting the Customer first.

■ Customer-Driven Marketing

Many businesses seem not to have been created for their Customers. They exist to produce or manufacture or process; they have to buy, to administer, to look after their staff. They have to pay suppliers and bill their Customers. And, oh yes! They have to sell. To such organisations, making every major decision a 'Customer first' decision is very difficult. And even when the decision is made, implementing it is also arduous.

The time it takes to set Customer-driven marketing in place will depend not just on the size of your company, but also on the number of people and locations involved, the amount of restructuring and reorganisation that has to be done and the drive, commitment and energy of your people. This is a programme that will probably take quite a while – a year at least, maybe two or three or, in extreme cases, more. The key question is how much of a march you can steal over your competitors by getting started quickly.

## And a whole heap of courage

Customer driven marketing also needs courage and, I would add, perseverance. For the first two, or even three, years little benefit may be gained, while probably most of the set-up costs will be incurred.

After three years' investment in Quality, Rank Xerox reported no visible improvement. In the fourth year they began to see real gains and by the fifth year, a veritable firework display of benefits; profits up 40 per cent, return on assets effectively trebled, unit costs of components down by 30 per cent and, most important of all, Customer satisfaction up 35 five per cent. Rich rewards!

However this all goes to prove that old habits die hard – especially bad ones.

## The unique problems of the British

Since Britain joined the EC I have tended to describe myself as a European living in Britain. However, a true Brit through and through, I find that the next few paragraphs truly disturb me and cause me great problems to come to terms with.

The world of business and commerce is moving towards quality, not just in marketing, but throughout its disciplines. Sadly Britain has found itself with a severe handicap; for the British appreciation of quality standards is, I believe, by far the lowest of the major European industrial nations and no better when measured on a world scale.

Britain is going into its third decade of falling and failing educational standards. The young Thatcher government, when it came to power, inherited an educational timebomb which it failed to defuse. Instead it concentrated on other, more market orientated problems and failed to get the support of the, predominantly socialist, teaching profession. Britain's education system is now in chaos and shows no great signs of recovery. But worse, the country now has whole generations of unsatisfactorily educated young people whose perceptions of quality simply do not measure up to most of the rest of its competitors, whether you measure on a European or global scale. The problem now is that Britain stands apart from many other countries in the world markets. It starts with the consumer where British mass markets are the least discerning of all the major players.

In 1993, Gerald Ratner, at the time CEO of Britain's biggest jewellers, Ratners Group, addressed the British Institute of Directors Annual Convention declaring that his business was founded on selling people what they wanted; in his own words, 'total crap'. Having the day before announced record profits of $192 million produced from 1000 stores throughout Great Britain, Ratner astonished his 3000-strong audience by revealing his views of his Customers.

'We sell things like a teapot for two quid (£2) or an imitation book to lay on your coffee table. The pages don't turn, but they have curled up corners and genuine antique dust. I know it's in the worst possible taste, but we sold a quarter of a million last year.'

'We also sell cut-glass decanters complete with six glasses on a silver-plated tray for £6. People ask me how can you sell this for such a low price? I say, 'Because it's total crap'.

'We even sell a pair of ear-rings which are cheaper to buy than a sandwich. But I have to say the ear-rings probably won't last so long!' The following day, the stock prices in Mr Ratner's business rose substantially on the London Stock Exchange. However, I'm pleased to say that Mr Ratner was later removed and the company had a hard time, having to change their – long established and extremely well known – trading name as part of their recovery plan.

I guess many could rightly ask whether this is so very different to Procter and Gamble's (P&G) treatment of their orange juice-buying Customers in the US. For years their premium brand of concentrated orange juice has carried the word 'fresh'. While I'm sure if you ask P&G if they want to treat their Customers honestly they will say that they do, you have to ask why it eventually took the US federal government to require them to take the offending products off the shelves.

In many European businesses too, such apparent duplicities exist. Indeed, the belief in quality as a necessity hardly exists at all; it seems to be viewed almost as a luxury and a practice for those who want to be at the very top of the tree – a place where many Brits think the whole thing is just too much trouble.

*The Economist*, a highly respected weekly business newspaper, in a leader, urged that was what was needed was to 'offer the promise of

■ Customer-Driven Marketing

reward for excellence rather than the certainty of getting something for being so-so'. Yet, Britain often seems to pride itself in being the best in Europe at being so-so.

Britain has an awful lot of middle; there's enough pride left to want to stay off the bottom, but absolutely no perceived need to be at the top. The 'middle's OK' attitude becomes most obvious when we come under threat. Give the Brits a war to fight or the most difficult recession in history to overcome – no problem! Out comes the latest version of the 'I'm backing Britain' campaign and the foot hits the floor. But no sooner has the corner been turned, than we want to put up our feet, have a cup of tea and get back to the telly. And there we are in the middle again.

When you're up against American drive, French creativity, German quality and Japanese or Malaysian everything, Britain has to realise that this is not something which can be attended to in fits and starts.

### Quality starts at birth and at home

The fact is that the British education system is delivering lower quality young people to industry and commerce than it needs to compete in the global market. British standards are dropping when many of its competitors are rising. Thus, British industry has the problem of training its young intake to get them up to speed before they can use them. This decline has been taking place for a decade or more and, whatever the colour of the governments of the future, it will take at least a decade to correct.

The correction, however, does not lie simply within British schools. Quality is a way of life and the value standards generally in Britain no longer demand sufficient quality. This problem I believe dates back to the 1960s. My generation is to blame!

I would love to have to confess that I am some arrogant, pompous, cantankerous old rat, and that my view is the result of being mugged by some hooligan in the subway on the way home. Sorry, it's not that! These are the views of someone who travels the world as a trainer and consultant, and sees the literate, articulate, educated, enthusiastic and most often multi-lingual youngsters that other countries enjoy.

I wish there was an answer to this dilemma. The only one I can suggest is to be ruthless in your recruitment, generous in your training, fastidious in your monitoring of standards and as demanding as possible in all matters of quality.

I should repeat that this British predicament causes me pain. Nothing would give me greater pleasure than to heap praise on British young people, and junior or trainee workers, executives and managers; but it's just not possible. I further realise that not everyone is at fault and there are many shining examples of well brought up, well-educated, socially and culturally admirable young men and women; but, sadly, they exist in

% Educated workforces

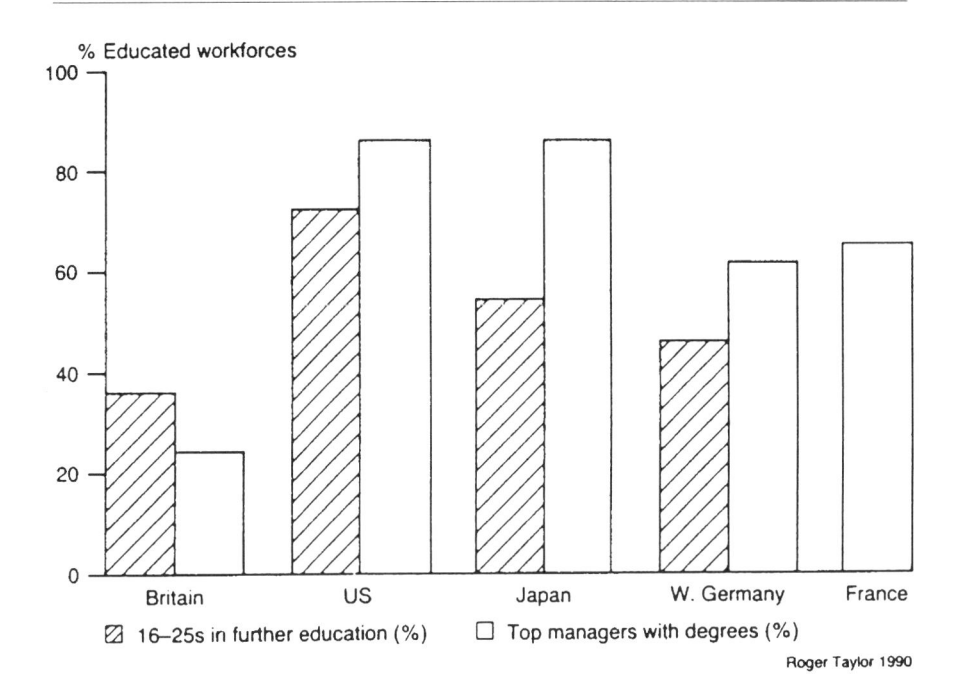

**Figure 12.1** *Education at work. This figure shows where Britain stood against its competitors in relation to managers with degrees and young people in further education. Compare its position with the US and Japan in particular.*

nothing like the numbers Britain needs to hold top positions in global industries and commerce in the next two or three decades.

Later figures in 1996 suggest that things may be improving. However, British industry and commerce is still complaining vocally that the quality of student is lower than they experience in other countries and certainly lower than they need. Students appear to have reasonable knowledge in their subjects but lack commercial awareness which could reasonably be imparted while in education (I believe this to be a joint responsibility for industry and academia), and basic literacy and numeracy.

## Ultimately, quality suffers no dropouts

The quality of young people is important because Customer driven marketing is a practice for businesses of every size – from one-man bands to vast multi-nationals. It is a culture, a philosophy, a creed as well as a strategy and a system. It is also by far the most competitive action you can take. However, it is not a movement from which you can opt out. 'Quality is not for me' will be an epitaph, not a decision.

■ Customer-Driven Marketing

## Quality turns back the clock

Before there were so many of us sharing this planet, businesses delivered quality as a norm. Shopping used to be a pleasure; recognition an everyday occurrence; customised service the way it was; courtesy and value part of the deal. And that is where and what we have to get back to. This is a numbers problem. If we all had fewer Customers, we could devote more time to them, think more about them and dedicate more of our resources to their problems. It is therefore a conundrum which many of us will solve through computers and technology, the database being a prime example. The other method is actually to arrange fewer Customers; to break your marketing thrust down into smaller units which will market to smaller groups of Customers.

At one time I found myself referring to the past, the way things used to be, how our parents and grandparents experienced things, so often that I began to be very self-conscious about it. I sounded more like an ageing historian rather than someone fascinated by the way business is changing for the future.

Yet it's not coincidence. In the past it *was* better in quality and service terms and it will be again. All we have to do is recognise the gravity of the problem, appreciate the speed with which we must get started and understand the lengths to which we must go to get back to the future for Customer driven marketing.

This chapter draws to a close Part Two, in which we have reviewed some of the key issues that will affect marketing as we start an exciting new millennium. Next we will look at the steps we must take to prepare for marketing in the age of the Customer. But first here is our chapter review:

- Great pressure will build up on prices and margins. The need to be competitive must be balanced against the desire to maintain product development; to meet the demands of the Customer; to cope with decreasing media effectiveness; to go international; to meet the costs of increased Customer care programmes; to increase the budget for corporate image and positioning; to build and maintain a database; and to spend more on recruitment and training.
- Customer driven marketing is a process which requires time and perseverance and persistence to yield its rewards.
- A great deal of courage is required by the board and senior managers since the payback for Customer-driven marketing is slow but, when it comes, rich and long term.
- Britain has a severe quality handicap which will be industry's problem to sort out in the short term. In the long term it can only be hoped that quality becomes a way of life in more ways than one.

- You can't duck the quality race. It's merely a question of when you get started.
- To put the quality into marketing will, for many, be a restoration process. We're headed back to the future as fast as we can!

## Part Three: What's new, what's different?

# 13

# The trends that take us to tomorrow

Part Two identified many of the changes you will see taking place in marketing during the years to come, discussed some of the problems you will face, and looked at some positive ideas which might hold the key to the ways you react and respond to threats and opportunities; and we saw how those will abound in the agitated yet challenging and stimulating times in front of us.

By the end we had painted a picture of an inevitable outcome – business will get harder, but marketing will get harder still. Is this the kind of gloomy scaremongering you buy books for? Certainly, whether we like to face it or not, it doesn't get any easier out there in the future; therefore I would like to look now at some of the preparations we can make. At least if it's going to rain we can get our waterproofs on!

This next section is to help move us into preparation mode and it contains plenty more ideas; but, particularly, they are ideas which identify the major issues to think about and what you can do towards them. All of this should help you to review your own practices and adjust them to the ways which will maximise your success in the new marketing environment, perhaps even sow the seeds for a few miracles.

Some of the issues we'll consider are quite unexceptional, pragmatic ideas; others are conceptual or philosophical; but all of them are critical to marketing effectiveness. We will consider new criteria for choosing what is currently called an advertising agency: we will look at how many agencies a big budget marketer should have – and, where it's more than one, how the work should be divided among them. We'll endeavour to form a closer, more detailed understanding of the ways which selling and marketing will change; and take a look at the fundamental processes of buying and selling; finally in Part Three, we will examine new concepts as Granular Marketing is explained. This all leads into Part Four, where methods are demonstrated by which you will most successfully implement the kinds of changes which the future needs from you.

## Connecting the dots

One of my most frequently used slides for the beginning of training sessions is taken from a cartoon strip. A prisoner lies festering in a dark, damp medieval dungeon. Peering through the bars of the tiny hole in his cell door, he calls out to his jailer. With obvious pride he explains that he has just finished a book he has been working on and proffers it to the jailer. The next two frames show the prisoner waiting expectantly for the praise and congratulations he is sure will come – the jailer on the other hand is clearly puzzled, unable to make any sense of what he sees on the pages of the book he has been handed. He turns to the prisoner who, seeing his puzzlement, explains, 'You've got to connect the dots!' In a sense, before we move on to the next layer of information, that's what I would like to do now; otherwise, we run the danger of, as the saying goes, simply being confused – but at a much higher level.

## The rise and rise of the Customer

Surely, it is the return of the Customer as the driving force of marketing which is behind the need to return to quality marketing practices. That's not to say that Customers place quality first in all their purchasing; of course not. They are often looking for a value balance which may include many factors. However, the new breed of marketers are convinced that, when you look at today's marketing environment, capturing the Customer's heart, trust and loyalty is a highly potent cocktail which has fascinatingly attractive after-effects. It certainly is, for example, extraordinarily strong at locking out competitors. In an age when 'We'll beat any price in town', and 'Instant credit' signs have become commonplace, marketing seems to have reached a stage where duelling competitors, having run out of ammunition and broken their swords, are now reduced to rolling round in the mud slugging it out until one of them finally drops. Is that marketing? I think not. It's the result of a business which has worshipped quantity at any price, and which has done so for so long, that every last drop of quality based thinking has been wrung out of it to the point that it is absolutely quality parched.

Take a look at the state which this transaction marketing, 'close that sale' mentality has left as its inheritance; there you can see the roots of so many of the problems we have given ourselves.

## Develop a quality lock

So this is the start of our new cultivation process, almost a barren desert. No better place to start! And in this desert there is beginning a strong wind of change. It is blowing now and it is the wind of quality. It carries the message that the bond created with the Customer is far greater than the sum of the transactions.

For those who change direction first it holds the most difficult task but commensurate reward. Those who establish the strongest, most enduring relationships now will be those who hold the high ground. It is very difficult for a competitor to wrestle away a Customer who enjoys a broad based satisfying relationship with you. It is very easy to steal a Customer who buys on price. Those who inherit the task of attacking competitors which have developed a quality lock on their market will have a daunting task ahead of them. It will cost them much dearer in time, effort, resources and cash.

However, let us also remember at this time, the principle of marketing as a four-way process; it should encompass not only your market but your people, your shareholders and your suppliers too. This will add longevity, loyalty and endurance in these areas, thus affording safety and stability to its practitioners.

## Trends to turmoil

So why is all this necessary? Is the argument in favour of a return to quality purely a flimsy emotional cry ... or are there really things happening out there which point to it unequivocally as the way we need to go forward?

Certainly if you look at the way things were headed as we left the 1980s you could be forgiven for becoming pessimistic or depressed. Throughout the world we witnessed many trends which suggested that the rewards of marketing, as distinct from the rewards of selling (as defined and differentiated in Chapters 7 and 8) would make a change of direction necessary. The notions of a chaotic, unpredictable business environment are well forecast and much advice issued. Indeed, for many, this was their starting point for the quality rationale. It remains a complete mystery why so very, very few extended that to include their advertising, sales and marketing, especially when so many miracles lie waiting there. None the less, the beginning of the 1990s saw the global ranks of marketers in the developed world facing an array of problems to handle.

Think about it. While the world saw increasing see-saw swings in its economic fortunes, many marketers found themselves with the twin dilemma of mature markets and parallel products. Those same markets were becoming more and more fragmented and diverse, while the media were offering less and less effectiveness. In terms of distribution channels, not just in the US but right across the world, we saw a startling level of change developing in their patterns which in turn provoked power shifts that were often as rapid as they were short-lived as they were ill-conceived. Many quite large and previously soundly based businesses were acquired by rapid growth corporations which found themselves over extended and caught unawares by violent interest rate fluctuations. Suddenly even some of the most solid and dependable names became a whole lot less solid and dependable. This unsatisfactory state soon led to a consequent nervousness in the tents of the money lenders. And rightly so. They had lent too much too easily for too long. Soon, with their minds refocused on the financial picture and belt-tightening, companies found themselves drawing in and cutting back, just at the same time as the wholly materialistic greedy business of transaction based selling backfired and led them into markets which had forced Customer expectations to rise, while often also becoming more price sensitive.

The timing could not have been worse – competition, both domestic and overseas, was mounting while simultaneously their weapons were proving less effective; marketing effectiveness was declining, while the pressure was pouring on with constant changes in technology, costly in themselves, but more difficult still when you saw how those same technologies shortened the life cycles of products and services. A competitive advantage got more difficult to gain, more expensive to establish and lasted for shorter and shorter periods.

I rest half my case! This is the half which says circumstances, whether accidental or created by marketers themselves, have led us to a point where the only logical solution in all this turbulence is to create stability: to bring back practices which reflect long-term criteria and professionalism.

If that wasn't enough evidence to support Customer-driven marketing based as it is around the creation and maintenance of relationships not transactions, there is another convincing case which requires simply that one reads the signs and considers what to do next. Again I believe Customer-driven marketing is the only logical answer. See if you agree.

Let's return to those issues raised in Chapter 8 (on pages 124–5) when we discovered the array of corporate, product/marketing and marketing mix strategies (Tables 8.1, 8.2 and 8.3) produced by Professors Stern and Kotler. Look back and consider how many of those from the 1990s column point in the same direction. With only two or three exceptions which, as it were, rest in a neutral position, the remainder stand together pointing clearly towards the ways of relationship-centred activities. For example take niche and customised marketing and product positioning; Customer, competitor, channel orientation; strategic mission for each product; and product line rationalisation; the multiplex sales force; targeted and co-ordinated communications; pricing based on Customer perceived values; suppliers and distributors as friends; governance structures; strategic alliances and synergistic diversification. Each one of those and others, if they don't actually suggest or support relationship marketing values and ideas, will prosper and flourish best in such an environment.

What's more, we are sufficiently well on with the game to be able to turn to Kotler and Stern and ask them: 'Were you right about the 1990s, eh? Did your predictions turn out the way you thought they would?' Let me save you referring back to check it out. It's uncannily accurate. Their predictions have come to pass, plus or minus a little, exactly as they said they would. I think this gives us cause to be as confident as one can these days, at least about our strategic environment for the next few years.

That's the other half of the case. Once you have understood the significance and force of its direction, its inevitability is clear. It's happening. And it's happening now. To add weight to all of this, consider the table here which shows again the full list from Chapter 8, this time with the addition of a key which enables you to identify which and how the factors correlate. It's a formidable network of synergy, serving to add one final compelling force to my arguments.

If you draw the conclusion that there is no time to be wasted in adopting Customer-driven marketing practices, then we would be in accord! Let's move on to look at some of the ways you can start putting the quality back into marketing. Before we do, here is the summary of this chapter:

- The evidence to support the adoption of Customer-driven and quality techniques in marketing is quite overwhelming.
- As the 1980s ended, the trends in the business environment consisted of two predominant types: the first were the results of marketing's over-obsession with quantity for three decades or more; the second more circumstantial, but totally endorsing of the new quality directions.
- Of the major informed academic projections, once the picture has been pieced together, these too suggest the same path. Quality must return to provide the deeper, longer lasting relationships which will satisfy the Customer's needs and provide the stability, sales and profitability which is required to finance them.

■ Customer-Driven Marketing

**Table 13.1** *The synergy of strategies*

| Line no. | 1990 Strategy | Correlations |
|---|---|---|
| **1. Product/market strategies** | | |
| 1.1 | Niche & customised marketing and product positioning | 1: 2 3 4 5 6 7<br>2: 1 2 3 4 5 6<br>3: 1 2 3 4 5 6 |
| 1.2 | Customer/competitor/channel orientation | 1: 1 3 4 5 6 7<br>2: 1 2 3 4 5 6<br>3: 1 2 3 4 5 6 |
| 1.3 | Product line rationalisation | 1: 1 2 4 5 7<br>2: 1 2 3 4 5 6<br>3: 1 2 4 5 |
| 1.4 | Strategic mission for each product | 1: 1 2 3 4 7<br>2: 1 2 3 4 5 6<br>3: 1 2 4 5 |
| 1.5 | Selective market coverage | 1: 1 2 3 4 7<br>2: 4 5 6<br>3: 2 4 |
| 1.6 | Global marketing | 1: 1 2 3 4 5 6<br>2: 1 2 4<br>3: 1 2 3 4 5 |
| 1.7 | Local marketing | 1: 1 2 3 4 5 6<br>2: 1 2 4 5 6<br>3: 1 2 3 4 5 6 |
| **2. Marketing mix strategies** | | |
| 2.1 | Decision support system research | 1: 1 2 3 4 6 7<br>2: 2 3 4 5<br>3: 1 2 3 4 5 |
| 2.2 | Competing on quality, design and services | 1: 1 2 3 4 6 7<br>2: 1 3 4 5 6<br>3: 1 2 3 4 5 6 |
| 2.3 | Pricing based on Customer perceived value | 1: 1 2 3 4<br>2: 1 2 4<br>3: 2 |
| 2.4 | Suppliers/distributors as partners | 1: 1 2 3 4 5 6 7<br>2: 1 2 3 5 6<br>3: 1 2 3 4 5 6 |
| 2.5 | Multiplexed salesforces | 1: 2 3 4 5 7<br>2: 1 2 4 6<br>3: 2 4 5 6 |
| 2.6 | Targeted and co-ordinated communications | 1: 1 2 3 4 5 7<br>2: 2 4 5<br>3: 2 6 |

*Table 13.1 continued*

| Line no. | 1990 Strategy | Correlations |
|---|---|---|
| **3. Corporate strategies** | | |
| 3.1 | Synergistic diversification | 1: 1 2 3 4 6 7<br>2: 1 2 4<br>3: 2 3 4 5 6 |
| 3.2 | Implementation excellence | 1: 1 2 3 4 5 6 7<br>2: 1 2 3 4 5 6<br>3: 1 3 4 5 6 |
| 3.3 | Economies of scope | 1: 1 2 6 7<br>2: 1 2 4<br>3: 1 2 4 5 6 |
| 3.4 | Governance structures | 1: 1 2 3 4 5 6 7<br>2: 1 2 4<br>3: 1 2 3 5 6 |
| 3.5 | Strategic alliances | 1: 1 2 3 4 6 7<br>2: 1 2 4 5<br>3: 1 2 3 4 6 |
| 3.6 | Co-ordinated business functions | 1: 1 2 7<br>2: 2 4 5 6<br>3: 1 2 3 4 5 |

This table identifies the quite staggering synergy between the strategies when relationship building and total quality marketing are the objective. To use the table: each of the strategies listed has a strategy-type prefix and a line-number suffix. To identify the strategies of importance when considering the quality issues, the corresponding numbers are given in the right-hand column headed Correlations. Remarkably, of the potential 57 lines, 37 have more than 5 correlating strategies. This illustrates the strength and cohesion of the force behind quality concepts in marketing for the future.

# 14

# There's a new kind of client looking for a new kind of agency

Here it comes again! Another idea through which we're going back to the future. In the 1950s and early 1960s the major advertising agencies right around the world claimed to be 'one stop shops'. They wanted to be all things to all people; they failed, but tried quite hard. They laid claim to corporate image, to general brochure and leaflet work, to all sales promotion activities, branding and packaging, and direct mail. You name it, they did it or said they did. They had merchandising departments, public relations departments, some even had marketing departments – marketing in that context proving to be a euphemism for 'below the line' or marketing services. Yet what they were good at was advertising. Above the line they were all powerful, below the line all greedy.

The expression 'Jack of all trades, master of none' was never more appropriate. The skills they applied below the line were often ill-conceived, ill-planned and ill-informed. Watching the appalling mistakes and waste, the business quickly spawned a highly skilled, efficient and competitive host of marketing service suppliers who have been there ever since. Some of them pulled together a set of discrete disciplines to which they could apply discrete skills. Direct marketing agencies are a perfect example. In the 1960s, so frustrated by the mess the big agencies were making of, particularly, the strategy and creativity of their discipline, many mailing houses, specialist printers, house-to-house distributors and their counterparts set up their own competitive sources. They quickly improved the results Clients were getting and, since they often sold to Clients direct, effectively positioned themselves in competition with the agencies and became rivals for the budgets.

## There's a new kind of client looking for a new kind of agency ■

Apart from improving the strategic use of marketing services and increasing the cost effectiveness which resulted, little else positive was achieved. Indeed, a holy war started. The above the line were on one side – the establishment – well backed and financed by the City in London and Wall Street in the US; arrogant, in control, the natural home of 90 per cent of the budget. On the other side – the wrong side of the tracks, the unshaven vocal and rebellious rabble that was below the line. Even the phrase itself gives away the 'bad smell under the nose' way with which classical advertising people mouthed this distasteful description. And just to make absolutely sure the below the liners knew their place, the agencies asked them to use the tradesman's entrance, and deal with the print buyers and media buyers.

Ultimately, it was the Client who was to make a decision and, in so doing, start to resolve the issue. Ironically, it leads us back to the 1950s.

### Divided we stand, divided we fall

The marketing services specialists and their allies were not to be so easily discouraged. They had ambition, they had valuable and demonstrably cost efficient skills and they had the conviction of the underdog with all the energy, enthusiasm and cunning that being shown the tradesman's entrance was to engender. Yes, perhaps I should add resentment. Through the 1970s, the below the line voices got louder as their skills became more polished and accomplished. Gradually they started to squeeze the agencies by their jugular vein; in other words – their budget share. The 'Battle of the Budget' had begun!

It was a two-faced, hypocritical holy war. On the surface both sides claimed friendship and co-operation, while underneath they spat venom at each other. The below the line specialists were creatively incompetent, undermined brand values and were often strategic vandals. They were no better than greedy guerrillas. The above the line were arrogant, overpriced, over-rated and over-obsessed with television. Like all good holy wars – or rather bad ones – both sides were right, both sides were wrong.

So, by the late 1970s, marketers were faced with a choice of classical ad agencies for their account – which was essentially their mass media spend; together with their choice from a wide range of specialist suppliers. There were effective, highly skilled sources for corporate design, packaging, public relations, sales promotion, sponsorship and events, and of course the major growth area – and some would argue (foolishly in my view), the contender for the throne, direct marketing.

Strangely, I don't think the war will ever be decisively won or lost. Individual Clients may choose one way or the other for a time, but broadly, across the business, another revolution will occur. The best will be plucked from both or all sides.

■ Customer-Driven Marketing

## Clients must take the initiative

The fact is that, strategically at least, the Client was the loser – neither the above the line or the below the line side was providing unbiased strategic advice. They were both providing advice which was almost always biased (not unnaturally!) and almost always tactical. Inevitably the major criterion for any proposition placed before the Client was to secure the spending and thereby the welfare of the proposer. Which agency in their right mind would advise a Client to reduce his budget by 50 per cent and hand it out to the specialist; which specialist was going to tell the Client that he was overspending on sales promotion, a fraction low on direct marketing, should hold it where it was on PR and up his radio and national dailies? Thus the Clients made the decisions, some better than others, naturally.

## Where are we now; and where should we go?

The position is now confused. Some agencies have 'acquired' specialists. Of those, some have merged them in; others keep them as service companies within the group; others still just take an interest and let them operate autonomously. PR and design have managed, by and large, to remain distinct disciplines, whereas direct marketing and sales promotion seem to be confused by many companies, one as a function or technique of the other. There is some overlap, of course, but really the confusion has little logic, other than that they are both still largely deeply rooted in the business of quantity based selling; but then isn't all marketing at the moment?

To make Customer-driven marketing happen we need two important strands: refocusing and managing individual Customer relationships, and integration of marketing and sales to deliver their effort seamlessly. Therefore, it is necessary to return to the one stop shop concept, with one less than subtle difference. Instead of the agencies merely wanting to do it all, they genuinely have to be able to deliver. In order to deliver, they will need to acquire or merge with -- and *fully integrate* – the specialists. This means the disciplines may have 'centres of excellence', so to speak, within the agency, but there must be competent planning, creative and implementation skills available to the Client on a day-to-day basis. Thus, agencies will need creative and media and account handling personnel who are trained and skilled on a much broader, more general basis. Specialist service suppliers will need to have the vision and confidence to abandon their single skill specialisation and take their rightful place in the establishment. Clients may thus – as they need to reduce the size of their marketing department anyway – let go of the buying and administrative roles they have developed to deal with all the marketing services suppliers; then they can consolidate and pull back to the functions of control. Clients must become judges again, not referees. Thus we shall see the gradual transformation within the establishment block, from advertising agency to an integrated service marketing agency.

This now poses two further questions: where should the strategic thinking take place; and how will big accounts be divided up, if indeed they should?

## Where will the thinking be done?

Those agencies who can demonstrate a truly integrated service, no doubt will deserve an opportunity to be involved in the short, medium and long-term strategy. Indeed, I suspect one of the spin-offs of the new wave Client is that they, like the rest of the world, will become aware of the benefit of longer term relationships; thus most Clients will place more value on the teamwork and spirit that develops on both sides when practising quality Customer-driven marketing methods. However, I remain uncertain from the Client's point of view that the agency – integrated or not – is the best place for planning. I believe the optimum place for such planning will be amongst a new breed of 'super consultants' and 'strategic business planners' which we are already beginning to see develop – often specialising as they will probably have to continue to do – in certain fields. Indeed, more and more of my own time with Clients is taken up with just such work. However, to ensure the value and validity of such outside help, it is incumbent upon the consultants to be right with the leading edge and completely familiar with the Client's business. Clients may not all want to go to the leading edge, but they should know how far away from it they are!

My preference for the independent planning and strategic counsel is not founded on the basis that agencies are unable to prepare strategic plans; nor that they are incapable of the quality levels required. I am sure they will acquire the necessary people and, in time, manage to retrain their staff accordingly. My concern is that I remain sceptical that those who profit from the way the money is spent are the best people to decide how it should be spent. As I have demonstrated, agencies have already proven that this is an irresistible temptation for them. I think this represents a strong case for a separate strategic planning function and I am sure there will be a mushrooming of such consultancies and plenty of work for them. My experience has been that the only major snag in using separate planners with the agency implementing the plans later, is that of accountability for successes and failures: which is responsible, the plan or its implementation methods, tactics and ideas? The best advice I can give is to understand that using an independent strategist does not preclude agency involvement. I would encourage a group from the agency in the planning sessions thus developing tacit acceptance of the plans, increased consideration of the implementation issues and, if no more tangible link, at least a spirit of mutual commitment to, and accountability for, the plans generated.

Talking with Peter Thompson, chairman of Grey Integrated in London, it is interesting that his business now finds itself competing with management consultancies to pitch for corporate strategy work. What's more, Peter is quite happy that the agency should involve itself in strategy for a Client without necessarily getting involved in, or pitching for, the resulting agency work. Grey Integrated lay claim to being one of the few (Peter would argue the only!) truly integrated agencies in Britain.

I guess what is at issue here is the definition of the word 'integrated'. There's more on this in Chapter 23, where we examine the notions of Integrated Marketing and Relationship Marketing in more detail. However, briefly for the topic here, let me explain that I see relationship marketing to be descriptive of what we are trying to achieve and integrated marketing about how we do it. The former is about style, nature and content, the latter about method and process. You can use integrated marketing processes without necessarily requiring them to deliver relationship marketing objectives. Although I'm not sure why you would want to do so – that's a bit like visiting France and not sampling the wines or cheeses!

You cannot, however, deliver relationship marketing without integrated marketing. There is a school of thought around at the moment which believes integration to mean some kind of sophisticated campaign planning. Several times I have sat with groups of both Client and agency folk who believe that, somehow, if you have a multi-media campaign with a response element which triggers a follow up of a linked and efficient fulfilment process, coupled with well-timed telemarketing or sales follow up, this is integrated marketing. It is not. It is sensible marketing. It is usually also effective and possibly even efficient marketing. But that is all. It is certainly not integrated marketing.

Similarly, if you use the same agency to produce the television and press ads, plan and buy the media, arrange the response handling, create the fulfilment packs, write the telemarketing scripts, and produce the sales aids, this does not make them an integrated agency. It makes them an agency which can do a lot of different things – and co-ordinate them well. They are merely capable of handling a well-planned and comprehensive campaign.

## How can you tell an integrated agency from one that merely claims to be?

Easy! Take its lid off! If, when you look down inside, you don't see the disciplines all lined up as profit centres, they are at least trying! The financial and economic dynamics which require profits to be made in a discipline-led way do not encourage integration. Without exceptional management, here you still have warring tribes jostling for victory. To offer and deliver truly integrated marketing, an agency handling the full spectrum will need not to care where the profit is made. This is quite hard for an agency, especially with conventional fee and charging systems. For them, the answers lie in new billing methods as well as structural reorganisation. Clients who are looking for genuine integration will need to be more flexible in their negotiation and accept changes in the way they compensate their agencies for work. As long as the deployment of the media makes a difference to their profits, then my inclination would be to steer clear of an agency as the sole provider of outside strategic marketing or corporate wisdom and counsel.

Frankly, any forward thinking agency or an agency group could take the lead with this – as long as they can overcome their own internal politics and prejudices. The important factor is not that they already have the skills within a group or that they have the cash to go on a buying spree. The most important ingredient of success is that they can find enough skilled people to operate across the disciplines without any bias for any particular one of them. Unfortunately, bias, as well as expertise and experience, have a habit of growing up together and lodging themselves firmly in the heads of the Elders, whereas, innocence and open-mindedness are often found only in those too young to be allowed to lead.

## How should Clients decide which agencies get what?

There are some ideas now in use which can be improved upon as you move into Customer-driven marketing. Let's take a typical arrangement at the moment. Suppose you're a company with four brands or product groups. Often each of these will have the freedom to choose their own agency; similarly each of those same groups will appoint, or less formally, buy regularly from, their own choice of secondary specialist agency, backed up or supported by a whole host of PR, direct marketing, sales promotion, research and design specialists.

In organisational terms, Clients seemed to have developed the people and the systems to deal with this, and when one considers the brand or product group issues, it often works well. However as we move into the 'brand behind the brand' and the need becomes greater for a consistent corporate voice, so such processes will break down or underperform. It makes no sense to have a corporate message diffused, distorted or interpreted countless different ways. It confuses the market and works badly for the company.

## A simple idea solves a complex problem

Shouting at the market in ten, 15 or 20 different voices just becomes one more dimension in the build up to the Communications Traffic Jam. There is a simple answer.

■ Customer-Driven Marketing

I have always taken the view that there are only three kinds of Customer: the existing Customer, the prospective Customer and the lapsed or past Customer. It is generally accepted and agreed that in terms of effectiveness from the marketing unit of currency, the highest return will come from existing Customers (typically, as we have already learned, a performance difference of some 500 – 1500 per cent) and the lowest return from prospects. However the second highest return comes from those so many people seem to overlook – or write off – the lapsed or past Customer.

Examining this, I have concluded that if – and only if – you are able to work with an integrated agency, the best way to divide the workload is by appointing them – across the product groups or brands – making them 'guardians of the relationship'.

## Vertical or horizontal slicing?

In Figure 14.1 'Vertical or Horizontal Slicing?' you can see on the vertical axis a corporate range of products and brands. The managers of each of these can fire off advertising communications or activities at will. This method of slicing the market makes good sense to the company and little or none to the Customer. It is essentially a product driven process favoured by product managers in product driven businesses. I call it vertical slicing.

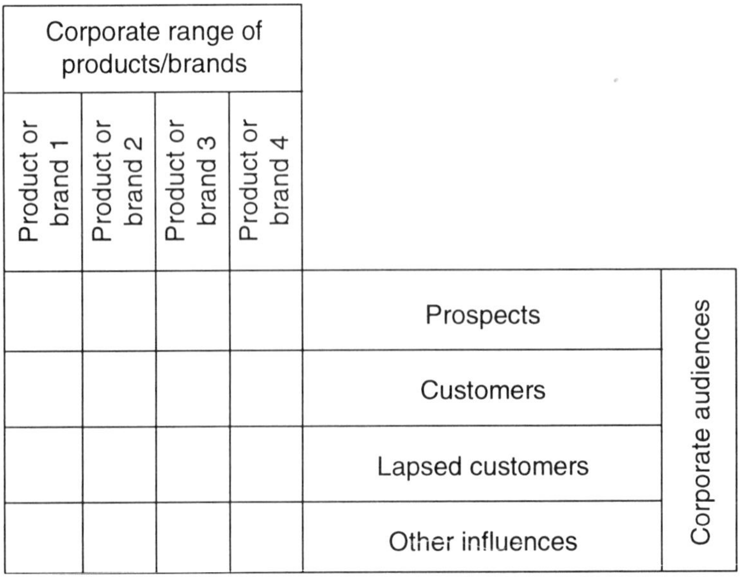

|  Corporate range of products/brands  |||||
| --- | --- | --- | --- | --- |
| Product or brand 1 | Product or brand 2 | Product or brand 3 | Product or brand 4 | |
| | | | | Prospects |
| | | | | Customers |
| | | | | Lapsed customers |
| | | | | Other influences |

(Corporate audiences)

**Figure 14.1** *Vertical or horizontal slicing?*

Horizontal slicing is my preferred method: here we divide the marketplace up by the nature of the relationship we currently have with each individual consumer or each individual organisation. This will nearly always be the first segment of any segmentation hierarchy or matrix. This is a Customer-driven process which will be the choice of Customer-driven businesses.

It is quite plainly pointless trying to decide the style, tone or content of any communication which respects relationships if you don't know what kind of relationship it is. Similarly, to keep those tones and values, dividing the remit of agencies by horizontal lines brings consistency and enables you to seek a choice of requisite agency skills to reflect the objectives you have for each agency group. They are themselves aligned to Customer groups where the relationships are in the same stage – prospecting and acquisition, growth and loyalty building or rescue and restoration. We'll come back to horizontal and vertical slicing again later in the chapter when other issues endorse the idea of the horizontal approach.

Casting your mind back to the thoughts expressed concerning the communications traffic jam, you can well understand that, if messages are confused before they leave and confused again as they leave the business, the result is going to be mayhem from the Customer's point of view. So, rather than have our communications disturbed and distorted, we need to find ways to improve their integrity.

There is no doubt that integration or fusion of the advertising, sales and Customer service messages is one very positive step forward. One of my Clients is a large company in the process of implementing integrated marketing country by country throughout Europe. There are many serious issues which arise in such large organisations, not the least of which is some structural awkwardness. For example, in this case, the Customer service team currently is to be found as part of their logistics team.

It must be realised that integrated communications, as a fundamental factor in the overall process of total communications management, are prerequisite to the concept of relationship marketing. However, the most common stumbling block I have seen is that the long-term objectives of relationship marketing, like so many quality issues, require agreement, acceptance and commitment at the very highest level. At the moment, awareness of the blossoming reimportance of relationship and integrated marketing is rarely understood, let alone recognised, among the board; therefore marketing directors, however committed they may be personally, can have great difficulty in carrying their colleagues along with them. Often only one, possibly two, of the board will truly appreciate what is at stake. It is no surprise therefore that the lead is being taken by those companies who already have either a marketer at the top or a healthily pro-marketing environment on the board. Good vision is cer-

■ Customer-Driven Marketing

tainly a useful lubricant to the right decisions here. Marketing miracles come most readily when an organisation gives their fullest commitment to it and, therefore, is no different to any quality initiative.

In the coming years, the influences which we have already discussed will push two options to the front. There is no doubt that the first of these is a compromise which will enable a quite workable face-lift to be carried out.

## Option One: More people

In order to deliver the new relationship style of Customer service – and therefore the intensity of staffing required to provide the optimum server/Customer ratio – marketers will have to restructure their front line (the array they display to their Customers). Supervision and monitoring of this extended, as it were, broadside exposure of their front line would be handled on a database; Customer communications of whatever type will be focused via, or in support of, the individual Customer servicer or Customer services team, but always through or acknowledged by a database.

This will lead to an increase in teams, in many ways structured in the style familiar to marketers, similar to those found inside advertising agencies: a triangular-shaped team with three or four levels. However, I described this as cosmetic and a compromise. And it is so. For on a short-term basis it will enable the Customer to feel as if he is getting more service. What is actually happening is the Customer is getting more attention. This is not a problem in itself, but still far short of what is needed for a truly effective relationship to develop. For such service teams are usually long on bonhomie and rhetoric but short on the authority and decision making capability that is needed.

So why is this a compromise? Why is it less likely to succeed? Consider this scenario. In comes a wealth of new communications technology. This is irresistible to people involved in Customer service. And, understandably, after all, a lot of the time the pressure to accept or adopt new-tech communications methods or media comes from the markets or Customers they serve.

Next let's fuel this with the certain knowledge that the easiest way to show a quick, or cosmetic, increase in Customer care or service is to communicate more, stay in touch, keep the Customer informed. This means, of course, that in order to make the necessary impression on Customers, more people in more departments will want to communicate more ways through more media. And if you're dealing with an organisation, more people will receive these communications across correspondingly more departments. Think how this becomes a recipe for confusion and irritation. Simply stir in the media and technology explosions we see happen-

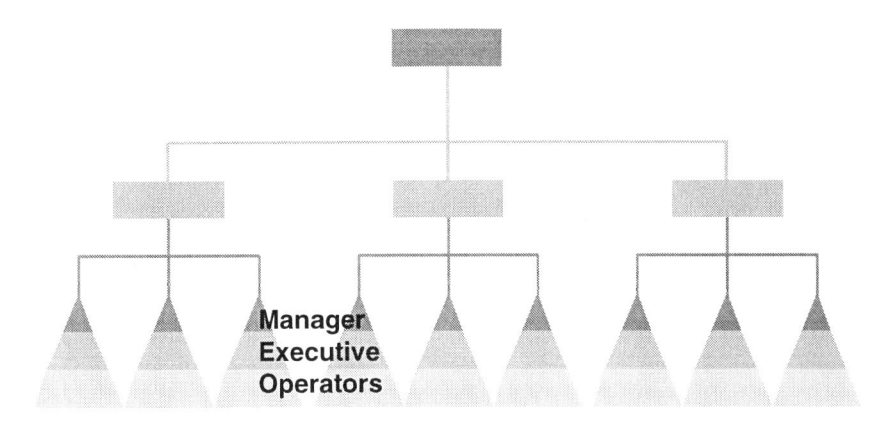

There's a new kind of client looking for a new kind of agency ■

**Manager**
**Executive**
**Operators**

**Figure 14.2** *The modified hierarchy – the micro-hierarchy within a hierarchy*

ing in parallel and bake well. Soon you'll have a perfect disaster in the making. It's all covered in that confection of the future – the Communications Traffic Jam!

## Option Two: More sense

Option One is only for those who want an interim measure to Option Two or those who are content with the cosmetic improvement. It is a bit

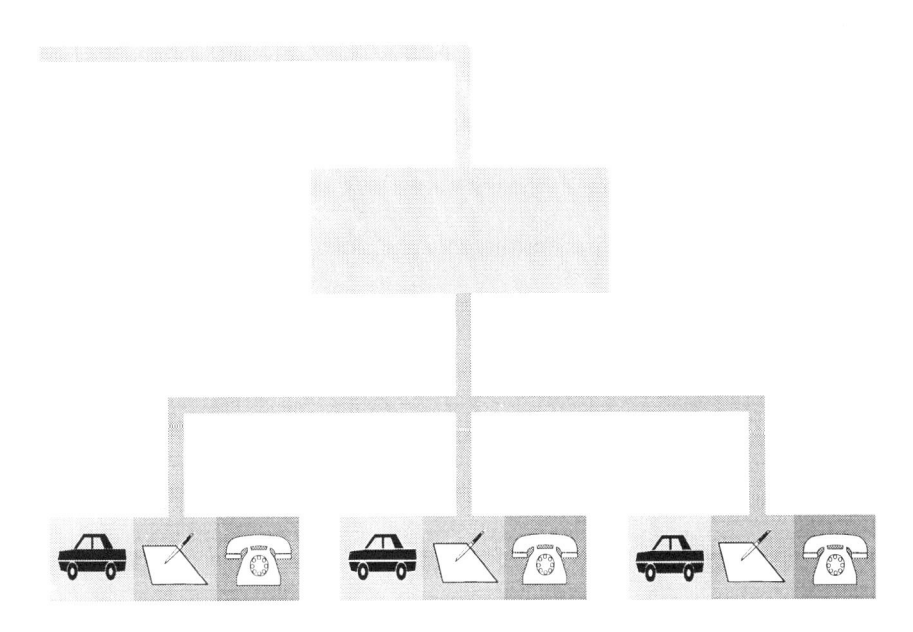

**Figure 14.3** *A common division of labour within a Customer service micro-hierarchy*

207

■ Customer-Driven Marketing

of a quick fix! Option Two is for those who want the real thing; but it does mean you must seek out suppliers who offer you integrated marketing services. Then appoint them as guardians of one of the three basic relationships. Reverting to my 'Three Kinds of Customer', you will see that in your forward marketing thrust, you are basically cultivating three corresponding categories of relationship as illustrated in Table 14.1.

**Table 14.1** Relationship styles and objectives

| Category | Style | Objective |
| --- | --- | --- |
| Prospects | Warming | Acquisition |
| Customers | Satisfying | Growth |
| Lapsed and past Customers | Restoring | Reconciliation |

To maintain the integrity of corporate voices, the responsibility for communications should be divided within these relationship objectives. Thus one agency might be appointed guardian of existing Customers; this agency will have demonstrated their ability to create powerful advertising and sales messages which respect the Customer, understand their needs and which speak with one corporate voice. As with the other two categories, this cuts across all brands, products or services. Only where there is no 'cross-talk' or cross-selling opportunity with brands would division of guardianship by brand be recommended.

This clearly suggests that the formal division between the disciplines (advertising, sales promotion, direct marketing and PR etc), running as they do in tightly defined alleys, must dissolve or at lease assume far less priority. The overall basket of media, and the uses to which those media are put, will fall along with the whole gamut of Customer service activities into a total communications management environment. There, with the marketing database as its core resource, the individual relationship with the Customer will take its rightful place as the driving force. This should provide a perfect culture for optimum Customer service levels and standards. In those companies where marketing and sales remain uneasy bed partners, such new thinking will be difficult to accept since they must clearly come together as one redefined effort.

So, the new picture will include fused sales, marketing and service teams also dividing their efforts into the three steps of acquisition, growth and reconciliation, each representing the full basket of products and services to Customers – even if one is selected at any give time for tactical, timing or other reasons.

Agencies must cease to divide themselves into the worn out departmental thinking of the 1960s, 1970s, 1980s and 1990s. What most affects their achievement for Clients is the weighting of the message and media, dependent upon which of the three objectives and relationships they have been given custody.

This is a necessary return to some of the ways of the past. However, this time it is imperative that the ability within agencies is there to deliver the specialist skills required across the board by today's marketer. This change will cause the development of very different agencies. With the added dimension of the Customer relationship as a specific briefed criterion of effectiveness it should breed a more professional, less cynical and less exploitative type of organisation. In the prospecting area, I suspect sales promotional techniques will continue to prevail, feeding on the human weaknesses which have been their diet for so long. Thus this particular style of agency may be the nearest to the current style.

Of course, many agencies will claim to be master of all three styles; indeed, they may well prove this capability. However, my suspicion is that the styles – warming, satisfying and restoring – may become, as time passes and the specialisations build expertise, very different in practice. I believe you will witness this change – indeed we are already experiencing it. Failure to move to horizontal slicing of corporate audiences will be a real miracle inhibitor, as you will read later. Integrated marketing communications will not work well with the old product driven concept of marketing.

One of the points raised by reorganising this way is what happens to the brand and, as I mentioned earlier, the increasingly significant 'brand behind the brand'? I accept that this difficulty, creating cohesion and harmony between the work of different agencies and other suppliers, still exists. However, my belief is that any lack of cohesion in brand delivery by your agencies is much less discernible to Customers if it takes place at the time of natural shifts in the relationship stage than it is if it happens constantly during the relationship while I am bombarded by communications from various product streams.

Returning to Peter Thompson at Grey Integrated in the UK, he told me how, worldwide, Grey are tackling this with a template for developing what they describe, and indeed have trademarked, as Brand Character. The three core strands are Product, Positioning and Personality. Grey will work with the senior management of a business to develop a set of uniform key corporate beliefs or goals and they will facilitate this debate until there is unity of understanding and commitment from the group. From this a short set of words or a statement is created which defines, describes or gives meaning to the Brand Character. Peter told me that this will enable the agency to communicate the brand with 'one single spirit', its very essence. Further to bring this to life and give shape, dimension and feel, Grey often accompany this with a video or film which is made especially to capture that 'spirit'. The 'spirit', Peter tells me, is

■ Customer-Driven Marketing

just as valid for examining every corporate strategy and all the corporate decisions of a Customer-driven business as it is for creating marketing communications.

Garth Hallberg of Ogilvy & Mather (O&M) in the US relates how a similar concept is being used by his agency on a worldwide basis – they call it BrandPrint. Similarly, he describes how the BrandPrint gives 'a distillation of the brand in words and images, down to its rock-bottom truth'. However, whereas Grey Integrated strap their Brand Character to an integrated marketing process, O&M's has been developed as a companion tool to another O&M invention – 'differential marketing'. I got the impression that the O&M concept was a repackaging of some fundamentally very sound thinking, but I couldn't find a great deal of difference between the 'new' O&M concept of profit segmentation and the value/profit hierarchies used by mail order businesses 30 years ago. So it seems I'm not the only one suggesting we are going back to the future! At least these days we have the data and computing power to enable the data analysis and manipulation to be done – and, when it is done, for an affordable price in a realistic time.

The more I listen to some current marketing 'experts' (sorry, Mr Hallberg!), the more I begin to feel that we have reached a point where, to some extent, we are just trying to make the blindingly obvious – common sense – more and more complex. We don't have to. Technology and electronic media will cause enough complexities of their own. The whole notion of Customer-driven marketing is simplicity itself. For all the simplicity, in today's increasingly competitive business environment, it is none the less still hard to achieve. Unlike many of my peer group, I have never had the luxury of a David Ogilvy quote on any of my book jackets. I guess I never will now!!

## In comes the new wave

The problems and opportunities with communication of the brand exist whether you use the old methods or the new. What will change a great deal however is the marketing business itself and how advertisers and marketers relate to it and the demands they make of it. There will surely be a new wave Client needing a new wave agency.

The heydays of many of the distinct or discrete marketing disciplines may soon be over. Will we see the death of direct marketing, the demise of PR or the end of sales promotion? I don't think so! There will of course be many special cases or smaller Clients who will continue to use the resources of marketing services as we know them now. But in some years' time the serious spenders will have gone back to the 1950s and once again appointed their agencies to do it all. These agencies are being born right now. They are the result of new ideas, new thinking, new

Customer needs and desires, new technology and a new environment.

## The problems of promotionally led prospecting and acquisition

Later we will reflect together on loyalty building and discuss what makes Customers loyal. If one thing has become very clear to me during my work over the last few years, it's this. Some prospects have a much greater propensity or potential to become loyal than others. Attracting the higher loyalty potential prospects is greatly influenced by the kind of marketing which stimulated their interest in the first place, by the proposition which is put and by the way the sale is made. It is discussed elsewhere more fully, but it is a bit like that old expression 'You are what you eat'! In other words, if you advertise using, for example, heavily discounted prices, then you attract people shopping for discounts. If you use heavy sales promotion or give-aways, similarly, you build a clientele of those who respond to promotions or free gifts. Few companies understand the full implication of this and the vast majority I see are actually using methods which attract low loyalty potential new business to them and then subjecting these new Customers to loyalty schemes which fail to tap a potential which isn't there in the first place! No marketing miracles there.

Yet by understanding the notion of lifetime values, basic profiling techniques can be used to shift your marketing to the higher potential ground. This is miracle territory. Here you can flourish. Here you can begin to grow a future for yourself which is rich and abundant.

## What of the product manager?

I suspect that the days of the function of product manager as we know it are numbered. The days of the market or 'customer group' manager are beginning to be realised. For while the product manager usually has a corporate orientation to the market, the other has a market orientation to the Customer. This is the stuff of new wave Clients. With a bank of product managers, Customer communications lack flow, cohesion and integrity for the Customer. For each product manager has his own priorities – product priorities. With a bank of market or Customer managers, each has his own priorities too – but they are always Customer priorities.

In this chapter it became clear that a new wave Client is emerging and this will demand radical changes in the services and skills of their advertising agencies. And more...

- Three decades, the 1960s through to the 1980s, saw agencies specialise more and more in television and Press. A capable and increasingly strong marketing services industry grew up behind them. This led to

■ Customer-Driven Marketing

the Battle of the Budget, a phenomenon which defies the Client's best interest.
- Customer-driven marketing, in its aim to focus on relationships, requires the return of the one stop shop, but this time with highly developed skills, a marketing agency which understands integration.
- Agencies do not have a good track record of impartiality and unbiased advice. Clients may decide to take the strategic counselling to more impartial advisers. Benefit in this instance will derive from involving the agency in the work of developing the strategy.
- You can use integrated marketing processes without necessarily requiring them to deliver relationship marketing: you cannot, however, fully deliver relationship marketing without integrated marketing.
- To offer and deliver truly integrated marketing an agency handling the full spectrum of disciplines will need to operate without concern as to where the money is made.
- Integration will become a most important goal of agencies. Clients who find satisfactorily integrated services available will use new methods to apportion the work; one of the most effective ways will be through appointing them guardians of a relationship, thus harmonising the objectives of both organisations.
- To enable integrated and relationship marketing – and for apportioning work to agencies – it is better to switch to horizontal slicing of the audience as opposed to vertical slicing.
- Marketing work will become increasingly specialised in the three areas which recognise the three types of Customer: prospective, existing and lapsed.
- Customer service teams face two options: the first is to increase manpower to provide a better Customer/servicer ratio. However this is usually only capable of cosmetic, short-term gains. The second option is to rationalise the sales and marketing forces in the same way as the new agencies. This method provides powerful, sensitive marketing with integrity of corporate and brand voice.
- Companies with a marketer at the top or where a pro-marketing environment exists on the board will make these changes fastest and will steal a valuable lead on their opposition.
- Few companies appreciate how to distinguish between high potential and low potential Customers in respect of loyalty, and equally few understand how this can be used in the acquisition of new business. There is a direct and powerful link between the nature of your marketing and the new Customers you attract.
- The function of product manager could soon become quite rare. They will be replaced by market managers whose priorities are Customer priorities.

# 15

# Marketing: the new objectives

Customer-driven marketing – the notion of driving marketing by quality issues – is different to quantity marketing. It's harder for a start. It requires greater degrees of professionalism, better use of intelligence, more understanding and more information.

Providing the information is perhaps the easiest part of all of these – databases to the rescue! However, professionalism, intelligence and understanding require not only that we do our job better, but that we do a better job. In other words the new Customer-driven quality ethos must attach to both what we do and the way that we do it. This means it is essential that we build quality through defined objectives in both those areas. Conventional management techniques already provide us with the means to achieve these ends. However, I did find myself in a project definition meeting the other day which was addressing radical product change for a Client in the financial services field. 'Why', I wondered to myself, 'do we set about instigating or developing change in the same old way?' It's a question I haven't satisfactorily answered for myself yet!

The major channels which will help us to boost quality will be our personnel selection processes, training, the correct formulation of job descriptions, corporate or departmental structures, and the reward and appraisal systems. Four of these in particular will be powerful in effective refocusing for quality goals. They are selection, training, structures and reward systems; the latter two so much so that you will find them covered in more detail in Chapters 21 and 22. However the accent that quality places on recruitment and training needs thought in two contexts.

## Quality loves people people

'People who need people are the luckiest people in the world', the song goes. And it's absolutely true. If you're looking to create an environment which cultivates relationships, so you will have to ensure that you have the right people up front. Yet so often in life you find a dragon as your doctor's receptionist. These are people who seem to confuse officious with efficient. They build up defences against Customers. You see them in department stores, restaurants and in countless of the classic hierarchies. Yet, buried in the throbbing heart of many corporate epicentres you often find a one-man dynamo, a person who knows everyone, likes everyone, talks to everyone, makes friends with everyone and who seems to be the social catalyst of the whole building. This is the natural person to be out front making friends of the Customers.

It is more necessary than ever to consider each person's ability to relate to people as a criterion in their work which will, after all, be the business of building and managing relationships. This is not simply the question of smiling, being nice and saying the right thing, although that seems to give many businesses a hard enough problem. It is a question of understanding the Customer, looking at the longer term and creating the kind of atmosphere in which trust, loyalty, respect and even affection can develop. The chemistry between the individuals will be more vital, the closer and longer the relationship becomes.

The impact on recruitment here is clear; we must seek out and favour the kinds of people who can do that best. And, for those many companies in the process of restructuring, breaking down their hierarchies and flattening out, this gives them a hard task. The temptation in such cases is to take the middle management and redeploy them at the front end thus, as IBM did in the early 1990s, increasing the number of people available to deal with Customers in one context or another. Yet the fact is that many people who have been obsessed, sometimes for years, with the internal workings of the company may have become corporate introverts. That is to say the corporation, to whose welfare they have been dedicated for so long, assumes greater importance to them than the well-being or goodwill of the Customer.

Consider how this affects them. For example if you look at the difference in approaches towards a late payer between someone in the accounts department and someone on the sales team, you'll appreciate my comment. One sees the Customer as a lawbreaker dedicated to withholding money which rightly belongs with their employer and which causes cashflow problems; the other is trying to tread on eggshells, knowing he has to get the money in, but not wanting to risk the next order by raising awkward subjects or by threatening. Neither one of these is wrong; and yet they both are. They have to get the money in. So it is in both cases right objectives, wrong mentality.

In relationship building the mentality of the individuals towards the Customer is critical. To some extent this can be dealt with by training, but inevitably also one is looking for the actual capacity and propensity within that individual to relate to other human beings – Customers; the most important kinds of human being there are! Thus we learn that the delivery of quality to Customers starts with quality people. Quality means not just how they perform against conventional targets, but how well they perform in their human interactions; how good they are at building and sustaining relationships that work.

Effectively all of this tells you that many of the staff you would ideally like to redeploy while restructuring may not have the necessary people skills, even though they have experience of your business in abundance. People skills can be enhanced by training but they cannot easily and successfully be implanted or bestowed on someone who just doesn't have them in the first place. If somewhere cannot be found for such staff where they will not be damaging or inhibiting, they must be compassionately assisted in moving on to new pastures.

## Increased training levels

The biggest problem for sales and marketing people in these new flatter structures is that the training ground (previously, to a large extent, in climbing the corporate hierarchy) has disappeared just at a time when the new objectives require even greater levels of training.

Thus it will be important to ensure that workloads and timetables leave adequate time for training and education; that the resources, facilities and budget are available; and that the motivation is there for the training to be accepted and adopted by those who participate.

## Relationships not transactions

To a great extent quantity objectives have forced marketing to become a function which concentrates on trying to create a number of transactions. The new desire is to establish the requisite number of Customer relationships which will in turn create the sales throughput. Thus, if your marketing is to become Customer-driven, you will have to understand that your work must create the means for such relationships to grow and prosper and that the transactions will result. Understanding how this affects your business is important. Look at the locations, the atmosphere, the staff, the facilities and the circumstances in which your Customers will find themselves, and question whether you have created a forum for transactions or relationships. Also, take a look at the processes and techniques you use.

■ Customer-Driven Marketing

For example, how do you use sales promotion? Many marketers find that the more aggressive the techniques used in generating new Customer transactions, the less substance the business generated has for the future. Let's consider this along with some other interesting facts...

## What makes advertising work?

While considering the new objectives of the marketer, let us not become totally obsessed with quality. Let's think about quantity too. In direct marketing, the media and style of so many campaigns enables you to test quite scientifically and indeed quite economically all manner of variations to see which perform best. Although, on discovering this, lots of advertisers get quite carried away and start testing very trivial variants such as the colour of the letter signature – which in most cases will make no difference at all or so little it is barely perceptible. They soon learn the test of experience! This tells you that big things make big differences and little things make little differences. Aha! But what is a big thing? In the creative category, for example I, like many other direct marketers, proved conclusively many years ago that advertisement headlines generally work better under photographs than above them. Yet, strangely, the advertising industry persists, as it has for years, in preferring the reverse notion.

One particularly interesting set of statistics which I use as a discussion point in many conferences is those gathered by a leading international direct marketing agency through a most comprehensive analysis which they carried out. They were trying to establish which factors most affected response rates and in what proportions. Here are their findings:

response device, 20 per cent;
creativity, 35 per cent;
timing, 100 per cent;
the offer, 200 per cent;
the list, 500 per cent.

I understand these figures were gained by measuring the best and worst situations. Thus, for example, if a mailing with a badly conceived reply device would pull an index of 100 and a mailing identical but with a good device 120, the result was a response uplift of 20 per cent. The results were taken from many, many efforts, and the agency concerned was convinced of the validity of the results. To be clear about their findings, the first figure suggests that you will get a response improvement of typically 20 per cent (ie from, say, 2 per cent to 2.4 per cent) simply by thoughtful and informed attention to detail on the reply card or response device you are using. From experience, I know this to be so; and those in the financial services or insurance fields where applications can tend to be quite long and complex will also know this to be the case.

The next one down, however, is something of a poser. Can it really be true that the total difference between indifferent and stunning creativity should be just 35 per cent? Whenever I discuss this with creative teams they either take umbrage or just don't believe this figure. It does take a little while for creative sensitivities to work it through. Yet it is interesting that, according to these figures, correct timing is almost exactly three times more important than the creative work. Perhaps many sales people will find that one easy to relate to. Yet the offer or proposition is a remarkable six times more powerful at making the advertising effective than the creative. To be fair, especially in the direct marketing context, many would argue that the two are inextricably woven together. However, when you think of the number of advertisements which carry a message but don't make a proposition or offer, it is easy to see how underrated this simple concept is.

The last figure is interesting; it suggests that finding the right audience for your ad is two-and-a-half times more effective than the proposition, five times more critical than timing and an astounding 15 times more important than the creative.

This surely must question the current method of choosing an ad agency and the enormous priority given to creative skills in the selection process. On the face of it, here we see the relevance of their abilities in the creative process reduced to a relative also-ran.

## How do you choose your agency?

Rather than keep fellow proponents of the creative discipline in misery, let me say straight away that the figures lie! There's more to it than meets the eye.

Yet before we burst the balloon, let us ponder a while on what I consider to be a most significant thinking point here. When pitching for business, agencies are rarely asked to give more than a cursory run down of their media or strategic or planning skills. Because it's the most fun and, to many the most interesting, absorbing and entertaining, creativity rules. So in case the following should be thought to be dashing to the rescue of creativity, may I also make the plea for true weighting to be given to the other skills. Important as creativity is, it is certainly not all important.

## Creativity works to more than the sale

The catch, if that is what you can call it, in the figures is that they relate, in direct marketing terms, to what actually affects the response – and the response alone. They place no value at all on the pure advertising effect of the campaigns. Since most direct marketing and certainly most classical advertising has an effect on brand and corporate values, which of course are largely to the credit of the creativity, we must generally give it a better rating than 35 per cent suggests. However, I feel obliged to say that, in my experience, this is none the less one of the most over-priced and wasteful areas of the marketing world and needs a great deal of tightening up. For, as Raymond Rubicam, co-founder of Young and Rubicam and one of the forefathers of the international agency scene, once so succinctly put it, 'The object of advertising is to sell goods. It has no other justification worth mentioning.' Effectively that statement, although made many years ago, remains true; however, with the increased value that Customer-driven marketing places on brand and corporate strength and loyalty building, we will once again see greater strategic and tactical emphasis placed on these aspects of marketing.

## Creating sales that stick

I've always been a great believer in the idea that a first sale is only complete when the second sale is set up. If you feel the same way, you may have experienced a phenomenon which is well accepted in direct marketing and well known but rather less frequently worried about in selling.

The more promotion you use to close a sale, the higher the incidence of, first, the sale failing to complete as Customers cancel (or perhaps gather the courage or self-resolve to withdraw); secondly, the more worries, complaints and attempts to retract one gets during the 'buyer's remorse' period; and, thirdly, the less likely it is that the Customer will proceed to a second or third sale eventually leading to optimum lifetime values.

On a rather pedantic technical note it should be said that some direct marketers would argue that a 'flimsy' low commitment first sale is better than no sale since it gives the opportunity to create a more solid basis through the ensuing dialogue. This could be generally correct. However, the point to which I would like to draw particular attention is that the logic for the phenomenon also holds a moral. The more manipulated a Customer has been to pressure the sale through, the less receptive they are to the second approach. Moreover, companies that adopt heavy or continuous highly promotional methods tend to attract the kind of Customer who responds to them. By definition these will often be the kind of 'scavengers' who have less loyalty to give and who, therefore, will be more easily moved on by a better offer or bigger discount from anyone else. These people can collect premiums, gifts and incentives like squirrels gather nuts.

If your business survives on such people and can stand the cost of marketing to them or can sustain the high level of expensively gained conquest business, then this will not trouble you. You are a 'high activity marketer'. It is only when you crave marketing miracles that you will start to consider new thinking. Then you will want to understand the costs of not working on Customer loyalty: and it is at that moment that you might take fright. This is an issue we will deal with shortly.

If you want to practise Customer-driven marketing and be in the business of building sales through building relationships, you will appreciate that less will make more in the end. You must become a 'high focus marketer'. High activity marketers use exploitation selling. It is an aggressive process which bribes, cajoles and tempts the prospect with lots of 'goodies'! But the same 'goodies' used to tempt the less likely into buying will often be more effectively used as loyalty rewards or benefits.

## Apples don't grow on companies

When you consider how to add quality to your organisation's marketing it needs to be appreciated that marketing businesses and apple trees don't have too much in common. Apple trees can regularly produce quantity and quality. Businesses have been obsessed with the delivery of quantity for so long that quality goals will cause them stress and require much effort and commitment from all concerned. However, the return of quality objectives to marketing yield a benefit for the company which becomes a real treasure chest of an asset. By using its Customer-driven marketing process across its four dimensions, it engenders stable, durable relationships which, enhanced by quality products and services, will lock Customers, staff and suppliers together around the corporate core.

When one decides to incorporate such objectives they must be built in on a formal basis which enables success to be monitored and analysed. Although many of these objectives will be philosophical and cultural, it is still essential that they can be controlled and measured.

In thinking about the new objectives of the marketer we have considered:

- Customer-driven marketing is harder than conventional quantity marketing. It seeks greater professionalism, intelligence, understanding of the Customer and information. Of these, information may prove the easiest using database solutions.
- Quality building systems, techniques and procedures must affect both what we do and the way we do it. This will place greater needs on, and challenge conventions in relation to, staff recruitment and selection, training resources, structures and reward systems.
- Quality marketing practices place increased values on the human interaction, chemistry and involvement since they are less focused on the generation of transactions and more on the construction of relationships.

## Customer-Driven Marketing

- Companies who are restructuring to provide increased levels of Customer involvement should bear in mind when redeploying staff that they will need people skills in abundance.
- New flatter company structures, missing the hierarchical ascension, have effectively gained much, but lost a valuable training ground with a proven track record. It's been used since time immemorial. Thus replacement training opportunities and resources must be made available.
- Marketers must create forums which cultivate relationships rather than simply generate transactions.
- In the above respect, marketers will need to adjust their objectives to require less promotion and build more solid business. A business that uses exploitation processes attracts a less loyal type of Customer who can be more easily tempted away by others. Quality marketers enjoy longer lasting, more profitable, more satisfying relationships with their Customers.
- In choosing ad agencies, the value of creativity in generating business is less than in image, corporate and brand building. When selecting an agency, their ability to identify and reach markets is increasingly valuable. However, the value of the creative input will continue as the need for more loyalty to the brand and the company increases.
- Companies who appreciate and use Customer-driven marketing concepts build Customer loyalty as an asset for their business. However, to succeed in implementing quality techniques, companies must be sure that they are adopted on a formal basis, and that such new cultural and philosophical objectives must be set, monitored, analysed and rewarded.

# 16

# The shepherd? He works in sales

I predicted earlier that the practice of selling has a lot of change to make; however, in writing this chapter, I am aware it needs to be sensitively handled. There is a danger that many groups of sales people might be alienated because they interpret the comments I am about to make as, at best critical, at worst, offensive. This would be completely counterproductive, and sales and marketing should be totally harmonious processes. However, there are many changes already taking place which dictate a change in selling style. By implication the proposal of new methods seems to criticise the old ones; in this case that is true. The old ways were appropriate for their time. They are not now. This is a point which may become clearer when you consider the Three Generations of Selling.

At first glance, to a sales person who has matured during the 1970s and 1980s especially, this view of the future might seem a little lacking in aggression. Again, that's true. The sales style that goes with Customer-driven marketing is softer. It's assertive rather than aggressive; anxious to serve the company's own best interests through serving their Customer; accepting that the rewards take longer to build, but are greater when they come.

Although I describe the selling style as softer, the new selling methods are harder to achieve. They require long-term commitment from the top and selfless dedication to the Customer by all the individuals concerned. To be clear, I am not suggesting that all sales people and organisations will change to these new methods. I expect to see plenty of all three generations around in the future. However, I expect the new style to predominate over the timespan which this book covers. But some organisations will prefer to stay with the methods they know, the familiar

■ Customer-Driven Marketing

ways that have served them well. Others will move ahead with time, learning the newer, more caring processes and appreciating the stability and value this will add to their company, their career and their life. Customers definitely prefer the newer methods and this may indeed provide the greatest impetus for change.

## The three generations of selling

As you look back over the past decades, perhaps remembering some of the strategies we saw in Tables 8.1, 8.2 and 8.3 covering that time on pages 124–5, it becomes clear that the business of selling did not escape the helter-skelter down the quantity route. In fact during the eras of mass production and mass marketing, it would be fair to say that selling was in the front line. As the quantity target pressures built up, it was the refinement of sales techniques and promotion – the ability to manipulate markets and exploit sales opportunities to a greater degree – which carried both the greatest workload and the greatest responsibility. It was not uncommon in many companies to see the marketing department reduced from its strategic and principled role, to a mere inventor of constant merchandising, promotional and incentive programmes. It is no wonder that the infamous idea of marginal costing sprang to popularity in these times.

These were days when the Customer is king was a means to an end: the end being the heavily disguised truth that the product was actually king. When you glance down the 1960s column on the tables in Chapter 8 you can clearly see the facts there: a growth mission for all products; random product lines and products; competing on product features; pricing based on cost; generalised sales forces; heavy advertising and hard selling. But look at the second line of Table 8.1 which starts 'Product orientation', becoming 'Market orientation' developing to 'Customer/competitor/channel orientation'. So be it!

## The first generation of selling

As we move through the 1990s, any lingering doubt that we live in a 'benefits' society will fade. We buy things for what they do for our lifestyle. In the 1960s and early 1970s we were deeply embedded in a 'features' society. The ads for cars carried checklists inviting you to compare feature for feature. We switched from black and white television to the newly featured colour. In the 20 post-war years across the world we came from scarce availability to overloaded markets groaning with products that needed pumping down the distribution channels with great effort and energy. Eventually many markets moved into glut. The consumer revelled as prices dropped and gradually we saw the two-car family, a television in several rooms and the dishwasher. It could be argued that what I describe as the first generation of selling was not the first at all. It developed during the age of glut; a natural evolution from the heavy advertising, heavy selling time. I call it the first generation because it was the predecessor of the following generations as surely as ape preceded man.

In searching for a word to describe the style of selling of this era, the word 'muscular' comes to mind and seems to fit admirably. To be sold to was almost to be press-ganged. Lessons in selling were given by guru figures who presented themselves to avaricious hundreds of life assurance sales people worshipping them as if they were indeed some new god; masters of their universe; kings of the silver tongue and the smooth psychology that left a Customer with no more 'No's'. So the only result was 'Yes'. Conquest. The commission register rings up another sale.

When you consider the language of this generation it was aggressive and, in its literal sense, offensive. They 'attacked' a market. Their whole modus operandi was military. Of course, it led to some jolly good annual sales conferences. Great praise was heaped upon the sales person who browbeat the most Customers to take the most goods. But nobody stopped to think how the Customer felt about all this. Why bother? The sale was everything. The commission cheque was mere confirmation that winning the great sales race was what life was all about.

It was all very simple in the days of the first generation. You sold product and people bought its production; or if you were a consumer, its features. We bought lawn-mowers because they cut lawns; pop-up toasters because they popped up; copiers because they copied; typewriters because they typed. Gradually, through the latter part of the 1970s and into the 1980s, a new generation was born.

## The second generation of selling

This was the time when selling started to deal with the notion of added-value. Those who had learned that competitive discounting led to a war of attrition turned their attention to increasing Customer satisfaction and looking beyond the product.

The five-year warranty and extended service packages were invented. Computers came with software and games. Televisions (and just about every other domestic appliance possible!) came with infra-red remotes. 'Have a nice day' came to Europe. Those who bought copiers because they copied bought them now because they copied faster, collated, printed front and back, on plain paper and came with a service contract. Those who bought typewriters because they typed bought something entirely new. It was called a word processor. It was absolutely useless, unless, of course, you bought the added-value package. That gave you the equipment plus a training programme. And as a result, now, one

■ Customer-Driven Marketing

word processor operator could do the work of two or three typists. But only with the training.

Suddenly the added-value age was upon us. It sold the product but with the skills that helped you to get the best out of it. Suddenly what Customers were buying was no longer the product. It was increased productivity.

The selling style for this generation I call 'cupped hands'. For many consumers, added-value brought the promise of better service. However, in this generation it was a fairly cosmetic operation. It culminated in the seed corn of the quality age. Hotels started to put photographs of their management in the lobby. Name badges became the order of the day. Banks allowed their tellers to smile. The shopping mall was discovered in Europe. The Customer mistook this patronising lip-service to service for the real thing and was momentarily content. Hip organisations trained their operators to answer 'Good Morning. Thank you for calling the Hayling Island Post House. Sharon speaking. How may I help you?' Telephone companies announced record profits! The Customer service campaign – the non-thinking person's answer to *In Search of Excellence* – was under way. However, the thinking man and woman were at work looking into the way genuine change needed to happen beneath the cosmetic, the veneer. And they found a miracle waiting to happen. As so often seems the case, it had a problem attached! However, without solving the problem, the next generation could not happen.

## Preparing for the new age of selling

I remember sitting with a sales manager of a Client company. He had been with the business for nearly 30 years. The vast majority of that time he had been on the sales side of the business and for some years he had led the sales team at one of the top selling branches in the business. I was there to give a talk to his team and their support staff about 'the new way' being the style and culture shift the company was making to bring their practices into line with the Customer philosophy as set out in their mission statement. As he summed up at the end, he turned to me and, in front of his team, said, 'I agree with every single word that's been said here today. And...' he turned back to face his assembled team, '..And that's why I'm going to need help from all of you. I know the old way like the back of my hand. I've been the best or second or third best in this company every year for damn near two decades. As I've been doing the old stuff the longest, I reckon these new ideas will take a while to become second nature to me. So I need your help to make sure that I make them happen. And you need mine. So we're in it together. Just like normal!'

Our friend had raised a very moot point. He had realised that as a sales manager he had the dilemma of being simultaneously the person who had to build conviction, commitment to, and skills in, the new culture and style of selling whilst also being the team member who was most entrenched in the old ways. The last 20 years of his working life had constantly reinforced and confirmed that he was succeeding by getting it right and by being good at selling. Now, suddenly, he was to become, for his team, the changemaster of something new and different. I knew what he was thinking as we had talked earlier. His unspoken question was this: 'I know it sounds right. But will it work?' Doubt is an uneasy place from which to lead change.

## How do many sales managers get to be managers?

Many sales managers get where they are by proving themselves to be good sales people. Over a consistent period of time they outsell the others in their branch or area and so they become the natural candidate for elevation. In recognition of their ability to sell, they are rewarded with a harder job still, promoted to do something they know little or nothing about – management!

Many people argue against this system, saying that you lose your best sales people while, at the same time, creating a poor inexperienced manager. Suddenly, they say, the sales superhero has to transform from a self-motivated individualist to a team motivated team player; from an action centred doer to a sensitive teacher and coach; from an outdoor king of the road to a desk-bound, paper-pushing administrator.

Right. Right. Wrong. In that order. Yes, a team player ... better still, a team leader. Yes, a coach and trainer. But desk bound? An administrator? Paper pusher? Only if something is radically, radically wrong.

## From master sales person to mentor, motivator and manager

Those who criticise the notion of top sales performers becoming sales managers seem to make a fair point. Yet, if they're right, why do so many, many companies go on doing it? Why do so many sales directors keep choosing them? Why do CEOs keep approving it?

The answer is because, in many cases, it works. It works because top sales people are usually bright, intelligent and people people. Such men and women like new challenges and can learn. But most importantly they can sell themselves and their ideas. This is one of the greatest characteristics of good leadership.

However, the good and effective sales managers must quickly catch hold of the value of strong and powerful leadership, and what, in today's management culture, 'strong and powerful leadership' means. Tomorrow's sales manager will have to support their team in the 'new ways' and lead by example.

Leadership in today's climate is about recognising just how much of the management task is in the mentor and motivator roles. And it's about realising how very little lies in telling people what to do. Instead of telling people what to do, we help them to know what to do. We help them to acknowledge and understand their own successes and failures. We help them to find their true potential. We support, counsel, encourage, demonstrate and coach.

Not many of those old-fashioned sales leaders would recognise this kind of language. Look at the last few words of that extract again – 'support, counsel, encourage, demonstrate and coach'. It's rather different to the ways of the past. And, unfortunately, as I have pointed out earlier, many of the people – and I don't just refer to sales managers here, but all senior sales, advertising and marketing people – who have to make the decision for this change and lead it through are those self-same individuals who climbed the ladder using their old skills! It's catch-22! Those who can make it happen are leading us into...

## The third generation of selling

It had to happen. If you return again to the 1990s column of Tables 8.1, 8.2 and 8.3 (pages 124–5), you can see the evidence stacking up before you:

- niche or customised marketing
- implementation excellence
- customer/competitor/channel evaluation
- product line rationalisation
- strategic mission for each product
- multiplexed sales force
- competing on quality, design and service
- priced against Customers' perceived value
- the product of strategic alliances.

We're undoubtedly heading into the age of individualisation and back to relationship values. But beware, for in both the consumer and business markets, the Customer's expectation has changed and so, to a degree, has what they're out there buying.

Take the business market. In previous generations we saw the typewriter become the word processor; and we saw how it was the skills that went with that which gave it the added value of increased productivity for the Customer. Here, in the third generation, the seller and the buyer join together to decide what the buyer needs and how best it can be supplied. Thus the company who sold the word processor would now sit down with their Customer to decide together how the seller's skills can best be made to work together to fill the buyer's needs for the future.

Thus our word processor manufacturer might find out that his client, as a publisher, is looking to computerise his typesetting so that it can run from keyboarding as raw journalistic input, be checked and edited by a third party, then be moved down the line to typesetting and page make-up and on again to print. The publisher is thus looking to buy the seller's know-how – the equipment or hardware becoming a secondary part of the whole process.

## Is what you are selling what people want to buy?

For more and more markets, the product is becoming a know-how product. Oddly, since know-how is being sold and ideas, therefore, are being bought, it seems to me that selling's evolutionary process has finally arrived at a conclusion where, possibly in many markets, the two have become the same for the very first time. Both represent opportunity. That is what is being sold and that is what is being bought (Table 16.1).

This concept of know-how as a product is fast gaining recognition in many business markets and in certain consumer markets such as financial services. It has an irrefutable logic. Which makes more sense to you? Consider the choices:

1. the machine itself – a first generation product;
2. the machine tailored to your specification or with the added value of skill opportunities to get the best out of it; or
3. the machine designed to do a better job for you tomorrow because it was the result of a team effort by the brains at the buying company with the brains at the manufacturer?

So this is the first part of the age of individualisation where the third generation of selling excels. Yet individualisation promises more – it promises recognition, and a level of personal service which is both enticing and captivating.

Table 16.1 *The three generations of selling*

| PHASE | TECHNIQUE | WHAT YOU SELL | WHAT THEY BUY |
|---|---|---|---|
| **FIRST GENERATION** | Selling | The product | Production |
| **SECOND GENERATION** | Added-value selling | The product with skills | Productivity |
| **THIRD GENERATION** | Multi-discipline marketing | Know-how (opportunity) | Ideas (opportunity) |

■ Customer-Driven Marketing

### The new strength of the retailer

It is this area, highly personalised, all-embracing service, that I see as being the big growth area for the retailer of the future. Again, like so many aspects of TQM, it requires courage and conviction to commit to it as a direction.

A Mintel report, 'Retailing and the Shopper' produced at the gateway to the 1990s, looked specifically at Britain but drew some conclusions which can certainly be projected into 'Western' Europe and in some respects almost globally.

They foresaw that the 1990s would see a dramatic return in the high streets and shopping malls of better choice, service and quality. A director, Frank Fletcher, was quoted as saying that 'In the 1980s the Customer has been King in name only. But the consumer can still only buy what the retailers let them.' That's a pretty powerless King! He continued, 'In the 1990s, the stores that truly make the Customer King will be the stores that succeed. Life will not be easy for the retailer ... who will have to work very hard indeed to persuade shoppers to part with their money.' This was a problem exacerbated no doubt by the richer, more affluent, well-equipped consumer facing a boring row of parity products and less real need to spend.

This promises an interesting trend back to the specialist or expert retailer who can demonstrate a discernible difference through choice or through service. It's a definite arena for relationships rather than transactions.

### Do retailing and niche marketing go together?

This is an interesting question to which I have no doubt whatsoever that the answer is 'yes'. However, the larger and more widespread the retailer's product range, the more difficult niche marketing would appear to be. This is a fallacy, probably most widely spread by a common misunderstanding of the term niche marketing.

I won't embarrass the rather well-known business commentator and frequent marketing columnist by naming him, but he was none the less the author of a searing indictment of the concept of niche marketing in retailing. As Britain groaned its way through the 'ghost' recession of 1990 (Mrs Thatcher kept assuring everyone, including both her chancellors of that year, that there wasn't one!), this columnist pointed out the extraordinary risk of niche marketing to any retailers considering what he felt to be a step in the most 'over-rated and hazardous' direction. His evidence, had it been in favour of the right argument, would have been compelling. He pointed to the demise or hard times of the small but ubiquitous Sock Shop, Tie Rack, Knickerbox, Paperchase and Cookie Kiosks.

Speciality retailing and niche marketing are at opposite ends of the spectrum. One takes a 'niche product', as it were, and places it before an unsegmented market (save for the outlet locations); the other, through one means or another, identifies or targets a small, homogeneous group of consumers and develops products or services that meet the needs of that group in relation to the common factors that make up the homogeneity.

The speciality retailers that suffered most are likely to be those that failed to niche market and, therefore, when hard times hit, were unable to consolidate their major or frequent buyers around them because they had made no effort whatsoever to get to know them or even simply to identify them. Thus, they could not materially reduce their resources without similarly reducing their market exposure and consequent sales.

Retailers, who have already demonstrated a great ability to segment internally and backwards through product groups and departmental thinking, must for the future examine and practise the methods of Customer group and individual thinking.

There is an interesting side issue which stems from the failure of speciality retailers to appreciate the wider benefits of marketing and the consequent strength and resilience marketing could have added instead of leaving them so vulnerable. The issue, or rather question, raised is why investors find such high risk businesses so attractive. My belief is that the City is using outdated methods to assess sales and marketing capabilities from an investor's point of view and may thus have become a little naive and vulnerable itself.

The large national and multi-national retailers must about face. They have become over-obsessed with asserting their strength over the manufacturers. This has resulted in the biggest example of cutting off one's nose to spite one's face the business world has ever seen. It has pushed many retailers throughout the world into a price-cutting syndrome coupled with an over-use of advertising and promotions. This in turn has backfired on the consumer and the manufacturer. The manufacturer has found his margins squeezed, lost control of his business and is unable to invest sufficiently in quality and product development. The consumer has been given less choice, less service and poorer value.

The third generation of selling, building relationships with Customers and treating suppliers as partners, is a mix which will return the retail world to its correct perspective. It will enjoy the cost-saving benefit of long lasting, stable, loyal relationships with its Customer and will work together with its manufacturers and suppliers to meet the increasingly demanding requirements of its Customers. This will place the Customer back as the centre of attention; give the retailer back his ability to serve and provide individually tailored advice and counsel; and enable the manufacturers to regain control over their margins and thereby restore

■ Customer-Driven Marketing

the investment levels to their optimum. I wonder who has the courage to do it first?

The large multiple retailers in Europe and to some extent in the US and South Africa have set themselves up. They increased the Customer's perception of price as a factor in purchasing and suffered ultimately because of it. Now, as the world outside retailing moves towards quality and vastly increased levels of priority for Customer service and Customer care, retailing, bereft of sufficient margin, will have to rethink its position or be out of step with communities upon whom it relies.

As we related this and other ideas to the shift in selling style, we saw that:

- Selling is entering a time of a softer style than has been used for 30 years or more.
- The Three Generations of Selling tracked the styles through time and identified know-how as a major new 'product' for the future.
- Certain retailers in Europe and the US may suffer through their obsession with controlling their suppliers rather than committing to and caring for their Customers.

# 17

# Listen to me. I'm the buyer!

We have seen that Customers have and will continue to become more demanding. We have learned that they (we!) will be looking for better service, better Customer care, and a more individual approach to both the handling of their business and the products and services that are offered to them. Yet, if we are going to see a time shortly when the Customer rules, how will this manifest itself? What precisely will they expect? What will we have to do to get their custom in the 'Age of the Customer'?

Of course each Customer will react differently. Each market sector may react differently. Particular countries will retain, possibly even increase, their national idiosyncrasies. Yet it is still possible to predict in general the ways that buying and selling will change. That is the subject of the next two chapters; we'll take the buying process first.

The environment to which we are changing is itself an environment of change; frequent, indeed relentless, change for businesses whatever, wherever their markets. And while we cope and learn to deal with all this change and the new demands of our Customers we must also address the fact that we have to deliver more intimate relationships, individual recognition and satisfaction, and Customers will require to be understood.

## So what are the demands?

In some ways all the changes in buying explained here could be seen as increasing demands. However, I feel there are four particular areas where there will be heightened expectation of marketing by Customers.

■ Customer-Driven Marketing

First, our Customers will undoubtedly adopt more and new communications media as they become available. And in this electronic age one should expect new media to continue to proliferate. I anticipate that this will happen faster within the business community.

Yet having said that, and to digress slightly for a moment, there is also a widely held belief that we will see a vast increase in those 'in-between' businesses; freelance or independent consultants and specialists, many of whom operate from home or from practices and who work in effective but small teams. The predictions are that SoHo's as they are known (Small office, Home office) will grow to three to five times their present level by 2005. Certainly if you look at the demassification and restructuring going on, couple this with the need to stay flexible and the increase of know-how as a product, one can understand the logic and therefore the prediction. It simply means that the advice given earlier for marketing directors, that it's better to have a big budget than a big department, may stand up just as well for other business disciplines too. There is also a widely held feeling that the training industry will, as it tries to cope with the vast new levels required of it, show massive growth in the same smaller consultancies. There is a consequent threat that, under the pressure of all this, trainers and training will not be able to cope, leading to failures in quality standards.

Returning to the changes in media through which Customers will want to deal with us, it would be foolish to think that the changes will only occur in the business markets. The consumer too will enjoy and embrace the proliferation, but in a different way. Here it is likely they will see it as choice. Therefore businesses who deal with the consumer markets will need to add the new media and communications opportunities to their range in order to satisfy the wider band of users they have.

The second category of increased demand is that of access to know-how and specialists. One of the effects that IBM appreciated as they restructured was the wealth of know-how and information which had previously been lost, locked up in the hierarchy, unseen and unavailable to its Customers. As they flattened out and moved these experienced people to positions where they came in touch with the Customer and their need, so they released a value for the company and for its Customers which had never been exposed before.

Thirdly, I believe that Customers will seek more information from their suppliers and less data, although it may be that this demand will be satisfied through the partnership style of relationship and therefore become a mutual development process. However in general the point remains the same. Customers will expect specialists and knowledge workers to be in the thick of it with them, rather than at a distance, say at the corporate base.

Fourthly, corporately and individually, with the relationship increasing expectations of loyalty, commitment and enthusiasm on both sides, Customers will expect nothing short of devotion. I described it earlier as heart, mind and soul.

Inevitably these four heightened demand levels will need a medium through which they can be delivered and satisfied. That, of course, is the relationship itself. So next we turn to the Customer's expectation of that relationship. How will it change? The answer, in a word, is intimately.

## Going for more intimate relationships

As the spotlight is turned on to the human interaction, relationships will become more personal and less corporate. Teams will become partners in problem solving, so there will develop three teams in effect: the buying team, the selling team and the combined team. I prefer to drop the buying and selling terms, finding the words 'commissioner and marketer' more appropriate. This often has me accused of going too far!

Thus, also, within this more intimate style, we see that the marketer must be more educated and informed about the buyer, their company, their systems and processes and their markets. In turn, the marketer will be expected to use these changes to the benefit of the buyer. For example, in the field of service expectancy, four categories can be identified where we may anticipate major demand spirals. These are:

- improved stock/availability
- better distribution
- faster delivery/reaction time
- more customisation.

It can be at once appreciated that there appear some paradoxes even in these four areas; improved stock appears to fight with customisation. But, as demands, they exist none the less, so the speed ideas in Chapter 4 may after all become less of a fad and I may have to eat my words.

## The need to be understood

As the amount of automation, technology and computing increases, the market will constantly remind us that the building of satisfactory relationships has its practical and material dimensions, but is first and foremost an exercise in human chemistry, dynamics and interaction.

Customers will ask us to understand them as the individual people they are and treat them accordingly. This has two particular aspects. First, we must understand that behind their demands of us lies a simple desire on their part to meet the demands of their marketplace or their families and lifestyles and, secondly, we must understand the pressures they work under. How can we help take that pressure off; or, at least, help them to handle it? How should we adapt or adjust what we do to take account of it?

I ask my audiences, 'What will be the biggest hurdle for executives and managers in the future?' It's a revealing process! One popular answer is 'getting to grips with technology'; but by far the most common fear voiced is that of stress. It's a problem which takes a mounting toll. Handling and dealing with people in a normal state can be a complex and interesting business. When almost the whole business world is witnessing record levels of stress and still climbing, this will require more understanding still. Stress incidentally is just one more unwanted by-product of the quantity age.

Stress is both an interesting and perhaps unlikely marketing topic which we could, perhaps should, spend greater time on. It is undoubtedly true that stress is a prominent and increasing feature of social and domestic life. For those in work, it is not as easy to leave stress behind as it is one's desk or tools. Workers take their stress home and share it with their family. Those out of work have stresses of their own to cope with. In London in 1995 I was a faculty member at the MCE Global Conference on Marketing and so was Lou Stern. In his speech 'Marketing in the Year 2000 – and Beyond' he pointed out what he believed was the biggest single problem marketers would have to deal with. You've guessed it! It was stress.

## Customers seek participation and involvement

For the future, Customers will not so much expect us just to supply or serve them. They will involve us in their planning; they will ask us to take part in their education and training processes; they will expect us to put our know-how together with theirs; and they will expect us to help them master technology. For the consumer marketers such as FMCG, some of these demands may not seem to relate directly. How, you may ask, can you be more understanding of Customers? How can you have more intimate relationships? How can you adopt new media, communications and technology?

If you really remain unsure, go back to the supermarket example in Chapter 4 or reflect on the incredible increase of Customer Carelines. The L&R Group in London, with the support of Mercury Communications, carried out surveys of Carelines in 1993 and 1995. Included in the survey were the US, Australia, Britain, France, Germany and New Zealand. Between the two surveys, the number of Carelines appearing on packaged goods in Britain leapt from 8 per cent to 22 per cent. In the US the figure remained consistent at around 80 per cent, being double that of any other country. It was also interesting that the response time in the US, in just two years, had dropped from 3.1 to 1.4 seconds. The hand of technology is at work again!

Yet there are fewer and fewer hands involved: in the US, 56 per cent of calls were answered by a voice or tone activated system and another 19 per cent by answering machine! Just 25 per cent were answered by a human being. That contrasts with New Zealand at 96 per cent and Britain the second highest user of automation but still a long way behind (or should that be in front?) of the US.

For FMCG brand owners – and many others – we should remember that there are two, sometimes three or more Customers: their wholesalers or agents; and then their retailers and their end-user/buyers.

To achieve the desired effect here, I tell people about Ripple Marketing, which is not as fancy as it sounds. It simply refers to the fact that you must develop marketing objectives which, while conforming to your loyalty building process for each of the 'rings' or 'ripples', also ensures that pure and clear brand and corporate messages are received throughout. Thus, as it has been throughout all recent history, assisting retail outlets to sell your products is fine; however, it is your product they are buying and your brand to which they are tying. You have a right to build an appropriate relationship with buyers of your brand. Carelines are a manifestation of this right as well as creating contact with Customers and giving them a voice.

'Heinz pull out of above the line to go direct', screamed the headlines of one the direct marketing 'trades'. It was actually rubbish! What happened was that Heinz in Great Britain had decided to invest in building a database of what they called 'The Heinz Households'. After all, as owners of several brands and product ranges, including WeightWatchers, it was a great opportunity to start building relationships with their Customers. Actually, what Heinz had decided to do was to pull back from mainstream press and television for a while to finance the database and name gathering exercise. This they did for a set period of time and then returned to a halo-effect spend back in television and press. However, the construction of the database over, they have dealt with the outlay and now the costs have settled back to maintenance and targeted activity. Heinz now can begin building relationships with these Heinz households. And as your baby progresses through from babyfoods to ketchup and beans and onwards, probably on to WeightWatchers products if their mailings are successful(!), so they will stay in touch with you and accessible to you. A lifetime relationship with the brand is built. As a result of their database building, Heinz are now in direct touch with 8,000,000 or more 'Heinz households' and the consequent sales increases will only be evident in one place other than at Heinz – that's in their retail outlets. Insurance brokers around the world might like to think about this story.

Brand owners must look at the qualities they bestow upon the brand and the way they position it. They must constantly strive to look at their opportunities to partner their distributors and retailers to build loyalty for mutual benefit. Where retailers insist on sole ownership of the Customers, it is, I think, still necessary to negotiate this view. Brand owners should find mutually beneficial ways of increasing Customer care and service and the gradual process of relationship building while honouring the retailer's stake in the Customer. However, brand owners need to be cognisant of the undeniable fact that, unless they radically alter their distribution channels – and 'going direct' has been a very prominent financial services route here – the intermediary, wholesaler and retailer may have more, often very damaging power over the consumer. In both a positive and potentially negative sense, in explaining the ripple marketing concept (where we differentiate the treatment for each layer of distribution like ripples on a pond), I always point out that the nearer you get to the end Customer, the greater the power and the greater the influence. Tell that to a centralised marketing department!

How to meet the demands we have discussed here for a retailer is easy; but what about the end-user? Here the brand owner must look at the qualities they bestow upon the brand and the way they position it. Furthermore they must look at their opportunities to partner their retailers and build loyalty to mutual benefit. Where retailers insist on sole ownership of the Customer, then, brand owners can resort to sensitive other means to increase Customer service and care, and through this begin the gradual process of relationship building. Carelines, enabling Customers to contact brand owners, are a perfect example of this and there should be no hesitation in gathering Customer data this way. However, those same brand owners must always remember that, unless they radically alter their distribution channels, the intermediary – the retailer – may have more, often very damaging power, over the consumer.

In this chapter, we have looked at some of the changes in buying criteria and expectations. We know that the Customer's changing perception of value will be of increasing significance in many areas and price less so. However we also considered that the changes in buying will raise Customer expectations and that they will require the following:

- *Satisfaction of new demands*
    — more communications, new technology, new media
    — greater access to specialists and know-how
    — more information, less data
    — devotion of mind, body and soul.
- *More intimate relationships*
    — more personal, less corporate
    — more educated and informed

        — more reactive to needs
        — higher service expectancy:
             improved stock/availability/reaction time
             better distribution
             faster delivery
             more customisation.
- The need to be understood
        — empathise with the human dynamics
             recognise demands and pressures
        — share growth path
        — assist education and training
        — help master technology.
- Ripple marketing tells us that each 'ring' of the distribution chain should be seen as a Customer and all should receive consistent brand values and attention.

# 18

# I hear you. I'm from sales!

As we have evidenced, the changes in selling are far-reaching. Undoubtedly the most influential factor behind these changes is the switch from transaction based work to relationship based work.

When our objectives change to include quality objectives, they will place in front of all others the strategy of building solid and stable growth for the corporation through these broad based, long-term relationships. This builds both brand equity and Customer equity for the business. In order to provide a safe and trusting atmosphere for the relationship to flourish, there are some ground rules, some changes to conventional thinking. For example I expect both parties to make each other quite openly aware of the financial, material and intellectual dynamics. There will be a shared understanding, a mutual respect for the desire to embark down a planned profit development path. This may not always happen willingly. Commission disclosure in the financial services, for instance, will rapidly assume global proportions. But in some countries it may come through government interference rather than being industry led.

Marketing is a flexible and reactionary process. Marketers must constantly research and monitor their activities, and they must analyse and establish values and directions. On the basis of such analysis marketers make decisions. This welding together of such practices behind the transactions within the relationship is a long-time procedure of the direct marketing fraternity and will become one of the most satisfying and rewarding processes for the classical practitioners to adopt as marketing fusion takes place. Also, marketing is now segment or niche orientated. We have seen duality, the apparent dichotomy of global branding, while markets fragment and demassify. Let us now examine the changes in 'selling' practices, which in general will become more 'marketing' in style.

## Building secure relationships works for both sides

Moving away from transaction led selling or, as I prefer to call it, exploitation selling to satisfaction marketing, pays much less attention and gives much lower priority to short-term volume sales missions. Now relationships are founded on the cornerstone engraved with the words 'Customer welfare'. Now it is all about welfare not warfare. Quite simply, we must dedicate ourselves to serving the Client's best interest on every level possible. Thus we can identify the four corners of the world in which selling products and services through Customer-driven marketing must operate. It's a cultural square where everything is bounded by quality, service, added-value and know-how. The mentality of the long-term relationship is one that requires that both parties share and are concerned about their own and each other's trends, threats and opportunities. An important feature, or indeed asset, of these relationships is their longevity and security. The security particularly, once created, breeds massive mutual confidence and commitment. This in turn creates valuable benefits in the quality and productivity of the work, but also provides a background against which risk taking and major investment (not words I usually place too close together lest they mate!) are suitably encouraged.

## A planned profit development path

The trouble is that while change is hitting businesses so relentlessly, chaos and havoc are underneath like starving alligators waiting for them to fall. This will require that business planning functions are modified to be less rigid; the area of planning is a prime area where we will witness the openness in dealings and discussions as profit development paths are opened up. In order to encourage the necessary atmosphere the future will see what are, by conventional standards, extraordinary exchanges of information from both sides. This will include:

- disclosure of personal and business goals
- disclosure of detailed corporate growth and development plans
- disclosure of personal and corporate reward, incentive and motivation potential.

Such discussion and collaboration encourages exciting unity of purpose and comradeship; it is also healthy for the 'third team effect'. Further, it correctly places the highest value on know-how as we accelerate into the third generation of selling.

■ Customer-Driven Marketing

The structures required to facilitate such relationships and the working styles they encourage are, however, necessarily different from conventional hierarchies since a much more broadside exposure is required to support and deliver these relationships. Yes, many differences are developing as we move away from the supply and demand style and towards mutual interest projects. Again, you will find these changes relate similarly to the consumer, especially, I suspect, the question of remuneration and rewards. This is a point which will have dramatic impact on the future as we will see in Chapter 21.

## Marketing becomes analysis based

Marketing already understands the value of certain kinds of research. However, the research industry throughout the world is becoming more innovative and experimental. This is just as well, for marketing will need it to provide information which is wider and deeper – and it will need this information both faster and more frequently. As planning becomes less rigid in its outlook, so the information on which it is based will need to be more adventurous and explorative in its scope, yet more reliable and sensitive in its delivery and interpretation. Thus, future research work will enable us to make more intelligent value perceptions and thereby value judgements and, of course, decisions. These will in turn improve the quality, design and service aspects of our products and services.

## Orientating for the niche

'People can be over-selective in their market selection', said the managing director and founder of the business. He is the dynamic head of a mail order booksellers specialising in business books. He went on to explain how a member of his team had analysed the sales of one book (let us invent one here, say, *How to be a Super Sales Manager*) and found that less than one in 20 of the buyers were sales managers. The rest were made up of a strange collection of sales and marketing people, smaller business managing directors and even – somewhat inexplicably – a dental hygienist! As a result his company had found that what many other direct marketers would consider to be a hopelessly scatter gun approach worked well. Basically, he suggested, the more people he let know about more books (of particular qualities and types, naturally), the more he sold.

He may have felt this to be true for his company, but it will not be for most marketers. It is actually not so much to do with the strange idiosyncrasies of his business, his Customers, his market or his products. It is actually to do with the way he deals with his Customers and the opportunity he has to get to know and understand them. However, his business runs on classic direct marketing lines and has a single dimension relationship with his Customers. And very successfully it works too. However, when you look at the take it or leave it, art gallery approach the retail book trade has adopted, this is no surprise. Moreover, getting to know the Customer can and should include building a picture of what they actually purchase, as well as what their job title, business category, demographics or psycho-graphics or socio-graphics suggest they might want to buy. What we are ultimately trying to assemble is as accurate as possible a picture of their needs and their personal and/or business objectives.

To operate successfully in a niche market, one must develop a relationship which gets you nearer to the Customer, better able to meet more of their niche needs. Otherwise, one is simply headed the wrong way down a funnel. You end up with fewer people buying fewer or single highly specialist products.

Niche marketing is to do with the ability to adapt (or abandon) hitherto mass marketed, mass produced items and to develop and tailor them (or create new) by adding value and specialisation to the smaller groups that make up your total market. What makes the groups smaller is the information you have about them and their needs. Thus, until my bookseller friend is ready to create individual relationships with his Customers, in the way that retail bookstores could (but usually don't), then he would never have known that the dental hygienist bought the book for his wife to celebrate her forthcoming promotion to sales manager.

However, to take that story on, why does it seem so ridiculous to so many people that the bookstore would not enable itself to get to know the individuals who are its Customers sufficiently well that it might be able to offer these two people choices for the future which match their jobs, their lifestyles, their leisure activities and their hobbies? And the store could provide them all wrapped up in a convivial and enjoyable chain of experiences – a Customer relationship, no less? You would have to tear me away screaming from a bookstore which made itself so much a part of my life. To achieve all this you basically need a telephone, a simple database and the kind of person who can genuinely cultivate good relationships with Customers. Isn't that surely what a large part of successful retailing is about these days?

Another aspect of niche marketing and the necessary relationships required to profit best from the concept is that it requires that the seller represents the full capability of the company to the buyer. This cuts across brands and across product ranges. What's more, niche orientation requires that, whatever we call our front end array – sales force, business development team, account managers, marketing departments, outlets, branches – their aims must reflect the relationship building objectives. Their teams are structured according to the niche or niches they serve. The only real conjecture here is how the teams are structured to achieve this, the main topic of the following chapter.

Along with all this, indeed almost a catalyst to the evolution, is the availability of suitable database support for such marketing structures. These facilitate the networking of information, the movement and transfer of data and the ability to adopt techno-creative marketing communications with the market, other teams and necessary suppliers.

When you put together the content of these last two chapters, the changes in buying and the changes in selling, there is only one clear direction. It is the same direction to which so many aspects of our future point. This means going back to relationship based, Customer-driven and quality marketing techniques. Also we have seen now the major ways in which the thinking and motivations of both sides of the marketing process will change. In selling these can be summed up as follows:

- *Building secure, long-term relationships*
  — customer welfare on all levels is the first priority
  — security breeds confidence and commitment; it also increases investment and encourages exploration.
- *Creating planned profit development paths*
  — mutual growth tracks for Customer and supplier
  — openness about:
  personal and business goals
  detailed corporate growth and development plans
  personal and corporate reward, incentive and motivational potential.
- *Marketing increasingly analysis based*
  — planning with less rigid boundaries increases the need for wider and deeper research, faster and more frequently provided
  — research needs to be more adventurous and explorative in scope while more reliable and sensitive in delivery and interpretation.
- *Orientating for the niche*
  — relationships are the media through which niche markets blossom and yield their maximum potential
  — niche marketing requires the ability to move from mass production to customised and tailored production *en masse*
  — what creates a niche is the information you have about the individuals or organisations and their needs; the more information, potentially the smaller the niches
  — niche marketing requires across-the-brand or across-the-product range selling and flourishes when one-to-one communications are the order of the day
  — the full potential of niche marketing is realisable through databases and the supporting software which enables the satisfactory operation of the optimum working structures and information networking.

# 19

# The concept of granular structures

In this chapter, we turn to the issue of organisational structure: in order to give you some guidance about the nature of the structures which enable Customer superformance to take place – simultaneously bringing benefits to the business which are all a part of the transformation to becoming a Customer-driven business. There are some alternative things you could do, as you will read. They are at best compromises and will not enable you to enjoy the optimum benefits which accrue from changing to the granular structure which is essentially a network of self-managed units operating with great autonomy. It's a corporate network of small businesses, in fact! Let's start with some background and then look at the compromise solutions and then, finally, I'll talk you through my granular concept in more detail.

## The far-reaching influence of quality

There has been inference and reference to marketing department structures several times throughout this book. We also have used the phrase 'backwards to the future' and similar other phrases a number of times, the message being that, in many ways, the Customer-driven marketing gospel is not new. It is as old as the hills and well tried and proven. This is undeniable fact. Although like world wars, thank goodness (and let us pray it stays that way), those who can recall what it was really like are growing fewer in number. For the majority of those in marketing, it is pure hearsay – or at least it would have been except for the fact that the true standards and values of the quality regime in marketing have been so shunned and spurned for so long, that they have been neither heard nor said.

■ Customer-Driven Marketing

We have already seen how quantity took over, and how and why the pendulum swung so ridiculously far the other way. It is no wonder the consumer is feeling enough is enough. I suppose the question here is why we can't turn back the clock and market like they used to in, what can quite fairly in this context be described as, the good old days. What has changed? The answer is nearly everything. The whole dynamics of marketing are entirely different: the numbers, the speed with which things are required and the expectation of Customers generally has changed out of all perspective. Moreover, as their just compensation for the exploitation they have suffered, Customers will expect the wrongs righted but to hang on to the 'rights' they have gained. The business world, too, is not made up of idealists and philanthropists; it will only consider accepting the return of quality and Customer issues as long as it can hang on to the quantity. I believe, largely, both sides can win with Customer-driven marketing. I also recognise that the corporate structures that delivered quality the last time round would collapse under the strain as we pumped today's quantities into the system. Unfortunately, making them bigger or more robust will not help either since they become too clumsy and unwieldy to provide the speed and reactions required in today's business world. Indeed, with flexibility as a keyword to survival for the future, this point could be well taken by so many of today's businesses who frankly still operate the same elaborate hierarchies and command and control systems which they operated at the turn of the last century. The systems have not been built to provide quality and quantity. They have only succeeded with one or the other. So there is a strong argument to look for new ways.

## Is it necessary to meddle with corporate infrastructures to become Customer-driven?

The answer is most probably. However, it is definitely vital to consider radical changes to the structures of sales and marketing. Yet it would be unwise, I believe, to have one type of structure throughout the organisation but another in marketing and sales. To a large extent individual answers here will depend on the nature of the organisation, the nature of the business and the way it interfaces with its markets. Tracking back to the Three Generations of Selling will help us to solve these issues. Consider the first generation and the structure of its sales and marketing division or departments. It has a classic hierarchical shape, from director to regional or branch sales and marketing managers to district sales or product managers through to the sales force. They operate via the muscular regime. This creed is that to sell more you need more people to sell. Their operating methods are aggressive and highly promotional. Their objectives are singular – to move product. The sales people work alongside a marketing team where, in the worst cases, a strong sales director will have beaten marketing into subservience and they will have become a support group providing promotional and marketing services on demand. In the less severe cases, the sales and marketing teams co-operate. It frequently happens without a great deal of respect on either side and, as a result, they don't often seem to like each other very much!

From this we have discussed the evolutionary change which developed with the second generation of selling. The idea was to present a wider spread to the market. It cultivated operatives who had a Client service mission. This pattern was achieved through simple refocusing of direction and by closer integration of the sales and marketing effort. Indeed this regime often became confused and argued about whose role started and ended where. The second generation is the 'cupped hands' regime at work. Its operating methods are kind, attentive to Customers and much more service orientated than its preceding generation. Its creed is service assistance; and its corresponding objective the added-value sale.

## Ideas like advertising agencies

Often second generation businesses would benefit from building Customer service mini-hierarchies. The mid-1970s to mid-1980s saw a global outbreak of these units like daisies on an early summer lawn. I have always thought that advertising agencies set the best example of this type. Their account handling structure – account executives, account managers, account group managers, account directors and account group directors – worked extremely well in the context of the big monolithic agency. However, there are danger points. The first of these is the way the communications path gets longer as the organisation is successful and expands. A group with four account executives, two account managers and an account director can be expanded to, say, eight account executives, four account managers, two account group managers and an account director with relative ease. The problem here is that, as the layers increase, the centres of inspiration and authority in such hierarchies, the leaders, are getting further and further apart. Thus life becomes an inevitability of small decisions and procedures where major decision making is tedious, cumbersome and slow.

The second danger point is a tendency to bureaucratic systems in response, usually, to the volatile, unpredictable and fast moving nature of the people involved and the work they handle. Those bureaucracies can also become self-fulfilling, with heavy overheads and low productivity, hidden by the amount of work they generate in perpetuating their own existence. It is strange how often these units, in many senses a team, have little, if any, team spirit.

The sales or Customer services units, when looked at in detail, are in fact simply micro-hierarchies within greater hierarchies. Where they are headed by a strong, inspirational leader they can be very successful. They tend to have executive and operational strata; the operational tier generally having three kinds of communications functionaries:

- the Ambassador – a traveller
- the Voice – a telemarketer
- the Scribe – contact through the database.

There have been massive developments here in databases, and sales direction and management systems are now coupled to Customer communications and transactions by computer. This leads to all manner of cost efficiency improvements from increased supervision and management effectiveness to better stock control and resource management. Looking at Figure 19.1, you can see what I mean when I tell you that this is essentially just a classic service team approach.

## Is the classic Client service team concept dying?

As a solution the fact is that the classical Client service team concept can still work very well. However, for the future it will work best for those who have found their natural place in the second generation. It provides a perfectly practical and viable answer for those who associate their needs or situation with those described under Option One: More People, in Chapter 14. However, the words I used in relation to that option were 'compromise' and 'cosmetic'. My belief is that, to move into the third generation, we need to see a new style of Client service team being created and I propose that such teams should work as granules within a broadside structure or a network structure; hence the term 'granular marketing' as we shall see shortly.

## What style of teams work best?

Staying with the second generation a moment longer, it should be remembered that, when choosing which business style will best suit the teams, the more traditional methods and techniques will work better with the classical Client services team. It is after all a hierarchy. It is with the new flatter structures where new management styles flourish. Yet in a hierarchy rank, authority, strict procedural ideas about control, transmission of instructions and reporting thrive.

This is not generally a good environment for experimentation and entrepreneurism which the third generation requires. Yet in the context of individualised product and Customer service, together with a need for increased sensitivity and responsiveness, it is clear why the reservations develop with the conventional first generation structures, techniques, cul-

## The concept of granular structures

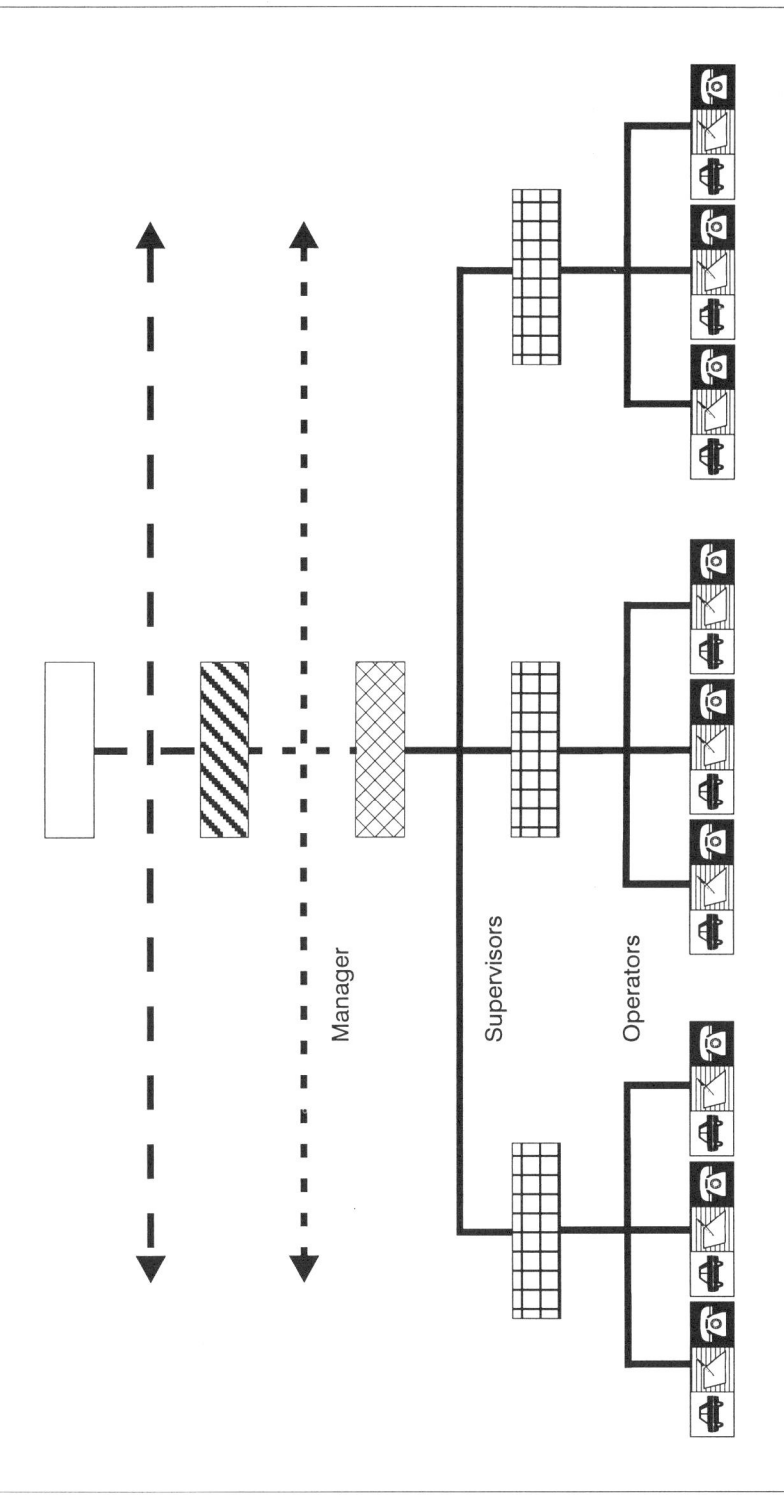

Figure 19.1 *Customer service units: hierarchies within hierarchies?*

tures and management styles – they were fine for the 'Age of Plenty' but are nowhere near enough for the 'Age of Sufficiency'.

The new marketing management style for the third generation is responsible: it can take decisions and be accountable for them. The new style is mature: it understands the need to become more business orientated. The new style is autonomous, adventurous and challenging: it stands ready to get close to Customers, to find new ways to satisfy their demands and it constantly questions beliefs, practices and dogma. The new marketing style is alert, free-thinking, strategy conscious and technologically competent and fluent.

### Getting closer to Customers

An important realisation of getting closer to Customers is that hitherto they have not known what they want because they have not known what they could have; they have simply taken the choices on offer. In business-to-business situations, as the relationship succeeds and the boundaries fall, one of the greatest fields for new product ideas, development and proving will be within the joint project work that develops. When Customers get to appreciate the boundless choice available with customisation, I expect industrial, professional and commercial progress to speed up tenfold by 2010. The technology is already sufficient to support such a jump. It may even enable us to reach this level earlier still.

I'd like to interrupt myself at this point to explore some other side-effects of customisation since they will impact greatly on the structure of the marketing department. The knock-on effect of customisation (indeed individualisation pushes this argument forward further still) is very substantial. One can predict a huge decrease in the commonality of the work done by marketing. In many cases industrial marketing will become a one-to-one process. There will be massive product proliferation as information networking reveals to other teams within the company the products of the intensified development work. It will in turn shorten product life cycles even further than they have already become under the influence of modern technology.

These three factors alone promote a fascinating insight into the changes that will eventually come to marketing. They push it closer to integration with the selling role and towards an inevitable conclusion that marketing could become a very diverse process indeed; almost an individual Customer by Customer process for many practitioners. Its primary information source would come from networking with other marketers in the same corporation or syndicate, with perhaps only a modest central resource for strategic counsel and training.

Most importantly, the marketing database must run from core to Customer and, as quickly as possible, the communications decision making process must be moved to the front line.

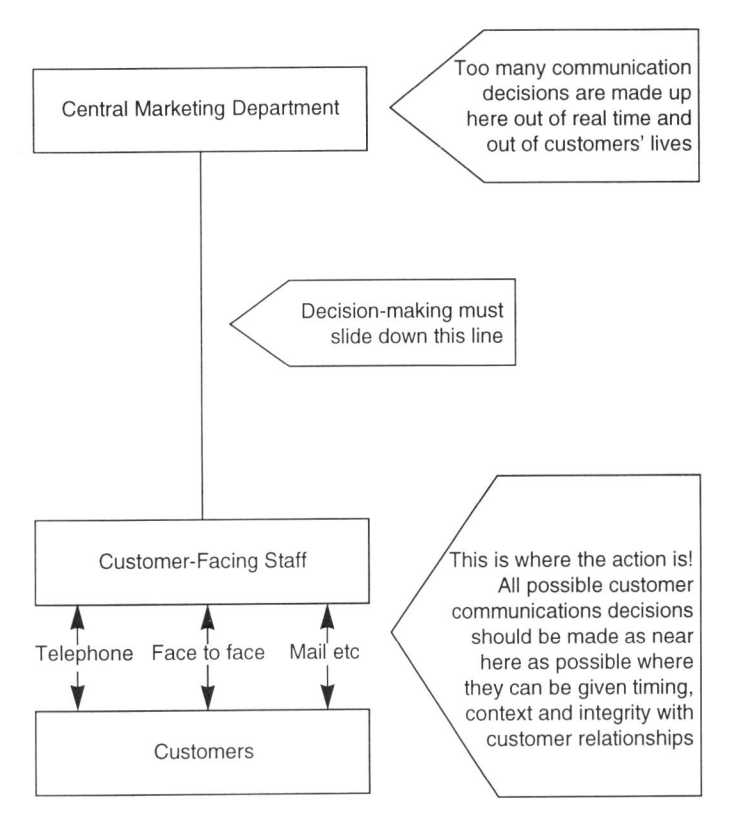

**Figure 19.2** *Communications decision-making must be devolved to the front line*

## Customer-driven marketing needs total communications management

Earlier, we discussed the notion that relationship marketing must use integrated communications to move the efforts of the sales and marketing teams into real time with their Customers.

From the way the signs are pointed, and with the ideas we've been considering, it is clear that the existing communications management and control systems are hopelessly outdated, unsatisfactory and inadequate relics of the past. Total communications management is a philosophical concept which suggests that you must organise your communications to reflect and honour the integrity of the closer relationships that are cre-

■ Customer-Driven Marketing

ated with Clients. Otherwise we create a magnificent five-star hotel with only one telephone line.

It was suggested earlier that the way you manage your communications presents a shaft of truth to the Customer about how individual and personal their service is. Every modern consumer has experienced this let down or the moment when one human response to your situation has given you hope of satisfaction – and the next mass produced missive shatters what seemed like a solution but is revealed as an illusion.

## Dear God, please send a new idea!

Having researched this whole area with masses of help and advice, and discussion for nearly ten years and that decade now of practical experience with my Clients, it seems that none of the conventional solutions fits. So the big problem with our third generation (which is a pseudonym for the future of our business!) is that it's a renegade. To solve the problem we need some new thinking.

The thesis of total communications management is simple: in order to ensure the integrity of Customer communications within the relationship (and to overcome the communications traffic jam) one person must be assigned responsibility for the communications an individual or with a group of Customers. The object of that assignment is to order and adapt both content and timing so that the actual reality of the Customer relationship makes a difference to the communication being sent. For classical sales and marketing structures, this is as implausible as it is impractical.

Therefore, in order to ensure responsive decision making and corporate flexibility, the responsibility must be devolved to the front line where the action or interaction is happening. Thus, the granular marketing unit, as I have called it, is born. It operates in the mind, body and soul regime. Its creed is a profitable partnership. Its operating methods are creative, committed and entrepreneurial. Its objective is to expose its brains. It is, inevitably, a self-managed team.

Adopting the granular marketing culture recognises the following:

- Buying decisions will involve more specialists. It equips each granule (Client service group) with as many specialists as demanded by the Client relationships or niches for which they have responsibility.
- In the future we will see many more trading partnerships where it is recognised that specialist know-how requires in-depth, intimate work from people who understand the larger issues – and therefore where their mutual development path will lead. Such relationships rely heavily on a build-up of mutual experience and are optimised by stability and longevity.
- We will see greater rationalisation of brand/product/service lines. This

must happen, as we have seen, to enable the customisation that the market will require and the individual treatment and recognition it seeks. Just as we have a unique computer number to identify us and stop duplication these days, so we will have a unique person to identify and manage the relationship. For that relationship to succeed at maximum effectiveness, we must be able to seem like a small personal business, acting almost as if we only had the one Customer we are dealing with at any one time. With granular marketing structures such idealistic levels are possible, but it requires that instead of sales or marketing teams we create small autonomous business units. We are dealing here with a switch from the ability to sell to the ability to cultivate business.

Figure 19.3 illustrates a typical granule; the segment, tones and patterns represent different disciplines. For example one might have sales/marketing, product development, administration and financial disciplines. The nucleus in the centre of each group is the leader who takes overall responsibility for the team's quality, effectiveness, performance and achievements. The segments can represent numbers of people or proportions of specialist resources. Notice each is different according to the segment or group of Customers it is servicing. When deployed, the picture is as described below.

First, in the forward direction towards the Client, *two* styles of relationship will be cultivated, interpersonal and intergroup.

Secondly, the exchanges take place via the matched specialists within the marketer and commissioner (Customer) groups.

The marketer and commissioner groups – essentially a deployment for business and commercial interaction – are two matched teams and the reason for describing them as 'three teams' is that each partner in the relationship operates as a team (Figure 19.4), but also they should all feel part of the same team with common goals. In consumer marketing, it could be argued that such relationship arrangements could exist with, say, families or couples. Certainly, there is no reason why the spirit of partnership should not exist. My travel agent, for example, considers herself a partner in my business travel and seems to be as concerned as we are that our travel arrangements are perfect.

Thirdly, the operation, management, analysis and success of each granule is highly database dependent. Its forward (Client side external) and backward (corporate side internal and external) communication requirements fall into four categories:

(a) *information* – these are to provoke inspiration
(b) *demands* – these meet the needs of the relationship
(c) *requests* – these meet the desires of the relationship
(d) *responses* – they satisfy both (b and c) categories above.

■ Customer-Driven Marketing

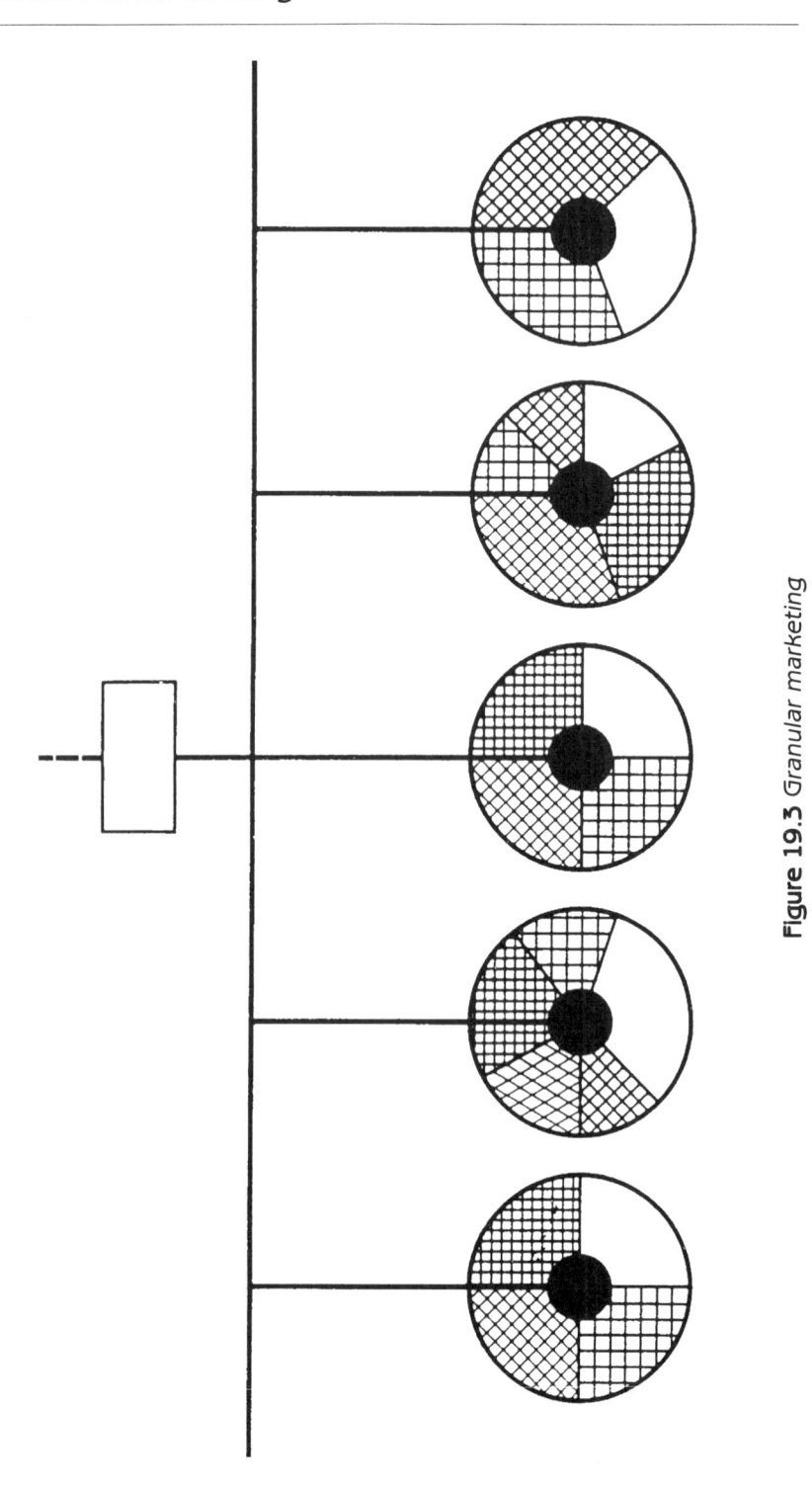

Figure 19.3 *Granular marketing*

## The concept of granular structures

Marketer         Commissioner
GROUP WORK

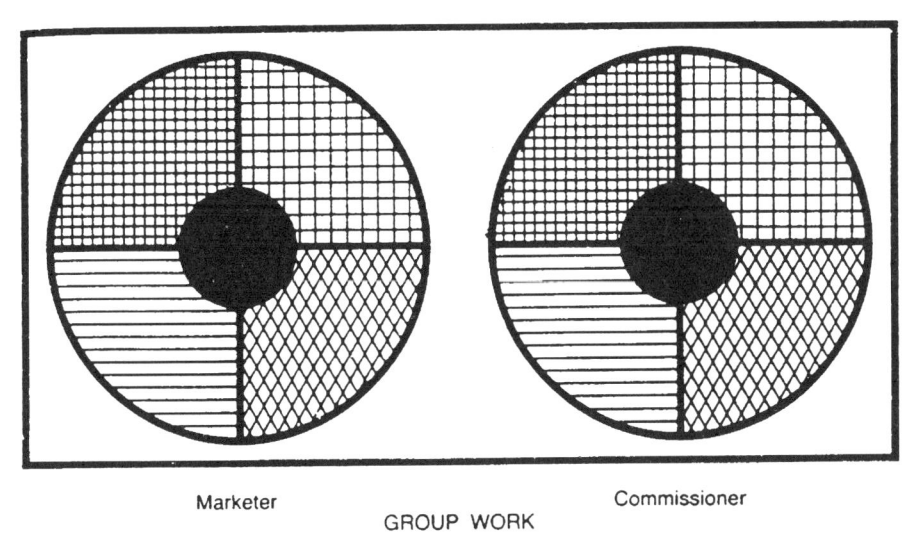

**Figure 19.4** *The marketer and commissioner groups: a total of three teams*

Fourthly, the resources of the granule are supported and augmented by two banks. The first is the Know-how Bank which supplies internal and external specialists. Similar to a centre of excellence, this is a centre of experience, expertise and knowledge. The second bank is the Infobank – the home of the database.

This is a triangle (Figure 19.5) and like any triangular structure will effectively collapse without any one of the three interdependent facets.

Knowhow bank         Data bank

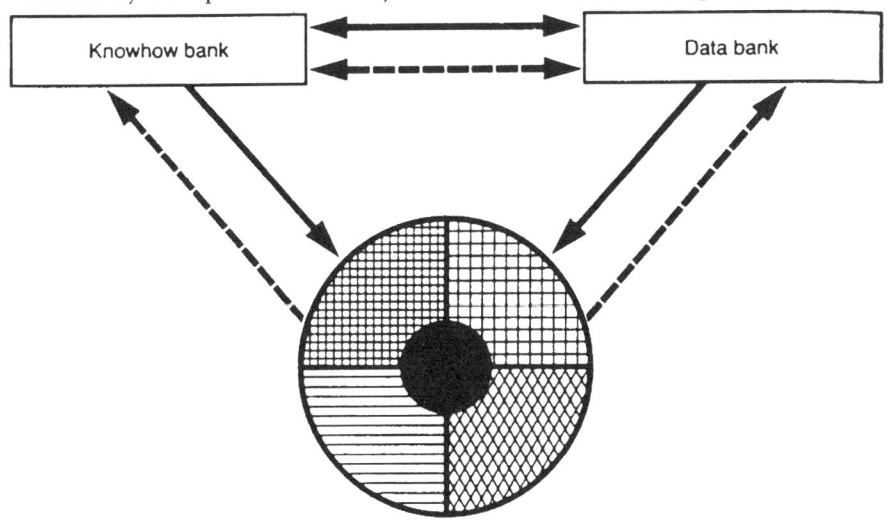

**Figure 19.5** *The granular marketing banking process*

But the most important part in the banking process – indeed, why it is so-called – is that it is two-way. Thus, it achieves its ultimate power and strength if the withdrawals do not exceed the deposits!

Here we have a fundamentally important view of the new structure. The structure itself consists of a diverse array of self-managed units which are, in essence, micro-businesses. However, we also wish to retain the advantages of a large business while gaining the flexibility, speed of response and decision making of a small business. When your business splits itself up into these Customer orientated small units, something magical happens. Instead of one business trying to solve its problems one way, it becomes a hive of experimentation and differentiation. The results of this must be gathered, retained and shared. If they are, you can imagine how the learning curve is improved. My experience suggests that it will increase almost in proportion to the increase in the number of units. Thus, for example, if the business transforms to become, say, 30 small autonomous businesses, the learning process can be improved almost 30 fold.

This has no benefit unless what is learned is stored and shared, hence the two banks – the InfoBank and the Know-how Bank. The first is the Customer information, the second is the knowledge and experience of the business. With the benefit of this learning curve, any business will establish and then maintain best practices at the speed of light compared with conventional competitors.

There remain three major issues in relation to decisions about new sales and marketing structures: are these units sales and marketing units or complete micro-businesses; how do they relate to each other and to the corporation; and how are the personnel motivated and rewarded?

## Micro-businesses or sales and marketing only?

As we have considered, the true product of the future for so many marketers is know-how. They will be selling to the head; an intellectual exercise. This will be true, even where, by the classical definition, the product is a manufactured item. I anticipate that where the marketing exercise has a product that is manufactured, granules will be primarily sales, marketing and service; although, depending on the nature of the product in question, they should be structured fully to meet all the needs of the Client which necessitate liaison and exchange. However, where there is no such production base – services and the professions – there are only exceptional cases where these units could not be complete micro-businesses operating with maximum power and responsiveness for their Customers' benefit. These units will effectively combine the best of a small business with the best of a large one. These two methods will look like Figures 19.6 and 19.7.

The concept of granular structures

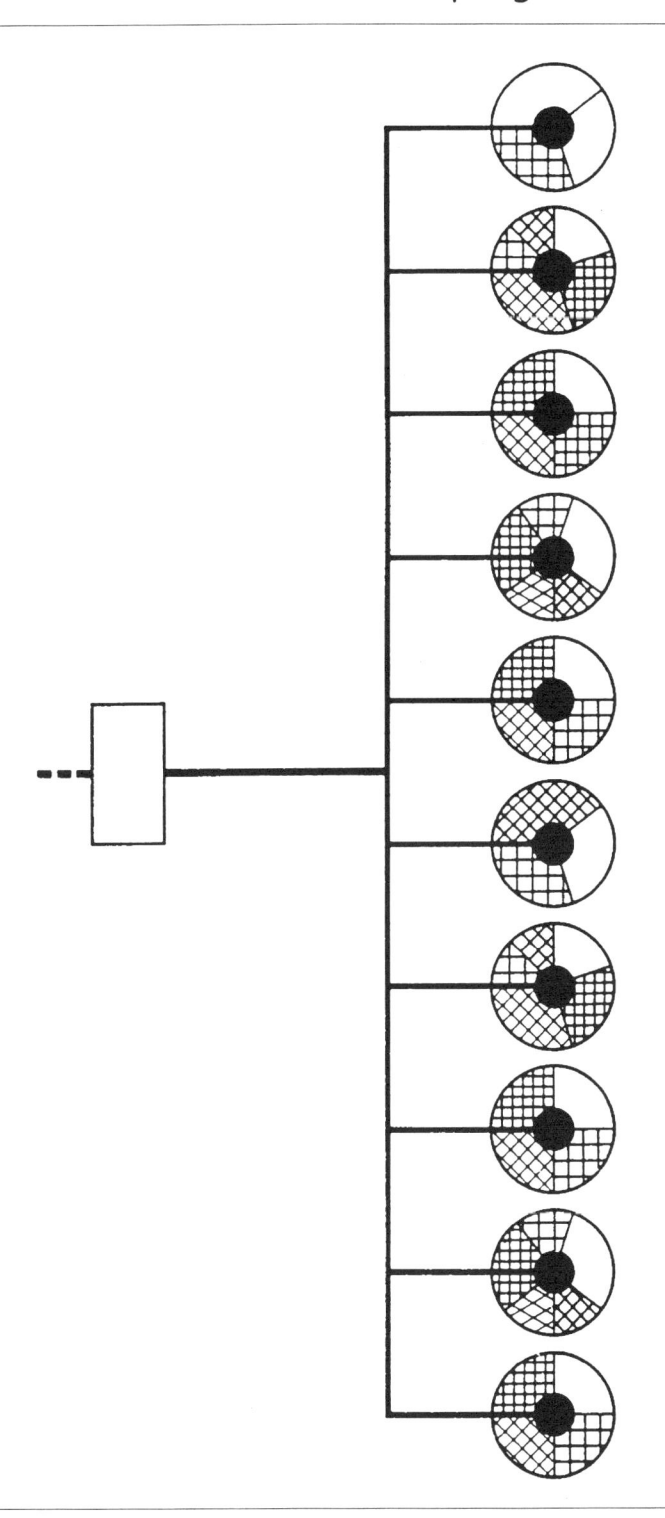

**Figure 19.6** *A broadside granular structure*

■ Customer-Driven Marketing

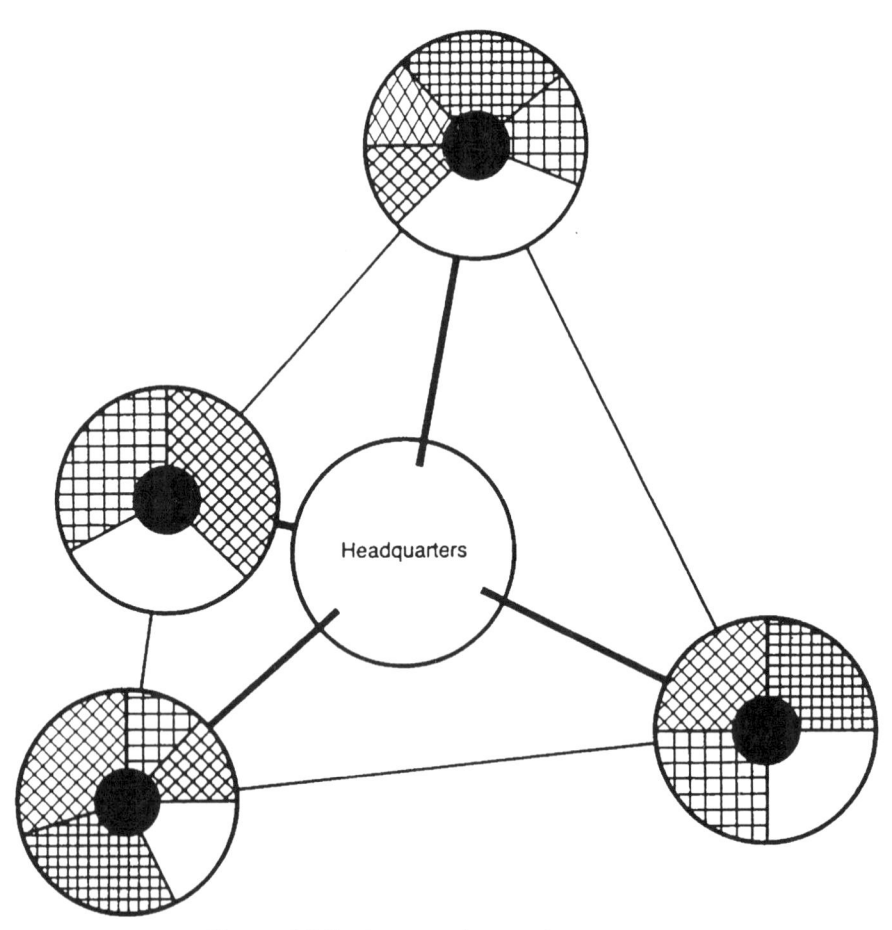

**Figure 19.7**: *A network granular structure*

The broadside array in Figure 19.6 has a line-tie to the business centre thus providing a pure sales and marketing extension. Effectively sales and marketing will operate here, almost as if they were a sales and marketing company within a group, even though they are actually not truly so autonomous. In the network array, an umbilical cord exists to the core business. This cord carries the 'banking' details and the performance review, and goal setting and other central resources. Granules are networked to each other to maintain a leading edge exchange of thinking and know-how.

### What have we achieved?

Let us review what we have achieved by creating such structural changes. Apart from providing the means for optimum relationship building, we can see that the old way:

## The concept of granular structures

- encourages individual effort
- discourages consultation and teamwork
- promotes directionally wrong and old-fashioned values.

We can also see that the new way:

- sponsors team effort
- encourages group activity
- provides the forwarding of the total corporate promise
- propagates relationship values
- seeks not merely to listen, but to understand the client/partner.

Just as the 1980s and 1990s saw the creation of centres of excellence, in the future marketers will create centres of empathy.

This chapter has dealt with some matters of structure and suggested some new ideas for you to consider. They may not all relate to your business; some may only relate to those you buy from rather than those you sell to and therefore help them better to meet your needs. Let me endeavour to summarise the major points:

- Customer-driven marketing is not new. However, the structures and methods previously used are now inadequate and inappropriate. New ideas must be found.
- The idea of increasing the intensity of the classic Customer service unit will continue to operate, for those business methods do not change. However, again, this solution is inappropriate for fostering relationships of the depth and breadth we will see in future.
- Teams are the perfect unit concept, however marketing will need a new environment in which to flex its muscles. It will demonstrate a new maturity which is more business orientated generally and more responsible specifically.
- The rate of product development that results from customisation will create a rate of progress that will compound the innovation rate technology has already created. This has three side-effects:
  – decisions will involve more specialists
  – trading partnerships will add intimacy and stability
  – rationalisation of brand/product/service lines assists customisation.
- Whether granules operate as wholly autonomous businesses or as sales and marketing units only, may depend on whether the business has the manufacturing of a product or not. Manufacturing or product businesses may choose sales and marketing units but with vastly increased freedom, influence and authority.

Part Four: Relationship and integrated marketing

# 20

# Change: nobody likes it, everybody's doing it

Not too many of us like change very much. And, in business, coping with change is a highly specialised task. So at this point I have turned to the best specialist I know, simply the most talented management consultant I have had the pleasure of working with. His name is Pip Mosscrop, a group director of Collinson Grant Consultants Ltd, the international management consultancy who operate from Manchester, England.

Pip is not a writer (he tells me), so the way the next three chapters of the book work is that we have discussed the issues together. I have then written up the results which Pip and I have discussed and edited; which is just as well for Pip, since the chosen writing style at Collinson Grant is somewhat different to my own ... and might therefore give him a few awkward problems back at base! Along the way, of course, we have reflected on our own material and blended in our two personal work experiences.

I would like to record here my sincere thanks to Pip Mosscrop and Collinson Grant for the time, expertise and information so kindly and freely given. It seemed hardly possible that, having set out by such extraordinarily different routes, we should find ourselves in the same place. It is quite uncanny and, I suspect, not a little comforting for us both. And it has continued to be that way for a decade or so.

## Changemasters

Change in itself represents a challenge to business. And we have already considered the notion that more radical and increasingly relentless changes are actually happening to businesses large and small. I have also demonstrated that classic corporate structures and hierarchies, whether throughout the company or just in relation to the marketing department, can create a lack of flexibility and versatility in sales, marketing and service situations which could seriously hamper or retard the alacrity with which marketers will have to operate in the future. This remains true whether one is thinking of maximising the prospecting and conquest geared activity or responding to the precise needs of Customers and seeking to protect the company from damaged or deteriorating relationships and thereby potential loss of custom.

Although it is a decreasing phenomenon, human nature, not good with change in the first place, seems to find magnification and amplification inside the booming chambers of big institutions and corporations. And occasionally the boardroom booms loudest and longest against change; tradition and precedent being more comfortable, less risky to deal with. Thus as we learn more and more about an age that requires flexibility of planning as well as flexibility of thinking and attitude, so attention must surely focus on the boardroom for the signal to address the future, consider new thinking and find new solutions. Leadership and direction, of which the boardroom is and will remain both the sanctuary and centre, have never been in a brighter spotlight than at this time. As autonomy and responsibility are encouraged for individuals, so leadership is an increasingly vital quality and 'management', for the business leader, less so.

It seems that every book or article I read is saying, just as I am in this book, that the drive for its particular topic or subject 'has to come from the top, it demands the attention, support and commitment of the CEO'. CEOs now face so many demands and are being asked for attention by so many people within the flatter structures that they really do have to manage their time with a great deal of skill and sensitivity. The benefit of such pressure is that it keeps their minds focused at the high level at which it should be and stops most of them slipping back into the old command and control ways. They simply don't have the time any more. If they let their attention slip from that high level, they either fail or the stress and pressure overcomes them. They burn out. The greatest risk here for the business is that the CEO fails to recognise the difference between 'running the business' and 'leading the business'. A major distinction is the great amount of people skills and people time required and, of course, as the pressures increase, these are exactly the qualities which tend to disappear first. Change stretches everyone wherever they sit in the business.

## Steps to changes

When you are considering changes, the following ideas will help you to judge and shape the task ahead of you.

## Step 1   Know where you are

First you must carry out a review or audit of where you are and where you stand. It may be necessary or helpful to seek outside help with this since impartial judgement and unimpaired observation are keys to a successful appraisal.

## Step 2   Know where you are going

Consider your ultimate goal for the change process you want to undertake. At this stage don't compromise this vision by letting history and experience cloud what can and can't be achieved.

## Step 3   Study the gap

The gap between step 1 and step 2 is the task at hand. Thus one can look at the gap as a corporate project and start to think about the methods and means.

## Step 4   Identify the phasing

Most projects of this nature fall or can be divided into phases with a natural feel or rhythm to them. Just in the same way as to cross a stream one might first put down stepping stones one pace apart, recheck the positioning again from the other side once it has been reached and then fill in or bridge the gaps to provide the completed solution.

## Step 5   Create a means for change

Just as in the preceding analogy, our bridge becomes a means through (or rather over) which one can get to the other side, so we must create a corporate means through which we can get from where we are to where we want to be.

Such a means might be created from training programmes, changes in management style, corporate or departmental structures, new procedures and changes to job specifications. These are the physical mechanisms which will provide our stepping stones. Gradually, as people get a clear view of the other side – where they are going – so they will, if the mechanisms are right, look forward to and feel confident about the journey. The bigger and more significant this is, in many ways the better – say, reorganisation or restructuring for example – and it will help to have a 'flag' to rally round being some kind of central theme or rationale. External threat is often used, but I would prefer to interpret it as a positive internal desire or need.

■ Customer-Driven Marketing

## How to find out where you are

The obvious place to start with such an examination is the Customer. However, I suggest that in many situations one finds a way past the 'professional' buyer if such an entity exists in your sector. It is the specifiers and highest level thinkers whose assessment will be of most benefit to you. If you have strong ideas of where you are, or if your own sales and marketing teams have developed systems to tell them, or if you rely on the likes of Nielsen figures or other similar research data, checking with Customers can help you to validate theories, discover the truth behind statistics.

Bypassing them may not sound respectful of the role of the buyer, but many corporations use the buyer as a protective ring or filter. I asked earlier how people feel about quantity driven sales people – here is some evidence! They build a defence structure – a ring of tough buyers – to protect themselves from those sales people who will do anything to get their commission. Since sales people exaggerate, we'll get some exaggeration detectors! Customer-driven marketing will cut through this costly negative and wasteful charade like the brightest, sharpest knife, leaving people to build teams which move them forward faster together rather than one side digging a moat while the other lays siege.

So one has the choice of building confidence with the buyer to let you through to the business or, alternatively, finding some way of approaching those you need to reach which does not cause damage. In the final resort, the CEO-to-CEO approach here has rarely failed since, in the greater order of things, both recognise the potential when it is genuinely there and the approach is justified.

## How to decide where you want to be

I see this as the task of creating a vision. Occasionally CEOs descend from a mountain clutching a vision as if it had been 'handed down'. Then they sell their vision to their team and expect everyone to climb on board. To me this is the wrong way. Vision, to me, should be created by the leaders of the business and it should be built by consensus. What should be avoided with a vision by consensus is that consensus is a great bringer of compromise and mediocrity. Thus the task of the leader of the leaders is to banish compromise and mediocrity and to specify the boldness of the vision.

## Assessing the gap

In assessing the task at hand or, if you will, examining the gap and looking at it as the project, it is vital to break it down into manageable segments – I'm probably not the first to describe these as 'bite-size chunks'. If the process lacks natural breaks, three-month or (if needs genuinely must) six-month periods represent good psychological units; enough to make tangible progress but not so much that one could be expected to change the world.

It is at this time that you will need to consider and create the shape of the vehicle or process which will be used to get you across the gap. There are some imperatives to assist with this.

### 1. Identify the right issues

In auditing where you are, it is critical that you identify the right issues. That is to say that your audit can be related accurately to the task ahead. Ask yourself, 'What are the few things that make the difference between success or failure?'

### 2. Seek third party help

History holds plenty of those who have tried to complete their task themselves and found that the one setback to self-assessment is that without checks or controls it can become self-fulfilling.

### 3. Understand the need to train and to develop experience

By far the most effective balance here will include an element of 'classroom training' and learning 'on the job' which is now more commonly regarded as a blend of coaching and counselling.

### 4. Head for a self-measurement regime

In this context it is a clear objective in new style businesses that everyone becomes an accountant and a marketer. That is to say they understand the financial dynamics of their success or failure or over or under-performance as well as the relationship it has with marketing. Thus, for example, a sales person will be expected to understand how price negotiations impact on margin, profitability, their budget and their pay, as well as how they affect the company's position with the Client in the long and short term. Moreover they'll need to consider how the way price is negotiated will affect the company's positioning in the buyer's mind.

To operate a satisfactory self-measurement regime, the standards must be absolutely clear; the effects of success or failure will be both powerful and direct; and wherever possible the reward system should be automatic. Self-measurement requires that people can relate their effort to the critical part of the initiative (the bite-size chunk) that is in hand. A degree of classi-

■ Customer-Driven Marketing

cal subjective assessment will complement such regimes, since it is likely that, as a part of installing the Customer or quality objectives, several 'soft issue' targets will be placed upon people. These are less tangible, qualitative and philosophical or even cultural. More of this can be found in Chapter 21 where we look at rewards. In effect, a self-measurement regime will play a major part in measuring the progress of change continuously and visibly.

### 5. Be open about goals, methods and achievements

There is a great deal to be said for openness in the whole matter of managing change. It tends to focus the minds of those who have chosen to come along with you. It breeds involvement, commitment and a sense of purpose. By breaking down the initiative into manageable tasks and applying self-measurement mechanisms to progress, the satisfaction and rewards are more readily obtained and the spoils shared. Success should yield generous rewards (not necessarily monetary) and failure must be firmly acted upon.

It is true of change generally that people tend to polarise, for or against. If they don't, you should encourage them to. For if they are not on your side they must count as against; if they are against, they must be helped to move on or to be found new tasks elsewhere.

It is a fact that in all elements of change there are generally casualties; people who don't fit or don't approve or who are not suitable on 'the other side'; that is when the gap has been crossed and you now occupy your new position – where you wanted to get to. Generally, the more senior the dissidents, the more damage they can do. Managing change as a process is much better dealt with 'top down' and requires, or rather works most effectively with, the full support, energy, enthusiasm and commitment of all who want to be involved – and without those who don't!

## Seven key factors in managing change

### 1. New lamps for old

Do everything you can to breed dissatisfaction, foster insecurity and distrust of the old (present) system. Flood the people involved with evidence and reasons for change. Create and stimulate excitement, enthusiasm and interest in the new system or process.

### 2. Grease the chute

Changemakers need lubricants – people or media who will openly and not so openly spread the new gospel, support views, become disciples of the initiative. Seek out the evangelists and give them plenty to evangelise about.

Often you will find teams are an effective way of coping with change: find your best evangelists and make them prominent or even leaders in the teams. These build to a critical mass and there comes a point where those resistant to change become 'in the wrong' as well as in the minority.

In the same way, changemakers need to seek out the healthy sections and build around them. Be fearless and surgical in dealing with the others. View them as lost causes; they are as potentially lethal as corporate cancers.

Winning the minds of those with authority, influence, desire or the freedom to change is a great facilitator and can speed change no end. And remember, you need full commitment right from the top.

### 3. Sell shares and go fishing

The more people who can claim 'ownership', the greater the dedication, commitment and involvement you will generate. The earlier this can be done the wider your net can spread. Harvest as many as you can and do all you can to help them deal with problems and overcome resistance.

### 4. Choose your costume

Which style will your change take – will you come across as the masked avenger, the pioneering spirit, the mad scientist, the brave foot soldier or the charismatic father of change? I found the work of Harrison and Theaker both interesting and amusing when, in 1989, *Dealing with Conflict* was published. They identified the four major styles as follows:

- *Blitzkreig / Charge of the Light Brigade* – Oblivious to previous history ... personal practices, interests and antagonisms are ignored ... fears are ridiculed ... conflict is bloody! ... tempers frayed! ... tears are shed! ... innovation fails ... prospects of other initiatives are sabotaged! (This can be an excellent idea if you are on death's doorstep but it obviously lacks credibility at other times!)
- *Borgia Method* – Intrigue and plots abound ... find out potential 'blockers' ... divide and rule ... work out ways of 'rubbishing' their views ... key decisions taken when they are absent from meetings ... papers only reach them at the last minute ... rumours are circulated about their personal habits, competence etc ... any mistakes are emphasised. (This sounds like business as usual in many companies! The big problem here is that it tends to absorb and waste vast amounts of resources and energy. And the wrong side quite often wins!)

- *Munich Method* – Appeasement Rules OK ... everyone must be 'nice' to one another ... avoid 'crunch' issues ... keep to the peripheral details ... everyone must agree ... therefore minimal change ... (Usually this approach is high on democracy and that is mistaken for low on leadership. High democracy needs strong leadership otherwise it vacillates in consensus, makes risk-free and slow decisions and everyone gets frustrated and fed up.)
- *Matterhorn Method* – All staff involved collaboratively ... conflict is necessary but needs to be controlled ... stress on benefits for the group ... team is greater than the sum of the members ... cult of the personality is avoided ... each member must have an opportunity to make a contribution and therefore have ownership ... (Some of your climbers won't be fit enough for this 'mountain' and others will be foolhardy. Often, while the leader is busy leading, others are simply swinging on a rope. This method can be highly motivating and successful but needs intelligent, sensitive leadership, careful planning and be sure only to take those who are fit enough with you on the climb otherwise they'll slow you down.)

## 5. Erect your scaffolding

Scaffolding – or support systems – of two distinct types is required for change to proceed most smoothly. The first is personal scaffolding. This provides the means for people to deal with their personal feelings and anxieties. Change is nearly always emotive and never more so than when jobs, territories, futures and securities are involved. And that's nearly always. The second type of scaffolding is organisational and must:

- avoid conspiracies by providing and widely distributing accurate information
- mould or reinforce positive ideas, actions and attitudes
- encourage, provide and respond to feedback
- give help, training, advice and counsel.

## 6. Send in the reinforcements

Successes – however small or apparently trivial – are successes none the less and should be made much of. Publicise them as far afield as possible. They all contribute to the 'winning team' concept and will further the spirit of compliance and co-operation. This may require special horizontal and vertical communications – and recognise both the formal and informal (grapevines!).

Visibly identify and reward the individual and team activities or actions which on an individual or a team basis support or further the change.

## 7. Become a pilot

Inside the cockpit of change you'll need to place instruments that measure the change, monitor your success and warn of deviations. You know your startpoint and you know where you are headed, so you've plotted the course. However, as pilot you need to be able to observe, calculate and make adjustments and amendments in order to achieve, not necessarily the smoothest flight, but certainly the most effective.

## Creating harmony of organisation and accountability

Payment and reward systems, as we will discuss in Chapter 21, are only effective if set in an appropriate context. The organisational framework in which people are managed has a dominant impact on how they perform. There are occasions when the structure can conflict with the reward system and discourage behaviour which would lead to greater earnings. It is essential, therefore, that team members are clear about their tasks and accountabilities for markets, products or processes. The style of the organisation sets the context for recruitment, selection and training.

The impact on motivation and performance of basic disciplines in recruitment, selection and training is underestimated. For those already employed by a firm, matching individuals to key tasks demands special care and attention to ensure that it uses people's strengths and covers their vulnerabilities.

Figure 20.1 (on page 270) illustrates the dilemma which many managers face. There are people of high potential who do not yet perform and there are those with low potential who do a good job. 'Workhorses' are a vital, but often underestimated, group of people on whom so many organisations depend. Stars are often the source of great pain and anguish as they manipulate one employer after another.

As Figure 20.2 (on page 270) shows, in designing the organisation for high performance, it is important to recognise the current style and structure. Directors and senior managers often speak the words of a performance based business, but behave in a risk-averse and hierarchical way. It is vital that measures of performance and the organisational structure are synchronised if people are to concentrate effort and emotion on the selling task and not internal politics. The larger the organisation, the greater the tendency for it to become status conscious. Bureaucracy generates excessive costs, slows response times and demotivates those who have greatest responsibility for selling products and services to Customers. Moving to a flat and devolved organisation, with simple, output based measures, results in a change of culture. Decisions can be speeded up, measurement of performance made fairer and the power of the individual channelled to achieve the required results.

■ Customer-Driven Marketing

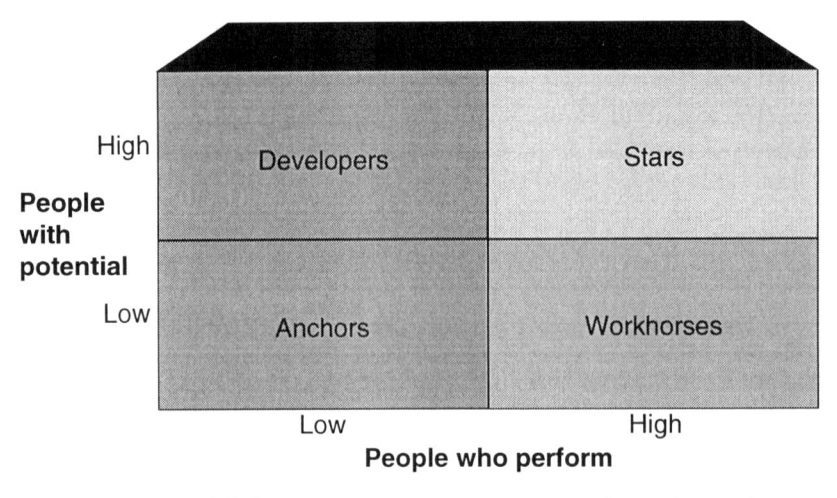

|  | Low | High |
|---|---|---|
| **High** People with potential | Developers | Stars |
| **Low** | Anchors | Workhorses |

People who perform

Figure 20.1 *Developing the organisation through people*

## What gets measured gets done

An activity which has not been recently measured can often be improved simply by introducing some form of performance monitoring. Whatever measures you implement, they should reflect the organisation's objectives and personal accountabilities and link, ultimately, right through the chain to the management accounts. Reporting of performance is often incomprehensible to those who manage it. There is little value in presenting information unless the individual who receives

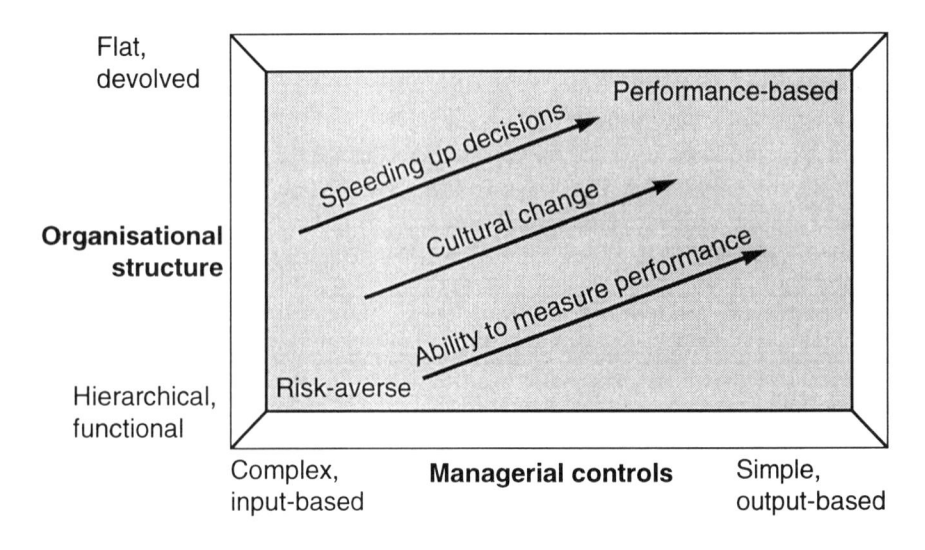

Figure 20.2 *Organisational design and performance measures*

it understands the message, and is willing and able to act on it. Reports should be designed for action, giving the individual or team as much feedback as possible.

The timing of reporting should reflect the nature of the action to be taken. The degree of analysis and its accuracy should be balanced with the speed with which judgements must be made. Consistency is often more important than accuracy. Employees are motivated when they are committed to accomplishing specific results in predetermined timescales. Their achievements must be measured and recognised. The reward system can only reinforce this commitment; it seldom creates it.

## The link between corporate values and individual behaviour

The arrow shown in Figure 20.3 illustrates the influence of the chain from values to behaviour. If people are to be genuinely motivated, the management culture has to be consistent with the objectives of the business. Conflicts occur when the behaviour expected is not in accord with the values espoused. To be successful, an organisation needs to set the values as explicitly as possible through statements of a vision, mission or strategy and reinforce these through the measurement process and the way people are rewarded. If attitudes are inappropriate, or unconstructive, then it is important to consider the deeper issues.

Assessing the perceptions of employees in an organisation can be a valuable way of raising the awareness and understanding of the barriers to success. A staff survey can be employed in a constructive environ-

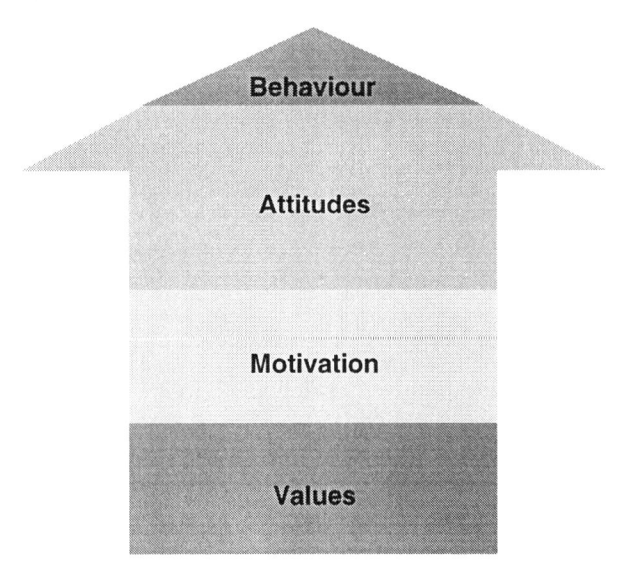

**Figure 20.3** *What makes people tick?*

■ Customer-Driven Marketing

ment but employees must be convinced that the directors are genuinely interested in responding to their concerns and negative perceptions. A survey is not a panacea and will create more problems than it prevents if it is done solely for cosmetic reasons. A successful survey should highlight what is going well and offer opportunities for employees to express feelings and pinpoint problems. Staff can also help to clarify priorities and explain the first steps towards solutions. Undertaken by an independent organisation, surveys can provide a valuable insight that would be difficult to obtain in any other way. The approach can be through a combination of written questionnaires, face-to-face interviews and discussion groups, depending on the needs of the business, the available resources and the sensitivity of the issues. A survey should not be undertaken unless its objectives – and how the results will be used – are explicit.

Feedback and action must follow the completed survey. Expectations will have been raised and doing nothing will make relationships worse. The way producers behave reflects their perceptions, not some kind of 'objective' reality. Communications, managerial action and measurement systems all contribute to these impressions.

The relationship between managerial style and the values of the business is illustrated in Figure 20.4. Unless the way managers do their work is consistent with the values of the business, there is inevitable conflict, undermining the performance of those involved. Empowerment is not a gift from managers who abdicate their right to measure performance. Empowerment should be earned when taken. It demands better, not flimsier, managerial controls. Managers need to provide permission, power and protection to their teams. Raising their performance demands

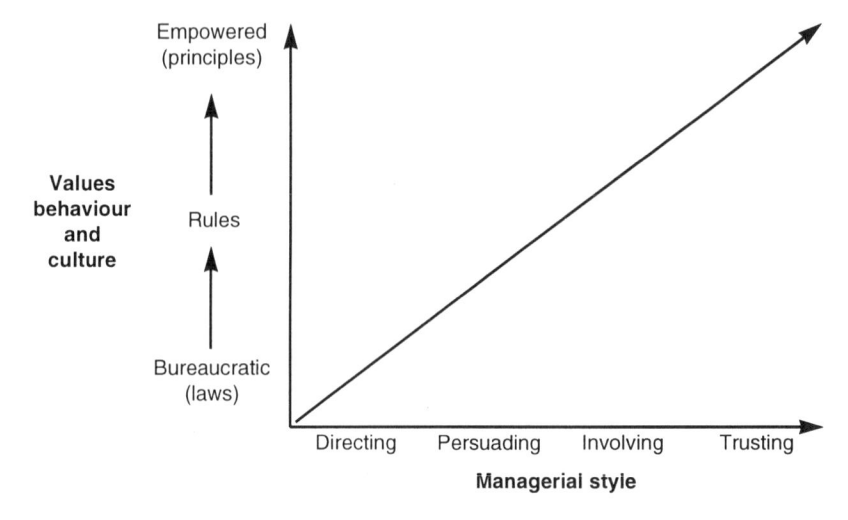

**Figure 20.4** *Managerial style and values*

understanding of their personal tasks and responsibilities, leadership by a champion, who is not necessarily a manager, and a credible path to a challenging goal.

## Getting organised for change

To organise yourself correctly for change, you will need four sets of people: a small steering group at the helm; multi-functional task forces investigating processes and principal changes; line managers who will be responsible for evaluation and implementation; and external facilitators (Figure 20.5).

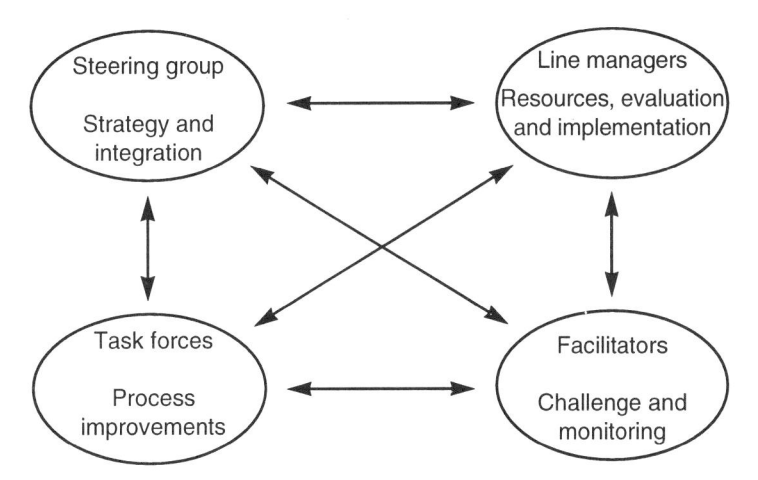

**Figure 20.5** *The organisation for change requires four groups*

Once key executives have given their commitment and the organisational framework is in place, you can start to analyse and evaluate the 'core' processes. In any business there should not be more than three or four truly 'core' processes although these may cover a long chain of related activities. The mapping can use specialised software although, to be frank, manual drawing, or the use of a suitable spreadsheet or graphics package, is often adequate. What is important is that those who actually do (or will do) the work participate in this task. You will find their knowledge and comments invaluable. The objective is to design new processes which:

- are Customer-driven, which reinforce long-term commitment to Customers and which work in harmony with the desire to build loyalty through relationship marketing activity
- offer flexibility without complexity in the marketplace
- design reliability and speed of response into all processes
- assure efficient throughput
- avoid and do not create operational and administrative bottlenecks.

■ Customer-Driven Marketing

Managers and staff are more likely than executives to be aware of ineffective methods or ideas and can be remarkably realistic about the repercussions for the organisation and for jobs. As with all reform, it is the middle managers who feel most threatened. Acceptance of the need and value of the Customer-driven transformation arrives with a growing realisation during the work that has to be done to create a genuinely competitive edge. Or, as one of my Clients so succinctly put it, 'to blow our Customers' socks off ... in the nicest possible way, of course!'

## Becoming Customer-driven is inevitably a complex task

Preparing your business to become Customer-driven will probably involve you in a great deal of change. As you have read during this chapter, change like this impacts in many ways. The issues are not silos; sometimes they overlap, sometimes they rub up against each other, sometimes they dovetail neatly together. In this chapter, in relation to change, we have noted the following:

- planning and measuring change benefits from six key points:
  1. know where you are
  2. identify, specify and agree the critical project stages
  3. communicate openly to gain understanding and commitment
  4. identify and implement managerial controls to measure performance
  5. reward achievement generously
  6. act firmly on failure.
- The Strategy of Change has seven steps:
  1. analyse past trends
  2. evaluate objectively the current position
  3. identify the ultimate goal
  4. break the task (gap) down into manageable critical steps
  5. determine and agree how each of these will be tactically achieved
  6. plan and manage the change
  7. measure progress continuously and openly.
- The seven steps to managing change are:
  1. rubbish the old, worship the new
  2. look for people and opportunities to lubricate positive opinion
  3. encourage others to become co-owners of the change
  4. decide the style of the change
  5. build personal and organisational support systems
  6. publicise success and team or individual achievement
  7. monitor, measure and control the change to adopt and adjust for the best results.
- It is essential both to create harmony between the organisation and

accountability and to ensure that there is also harmony with people, in other words, you should fit 'square pegs into square holes' as far as people are concerned.
- Moving to a flat and devolved organisation, with simple output based measures results in a change of culture: decision making is faster, performance measurement fairer and the power of motivated individuals harnessed to the required outcomes.
- 'Whatever gets measured gets done': measures should reflect the organisation's objectives and the accountabilities of personnel. These should follow the chain through to link to management accounts.
- Behaviour is affected by attitudes; attitudes are formed by motivation; motivation should stem from the corporate values. A staff survey, constructively handled, can prove very useful in assessing and preparing for necessary changes. However, feedback and action must follow.
- Democratic, empowered organisations need more leadership not less. Corporate managerial styles should grant empowerment where it is earned but should not relinquish their duty to measure performance.
- You need to gather four sets of people to assist you with the change to becoming Customer-driven: a steering group; multi-functional task forces to investigate processes and principal changes; line managers for evaluation and implementation; and external facilitators.

# 21

# Getting the right rewards

This chapter and the following one deal with two of the most difficult aspects of Customer-driven marketing. For, in assessing what comes next for sales, advertising and marketing, there are still two critical factors – the structure of the business in relation to Customer needs and the motivation of the people it employs. These matters are difficult for most organisations because they do not consider or face change of this nature every day. Indeed most companies, let alone their marketing departments, would justifiably be lacking in this respect; specialist expertise and experience in such matters is understandably low. Hence most companies would be well advised to consider taking outside help and advice from consultants who will be able to bring both the necessary experience and expertise to support the required initiative and the vital objectivity of a third party. I constantly meet people from companies – often large ones – who, sometimes because they are disillusioned with previous outside help, have decided to try to cope with massive change programmes on their own. For some reason, this seems to be more common in South Africa than anywhere else. Perhaps it is to do with the weak Rand, but usually, in relation to the cost of failure, the argument for self-help is weaker than the Rand!

The first piece of advice in matters of such importance and proportion as rewards and structure might follow that given in the previous chapter; for even these projects can be broken down into bite-size chunks. And they can be achieved through a strategic transition process. Let us, however, concentrate specifically for the rest of this chapter on the rewards and motivation of employees. In the next we'll tackle structural matters.

Customer-driven marketing requires an enormous leap in the mentality of sales, advertising and marketing people. Indeed, I suggest that even those who do not feel it appropriate to follow, for example, the advice on corporate structure in the next chapter will, regardless, find it necessary to change or modify their reward systems. The primary purpose must now be to encourage and reward success; the secondary, where restructuring has taken place, will be to put back the other elements that will have disappeared. Remember that when hierarchies are abandoned for the new flatter structures, one element of the reward system has been effectively removed – promotion. The death of the middle manager casts a long shadow!

So, there can be no better time to step back from the task at hand and consider the role of pay and reward systems, both as a motivational tool and for nurture and propagation of our Customer and quality goals.

## Rewards – how they relate to the corporate mission

When projects like reorganisation or cultural shift are under way, the spirit to drive this through will come essentially from three sources. These are the reservoir of corporate pride, a sense of sacrifice in the common good and, of course, powerful incentives for excellent performance. Such incentives tend to work best when the schemes are simple and cover all employees. Typically these are geared to different factors, depending on the level of employee. Here are some examples:

- *Shop floor* — productivity, unit cost, quality and Customer service based.
- *Staff* — related to productivity or cost control
    — meeting Customer and quality requirements.
- *Management* — performance against unit costs and/or margins.
- *Executives* — performance related to return on capital employed and economic value-added
    — share options
    — customer satisfaction and loyalty.

It is vital that pay must follow the culture or mission, not lead (or even mislead) it, in effect, thereby, reinforcing objectives not driving them. Push rather than pull. A danger here is that with some of these issues we forget the big picture. For, if we are embarked upon a Customer-driven mission or have a quality perspective, this will affect our interpretation of, for example, rewards based upon productivity or cost control. It's not fast and cheap regardless – it's fast and cheap and perfect for the Customer.

■ Customer-Driven Marketing

## The politics of remuneration

When you lift the roof off any company, rather like a community of ants or bees, you can observe a society at work. The society, in matters such as remuneration, sets the tone of what are acceptable and unacceptable norms. As so often in life, pecking orders are established and so comparisons will be drawn. You might find this to be in relation to capability – skilled to unskilled; in relation to professional training – accountants to engineers; and in relation to geography – different areas of the country. As you move up and down the pecking orders so you will see the balance between cash and fringe benefits change.

Next you will notice that the society or community establishes dynamics which influence the style and level of pay. This is illustrated by the Remuneration Map (Figure 21.1). You will see how typical fast growing companies have high risk elements; mature companies place greater emphasis on benefits and bureaucracies have elaborate, defensive systems.

◄──────── INCREASING PAY COMPLEXITY ────────

**ORGANISATIONAL CHARACTERISTIC**

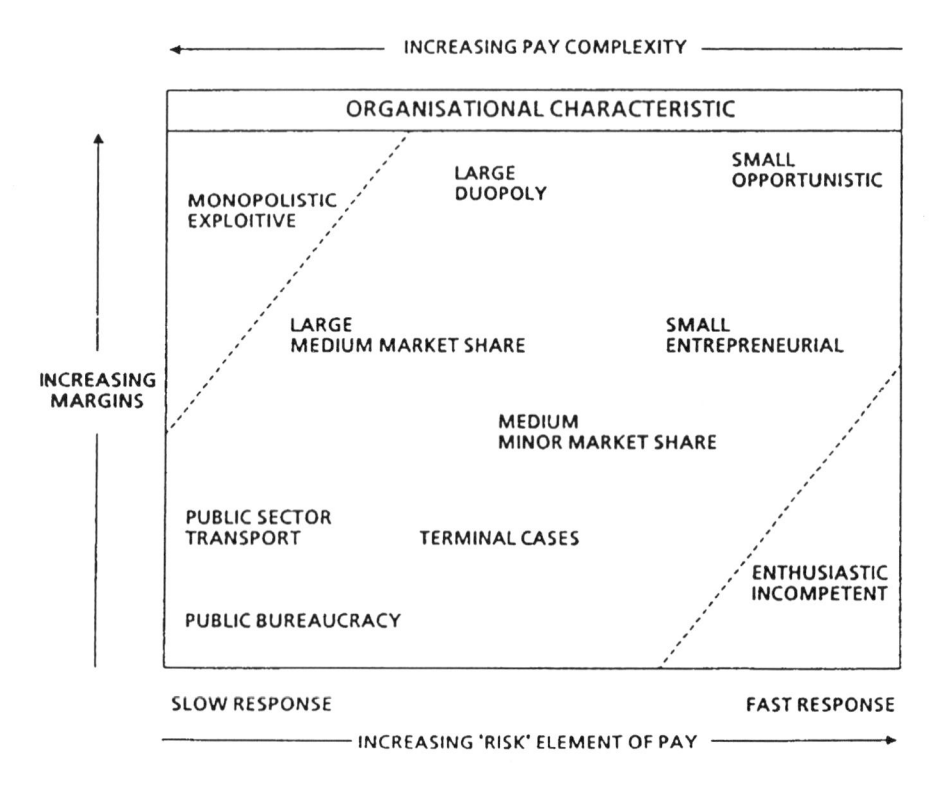

| | | |
|---|---|---|
| MONOPOLISTIC EXPLOITIVE | LARGE DUOPOLY | SMALL OPPORTUNISTIC |
| | LARGE MEDIUM MARKET SHARE | SMALL ENTREPRENEURIAL |
| | MEDIUM MINOR MARKET SHARE | |
| PUBLIC SECTOR TRANSPORT | TERMINAL CASES | ENTHUSIASTIC INCOMPETENT |
| PUBLIC BUREAUCRACY | | |

INCREASING MARGINS ↑

SLOW RESPONSE — FAST RESPONSE

──────── INCREASING 'RISK' ELEMENT OF PAY ────────►

**Figure 21.1** *The Remuneration Map: different organisational styles have different remuneration systems. It is vital they do not conflict.*

## Deciding the objectives of pay reform

Along with the implementation of Customer-driven marketing we have identified two pivotal roles for our pay and reward system: we want it to assist with the restructuring in some cases, but in all cases we want it to play a long-term and significant part in the transfer from quantity to quality objectives and from the hard to the soft issues.

One simple example will illustrate how this latter point is effected. Consider the change which occurs when a sales person is moved from commission on short-term sales to commission on long-term profits. All of a sudden the sales person modifies their whole negotiating stance, finding new less aggressive and friendlier, more caring, ways to lure. Plainly this shows that we can achieve our objectives and underpin our corporate changes of direction. However, we need to think how our people, not just the sales people, but all appropriate people can be made to concentrate on the relationship building.

Before looking at the factors we can use, perhaps we should consider whether there are any other objectives which should also influence our thinking. As well, of course, as its motivational impact in enhancing corporate pride or commitment and recognising business, marketing or sales performance, pay reform can also recognise:

- cost control or reduction
- the attraction or retention of key staff
- changing employee behaviour.

Of one thing you can be certain, it is the business need which will dictate the direction of change and that means ...

## ...Back to Customers, once again

Since the driving force in our decision making is now the Customer relationship, we can broaden the scope to consider what I call 'Geared Motivation'. This has three major aspects. First, it rewards business growth, not simply sales. Secondly, it brackets rewards. And thirdly, as I shall explain, it offers a range of 'gearing factors' which include more qualitative than quantitative factors.

The concept of bracketing rewards is fundamental to the Customer mission. By setting minimum levels below which little, preferably no, reward is triggered, one effectively sets a minimum acceptable performance standard or average. By setting maximum levels one inhibits overemphasis on aspects which might detract from the declared goals. This clearly could dissuade those who place too much value on the sales element and encourage them to focus on other aspects of their work. For example, a sales person who is paid 20 per cent commission up to 80 per

■ Customer-Driven Marketing

cent of target, 25 per cent up to 100 per cent of target and 30 per cent thereafter is basically going to screw every last sale out of anyone that steps in their path. Volume of transactions will be high, but quality of business will be low and repeat business will also be low.

Thus, equally it can be appreciated that, just as by putting a minimum bracket the minimum standards are laid down, so by putting a maximum ceiling for reward it is clearly demonstrated that selling to win more commission and to fulfil personal rather than corporate goals is not what is required. What is added now are the qualitative gearing factors. Let us take a look at what I mean by gearing factors:

- sales
- profitability
- spread of business
- longevity of relationship
- customer satisfaction
- customer loyalty
- customer loss rates
- share of spend
- problem-free periods
- research results
- initiative
- innovation
- team spirit/activity
- personal spirit/activity.

Of course, you can add more to these – to suit whatever your corporate desires are. Your selection of factors becomes the criteria against which employees are measured. However, none of them needs necessarily relate directly to sales or turnover (not even the sales factor); they could all relate to corporate performance, whatever way you choose to measure that. The disadvantage here is that the less direct and visible schemes become, the more trouble people have seeing what they have to do.

To be clear about the possibility that the sales factor might not be related to sales, let's take an example since it's confusing when you write it, let alone when you read it! You may choose to give a sales person a salary which, on target, is set to provide, say 80 per cent basic and 20 per cent from incentives such as commission. Of the 20 per cent rewards you have chosen your gearing factors so that actual sales turnover generated will provide one quarter of that, ie 5 per cent of total pay. However, the 'pot' from which the rewards are paid does not have to be a sales generated pot. It can be generated by items which are much more closely related to corporate success. Such a calculation will ensure that the time investment by the sales person is well thought out, but also that they know, at the end of the day, a happy, satisfied Customer leads to happy, satisfied employers, which leads to happy, satisfied employees. I said earlier that simplicity was a good quality to strive for in a pay and reward system; it is, but alas it's not always so easy to achieve. For pure courage and vision, and achievement of the notion of simplicity, although almost a decade old and rewarding a Total Quality drive, the Rank Xerox story referred to earlier is still fascinating, so here it is.

## Ranking quality higher

The Rank Xerox story is an interesting example since we can see how they were one of the first successfully to move quality objectives into their sales department as well as throughout the rest of the company.

There is a tale about Roland Magnin which I have not formally been able to confirm or deny. Thus, it might be more prudent to call it a fable. The fable suggests that, worried that his new salary and reward package might face a somewhat doubtful passage through the coming board meeting at which he would propose it, M. Magnin announced it first to the press, presenting his board with somewhat of a *fait accompli*. At the time, Magnin was chief executive of Rank Xerox. He was responsible for a change in focus which was to have a major impact on the performance of the company and enable the sales and marketing teams to adopt quality practices – indeed, more, it demanded that they did.

It was explained earlier that the use of Total Quality Management techniques have resulted in highly satisfactory performance changes within organisations chasing product, service and organisational improvements. Rank Xerox realised that more was needed. Magnin argued that even if the product was excellent, there would be no improvements if the sales people did not understand their Customers, get closer to them or even, for that matter, if after-sales and maintenance standards did not similarly match up. They also recognised that, whatever they did, it had to be a long-term or permanent programme. Indeed such initiatives always tend to start slowly and gather momentum as the enthusiasm and commitment grows, lubricated by early success. However, in the last respect – success – Rank Xerox had a long while to wait. And, in the early years of the initiative, they refashioned and remodelled thinking as they moved forward.

For example, profit had always been their number one and unashamed objective. Later this was changed to return on assets, but after three years of TQM methods, Customer satisfaction became the prime business objective. After one year of experimentation, Roland Magnin reported as follows.

■ Customer-Driven Marketing

## The first year

The scheme applied to the most senior managers in international headquarters and the European operating companies (135 people in total).

## The principles

The size of salary increases for these senior managers at the end of the year was influenced equally by Customer satisfaction and Customer loyalty. Customer loyalty was defined as the proportion of products with Customers at the start of the year which were still with Customers at the end of the year. This was measured internally by Rank Xerox. The calculation is:

$$\frac{\text{Products with Customers at the start of the year minus losses during the year}}{\text{Products with Customers at the start of the year}}$$

Products are weighted by their price and allowance was made where Customers trade in a Rank Xerox product for another Rank Xerox product.

Customer satisfaction was measured by external agencies through a written questionnaire which asked:

'Are you satisfied with the products and services provided by Rank Xerox?'

'If you need another or a replacement product would you seriously consider Rank Xerox as a supplier?'

'If asked, would you recommend Rank Xerox to business associates?'

The answers were compared to norms established through Rank Xerox's more extensive surveys of Customer satisfaction. The target levels for loyalty and satisfaction were each 85 per cent. It is interesting to note that this was one of the first experiments of its time which went so far as to measure both Customer satisfaction and Customer loyalty. Most other companies around this period, and for some time after, contented themselves with satisfaction as their yardstick. This is a notion which, as I have already opined, is fatally flawed.

## The link with salary increases

The results of the measures of Customer satisfaction and Customer loyalty determined whether senior managers received salary increases which were higher or lower than other staff in their country, with the override

# Getting the right rewards

that the results would vary by a maximum of four percentage points up or down. Here are two examples:

***Country A*** – Loyalty and satisfaction results are 25 per cent better than target. General salary increase is planned at 10 per cent. Therefore, senior managers receive 12.5 per cent (ie. 10 per cent plus 25 per cent of 10 per cent).

***Country B*** – Loyalty and satisfaction results are 10 per cent below target. General salary increase is planned at 8 per cent. Therefore, senior managers receive 7.2 per cent (ie 8 per cent minus 10 per cent of 8 per cent).

The general manager in each country has discretion to vary the increases for individual senior managers within the overall figure. The salary rises for senior managers at international headquarters were based on a composite of the results across Europe.

## The results

The results show that 89 per cent of Rank Xerox Customers said they were satisfied – and the Customer loyalty level was 85 per cent. On average this boosted the salary increase of senior managers by an extra 2.5 per cent.

## Changes for year 2

In the following year the scheme for senior managers continued with these changes:

- Greater weighting was given to Customer loyalty. This accounted for 70 per cent of the measurement, not 50 per cent.
- Customer satisfaction was measured as part of the regular, more detailed surveys and not separate questionnaires.
- The Customer satisfaction surveys measured perceptions of Rank Xerox against the main competitor in each product group in each country.
- The target levels of performance for loyalty and satisfaction were increased to 88 per cent.

## Extension to others

A bonus was introduced for staff at international headquarters. This was calculated on the same basis as the salary rises. The European operating companies were asked to introduce similar schemes suited to their national environment. As we have learned earlier in this book, the payoff was magnificent but longer and slower than everyone hoped or expected.

### Long-term results report

To remind you, in Chapter 12 we read how, after three years of dedication to quality and Customer satisfaction, the Rank Xerox team saw no significant improvement. In the fourth year they saw real gains start. In the fifth year profits were up 40 per cent, return on assets had trebled, unit costs of components had fallen by over 30 per cent and, very importantly, indices of Customer satisfaction had risen by 35 per cent. Rank Xerox were regaining some of the market share lost in the early 1980s.

The original problem at Rank Xerox had stemmed from the panic discovery that their rigging costs were about equal to the selling price of their Japanese competitors. This led to the realisation in due course that rigging was not the disease but a symptom; they had a corporate problem. The results they have achieved demonstrate that a process of leadership through quality can be highly effective, but that the effects will be boosted when quality reaches beyond the product and touches the Customer. Rank's evidence of increasing performance linked to its Customers' satisfaction and loyalty clearly substantiated that building relationships with Customers worked for them and that, over time, it is more profitable.

### Where to start

When setting the pay and gearing factors, it is always easier to start from the amount you want your people to receive when they get the job right and then work back to decide how your gearing factors will deliver that. So, if you want someone on target to earn £20,000 of which 10 per cent should be performance related, set the basic at £18,000, decide how you wish to deal with the rest. For ease, let's say the system will cut in at 80 per cent of target and cut out at 120 per cent. Thus this employee will not earn less than £20,000 (on target) nor more than £22,000. Systems like this can be operated to pay the rewards monthly, quarterly or annually if you prefer. Now all you have to do is decide on what basis the reward will be allocated.

### Describe the job you want done

We cannot consider pay and reward systems without a word about job specifications since the two should be locked together. When you change what you need from your staff, it is essential that the new elements are incorporated into their job specification (and for that matter the old removed). Each aspect should be discussed in detail with the employee and, where relevant, the correlation with the reward system clearly explained. Where subjective judgement or assessment is to be used (and that's probably in a great deal of areas), the methods of measurement and control must be abundantly clear to the individual employees. Also, they must be just as clear about new operational procedures. As they become more flexible and less prescriptive, there is a growing interest in describing jobs, not just as tasks, but also in terms of competencies. A draft outline job description is included (Figure 21.2 on page 286).

When preparing the job descriptions, try to remember the 'tight/loose' idea and give people more freedom to move, but in a more tightly defined direction. One way you can prove whether you have constructed these mechanisms properly is to ask each member of your staff to describe to you how they would relate these changes through to each Customer and, therefore, how they will treat that Customer differently. If that is not possible – perhaps because of scale – get them to nominate a representative number of Customers or representative clusters of Customers and then feed-back to you in exactly the same way. This is because, when they are presented with their new job descriptions, you need to be sure they understand what they must do differently: how will it change their behaviour, decisions, actions, responses and feelings?

When considering the remuneration strategy for your employees, whatever their grade, there are four factors which should be pulled together by pay: the style and culture of the business, the objectives of the business, the structures and societies in which your people work, and last, but always first in fact, the delivery and satisfaction of what your Customers want and need of you.

## Changing systems of remuneration

I don't need to remind you, I'm sure, that pay is a sensitive and emotive issue. This is **remarkable** and always confusing when you set this against where employees rate it in relation to their motivation. In a survey by the UK's Ashridge Management College, employees cited the challenge and interest of the job as their most important motivation, followed by authority and freedom to carry out their tasks. Salary was ranked third, yet it is often the topic about which people will be most vocal and emotive.

Thus, changes to existing systems should be planned and executed carefully. To assist you in that process, I have no hesitation in proposing the formula from Chapter 20. That's to say examine where you are, decide where you want to be and see the gap as the task at hand. Bite-size chunks may come to your rescue again and there is no reason whatsoever why one cannot run a transition period for, say, two or three years, achieving one or two steps at a time towards the end result.

■ Customer-Driven Marketing

| Outline job description |  |
|---|---|
| **Job title:** |  |
| **Reporting to:** |  |
| **Job purpose:** |  |
| **Scope:** |  |
| **Principal accountabilities:** |  |
| **Key performance indicators:** |  |
| Signed: | Date: |
| Authorised: | Date: |

**Figure 21.2** *An outline job description*

## Performance related pay – remember the team too!

If there is a warning to accompany performance related pay it is that it has been criticised for over-compensating individuals and detracting from their performance as team players. In connection with becoming Customer-driven there is a definite balance to be performed here since in the granules – the self-managed units – it is likely that you will wish to team up sales and service people, and measure their joint performance with their group of Customers. So the teamwork aspect should be thought about fully and not diminished or distracted by the scheme you design.

In businesses with many small sites, treating offices as one team can have benefits in encouraging co-operation between employees and the sharing of workloads. People can receive payments for their individual performance as well as for their contribution to the group's achievements. A reference period should be established against which future performance can be judged. The nature of the changes that are required to earn the expected bonus or commission should be highlighted. Modelling alternative options by spreadsheet can provide a simulation of potential events, likely rewards and vulnerabilities.

## Putting the package together

It is a prerequisite that there is a sound understanding of your particular employment market. Surveys of pay and conditions, preferably carried out by an independent organisation, provide a sound and generally credible foundation. Since it takes time and, frequently a lot of money, to change a pay structure, plan to achieve it over a three-year cycle. The total costs of employment, including fringe benefits and related overheads (space, telephone and facilities) are not always fully evaluated.

The balance between basic pay, variable elements and fringe benefits needs to be carefully considered and, in particular, their contribution to motivating people to achieve the desired performance. As illustrated in Figure 21.3 (on page 288), 'career risk' is linked with the speed of change in an organisation. As this rises, the security of employment decreases, exit costs diminish and incentives and personal salaries become more prevalent.

The use of fringe benefits to meet the needs of individuals varies according to their seniority and the country in which they work. They are more common in Europe than in the US. Such benefits are under pressure as markets become more competitive and individuals seek greater financial autonomy. However, removing benefits such as company cars, free fuel, health insurance, telephone expenses, life assurance and pensions is notoriously fraught. Although it is attractive to attempt to design

■ Customer-Driven Marketing

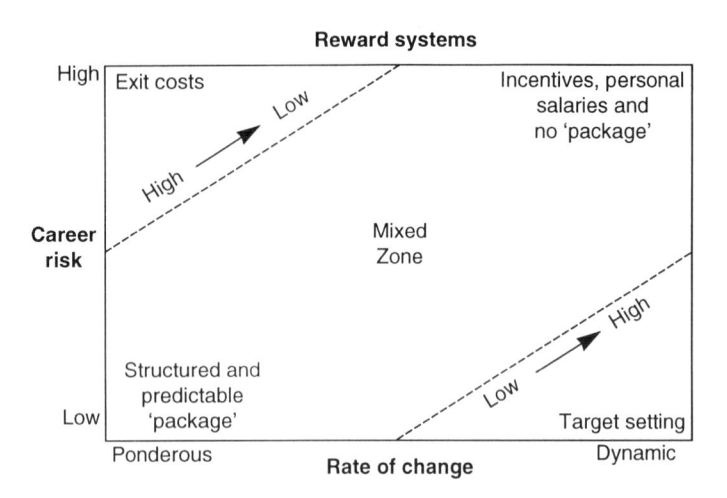

**Figure 21.3** Career risk and change are linked to pay

pay packages for individuals, managing the perceptions of equality can be a nightmare.

Even the most dynamic pay packages usually need some form of grading or job evaluation to establish the equity of basic pay. It is common to have regular personal appraisals, not always linked to pay, by which the performance of individuals is assessed against specific objectives. There is currently interest in '360 degree' appraisals. Managers subject themselves to assessment by subordinates and peers. This is not for the faint-hearted but certainly typical of the spirit of openness which flourishes in self-managed units. In my recent book, *Your Move – The Secrets of High Performance Sales Management*, I thoroughly recommended this process. To the subordinate, it demonstrates the desire to build an environment of openness and personal development; however, it is important that staff feel secure in this process and appreciate how it can help them to build confidence and stature. For the manager it provides valuable feedback, consolidates the relationship with his or her team, and provides fascinating insights into their style and how it is received.

This chapter has taken a fundamental look at pay and rewards in relation to Customer-driven marketing and described how you can think about what has to come next. Here is a summary:

- When structures are flattened, one of the great motivational factors for employees – promotion – is severely hindered. This focuses their minds on other aspects.
- Rewards should relate directly to the corporate mission. Simple schemes covering all employees are generally the most effective.
- Pay must follow the corporate culture or mission, not lead it. Figure

21.1 shows a typical example, demonstrating that fast growing companies have high risk elements, mature companies have an emphasis on benefits and bureaucracies have elaborate defensive systems.
- The major objectives to be influenced by pay reform are:
  — cost control or reduction
  — the attraction or retention of key staff
  — changing employee behaviour
  — enhancement of corporate pride and commitment
  — recognition of business, marketing or sales performance.
- Motivational elements of remuneration should reflect the desires of the Customers – the issues which are at the root of Customer satisfaction and loyalty. Geared motivation widens rewards from conventional quantity objectives:
  — it rewards business growth
  — it brackets rewards
  — it recognises, measures and rewards the quality and the soft issues.
- Job descriptions have a direct link to the pay and reward policy. New elements of the description should be explained clearly to staff and the relationship to the pay system underlined where appropriate.
- Job descriptions should be modified at the first opportunity to give employees as much freedom to move as possible, but in a tightly controlled direction.
- When presented with their new job description sales and marketing employees should be able to prepare a plan (in accordance with their new specification) for each Customer. They should be able to describe precisely how this will change their work, attitudes and feelings. Where numbers preclude this, they should be able to do the same but for a representative sample of Customers or, at the least, for individual clusters of Customers.
- Remuneration systems can be changed using the steps set out in Chapter 20.
- Performance related pay should support team or group activity.
- The balance between basic pay variable elements and fringe benefits needs to motivate people to achieve the desired performance.

# 22

# The relationship to structure

When considering the question of organisational restructuring, the first decision you face in becoming Customer-driven is whether the restructure should apply just to the marketing department or the whole organisation.

The fact that we are facing this issue raises two important considerations. First, we must realise – at least those who have any lingering doubts – that sales and marketing are not separate operational functions. They must integrate. We've tried co-operation – it ends in bloodshed at the worst, and frustration and exasperation at best.

I expect many companies, in practice, will cease to draw a distinction between the two functions over the coming years. There is so little merit in so many cases. It can already be argued that all marketing, in one guise or another, is selling; it is only a matter of time before the reverse should become true and that all selling will become marketing. At that point distinction loses reason.

The second consideration raised by restructuring to become a Customer-driven business (which is highlighted by the need to decide between a marketing or corporate change) is that this should not be a marketing department decision. It is a board decision. It impacts widely on the organisation and, if the restructuring is successful, will change the whole balance of the business, adding much greater emphasis and power to marketing. The reason why the decision should be made by the full board is simple. Without the complete buy-in of all, and without the direct, visible and total support of the CEO, it will fail. In instances where I have witnessed the process kept as a marketing decision and a marketing process it tends to be viewed by others as some kind of mental aberration by marketing or a power play to take over the world! Oddly, in one or two cases the biggest resistance came from sales!

## A new balance and therefore a new balance of power

At the moment convention suggests that a business has assets which are its buildings, machinery, plant, people and expertise. With manufacturing businesses the valuation of assets is traditional; with service businesses this matter is more complicated since often its people are a more important factor. However, in tomorrow's businesses we see two other assets which become significant. The problem for accountants is that these two assets are both intangible. The first is know-how and the second is Customer relationships. In the latter area some pioneering work is being done, and I expect to see accounting conventions come to terms with this new thinking. More importantly, we need to appreciate that as we move from transaction businesses to relationship businesses, the fundamental shift of Customer-driven marketing, so we no longer see individual sales transactions as the marketing units of currency. Focus is shifted on to the relationships being built. Customer relationships are more stable, more predictable, more reliable, but still at this time less quantifiable to accountants. Over time, as the power and effectiveness and therefore the value of these relationships starts to outshine the traditional methods, so this will create a shift in balance of the perceived assets and their values to the company.

For many, a new view will develop which is that the market is a greater asset than the business. In other words, instead of building a business and constantly looking for markets to satisfy it, the balance changes to the view that says we have the market – that is the power – we must look for manufacturing or service opportunities to satisfy it. So these are the two extremes of view; where your company positions itself is what matters. For the future, however, we can be sure of a substantial swing towards those which place quite significant value on the markets. A point which, incidentally, juxtaposes favourably with the 1980s trends of looking anew at the asset value of brands. Indeed, if one observes how investment decisions have been magnified since the notion that brands have quantifiable asset values, you can imagine how the same concept applies to Customer relationships.

## Will the board understand the decision it will be asked to make?

The extent of restructuring and the making of the decision by the board present, I believe, two substantial hurdles to marketers. The first is to get a sufficient understanding of the new concepts through to those representing (and usually protective of) their own disciplines and territories. The impact on them is extensive if it is to be a corporate restructure. For the

■ Customer-Driven Marketing

autonomous business units that result, operating as if they are in effect small businesses within businesses, will devolve marketing down to the front and will in most cases place marketing alongside the others in these teams. We are dealing with a potentially highly charged political issue! Thus marketers who are making such a case must have a full and clear understanding of all the wider business issues before they go to the board.

## Back to the Customer yet again

What should lie behind the structural shape of a company? What is wrong with a hierarchy?

Common sense tells us that if the majority accept, as does tradition, one common shape to solve all problems, then that shape must have more to do with its suitability to the problem solver than it does with the problem to be solved. For if the business world consists of problems which fall into four types – rivets, screws, nuts and nails – having a hammer will perform a task but it will be much more effective in certain identifiable cases. Those who argue for the hammer, in praise of hierarchies, will suggest that the well-being of the problem solver is important, since no good at all will come of a broken hammer. Those who favour autonomous business units, while agreeing that having all four of the necessary tools requires more skills, equally accept that the end result is vastly better since you find the right solution to the right problem.

Customer-driven marketing places the Customer first – even in this decision. For I believe the structure of the business should facilitate its primary function. The primary function of the business is to respond to Customer needs. The optimum way to achieve this is through flexible, agile, high energy, responsible teams. Further, to stay flexible to Customers and markets, the structures that are developed should themselves be under constant review. Is it necessary, for example, to require more of a structure than a two-year, perhaps three-year horizon? If it is, fair enough; but convention suggests, again for no valid reason at all, that a corporate structure should last a decade or more.

What do Customers want of us? How do they use our products or services? What will they need next from us? These are the real issues for determining a corporate structure. Find these answers and the board will find its structural answers.

## Elegance of form

There is one further idea which you might like to think about when looking at organisational structures. Draw them on paper, see how they look. For me, one of the great plus points of the hierarchy was that it had elegance of form. When the elegance was there it usually worked well.

## The relationship to structure

When managers had distorted the hierarchy to a shape lacking elegance, just as it looked clumsy, so was its performance.

This idea does not suggest that effective organisational structures always look good on paper or, even more ridiculously, that if it doesn't work on paper, it won't work in fact. It does propose that structures that look right are more likely to work right, hierarchies or otherwise.

### Aspects of structure

Redesigning structures for Customer-driven marketing will impact throughout the business. There isn't anyone who will remain unscathed or unaffected, but those to whom restructuring should make the most difference are your Customers. Remember again that flatter corporate structures make management and control both harder and more critical – this is where those 'tight/loose' controls come in.

A business operating to 'tight/loose' controls requires that its managers should have crystal clear business objectives to which they must work and against which their performance will be tightly measured and recorded. However, the ways that they may set about achieving their objectives will be subject to very loose controls, allowing them great freedom of decision making, activity, method and, necessarily therefore, responsibility.

Whatever the controls employed, other aspects of dismantling hierarchies are important. Indeed one can expect to lose some valuable benefits for which you must be careful to make provision in a new structure. For example, how do you harness corporate pride? How do you build corporate commitment? Both these important requirements must be engendered for an effective business that has confidence in its ability and belief in its standards.

Within a hierarchy these qualities tend to breed well since both the system and the culture enjoys, and often rewards, them but this is not the case with fragmented structures or autonomous business units. With these you have to take positive steps to encourage pride and commitment, and to help them grow. This is achieved through performance and communications – anything that can be done to build pride and commitment to the business unit is generally the best first step. It is important that these autonomous units do not become too wrapped up in themselves and therefore place all their allegiance and commitment within their own team. They must not lose sight of the fact that they are part of the total business and must maintain high key attitudes to corporate desires and strategies.

To some extent this can be underlined by performance and pay but effective information systems and communications are essential. This moves information and communications systems to centre stage. With regards to those the following are the key issues:

■ Customer-Driven Marketing

- Flat structures do not need elaborate committee networks but they do need an information network to encourage the free flow of information and give ready access to its sources.
- A conference technique can be used to integrate management. This has three benefits:
  — it provides clarity of purpose
  — it reinforces motivation
  — it subjects executives to 'trial by their peers'.

  The conference technique pulls together the key managers of the organisation. They will typically spend a highly charged and highly taxing period together, tackling the next year's plan. Basically, no one escapes until there is full agreement. Operating rather like a prime minister's cabinet (but probably with much greater effectiveness!), the team have to face all the issues of the business, fight all their departmental battles, assent fully and individually to the corporate objectives and agree the corporate priorities. There is no doubt this is a gruelling procedure but it is being used with great benefit to avoid the ineffective and frustrating reiteration of the budget process.
- Leadership development is by exposure rather than by training alone – we realised earlier that these flatter organisational structures, as the levels are reduced, take from the organisation a training ground that has for centuries proved highly effective and extremely cost efficient – the oldest example probably being the military. Thus provision must be made to put back this vital resource. In terms of day-to-day training, a resource can be created for 'classroom' training which will augment the coaching or on-the-job learning process. However, leaders need to be identified and brought forward. Businesses have found – as incidentally have many educationalists – that leaders need to be given a chance to shine; that given the freedom to operate, often leaders lift themselves above the crowd; and that the tougher the targets or tasks they are given, the greater the qualities and the ingenuity they display. If your system doesn't give such people a chance to stick their head over the parapet and be noticed without being shot at, you'll never know they were there. Often systems, procedures or traditions mask our potential leaders from us and leave them frustrated in an inhibitive regime where everybody is average – and sadly average becomes the accepted level. Leaders often may not be good at one or two of the steps convention says they must take. Or, one hardly dares to suggest it, perhaps they should skip a layer or an experience! It's about bringing out the best in your people and being sure that the system cultivates leaders, not squashes them.
- Operational communications follow the line of the profit chain; meaning that, instead of being organised by function as they are at the moment in hierarchies, communications are reorganised to follow a

direct process, eg Customer – marketer – product/service. At the moment complex chains of approval or agreement can be required to gain, say, agreement for some special arrangement for a Customer. I once tried to buy a toaster from British retailer Argos without a box. They had lost it and would not sell it to me without the box! I went off to finish my shopping and returned an hour later. As I did so, the store manager had just finished obtaining authority to sell me the toaster! The story he told me doesn't merit the page space, but I can assure you that the first thing I would have done with the box was consign it to the rubbish bin. As I suspect would most people. It is difficult to comprehend why this manager couldn't just make up his own mind or, for that matter, the young woman whom I was trying to persuade to take my money.

In order to obey the social etiquette, a sales person wishing to obtain something special for his Customer will approach a production person only by routing his request via his manager to the production manager and down to the production person. Indeed it is often much more extended. When lines permit or even encourage direct communication it is far more responsive to the Customer need. Of course, if the autonomous business unit structure is adopted, the perfect solution prevails since sales and marketing, production and administration are represented together within the SMU (self-managed unit). This also reduces time to serve and cuts work in progress and finished stock. The current 'hot' technique here is Supply Chain Management (SCM). Rather like integrated marketing, I have yet to find two people with the same definition of SCM! Essentially it is a concept that extends the view of operations from a single unit to the complete chain from raw material suppliers through to end Customers. SCM uses a set of practices to manage and co-ordinate the whole chain.

## Handling information systems

The information systems of the new structure will be critical. And information systems have some characteristics that should be recorded here. It is likely you will already have suffered these in some way – perhaps for many years! But let's recall them anyway:

- Computer systems can be essential. This sounds obvious. Indeed it is, so much so that most people place an expectation on the computer system which is preposterous and unachievable. Computer systems may be helpful, but a universal remedy they are not!
- Managers always seriously underestimate the preparation time required, the resources that will be needed, and the costly, time wasting, frustrating disruption that is created.

■ Customer-Driven Marketing

- Software is always late. Always!
- Inadequate thought and effort always go into the disciplines which should ensure data integrity and accuracy. This is always discovered too late, costs too much to correct and takes too long to become operational. It has been my experience that there is a critical link between the integrity and accuracy of data and its ownership. Data ownership should always be shared by those who provide it and those who use it.

## Broadside or network?

The final consideration of this chapter is whether you should deploy your new sales and marketing or business units in a 'broadside array' or as a 'networked structure'. The answer will depend entirely on the decision you considered at the beginning of this chapter. Are you planning to adopt sales and marketing units or autonomous business units? If sales and marketing, go broadside; if autonomous business units, because of their self-sufficiency, go network – as discussed at the end of Chapter 19.

To summarise, this chapter presented the following ideas:

- Businesses do not have to deal on a day-to-day basis with such matters as changes to infrastructure and pay and reward systems. Therefore it is unlikely that sufficient specialist skills about such sensitive and critical issues will be found in-house. Carefully chosen external consultants or advisers can usually provide a cost effective, more experienced and objective way to see the project through.
- The distinction between sales and marketing is about to disappear. We should assist it.
- The issue of reshaping to get closer to Customers reaches to the heart of the organisation; as such it is a board issue, not a departmental issue.
- The notion that Customer relationships have an asset value will change the power balance of companies and enhance the role and value of marketing.
- Marketing has a dual hurdle in presenting its case to the board: first it must make the directors aware of all the issues; secondly it must make them understand the deep and critical significance of this matter. In other words this is a matter of corporate life or death.
- Corporate structures should be elegant in design and must reflect the needs of the Customer. However, it is foolish to think of this in a rigid way: for the future structures will become more flexible, more responsive to Customer needs.
- Flatter structures benefit from 'tight/loose' managerial controls which give clear objectives and firm measurement but greater freedom of action and decision making.

## The relationship to structure

- Some benefits get lost when hierarchies are flattened. It is therefore important that specific provision is made for them. Vehicles must be found to harness corporate pride and foster corporate commitment to the total enterprise.
- With regard to information systems the following factors should be remembered:
    — elaborate committee networks are not required
    — a conference technique can be used to integrate management effectively. This provides clarity of purpose, reinforces motivation and subjects executives to trial by peers.
- Leadership development is by exposure as well as training. The whole process of 'growing' people is different outside hierarchies. We must give potential leaders the opportunity to shine otherwise they may simply get absorbed into the mass. Good people respond to tough targets and assignments, making them reach heights they may not even have realised they could achieve themselves.
- Operational communications should follow the profit chain not the business disciplines and should be free of social and political precedents.
- Regarding the planning and implementation of new information systems, these factors are common:
    — systems are helpful but not a universal remedy
    — no computer systems are easy to get in, up and running
    — time, resources, disruption and costs are always underestimated
    — software is always late
    — data accuracy disciplines are never good enough
    — data ownership should always be shared by those who provide it and those who use it.
- If Customer-driven marketing ideas for relationship building are to be implemented on a departmental basis, a broadside array is recommended; if on a corporate basis, use a network structure.

# 23

# How to develop integrated marketing

I think we should change its name to start with. Let us call it integrated sales, marketing and service (ISMS). My definition of this is 'the seamless delivery of sales, marketing and service to the Customer in complete harmony with the relationship and in real time'.

One of my Clients, after much debate, came to this definition – 'integrated marketing means achieving synergistic effects between different means of communication through integration of goals, messages, execution and timing. The goal is to create a long-term relationship with Customers through a mutually productive and profitable dialogue. Each activity also has a short-term measurable goal. Goal fulfilment is always measured in an organised way.'

That definition is somewhat more explicit and pragmatic than mine and was followed by these answers to the question 'What is ISMS?'

- Using sales, advertising, telephone and mail in the right mix.
- Integration of marketing activities for improved synergy.
- Using a marketing database for managing the activity.

Next we set about identifying the stepping stones. The list which follows is authentic and was created from a project definition gathering – and, as such, is in no particular priority, includes a few peripheral issues and puts the numbers last. I have not included it because it is definitive or prescriptive. I have included it because it is typical. Indeed, it would not do for any other business because every starting point is unique. Just as yours will be. And their destination was unique, just as yours will be.

The following projects or activities emerged:

1. Create one single Customer database.
2. Clean up the database.
3. Categorise and grade Customers.
4. Resolve how to handle actual versus potential sales.
5. Improve telesales facilities and capabilities.
6. Install the new database system in all countries.
7. Find and include all relevant Customer information on database.
8. Set up continuous Customer satisfaction procedures including measurement and analysis.
9. Devise accurate measurement processes to analyse cost/results of marketing activities.
10. Define all Customer activities and communications and audit to uncover improvement areas.
11. Co-ordinate all (sales and) marketing activities by Customer.
12. Agree the uses of existing data and needs for new data.
13. Educate and train the sales, and marketing and Customer service teams.
14. Involve the above in the creation and development of ISMS.
15. Take very seriously information from the sales force about Customers: to find ways to encourage the information flow.
16. Decide how best to use the above information wisely to enhance Customer relationships.
17. Make Customers aware of ISMS and to enable them to feel the benefits as quickly as possible.
18. Encourage sales and service teams to take a 'room for improvement' attitude to complaints or potential complaints.
19. Improve complaint handling and response times.
20. Install a new bonus system across the business which is related to and reflects upward and downward movement of Customer satisfaction.
21. Gain the total commitment of the whole organisation.
22. Encourage advice for service improvements from the whole company.
23. Create and maintain the spirit for and excitement about ISMS.
24. Identify the key performance indicators and develop the monitoring and measurement systems.

## Integrated Clients, definitely. But what is an integrated agency?

One of the great confusions about integrated marketing is that it means different things to different people. I have worked internally with a number of Clients and facilitated meetings to determine their definition of integrated marketing. With each group we come to definitions which, if taken to one of the other businesses, would not fit at all. Thus, I believe integrated marketing should be a custom-built solution for your business.

■ Customer-Driven Marketing

It is a series of processes designed specifically to fit your advertising, sales, marketing and service objectives and deliver them to your market. The result is relationship marketing.

This already uncovers one of the fallacies about integrated marketing. How can agencies, predominantly ex-direct marketing agencies (and many of them not so ex!) call themselves integrated marketing agencies? Integrated marketing is not something an agency can supply – it is a corporate marketing function. True, agencies can supply those who are using integrated marketing techniques, or at least a few agencies can. When they work with a company using integrated marketing, actually what is being asked of them is to have a strategic understanding of how marketing works in a business that communicates with its market in an integrated fashion. This means that the agency must be capable of all the usual functions and certainly should be well equipped with 'direct' communication skills which are essential to integration. However, the agency must also be able to administer for, and cope with, a vast diversity of much smaller – in size and budget – tasks. The 'integrated' Client uses very narrowcast communications. Such a Client will be endeavouring to transmit as many of its communications and messages to enhance, as near as possible, one-to-one Customer relationships and will inevitably be using TCM or some other method of communications management.

To be clear, integrated marketing is not sales, advertising and marketing activity that all fits together neatly; it is marketing activity of any kind that has integrity with Customer relationships and encompasses the service aspect of the Customer relationship. These activities and messages are inseparably bound together with the Customer relationship – *they make sense to that Customer*.

When 'it all fits together' – even if it all fits together well – we have good campaign planning. If the ads on television support the mailing, support the retail activity, which harmonises with the point-of-sale materials, which tie in with the sales presenters and the sales people give out the same message, that's admirable. If lots of Customers buy and find that everything that was said was true and they are happy – you had a good campaign. It all fitted together. What I have just described is not integrated marketing, it is simply an example of an effective and well-planned campaign. It is not a new idea, it has been around for years. What is missing is any connection to the nature and state of the Customer relationship.

## One-to-one can be a state of mind, it can be a way of life

All Customers deserve integrated marketing as a state of mind, but not all of them will get it as a way of life. Indeed, not all of them want or expect it as a way of life.

If I am a casual buyer of your brand of toothpaste, perhaps I buy it when it's on special offer, my demand is basically limited to the product. You can do things to change that, but you have an uphill climb because I'm a price-shopper. If, on the other hand, I buy your toothpaste regularly, I'm brand loyal, and demonstrate the desire to be so, potentially for life (or as long as I have teeth!), I have a different perception or expectation of you. You are more important to me and I am hugely more important to you. You should know who I am and I should feel I can talk to you and you want to hear from me. Equally, I may buy other products from you – different brands – and actually, the sum total of my commitment to your business, even if it is made up of a great number of individual purchases, may be potentially quite substantial. I am, to a degree, corporately, a fan of yours. With conventional marketing I'm a no-name. With Customer-driven marketing, I am someone special. And I know it and appreciate it.

A primary part of the task here is to develop mechanisms which identify and grade our Customers against their expectation and their value or potential value to the business.

Given the opportunity to communicate, share their feelings or voice an opinion, higher loyalty potential Customers often identify themselves. They respond to you and, in effect, say 'Here I am. Listen to me. Speak to me. Recognise me.'

I have a Client whose marketing budget runs into tens of millions of pounds. They have a clientele some of whom could spend as much with them in turnover as that marketing budget. Equally, some may not spend more than £1000 a year with them. How should this Client deploy integrated marketing? Are they expected to deal with small spenders in exactly the same way as those businesses which spend tens of millions with them? Plainly, they are not. Even if they were crazy enough to want to, they simply could not afford to.

Customers need to be graded. I have seen businesses do this by turnover, volume offtake, that is, the volume of units sold without taking discounts or special offers into account – I don't recommend this method – and by profit, actual and potential. The grades need then to be matched to a set of Customer service and delivery levels which exceed Customer expectations, while being profitable to you. If this sounds like something of a balancing act, that's fair enough because that is exactly what it is!

## Customers can go down as well as up!

Much to the upset of some Customer-facing staff, this grading process has a hard edge. The only way is not up! Customers can be downgraded as well as upgraded: thus they may need sensitive handling when service levels decrease and competitive service positioning should be watched to

## ■ Customer-Driven Marketing

ensure that you are not withdrawing something which a competitor would be prepared to give. On the happier side, the desired direction is up, which means increasing the service levels and maintaining them when it tops out. To be explicit about this, remember I am proposing variances in the level of service here, not the standards. The business should only have one set of service standards. It is slippery ground indeed for one organisation to run more than one set.

I said that downgrading can cause some upset with Customer-facing staff. It's simply that downgrading is obviously more arduous and a much less pleasant thing to do, rather like asking a sales person to collect a late payment cheque from a Customer. Many would rather leave the debt-chasing to the accounts department! However, the company does not have a bottomless purse and it should be appreciated that those who get too much service deny others their fair share.

Some of those Customers will expect and understand that they will be spoken to *en masse* via television or the press. Others, will demand to be 'account managed' or given personal attention. The task of individualisation is to take the five strands of relationship marketing – price, product, delivery, service and recognition (more on this in the next chapter) – and provide the availability to those as far down the pyramid of expectation as possible. The challenge is to exceed Customer expectations at all levels, profitably. Cost-to-serve is an important issue here. When you come to considering the levels of service and the cost of those activities, remember that your general direction is upwards. We are looking to increase sales from existing Customers – thus, if you are going to err, err on the generous side! And this is where some assessment or knowledge of the potential is helpful. Preferably this grading process should be carried out by Customer. If you are a large business with many Customers, you may decide that your base level precludes much or any individualisation. And it is precisely at this level where one-to-one becomes philosophical rather than actual. And this is where I take issue with those who talk about a one-to-one future. It will be for some, but only if they, or rather the relationship, merits it!

### So who is trying to have a relationship with whom?

Bags of salt! Regular old table salt. I have vowed to be totally loyal to the brand. I might buy perhaps 50 bags in my whole life. Total value: next to nothing; service expectation: none; relationship expectation: none. So does that mean the salt business cannot use integrated marketing? With me, the consumer, it does. The only chance anyone has with salt is the retailer. And he has plenty of reasons! He has a real chance at locking me in to a major portion of my household spend. So what of the salt company? Well, they are anxious to secure the business of the wholesalers

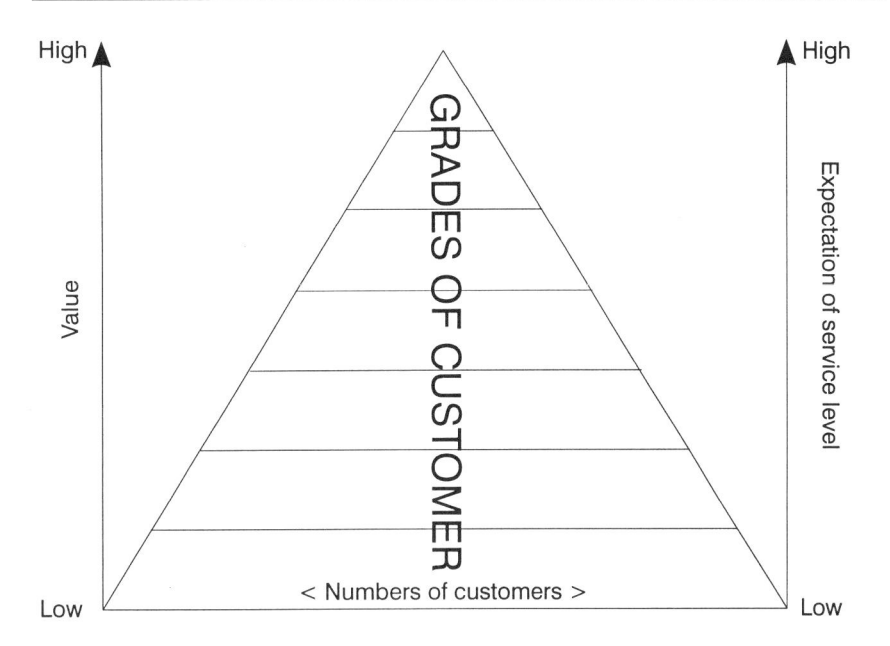

**Figure 23.1** *The pyramid of expectation. As Customer value increases so does their expectation of service. Customers can be graded by actual and/or potential sales or profit contribution*

and retailers who buy from them and, yes, integrated marketing is perfect. The wholesalers and retailers, unlike me, both merit and will welcome the full benefits of a Customer-driven marketing approach.

## It's about to get a whole dimension more complicated

The whole puzzle now goes into another dimension when we look at the various patterns of purchasing and contact that operate within your business. For, just to complicate things, some Customers wander in and out of full service requirements.

Take an estate agent, for example. Do we want or expect the agent to stay actively trying to satisfy us right throughout the ten years we might live at a house before we move on again? I hope not. If all our suppliers did this, we wouldn't be able to get to our doors for mail or have any time for personal telephone calls. We would have come to grief in the communications traffic jam.

I argue that it would be prudent for the estate agent to stay in touch, to keep us informed of their value to us. Hardly any of them do. They seem to expect that any loyalty they created in one transaction is automatically retained until the next. Of course it rarely is!

■ Customer-Driven Marketing

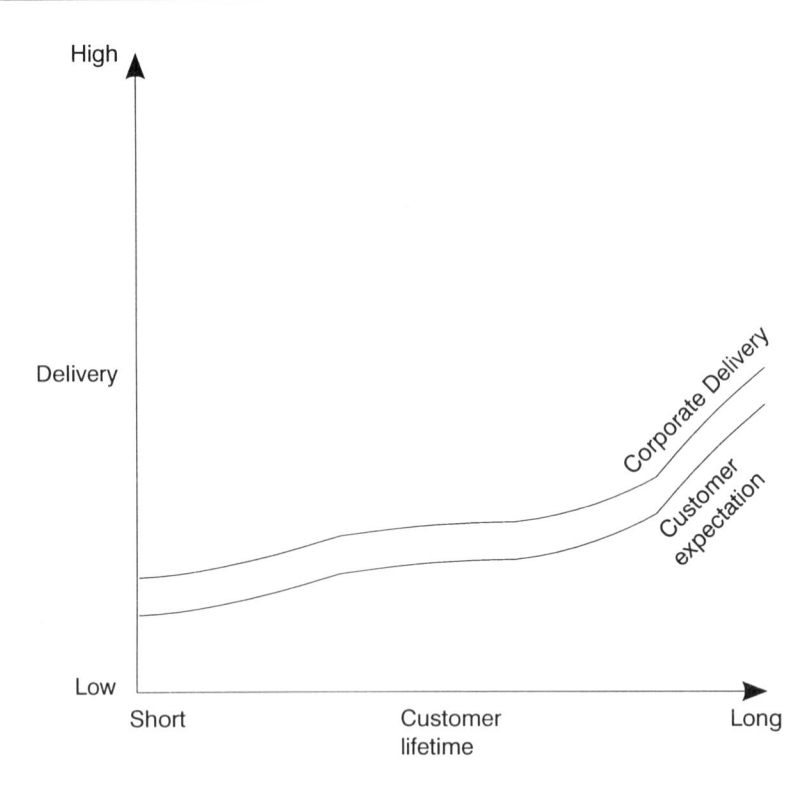

**Figure 23.2** *Actual corporate delivery level (of promise) should be pitched to exceed Customers' expectations which will vary up and down. This chart shows a successful pattern with delivery mirroring expectation but always above it*

So with some Customers, the expectation increases around a need or desire. Again, this would affect, for example, a car purchaser or someone who had just acquired a new dishwasher. There is little point generally in sending me details of a new model days after I have purchased another. However, awareness of the new model as part of a Customer contact programme is both sensible and appropriate. Customer-driven marketing would enable the car seller to know when one family has two of the same make and, for that matter, the dishwasher vendor or manufacturer to know when a household has washing machines, dryers and other devices of the same brand.

## What has all this Customer service grading to do with integrated marketing?

Good question! And the answer is, a lot. I described integrated marketing earlier as 'the seamless delivery of sales, marketing and service to the

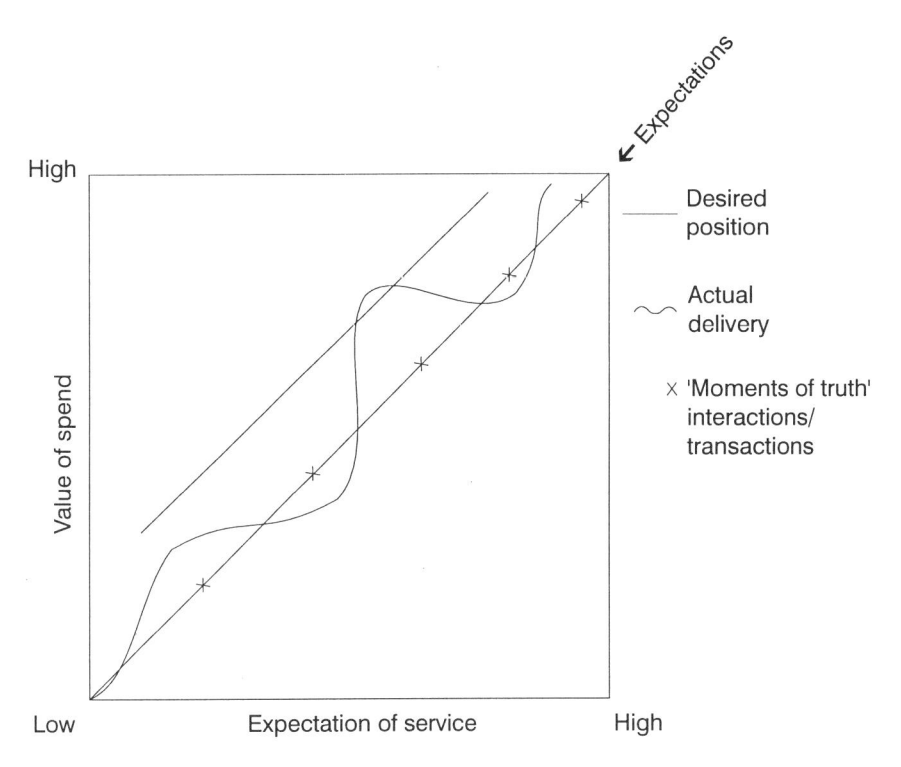

**Figure 23.3** *Failure! As transactions take place, corporate delivery rises and falls but all below Customer expectations and only once barely meets the desired position.*

Customer'. The three, currently differentiated functions of the business – sales, marketing and service – have to become welded together. How can we possibly weld service into sales and marketing if we don't have some notion of the service levels this has to include? Answer: we can't. However, now we have decided our service levels we can start looking at how we deliver the service, how we integrate our marketing and how we wish to make those all-important sales to the Customer. We can start to determine and take feedback from Customers on frequency, method and style of contact. This adds to the value balance in line with that Customer's needs and expectation, and brings order and reason to the communications within the relationship. This is why Customer decision making has to move to the front line, along with marketing and the database. It's also why Customers need to be aligned with, and kept in touch with, the individuals who are responsible for them and why communications must be, or be seen to be, channelled through those same personnel. And the more consistency there is of those personnel, generally, the better chance we have of building corporate and brand relationships. This alignment, without the integration, is perceived by Customers to be shallow and inconsequential. It denies what is happening between them and those claiming to look after or service them. It equally denies your staff the opportunity to take responsibility for Customers and do the job of Customer-driven marketing.

The responsibility to which I refer is not simply to Customers. These people also have the responsibility to increase sales, deliver profit and protect margins by adding value. However, the Customer-driven environment, as you will see in the next chapter, tends to create an atmosphere where people approach you to buy. This contrasts dramatically with what we have suffered through the previous decades when we studiously made things far tougher and more expensive for ourselves as we went off track down the route of high activity marketing.

## New tasks, new divisions of labour

In essence, the communications which we have to manage can only fall into two broad categories: inbound and outbound. The inbound are relatively easy to manage since they will generally be through a limited – or limitable – number of media. Typically we could still say for many businesses these will be written (letters, faxes and e-mail), by telephone or from face-to-face contact. Outbound is more complex, because the choice of media is much wider. The more you move from individual messages, the harder it gets to operate in real time for so many relationships and the more the classic media choices stand winking enticingly at you. To some extent, your choice of media will now be much more affected by the nature of the message. Is it more appropriate to use one of the narrowcast set of choices or the broadcast? To be clear, one-to-one is the ultimate narrowcast! There are already an enormous number of communications to Customers which are dispatched in thousands and which are missing opportunities to consolidate the relationships between individuals. Why do personalised mailings go out to Customers signed by anyone else other than the front line person who usually deals with them?

In essence, we have to ensure that three vital activities can take place: we need to hear what people have or want to say; we need to be able to respond when they want; and we also need to speak to them from time to time. By speak and hear, in this instance, I mean by any communications medium from individual face-to-face to broadcast television.

The critical issue is that what remains to be done *en masse* does not usurp what is happening at the front line.

## How to weld sales, service and marketing together

People who are effective at selling must remain doing what they do best. And the same applies to the service and marketing people. However, it is structure which is important. The task of integrated marketing needs the welding. And the welding of the three disciplines is achieved by three basic steps.

First – and this is the priority – align the people with their responsibilities. Their responsibility is clear, it is to build loyalty through their relationships with Customers. The key issue is Customer relationships. They must be managed and developed by those who will do the work. So don't sit sales people with sales people and service people with service people and hope they get the Customer task right. Sit sales people with service people with marketing people and charge them with looking after the same group of Customers together. Then the task, the goals and the alignment are in harmony with your real objective, your first priority. This is exactly as explained in the granular marketing concept in Chapter 19.

The next priority is that the front line staff have the information to do the job. The database is therefore a critical factor. If any one of the three functions cannot access Customer information which is both accurate and up to date, they cannot possibly succeed. They must also, then, take responsibility for the data quality. Now we are beginning to have integration!

Lastly, let them work out their own responsibilities and demarcation lines. The important thing is their commitment and dedication to the Customer. That is all.

## The final words go to Customer communications

I have placed the view before you that as the communications become more narrowcast, the management of them must also move as near the front line as possible. However, there is no point in it doing so unless they add relevance and timing to it. For example, front line people should be able to deselect Customers from, say, a mailing, on the basis that they think it would be better to call the Customer first and tell them about it perhaps following up with a (their) choice of further information through the post or by visit. As long as they are adding relevance, power and timing to the message, it is up to them whether it works. It's their responsibility.

In this chapter we have seen that integrated marketing is as individual to your business as the results of it are to your Customer relationships. In summary, this means the following:

### ■ Customer-Driven Marketing

- Integrated marketing is a custom-built solution for your business. It should be designed specifically to fit your marketing and service needs. The objective is to deliver relationship marketing.
- Integrated marketing should not be confused with effective campaign planning. This is a notion as old as the marketing hills – and a very effective one! The true concept of integrated marketing is one that brings order, sense and relevance to the communications and interactions as judged against individual Customer relationships.
- Integrated sales marketing and service (ISMS) welds the sales, marketing and service functions together to provide seamless delivery of the corporate promise to the Customer in complete harmony with the Customer relationship and in real time.
- One-to-one can be a state of mind – a goal to aim at, a philosophical desire – for some and an actuality for others. Not all Customers merit one-to-one treatment and not all expect it.
- Customers have to be graded by turnover or profit, actual and potential. The grades are matched to a set of Customer service and corporate delivery levels which exceed Customer expectations while being profitable for the business. Customers should be downgraded as well as upgraded. It is important that, whereas service levels may vary, service standards do not.
- Customers' expectation of service increases broadly in line with their spend – or with their value to the business. The task of individualisation is to extend the five strands of relationship marketing – price, product, delivery, service and recognition – as far down the pyramid of expectation as possible. This calculation should have relevance to the cost-to-serve.
- For some businesses, Customer's expectations of service vary set against their needs or desires.
- The grading of Customers to determine appropriate service levels is important to integrated marketing in order to ensure that when sales, marketing and service are welded together, the levels are understood and commonly worked towards.
- The alignment of staff, not by discipline, but by Customer groups, is critical. They will share Customer objectives but they will also share responsibility for sales, profit and margin protection. It is this structuring which provides the welding of sales, marketing and service.
- Customer communications divide cleanly into inbound and outbound: inbound are comparatively easy to manage because of clear and limited media choice. The nature of the outbound message should have greater influence over media choice. Every effort should be made not to usurp what is happening at the front line. As many communications as possible should be channelled or be seen to be channelled through front line individuals.

- The Customer database is critical. Therefore the teams of realigned staff must take responsibility for data accuracy and data quality. Within their teams, they should agree their own demarcation lines for work and responsibilities.
- Front line staff should get as much control as possible over Customer communications, but it is incumbent upon them to add relevance and timing.

# 24

# The facts and fallacies of Customer loyalty

In Chapter 14 I suggested that many marketing experts of our time were taking simple, long-held marketing knowledge and beliefs and making them more complex than they actually are. Many, it is certain, manage to find ways of explaining and describing fundamental truths in the most complex ways. In relation to Customer satisfaction and Customer loyalty there seems to be a lot of this going on. I remain undecided as to whether it really is more complex as we move further into the soft issues, and the genuine intricacies of the human psychological aspects come into closer focus, or whether my peers and I are guilty of complicating very simple issues. Maybe a deal of both is true – I will leave you to decide for yourself as you digest this chapter.

### The waitress was a singer

I was on the road home. It was late and I was hungry. Soon I was sitting in the rather shabby branch of a British chain of roadside restaurants. Like many Britons I was praying the government were right and that the beef was not a risk, as I chewed my way through a tasteless and rather tough piece of steak. It was marginally better than staying hungry. About half-way through this the young waitress who had taken my order and served me, reappeared. She sang to me. 'Is everything allllriiight?'

I don't know who teaches these, mostly, young people to sing to their Customers. Switchboard operators and receptionists do it a lot too. It's as if they somehow equate the singing tone and extended vowels with a caring attitude. I looked at her, smiled and replied, 'Yes, it's fine, thank you.' She had just sampled Customer satisfaction. The truth was that the steak was well below acceptable and I was toying with the idea of resoling a pair of favourite old shoes with the remains of it. My real reply should have been 'No. It's awful and I'm not coming here again'. Customer loyalty index? Zero.

Well, why didn't I tell her? Because, because. Because I was tired. She was at the end of her shift. They were waiting to close. I couldn't be bothered. It wasn't her fault. Etc. Etc. You know how it is! But I still won't go back there.

This is an important point – and, for me, renders tenuous Customer satisfaction (what I say – 'yes, it's fine, thank you') and leaves it deeply subordinate to Customer loyalty (what I do – 'I'm not coming here again'). There are plenty of people who will tell you that satisfaction levels are linked to loyalty levels. I find that rather like saying that a swimming pool *looks* warm enough. There is nothing better than sticking a toe in and feeling it to find out. Of course they are linked. There would be little loyalty without Customer satisfaction. However, some leading consultancies have given advice to their Clients which seems to propose that managing Customer satisfaction is enough. It is not. Later in this chapter we will see that it is just one of the components. You have to get Customers well towards the top end of satisfaction levels before there is any kind of robustness and loyalty is created.

## The inescapable truth of Customer loyalty and the five strands that create it

Loyalty is, inescapably, the truth of your success as a business. There can be no more telling benchmark by which you can be measured and judged. It is the sum total of the effect of your business or organisation on its Customers and their response to it. This means that 'the Customer' is, and must always be, the reason for our existence. There is no other reason. In business we have no other purpose. This is the inexorable rationale for the Customer-driven business. It explains, for all those business leaders who can't seem to make up their minds, why it is wrong to stand up in front of their staff and tell them that they are the most important asset of the business. They clearly are not. It's the Customer who has to be first and foremost because, without Customers, who needs staff? Any business leader with enough money can certainly have as many staff as they like with no Customers at all – but, presumably because they like their jobs, not many of them make that choice!

Satisfaction may be a vital component part of Customer loyalty, yet satisfied Customers leave your business and defect as well as dissatisfied Customers. More confusing still, loyal Customers leave you too.

The five strands to Customer satisfaction and loyalty are, however, common. They are:

## ■ Customer-Driven Marketing

- price
- product
- delivery
- service
- recognition.

Price and product tend to fall mainly into the area of logic whereas service and recognition are connected to the emotions. Delivery is a factor which, it could be argued, falls into either – I suspect, personally, it falls into both. Actually, these five strands make it easy to see why things have changed – first, not more than a few years ago, that set of five strands would have included distribution instead of delivery. The significant shift here is in understanding that when you market to achieve a series of separate transactions those transactions take place at the far point of your distribution channel. This is a product driven process. It distributes your corporate product. However, when you market to achieve a managed Customer relationship, then what we have is a means of delivering the corporate promise. Transaction marketing effectively switches on to standby between transactions; relationship marketing is permanently fully switched on 24 hours a day, seven days a week, ready and alert to every Customer interaction.

In relation to Customer loyalty, it is vital that we therefore work on permanent improvement of the corporate promise and that means all five strands. It means adding to our previous experiences which were logic based – product, price and some delivery issues (essentially those to do with distribution) – and supplementing them with new, 'soft issue' experiences which are emotionally based – service, recognition and those delivery issues which 'wrap' the product at distribution and stay connected with the Customer through their relationship with you.

My experience fully suggests that to move from building satisfaction to creating loyalty, you must work in the emotional issues of the relationship. This will gain the most leverage and make the most difference. It is this recognition which exposes the fallacy in the vast majority of so-called loyalty programmes.

### Bribery and integrity are like oil and water. They don't mix!

Most loyalty programmes rely, to a major degree, on bribery. This is like the villain in a children's play handing out sweets to the goody in the show. None of the kids in the audience are fooled. They don't trust the villain's smile or voice.

With some of my audiences, I mentioned to you earlier how I ask them to examine the difference between a personal relationship and a commercial relationship. You remember? I 'marry' someone from the audience. I say 'someone'. I've never picked on a man yet! Anyway, I use an entertaining role play to look at the phases of the relationship and to highlight the similarities.

Lately, I have taken to asking the same audiences the following: first, I ask those who have a loyalty card to raise their hands. Then I ask those who do not have two or more loyalty cards for the same type of business – supermarket, hotel group, airline, whatever! – to lower their hands. Lastly, I ask of the remaining raised hands, who uses all the businesses and frequently gathers loyalty bonuses from all the programmes? There are still a lot of hands showing.

So my next question is, 'If you found your partner had two more other people to whom he or she was also being "loyal" on a regular basis, would you consider he or she was also being "faithful"? If you do – keep your hands up.' I haven't had one yet.

These are not loyalty programmes. Most of them are heavily disguised sales promotions which use the mail and the shop (or whatever) to merchandise special offers and discounts. It's basically good, old-fashioned bribery! It has nothing at all to do with gathering the emotional commitment of the Customer so that they bestow their allegiance to you. It has nothing or little to do with winning over the hearts and minds of Customers. And, when I said earlier that it would be good to take a major portion of the prospecting or conquest sales promotion budget and use it to say 'thank you' now and again, this is not what I meant by a loyalty programme.

The truth is that, at best, all these schemes create is a bond. It's just a link, not a lock. Some may manage a quite strong bond. Yet the major benefit of such schemes is that they tend to increase exposure to, and sampling of, the corporate promise. As I use my airline miles or store bonus points, often I use them for more of what I have been getting already. I'll fly somewhere on holiday or buy something which means the operator of the loyalty scheme gets another chance to prove their worth and value, to deliver Customer 'superformance'.

## So, what wins hearts and minds?

Certainly, there is a place for discounts and special deals if they fit with your mission and your brand(s). However, the bulk of the loyalty building solutions will be found in the soft issues to do with service and recognition. It may be considered occasionally right or prudent to issue money off vouchers or make discount offers, but it is also to do with the style and tone of voice with which they are distributed on those occasions.

It is in delivering those aspects of the corporate promise to do with service and recognition where the hearts and minds will be won over. It is in recognising and treating Customers as the individuals they are, knowing their preferences and choices, understanding what turns them on or off.

■ Customer-Driven Marketing

This builds loyalty – and it also creates that 'quality lock' which locks them to you and locks your competitor out.

Loyalty is so much more robust than satisfaction. It permits dialogue. It tolerates flaws as long as they are sensitively handled, tangible action is taken to avoid them happening again and the apologies are sincere. Recently, following spinal surgery, I acquired a special new work station and chair which enable me to continue to work long hours when I am writing. The screen and keyboard are in a raised position which encourages me to sit in the correct posture for my spine. To the right of the keyboard support is a mouse shelf which I could not get to stay in position. One day I decided to take the relevant faulty part of the unit to the manufacturer, whose factory happens to be near my home. I was greeted with profuse apologies, offered coffee and asked to wait a few minutes. The factory manager soon arrived carrying the unit now with mouse tray correctly attached. More apologies! Then he said, 'I want you to know how grateful we are to you for taking the time to visit us and bring us this defective product. You have enabled us to uncover a small batch of keyboard supports which have mouse tray brackets that are 3 mm out of alignment. We will contact the relevant dealers and recall the units and rescue our reputation for perfection. I have a meeting in ten minutes' time with my production team to see how we can prevent such an error happening again. So thank you very much for bringing this to our attention.' After that more pleasantries followed and I went on my way, a happy Customer.

If any reader wants to know where to get a superb product to help you enjoy your computer and maintain a perfect spinal position, use my e-mail address and I'll put you in touch with them. They are excellent – and very switched on!

## The Customer-driven marketing model: the myriad miracles that await you

I have produced a model which takes you through the whole Customer-driven marketing process. From the model (Figure 24.1) it becomes clear how all these processes fit together in a virtuous, complementary fashion to improve the lot of the Customer, to lower marketing and sales costs, to improve brand performance and to increase business efficiency as a part of an holistic continuum. This shows just how many aspects come together to work in harmony: the Customer wins all the way through – and, just as importantly, so do you!

I suggest you absorb and understand the model for a moment, and then read the explanation that follows.

Note that I have numbered the panels in the chart and these numbers relate to the following paragraphs. Effectively, now you have a step-by-step guide to building and managing real Customer loyalty: a step-by-

# The facts and fallacies of customer loyalty

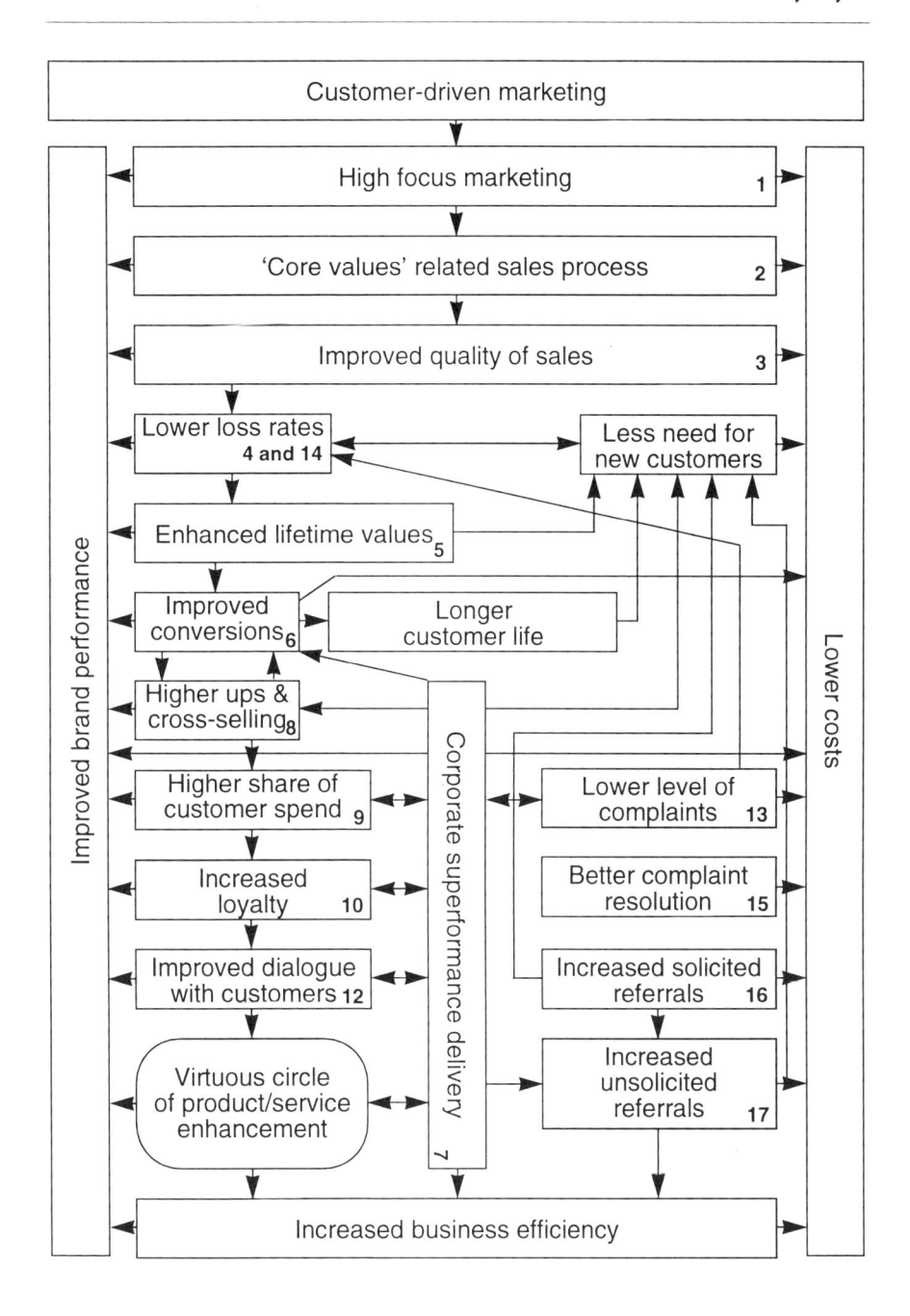

```
                    Customer-driven marketing
                              ↓
    ┌──────────────────────────────────────────────────┐
    │         High focus marketing                  1  │
    │                     ↓                            │
    │    'Core values' related sales process        2  │
    │                     ↓                            │
    │         Improved quality of sales             3  │
    │                     ↓                            │
    │   Lower loss rates           Less need for       │
    │      4 and 14                new customers       │
    │         ↓                                        │
    │   Enhanced lifetime values  5                    │
    │         ↓                                        │
    │   Improved          Longer                       │
    │   conversions 6     customer life                │
    │         ↓                                        │
    │   Higher ups &                                   │
    │   cross-selling 8                                │
    │         ↓                                        │
    │   Higher share of           Lower level of       │
    │   customer spend  9         complaints      13   │
    │         ↓                                        │
    │   Increased                 Better complaint     │
    │   loyalty      10           resolution      15   │
    │         ↓                                        │
    │   Improved dialogue         Increased solicited  │
    │   with customers 12         referrals       16   │
    │         ↓                                        │
    │   Virtuous circle           Increased            │
    │   of product/service        unsolicited          │
    │   enhancement               referrals       17   │
    │         ↓                                        │
    │         Increased business efficiency            │
    └──────────────────────────────────────────────────┘
  Improved brand performance  | Corporate superformance delivery 7 | Lower costs
```

**Figure 24.1** *JFR's Customer-driven marketing model – a myriad miracles for your business*

■ Customer-Driven Marketing

step guide to Customer-driven marketing.

## Seventeen steps to real Customer loyalty.

From this model we can see that the overall outcomes of Customer-driven marketing are lower costs, improved brand performance and increased business efficiency. It doesn't sound half as good as it really is and the secret lies, of course, in that the chart doesn't show volumes! This is a veritable treasure chest of miracles. Look at the issues which rain (sideways rain!) towards improved brand performance. On the other side, more rain! This time it's showering improvements to costs and, meanwhile, every issue leads to eventual increased business efficiencies.

1. High focus marketing, you will remember, is the process of focusing on those Customers in your prospective market who have the highest potential for loyalty to you. These can be modelled out from analysis of your Customer database. The strategic concept here is to secure dominant market share of those Customers who 'lock' with your core corporate and brand values – those things which differentiate you from your competition.
2. In turn, naturally, you must embed those core values into your sales process. This optimises the 'fit' between the way you attract Customers and what they want – or are buying – from you.
3. Once you get that fit, there is a dramatic improvement in the quality of business you gain. Effectively, you are now taking the cream from the marketplace and leaving the rest for your competitors to fight over.
4. In turn this has two effects which will be of enormous benefit for your business: first, you will have much lower Customer attrition; secondly, this will be a major factor in 'putting the plug in' as explained earlier. This, in consequence, will enable you to cut back on the high costs of hunting for new business from totally 'cold' prospects.
5. Next, from the model, you can see the natural follow-on is that Customer lifetime values are enhanced. If you haven't already started calculating and using lifetime values I encourage you to do so. For many of the people and businesses I have worked with, it was this notion which enabled them to start wrapping some numbers and reasons round the transformation process.

   The use of lifetime values seems to be almost like turning on a light to so many of those who remain unconvinced by the ethical, moral, cultural or philosophical rationales for the transformation.
6. Once you have defined and calculated your measures of lifetime values, you can start the process of managing them and beginning to appreciate the full benefits of what can be achieved. There are two significant uplifts you will get from managing Customer lifetime values

upwards. These are, first, with yet another natural by-product of this process cutting in, you will find that the conversion to sale ratios are improved by about double. You can imagine the effect this has on sales costs. They tumble!

Secondly, you will find that, simply being aware of, and managing, the process of Customer lifetime values brings the in-built benefit of extending them. In many ways you have discovered one of the true purposes and uses for Customer-driven marketing. Now that the light is turned on and you can really see what's what, the argument for delivering Customer superformance – actually exceeding Customer expectations with every transaction and interaction – begins to make supreme sense. The debate which the oldsters love, about whether Customers deserve, or are worth it, just falls away.

7. Now the earnest business of prolonging Customer 'life' by keeping them deliriously, actively and constantly satisfied with your business, the service and values you deliver and the products which you make or distribute, should become a permanent quest which will preoccupy, even obsess, all staff. And this obsession applies whether they are Customer facing or not. Customer superformance is a benign and wonderful concept. It must take place at every opportunity and will bring prosperity, growth and profit to your business.

8. You are about to kick start your business into the next phase of its development in becoming Customer-driven. Those improved conversion ratios pay off with much higher incidences of cross and up-selling to your existing Customers – the easiest, least expensive, sales your business can achieve. Again I ask you to recall the experiences we shared earlier. I related how it was common for the cost-effectiveness of moving marketing spend away from 'cold' conquest or prospecting activity to focus on your existing Customers to improve by five to 15 times – an average of a tenfold improvement.

9. With the simultaneous effect of Customer superformance and our improved conversion rates yielding more cross and up-selling, we find the all significant share of Customer spend increases rapidly. This is a great loyalty builder and a great way of measuring the success of your loyalty work. For that is effectively what you are doing here – loyalty work. It's real. It's attentive to Customers and it builds far more for you than any disguised bribery via a simple loyalty club, programme or scheme. Why? It's because Customers feel it, experience it and value it. It's so much more tangible a demonstration of the way you value them and their custom than a few mailings and a sporadic dissemination of discount vouchers from manufacturers you have been able to do deals with or routes you are having a problem filling. Customers have been there and done that. It's called the past. Customers, experiencing the last few steps I have described, begin to realise that now what is hap-

■ Customer-Driven Marketing

pening is about them, driven by and for their needs, aspirations and desires – and it is happening in tune with their lives.
10. Now you will start to see the loyalty factor climbing to levels you would only ever have dreamed of before – if you had been ready or able to measure it.
11. I am just about to use the word natural again, to say that, as the natural result, you have a vastly improved dialogue with Customers and this will begin returning benefits to you. They value you because you have amply demonstrated that you care about and value them. The word 'natural' here is interesting because if you look at the chart you will see how naturally these steps fit together. Given that you perform and listen and deliver, everything fits holistically, harmoniously into a natural order. It is this natural quality of the process that gives it such elegance and that makes it as right for you as it is for your Customers.
12. With the dialogue between you and your Customers enabling discussion, debate and free exchanges about their needs and feelings and encouraging honest, frank feedback regarding your efforts for them, you now arrive at a virtuous circle of product and service enhancement. With openness abounding, debate and discussion taking place, you can 'sit' with your Customers and discuss the future. You can discuss what you are getting right and wrong, what they want and don't want, what their views and feelings are. This will yield a wealth of new product development ideas and activities. In turn you can ask Customers for opinion and counsel. They feel involved, heard and recognised. And you can discuss your new ideas for products and services with them.
13. Turning to the chart again, now let's observe what is happening to the right of the Customer superformance panel. Once you turn the spotlight on to amazing your Customers at every opportunity, exceeding their perception of service and value, you will find complaints plummet to all-time lows. This is good news and bad news! On the one hand, it is obviously good news, Customers are happy with you and what you are doing for them. On the other hand, it is bad news because complaints are valuable opportunities to build Customer loyalty. Time and time again it has been shown that Customers who complain, get a real hearing and then have their complaint resolved happily and satisfactorily, will demonstrate huge leaps in loyalty and word of mouth recommendation and referral. It's perverse but true! Never fail to take any complaint seriously and to effect a resolution which leaves your Customer totally in awe of your desire to keep them, value them and respect their desires and feelings.
14. As you manage the complaint figures down, notice how this contributes to a further reduction in your Customer loss rate (on the left-hand side towards the top of the chart).

15. Handling complaints efficiently and effectively, of course, gives you valuable experience in how to react to unhappy Customers. The more you learn, the faster you act, the better you should become at complaint resolution.
16. All of this, supported by the radically improving standards in Customer superformance, brings you another naturally flowing benefit. Moving back to the lower right panels of the chart, we see how, once we have started genuinely to work the loyalty spell, we can actually – if gently and sensitively – ask the Customer to help us. We can ask them to provide us with referrals.

    A very up market retailer – you would instantly recognise the name even though you may be at the other end of the world! – once told me that seeking referrals would be impossible and inappropriate for her to do. However, within 30 minutes she had worked the idea through, considered the possibilities and was positively bombarding me with ideas for gaining referrals, any of which would have landed her new business in great volume! Anyone can do it. But don't move an inch away from your core values when you do.
17. Then, finally, we gain the full benefit of what I described earlier as the cheapest, most effective advertising you can buy – word of mouth. These are the unsolicited testimonials with which Customers reward those with whom they are wholly content, those who get it right, leaving them actively satisfied.

Before we finish this piece on JFR's Customer loyalty model, let me ask you to notice one or two more things – these are positively magic qualities for your business and perhaps the secret of the success of Customer-driven marketing. At the beginning of this section I listed the outcomes as: improved brand performance; lower costs; and increased business efficiency. I'd like you to just look at the number of arrows which point to increased brand efficiency and equally the number which point to lower costs. And, for that matter, while you're counting arrows, it wouldn't do any harm to note that there are quite a few pointing to the panel 'less need for new Customers'! Also note that everything in the chart moves towards increased business efficiency. That's why I describe this process as benign, virtuous and holistic. It is as near as you will get to organic. It enhances the lives of all it touches. That is why it works. It simply returns the dynamics of the business to 'reset'.

## How do you measure loyalty?

Loyalty at its heart – what people do as opposed to what people say – can be measured by their ultimate doing: their buying behaviour. However, to limit yourself to this is like planning a journey by the distance. You

■ Customer-Driven Marketing

take no account of what the road is like. To get the full picture, we need to access Customers' feelings as well as their actions. The problem here is that Customers, particularly disgruntled Customers, don't talk to you, they don't share their feelings. British Airways, who carried out their own research into this, discovered that only 8 per cent of Customers talked to their Customer relations people about the quality of service whether their experience was good or bad; a further 24 per cent did share their feelings with someone but the information never reached Customer relations; and the majority, 68 per cent, didn't talk to anybody. (I think they meant anybody at the airline with that last figure.) My experience suggests that the happy Customers do talk to two or three people and the unhappy ones to four to six times as many. British Airways decided, as a result, to facilitate the process and encourage Customers to talk to them in greater numbers. This is why they set up Customer listening posts which included internationally toll free surveys, Customer forums held and attended by BA executives, and actually putting Customer relations personnel on flights together with Customers. Their data, after all, had shown them that for every £1 invested in Customer retention, they received £2 back.

In a similar way, I have encouraged a number of my Clients to develop programmes which reward staff for uncovering Customer complaints or grievances. It is important though that staff who uncover complaints also have the power to do more than just hear and sympathise with the Customer as suggested in Chapter 23.

Taking this whole matter seriously, British Airways then installed an image-based computer system to enable global access to Customer case histories and to eliminate paperwork; they re-engineered their Customer service process down from 13 steps to three; empowered their Customer relations teams to use whatever resources were required to retain their Customer; and they invested in interpersonal skill training to improve the handling of Customers.

Customer complaint handling is now a four-step process at British Airways. Step 1 is to apologise and get an individual to own the problem; step 2 is to resolve the complaint quickly – their target is same day, they see three days as the longest acceptable; step 3 is to convince the Customer that the problem is being fixed to stop it happening again; step 4 is to do as many as possible of the preceding steps by phone.

The following three figures are the results of a Customer survey carried out by one of my Clients. What they demonstrate is the tangible link between loyalty and the intent to repurchase: I see this intent as a valuable measure of loyalty.

From the three figures opposite, we can see that this Client was in an unhappy state and there was plenty of work to be done. First, Figure 24.2 shows that they were no different to the rest of the world. If they were

## The facts and fallacies of customer loyalty

| Satisfaction level | % definitely/probably buy again |
|---|---|
| Very satisfied | 95 |
| Satisfied | 66 |
| Less than satisfied | 14 |

**Figure 24.2** *Customer superformance guarantees repeat sales*

| Satisfaction level following problem resolution | % definitely/probably buy again |
|---|---|
| Satisfied | 76% (over 5 times 'dissatisfied') |
| Mollified | 34% |
| Dissatisfied | 14% |

**Figure 24.3** *Resolving Customers' problems is vital for future business*

| Satisfaction level following problem resolution | % definitely/probably buy again |
|---|---|
| Satisfied (30%) | 76% |
| Mollified (50%) | 34% |
| Dissatisfied (20%) | 14% |
| Unresolved (37%) | 21% |

**Figure 24.4** *Effective problem recovery is powerfully good for sales (as well as relationships)*

actively satisfied, 95 per cent of their Customers said they would buy again. Figure 24.3 demonstrates that a satisfied Customer is more than five times likely to buy again. Figure 24.4 shows that (bottom left) 37 per cent of their Customer problems were unresolved at the time of the survey. This is a frightening figure! Taking the 100 per cent whose problems had been resolved, 30 per cent were satisfied, 50 per cent were mollified and 20 per cent were dissatisfied. I suspect the 14 per cent of Customers expressing dissatisfaction were probably prepared to buy again because, somewhere earlier, they had enjoyed a different experience and this demonstrates that Customers do have a certain degree of tolerance. Or it may be that they don't feel that they would get any better anywhere else! The figure of the unresolved who would buy again, you will notice, is higher than those whose complaint had been resolved unsatisfactorily – that is plainly because a number of them were still waiting in line to become dissatisfied!

The figures in these tables were used widely within the organisation both to convince senior executives that they should invest heavily and quickly in their equivalent of a Customer superformance programme, and to demonstrate to sales and marketing people that a rapid change of culture, style and method was vitally necessary and long overdue. The picture was probably worse than stated here and as revealed by the survey. My experience suggests that these figures usually overstate the case of repurchase. In the US research confirms this: somewhere between 60 to 80 per cent of car purchasers, interviewed 90 days after a purchase, said they would buy the same brand again yet, three to four years later, only 35 to 40 per cent actually do. The moral is clear – stay in touch and superform at every opportunity. If the opportunities don't arise, create them.

## Measure the old favourites too

By old favourites I am referring to those measures that have been used, particularly in mail order, for three or more decades. They are: recency – when did the Customer last buy (also measure when was the Customer last in contact); frequency – how often do they buy; monetary value – how much are they spending; longevity – how long have they been active Customers; and, wherever possible, share of Customer – of the spend of that Customer, how much goes to you, how much to competitors and how much more there is to be spent.

## Finally, how far will they go to help you?

Another valuable piece of information is whether that Customer will do anything positive or negative to assist you. Do they ever pass on positive or negative word of mouth, are they prepared to give solicited referrals or testimonials? With these questions, you are deep into the heart of soft issue country. Often you will find that Customers are more open, more honest in fact, about whether they would recommend you to someone else than they are about whether they would buy from you again.

The vital part of using Customer satisfaction to measure loyalty is that you should understand just how high the satisfaction levels need to be before Customers display real loyalty. If you index Customer satisfaction from one to ten, don't expect a significant level of robust loyalty until you achieve beyond eight on the scale. From six to eight they are still vulnerable to competitive offers and propositions, lower than that there is no loyalty of any value.

## And don't forget the other three dimensions of marketing!

In my past, I have had active experience of the value of building loyalty from my suppliers. And if your business is using techniques such as supply chain management, you will doubtless already have identified this issue for yourself. Frankly to gear up your business to superform for its Customers without entering into the necessary close alliances and partnerships with your suppliers is futile, within a short period of time they will seem to be living on another planet. Talk to them, involve them, gain their commitment and support – their loyalty will build as you work at the problem together and you share the responsibilities and benefits together. Remember the power of praise. Businesses are much better at sharing negative experiences than consumers; however businesses are much, much worse at handing out praise than they are at complaining!

In his book *The Loyalty Effect* (Harvard Business School Press, 1996), Frederick Reichheld reports that the average holding time for shares by investors has tumbled from seven years in 1960 to two years in 1996. This figure underlines just how little companies do to create loyalty from their investors which has never been more vital than it is today. Organisations needing to cope with change and market turmoil need to clutch at consistency and reliability more than ever. Without the support and loyalty of your investors, thinking long term, or merely longer term, is a non-starter. Reichheld maintains that you can fish for investors who share the same qualities and ethics as your business in just the same way, I guess, as I have been saying earlier. You should match the core Customer needs to the core values of your business to get the higher quality, more loyal Customer. Fishing for perfect investors this way sounds a fine ideal to me – if you are a private company and can pick and choose to whom you sell your shares. Otherwise, it's going to be considerably harder. However, there is absolutely nothing to stop you investing in communications programmes and loyalty building activity with your shareholders – why shouldn't they, for example, be proud to own your shares as well as expect to make money from them? Equally, there is nothing to stop you using very similar devices as we have been discussing for Customers to analyse, measure and manage investor loyalty. Reichheld seems to suggest that retaining or regaining private ownership is the answer. Again, I think this may lack a little in pragmatism, but it is right ideally. If you can't, get to work with an investor loyalty initiative – but it must build the genuine loyalty we have discussed.

## And what about your people – how loyal are they?

Loyal staff breed loyal Customers. And a company that wants to superform needs super-staff. Super employees are not created overnight. They are never super on their first day. If things go right, they improve as time passes. Customers love the consistency, the experience, the product or service knowledge – and they love to deal with people who admire and are loyal to their employers. Customers take comfort in that, it reassures them and endorses their own good feelings or perhaps makes them see that their bad experience is an exception and that, therefore, the company are approachable and might want to sort things out.

Economically, building employee loyalty makes as much sense as Customer loyalty. An employer with a high turnover of staff will find recruiting new people and training them is expensive, just as recruiting new prospects and converting them to Customers is expensive. These are different sums of money, but both very expensive. In the same way that it is foolish to fail to build loyalty with a Customer once you have made the investment to win them, so it is also expensive to lose good employees once you have recruited and trained them. The development of employee loyalty is fundamental to the success of becoming Customer-driven and to delivering a sound corporate promise. The quality of your people is vital. And the greater the reliance on technology and computerised Customer solutions, the greater, I believe, the focus is on the people, the human element of our interactions. You must, therefore, only recruit quality people and you must recognise that such people take their motivation, satisfaction and fulfilment from far more important things than just money. Another virtuous circle of Customer-driven businesses is the recognition that people who have the propensity to be loyal employees value and understand loyalty. Nothing will give them more pleasure and satisfaction than dealing with and cultivating that same quality in your Customers.

So, we draw to a close one of the most important and significant chapters in the desire to create corporate miracles, to assisting your business to blossom and prosper, to building a successful future for you and for your organisation. Be in no doubt, those who understand and learn and become masters of managing the four dimensions of loyalty will be among the most sought after and valued in the business world. To summarise:

- Customer satisfaction is interesting to your business and will help you to understand Customer loyalty. However, ultimately, it is Customer loyalty – what people *do* as opposed to what people *say* – which is the true measure of your corporate success.
- The five strands of Customer loyalty are: in the logic area, price and product; in the emotional area, service and recognition. The fifth strand – delivery of the corporate promise – falls into both.
- Loyalty programmes relying on greed or bribery or ill-advised sales promotional techniques are unlikely to build robust, sustainable loyalty.
- The Customer-driven marketing model contains abundant miracles for your business. It demonstrates the virtuous, harmonious and natural fit of the strategy and processes and explains just how these all

## The facts and fallacies of customer loyalty

work together to further the brand while actually decreasing sales and marketing costs.
- The 17 steps to Customer-driven marketing clearly explain that you should do the following:
  — Use high focus marketing techniques to select those Customers with the highest potential for loyalty.
  — Align your core values to the sales process.
  — In turn this attracts a higher quality Customer with lower loss rates and enhanced lifetime values.
  — That leads to vastly improved sales conversion rates with existing Customers. Sales costs tumble as a result.
  — Being aware that lifetime values carry an inherent benefit you, start to manage and take responsibility for the issue and this results in an improvement.
  — The natural consequence of the above is that you commence a programme of Customer superformance which sets out to exceed Customer perceptions and expectations with every interaction.
  — Now cross and up-selling takes on a whole new significance to your business.
  — Share of Customer is radically improved and has a marked positive effect on Customer loyalty levels.
  — Your dialogue with Customers becomes more valuable and useful.
  — That leads to a virtuous circle of product and service enhancement.
  — Complaints reduce in number.
  — Your expertise at complaint handling grows.
  — The numbers of both solicited and unsolicited referrals increase.
- Customer loyalty is measured by Customer satisfaction; recency, frequency and monetary value; Customer longevity and word of mouth – referral activity.
- To be involved in a process of Customer superformance and loyalty building without the participation, involvement and support of your suppliers as well as Customers, is a mistake and will yield failures.
- You can and should work on investor loyalty. Working on long-term Customer improvements to your business is difficult without investor support and understanding. Investors will respond similarly to Customers when you market the business to them. Their loyalty can be measured in similar ways.
- The final dimension of loyalty lies with your staff: quality of people is key and loyal employees value and exude loyalty and will breed loyal Customers.

# 25

# Here's an instant marketing miracle for you to start now

This will not be a long chapter. In fact, it is short but very sweet. It is potentially by far the most profitable chapter of the book. For some it will be the most profitable chapter of any business book they will ever read. If your business is typical, I promise you the next few hundred words can return you at least thousands of times what you have paid for this book – and, if you are spending millions, then it could quite easily return its jacket price a million times over.

This is not a wild or crazy claim. It is quite simply the reward you will get from refocusing the way you spend your marketing budget based on the information you have already been given in this book. This is, with no word of exaggeration, probably the single largest marketing miracle that you can perform for your business. What you are about to read has, quite literally, enabled me to turn companies round. In one notable case, we achieved massive increases in sales which almost defied explanation while simultaneously cutting marketing spending by upwards of 40 per cent. Imagine what that did to the bottom line! And Customers loved it. Well, they must have, otherwise it wouldn't have worked.

You don't have to be incredibly clever or skilled to achieve the kind of results I'm talking about, but, on behalf of the business, it does take courage. It takes courage not because I will propose that you take any risks: simply, because people – marketing people or other senior management – *believe* it will involve risk. This is only because they have been doing what they have been doing, have been accepting that the activities of the past were right or necessary, when really, they were neither.

## Not so much new as forgotten

You already know what I am just about to tell you. There is nothing radically new: nothing you don't probably already feel in your heart or accept in your brain. It is simply that the time has come to break the habits of the past and do something different. If there is a difficulty attached to what comes next in this chapter, it is most likely to be to do with your ability to persuade and convince others to come along with you.

One of my favourite sayings was delivered to me during a course of NLP (neuro-linguistic programming). It is this:

> **If you go on doing what you've always done,
> You'll go on getting what you've always got.
> If it's not working -
> CHANGE IT!**

The only problem with this notion is that it requires us to accept that what we've been doing was not right, or, rather, was not the best way. What makes this harder to handle is that what we have been doing has probably been the accepted practice of your business – and 99 per cent of all other businesses – for decades. It's not just you that is doing it – it is nearly everybody else as well. And we all know the rest of the world can't be wrong! And yet, almost whatever you read or watch or hear at the moment is giving us all the same message. It's telling us that there is so much rampant change around in every sphere of business that success is less likely to be achieved by doing better what we already do; it is about finding timely ways to approach and tackle our problems and opportunities. Well, this is a timely way – for there is no time like the present! Yet unlike new ways, this thesis has already been tried and tested for us. So, when someone says to me, 'The rest of the world can't be wrong', I answer, 'Yes they can!'

That means all the smart marketing academics; all the text books; all the writers and theorists; all the fancy international advertising agencies – all of them – and, for many years, myself included, have been wrong! The only people who might have got this right were probably the same people we talked about at the beginning of this book. The one-man bands, the craftsmen and women who weren't doing it because it made sense, they were doing it instinctively. As I said earlier, the bigger we get, the harder we seem to make life for ourselves. And the more we do, the more we seem to seek outside help or advice, the more we seem to think, somehow, someone must know better than we do ourselves. Well, the fact is they don't, as the Focus Game demonstrates.

What follows is absurdly sensible. It recognises the facts of sales and marketing life and experience.

■ Customer-Driven Marketing

Grab your courage – this could make you a fortune. Or, perhaps, it could shift your career up several notches. All you have to do is follow these guidelines ... and convince the others that you're right. And sane!

## The Focus Game

Often, when I am invited into a new business for the first time I will sit with a marketing, sales or managing director and I invite them to play the Focus Game.

You can see before you in Figure 25.1 a cross with '25 per cent' in each zone. Underneath each 25 per cent is a missing word with the first letter in place so that you can fill it in. The figures of 25 per cent are for the game only, ignore them when you apply the game to your own situation. They simply allow me to lead you through a short series of thought processes which are designed to get you to think about how and why we spend our marketing money at present and what the effects might be if we spent it differently. It is, on paper, just a game. But when you apply the thoughts it provokes, you will save marketing money on the one hand and radically increase your marketing productivity on the other. I cannot promise the proportions, but I can promise the effect, as long as it is done well. The combined effect is a miracle.

OK! Here we go. In connection with the first (top left) zone, the word is Customer. And my question is this: do you spend more than 25 per cent of your total marketing spend on your existing Customers? Invariably, the answer is 'No'. Well, why not? It seems to me quite crazy that if global experience tells us that we will get five to 15 times more effectiveness from money spent on existing Customers than we will on 'cold' activity, then it is plainly not bright to spend most of our money where it will achieve the least.

In the top right zone, the missing word is conquest. My question is – do you spend more than 25 per cent of your total marketing spend on conquest or prospecting or new business activity? Invariably the answer is

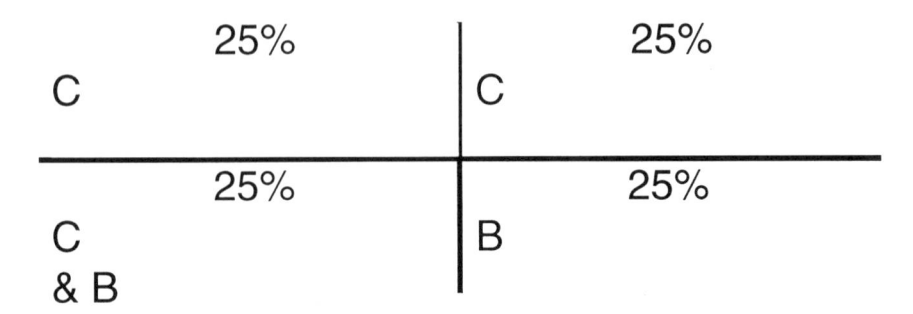

|  |  |
|---|---|
| 25%<br>C | 25%<br>C |
| 25%<br>C<br>& B | 25%<br>B |

**Figure 25.1** The Focus Game - Part One

'yes' and again, my response is – why? If our experience matches even the worst of the rest of the world, then by shifting, say, 10 per cent of our budget from this to spending it wisely on Customers, we would experience the equivalent of tripling the Customer budget.

Of course, this is where the big boys who frequent the peak television slots chip in with questions like, 'but what about awareness?' or 'but what about brand building?' I then ask why the two activities of prospect or conquest and Customer communications can't deliver brand effects. Of course, as we learned from the Marie Curie Cancer Care story in Chapter 6, they can. In fact they do! Moreover, we can pump them up to make sure they do even better than ever before. This is why the words missing from the lower left zone are 'Corporate. And brand'. And the question which accompanies this zone is 'Do you spend more than 25 per cent of your total marketing budget on corporate or brand issues?' And, again, the answer is always a whomping great 'Yes'. Yet again, I have to ask 'Why?' I can tell you the answer.

Your business, like something in the region of 95 per cent of other businesses, is running the bath with the plug out. All I am suggesting is that we put the plug in. All I want to do is get rid of profligate proportions of waste and really focus our marketing resources where they will do the most good. Most businesses are chasing round spending an unnecessary fortune on new business acquisition when they are sitting on a wealth of untapped business locked up in their own existing Customer base. Release this and not only do you put on business, but you do so at an incredibly low cost in comparison with completely new acquisitions which is probably one of the most expensive things any business can do.

Instead of complacently neglecting old and new Customers alike, and misguidedly setting off for more prospecting and more acquisition, we need to start the process of engendering growth, creating a bond, building a relationship, satisfying all the needs and building loyalty. And then we need to go on doing that for as long as possible. Acquisition (a role which, incidentally, our existing Customers are often happy to help with, but we fail to ask their help!) should be kept to the bare minimum to meet the business plan.

Oh! Did I forget to tell you what the word is for that fourth zone? It is BANK! For there is nothing else you need to do, nowhere else you need to spend. By refocusing to make sure that every penny works to its optimum level, you should have improved performance and reduced costs by, albeit theoretically, 25 per cent: but in practice it can be much, much more. So bank the difference!

Now you may not want to bank the difference! You may have much better ways to deploy your savings, but I ask you, how would your bottom line look next year with 25 per cent of your marketing budget added to it and sales going through the roof?

■ Customer-Driven Marketing

Let's go round that loop again. Let's look at each of the zones and really get to understand what the simple but rich suggestion is. We'll revisit this with a little expansion on the theory. We'll take the top two zones first.

While we do that, take a look now at the repeated model, Figure 25.2 The Focus Game – Part Two, and notice the bath which has been superimposed over the top two zones. You will notice the taps are in the prospecting and new business area, and the plug end is in the existing Customer zone. You will also notice the taps are both full on and the plug is out so Customers are draining out the other end. This is a really powerful visual image to work with while you are considering this concept. All you have to do to transform your business is to put the metaphorical plug in and then adjust the taps to the level you want. Or, as in some cases, you can keep the taps running and pull up a second bath!

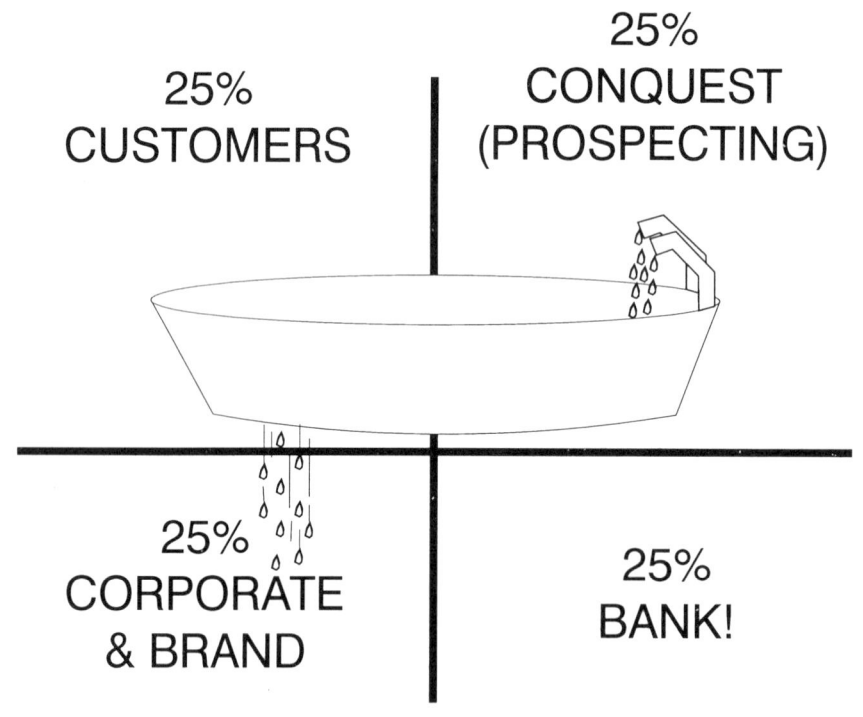

|  25%  CUSTOMERS  |  25%  CONQUEST  (PROSPECTING)  |
| --- | --- |
|  25%  CORPORATE  & BRAND  |  25%  BANK!  |

**Figure 25.2** *The Focus Game - Part Two*

## What we forgot to remember

Focus your thoughts solely on the top two zones – existing Customers and conquest or prospecting – for the next few moments.

Let's get right back to basics: in my recent book on the changing role of sales management in these changing times, I was reminding readers of something I call the Time Tested Time Test. It is quite simply one of those experiences or 'knowings' that has been handed down to sales people almost since selling began. In this form it is applicable to financial consumer markets but actually, if anything, it applies equally or perhaps even more to most other consumer, professional and business markets and anyone can adapt it to their own situation. It is basically a list, in descending order, of the most effective places you can spend your time if you want to end up with a big fat order book. To sales people this is one of those crazy things that we all know is right – but we have enormous trouble switching off that damn machine which seems to have been built in to us: the one that instructs us to seek out totally new Customers; the one that teaches us that a wealth of new Customers is some kind of Holy Grail we should head for.

Nothing could, of course, be further from the truth. Direct marketers proved it when they experienced those massive differences in response and cost effectiveness between their own Customer lists and those 'cold' lists they rented in. Sales people have experienced this across time and there are even jokes about the infamous drudge of cold calling. So look at the list below from a higher level. To professional marketers this reminds us that the further away we get from existing Customers the less fertile the ground gets, the harder it is to make sales. Here's the list – *The Time Tested Time Test:*

1. Visit and Review Existing Customers.
2. Other Visits to Existing Customers (Courtesy and Service Calls).
3. Family Referrals.
4. Other Referrals.
5. Orphans (Customers currently unassigned to sales people or intermediaries).
6. Lapsed Customers.
7. Other Corporate Leads and Promotions.
8. 'Cold' Activities.

As I said, this list was used by sales managers to help their sales people evaluate the focus or investment of their time and effort. Notice that it is only when we reach items 7 and 8 where we begin to step beyond the influence of Customers.

Here is your rationale equally for refocusing budget into those areas. That money moves across the model from the 'tap' side to the 'plug' side and, if achieved well, starts to put the plug in by increasing our share of the Customer spend, thus increasing sales and decreasing Customer attrition simultaneously. Now, and it can be quite suddenly, we find our costs decreasing and our business targets more easily achieved. Indeed, we are in the luxurious position of adjusting the taps to decide just how much

■ Customer-Driven Marketing

new business we really want. In many ways, I am as much concerned about 'share of Customer' as I am about market share.

Share of Customer, as discussed in the last chapter, is so much more revealing about how we are succeeding in the soft issues of Customer relationships – in other words, it is a handy measure of the solidity and value of what we are doing on the 'plug' side. Incidentally while, as has been discussed, share of Customer is a notoriously difficult thing to measure (particularly outside of the financial services business), it is also a powerful tool when used as a key performance indicator by sales management.

## Now for the brand and corporate issues: Zone Three

To return to the second circuit of the model, and to reflect upon the brand zone, it would be utterly foolish to believe that our brand, corporate or product work would ever be totally unnecessary because our Customer and prospecting activities were so brand conscious and so brand powerful. However, there is a strong case that money should in most cases be fairly drastically reduced in this area. Awareness and recall do not in themselves reveal precise information which reliably relates to sales. The power of what we might, for want of better words, still describe as the 'mass media' – by which I mean they cover slabs of our market *en masse* – can affect both existing and prospective Customers. The question really is how much more you can achieve when you strap brand work to other Customer or prospecting activity or communications. And the answer is you can achieve miracles! Some of this money is usually, therefore, channelled into the marketing effort in the top two zones of the model. Some slides sideways and becomes an element of the cost savings.

So, in essence, in this chapter we have discovered a rationale which can be quite quickly adopted to make us question how and why our marketing investment is deployed. With intelligent refocusing, marketing budgets can be made to work much, much harder, and this is done by finding new and different answers to the following questions:

- Why do we spend so little of the total of our marketing cash and resources on existing Customers when time honoured wisdom and many decades of experience by direct and other marketers guarantees us significantly higher returns?
- Why do we spend so much of our marketing money and effort on finding new business when everyone accepts that prospecting and conquest business is the hardest and most expensive thing we can do?
- Why do we not achieve significant brand building through all our Customer and prospecting activity and communications when these can achieve so much for so little cost and to such great effect?

## Part Five: Making your own miracles

# 26

# Checklists for success

One of the central themes of this book is that marketing can no longer be left just to the marketers. Marketing is now the concern of the whole business – no one can be left out, from the doorman to the business leader.

I almost wish that the expressions 'relationship marketing' and 'integrated marketing' did not have the word 'marketing' included. Yet unless we create an integrated process of advertising, selling, marketing and service which is focused on delivering one-to-one relationships with Customers, no business can become truly Customer-driven: these two are fundamental. However, this same combination of principle and process cannot succeed without the whole business believing and practising them. Marketing – the marketers or the marketing department – may sometimes be where the conviction, the belief, the initiative, the 'sell' starts – but where change must happen is throughout the business. Thus it simply will not work without the commitment and dedication and energy of the business leader. It doesn't matter what that leader's title is: it really does matter that they are prepared to reshape, reorganise, and reculture their business to dedicate themselves entirely to the Customer.

I have been working on these issues with my Clients now for a decade or so. It has been the most stretching, challenging and rewarding time of my life. But I must be honest. I think I have seen as many failures, or perhaps part-failures is more accurate, as I have outright successes. This shouldn't daunt those waiting in the wings. We can usually see quite clearly why ventures were less than successful or did not make the most of their opportunity. The old cliché proves correct again – hindsight is indeed a wonderful thing. And, with other people's experiences and experiments to observe and analyse, when we can learn from negative

■ Customer-Driven Marketing

outcomes or downsides, there is no reason why you need to follow them. Indeed, a while ago I was asked to make a speech at Management Centre Europe's Global Conference on Marketing. The speech was entitled 'Whether to drive your marketing by quantity or quality: a crusader's review.'

As I sat writing the speech, I created a catalogue of the failures and enormous successes I had seen in the past. It has occurred to me since that, for your purpose, it does not really matter what outcome your forerunners had. The successes can be seen as examples and the best ideas picked out. Other experiences can be turned to successes by learning the lessons that others have gone through for us. Let's just see them all as stones we can turn over and under which a miracle is waiting to happen.

Inevitably, I am about to summarise and reflect upon a lot of what has gone before. And for the closing sequence of this book that may not be such a bad thing. However, I want to encapsulate my thinking for you and to pull certain elements together. In my view, there is nothing you will read in the following that, if repeated, doesn't bear the repetition. Let's start with looking at why this book was written – and why I gave the speech I did at the Management Centre Europe conference.

## Why the crusade?

My crusade is an unashamed attempt to put marketing back on track. It is born, I suppose, from a megalomaniacal, arrogant, passionate belief that I have the answer and that most of the rest of the world has either got it wrong or is only just beginning to see it correctly. Correctly, to be quite explicit, means to see it my way! The crusade started in 1985 and will probably continue into my dotage. It is a consuming passion.

## What is the crusade?

Having been in advertising, sales and marketing for a period of more than 30 years, some years ago I had a mid-career crisis! I became convinced that marketing was over-obsessed with quantity issues and under-obsessed with quality issues. As a result, from a CEO's point of view, marketing was only helping businesses to 'run the bath with the plug out'. Marketing was returning a very poor ROI; leading businesses into short-term tactical approaches and thinking; causing businesses to suffer lower than necessary margins; and perpetuating inferior Customer service.

Remarkably, the global business world did not notice my mid-career crisis! Many businesses had started to accept that they should be market or marketing led. However, one of the most popular interpretations of this – mainly heard from marketing directors or marketing VPs – was 'do whatever Marketing say and give us even more money to do it with'. The extreme practitioners of this are now mostly out of business or under new ownership.

By 1989, I had become quite despondent that only a few companies seemed to want to follow me down the road of quality. Even though many wanted me to give rousing and inspirational speeches about it, they didn't actually want to do it. It was at this time that I heard Professor Lou Stern presenting the thoughts resulting from his work with Professor Phil Kotler and, as I reread his speech on a plane back from Johannesburg, I decided I now had concrete supporting evidence from two of the best minds in the business. They had, in effect, carried out a decade-by-decade review of 17 different aspects of marketing strategy (as presented in full in Chapter 8). Each aspect concluded with a prophecy for the 1990s. Now we can all clearly see that each of their prophecies has come, or is coming, to pass. It struck me deeply then, and cheered me on enormously, that 14 out of the 17 strategic trends pointed clearly to being driven by quality rather than quantity. Out of the way, quantity! HERE WE COME!

Maybe this crusade wasn't going to be so lonely after all. Maybe things were happening at last which would enable me to be re-enchanted with the profession of marketing.

## The transition story to date

These years later, it is fair to say that there is a business revolution going on and it is happening in some businesses around the marketing department, but in the more interesting ones, because of the marketing department. It is not only interesting, it is also great fun. There is nothing more fascinating, exciting and adventurous than running along the sharp edge of business practice experimenting with the future.

The business revolution you may be taking part in, or witnessing, is causing many companies and corporations to suffer severe headaches. But what is truly extraordinary is just how few of the headaches are actually occurring within the marketing department itself and how few of them have actually to do with what, classically, we have defined as the marketing process.

Here's where the major problems occur at the front line; in IT; in logistics; and with the Customer database. There are also problems in the boardroom and in the CEO's office – a point to which I shall, I must, return later.

Quality driven marketing, as we have considered several times now, works in what I call the 'soft issues' of marketing. It formalises and brings into the strategic spotlight those things which most effectively work to build and sustain Customer relationships as distinct from simply to sell. It

■ Customer-Driven Marketing

is quite common among my Clients to have formal marketing work or projects dedicated to such soft issues. They have targets. We measure and analyse our successes and failures.

Incidentally, let's remember here the point made earlier about measurement and Customer satisfaction. I feel measuring this, while often worthwhile and interesting, to be vastly overrated by management generally. This to me constantly proves itself to be an insubstantial and frail statistical measure. Just as satisfaction is an insubstantial and frail quality in Customers. It is easily shattered, easily withdrawn; easily transferred to others. Loyalty, however, because it must be earned and cannot by definition (or at least my definition!) be bought or bribed, is much stronger and more tangible. Satisfaction is fine measured as one of the strands of loyalty, but on its own, it can be rather misleading, if only because we tend to be self-satisfied with results that are too low.

## The key benefits of building quality-led Customer loyalty

Let me first run through some of the major benefits which I have seen accrue from a quality led approach to marketing which has a clear objective to cultivate, sustain and manage Customer loyalty for the long term.

- *Improved Customer service* – substantial lifts in loyalty here are the inevitable outcome. Often the whole notion of Customer service is redefined. It becomes an obsession to exceed Customer expectations, not just with every transaction, but with every contact. Only once have I sat with a group seriously considering that it was better to lower Customers' expectations rather than increase the performance delivered. Finally, they came to their senses!
- *Increased Customer satisfaction* – again, it is almost inevitable that significant improvements to Customer service yield significant increases in Customer satisfaction. Not always! One company I went into were busy improving services that the Customer didn't actually want in the first place!
- *Increased Customer loyalty* – as businesses shift away from the short-term objectives and practices of trying to set in motion a chain of single transactions, it enables them to get much closer to Customers and to have a deeper and more reliable understanding of Customer needs and desires. It enables those same businesses to recognise individuals, to respond to individual likes and dislikes, and to value and demonstrate its understanding of the individuals, families or organisations that are its Customers. Inevitably, this moves greater effort and activity into the 'soft issues'. There is a large emotional content to such work and when it goes well both sides feel good, and when it goes wrong, both sides feel bad.

- *Increased marketing effectiveness* – my experience over the years suggests that when marketing breaks its obsession with quantity and successfully addresses the quality issues, it effectively starts down a path which will enable it to improve its own cost effectiveness by up to 40 per cent. This can be quite a scary process for traditional or conventional marketers since they have to accept that the results of mass media brand building can be achieved in much more difficult, but much more cost effective ways. This makes their lives hell and does away with high exposure, lots of fun work and glamorous trips and treats. They have to roll their sleeves up! The pay-off is in miracles.
- *Increased corporate stability* - loyal Customers, the natural end product of Customer-driven marketing, display two valuable qualities which benefit corporate stability: they are much more consistent and much more predictable. In times of change – both discontinuous and continuous – and in times of market volatility, these two qualities have a greatly increased value. Indeed, there can surely be no safer haven, no greater shelter from the storms of the market place, than having the most effective possible relationships with your Customers, with your shareholders, with your own staff and with your suppliers. Achieve all four of these and you are about as safe as you can be. Loyal Customers are more dependable; they are more forgiving and tolerant (although I don't recommend that you challenge this too often!); and they behave very reliably. Again, the miracles abound.
- *Increased profitability and/or decreased or stabilised sales and marketing costs* – most businesses I walk into practise high activity marketing. As they shift over to a quality driver, we move them on to high focus marketing. High activity marketers are running the bath with the plug out. High focus marketing puts the plug in and works miracles. Among many things, it affords the luxury of long-term strategic decision making: we can choose between having another bath, a bigger bath or turning the taps down. High focus marketing also brings some problems. Politically, it challenges marketing directors and marketing vice-presidents. These people sometimes act as if there was some kind of psychological link between their egos or self-esteem which is connected to their budget or the number of staff they employ. They also fear that the improvements can't last and that the money, once it is redeployed, will never return. This is a valid fear. My experience suggests that, once the money is redeployed, it doesn't need to return.

These are some of the potentially substantial and significant benefits enjoyed by organisations which are prepared to let go of the traditional approach to marketing and shift into development and management of the soft issues.

■ Customer-Driven Marketing

Before we move on to the next batch I'd like to remind you of something I said earlier. It was:

> But what is truly extraordinary is how few of the headaches are actually occurring in the marketing department itself and how few of them have to do with what, classically, we have defined as the marketing process. These problems occur at the front line; in IT; in logistics; and with the Customer database. There are also problems in the boardroom and in the CEOs office.

As we move on to look at the next batch of miracles waiting to happen, I am sure you will begin to see why this is so. While you reflect on these things, let us also recall that, in advertising, sales and marketing, quantity and quality are like the North and South Poles. That means just about as far apart as you can get! The shift from one to the other takes time. I used to believe that two to three years felt about right, but my experience now suggests that this is not fast enough and 18 months is more appropriate.

## Batch two of miracles: getting rid of the inhibitors

I said that the transformation from being quantity led to quality led includes risk: it also requires radical change, experimentation, courage and faith. For the record, I have found that quality driven, or Customer-driven, marketing cannot work in businesses which have the following:

- *Command and control cultures* – businesses which are scurrying around following orders from the top cannot achieve the Customer focus or responsiveness required to succeed in a quality ethos. They are obsessed with upside-down values for these times and are generally too introspective, bureaucratic and Customer dysfunctional.
- *Centralised marketing decision making* – marketing and advertising as well as selling has to take place at the front line or as near as possible to it. Thus, centralised decision making of any of these three disciplines precludes successful work in the soft issues. For marketing and advertising, in the future, this makes a big difference. The task of the central marketing resource is to become a centre of excellence, the guardian of brand and marketing standards and a hyperactive training resource. It must also retain and develop and monitor strategy; indeed, this is a major obligation. None of these is easy when so many other marketing functions and responsibilities have been devolved frontwards. To achieve success, marketing must increase its ability to observe, listen and learn, and it must grow to be sensitive and skilled at the same time.
- *Lack of desire to re-engineer sales, marketing and service* – there has to be

corporate, not just sales, advertising and marketing, acceptance of the significance of Customer loyalty, Customer superformance and high focus marketing. These cannot be achieved by the old ways. These are enigmas to the old methods. Thirty years of experience has to be thrown out. The 'baby' and the 'bathwater' both need to go down the drain together. Everyone needs to cheer with full enthusiasm as they disappear, never to be seen again, and the 'plug' should go in the moment they disappear.

- *Separate sales, marketing and service teams* – to create seamless delivery you must get rid of the seams. It sounds obvious. It is obvious. Without multi-disciplined teams of individuals who take full responsibility for groups of Customers, failure is the only end result. Nothing less than an integrated process can be called integrated marketing: nothing less works to respect and deliver towards one-to-one relationships with Customers. Anything less is not integrated marketing. It is not enough simply better to rationalise or organise Customer – or, for that matter, non-Customer – communications and say that you have an integrated approach. You only have a semi-integrated approach. In some experiments I have worked on most Customer teams have also included other disciplines; for example, technical, product development, financial or production, sometimes temporarily, sometimes permanently.

In creating miracles, there is always a great deal of work to be done. Thus, some situations could develop for which we need to be prepared. The next list, and it is a long one, sets out situations or issues which have to be supervised or managed while you put your miracles into place. Hence, I have called it *'Your list of miracle enhancers and enablers'*:

- *The Culture Issue* – all managers at all levels have to realise what it is like to work in the new culture. Now delegation is often upwards. To some extent, the higher you are the harder it gets. Your only salvation here is that you can no longer get much higher. There is no height! The hierarchy has gone. But you can get smarter, more widely skilled and more accomplished.
- *The Database Issue* – for integrated marketing to facilitate a business to manage Customer relationships, it becomes vital that information runs 'from core to Customer'. The database must run from the strategic centre all the way through to where the business really happens – at the front line. It's a two-way highway operating in real time and has intersections wherever Customers may make contacts, or where Customer information – statistical or actual – may make a difference.
- *The Speed Issue* – businesses need to implement change with the maximum of speed. The biggest cause of speed failure is not that change takes too long, it is that the decision-making and the planning never

leave enough time for the work. Change programmes are often doomed to failure before they start simply because lack of vision and lack of courage extend the time involved with creating the vision and planning the change process itself. These become indulgences of hesitation and procrastination. Those businesses which have an inspirational leader, with strong convictions and a sense of purpose, will leap light years ahead of their competitors. There is more on this to come!

- *The Communications Issue* – all communications need to be handled with thought and openness. Referring back to the four-way marketing model, we can appreciate that communications with staff, shareholders and suppliers can be significant in a change process. However, the particular communications I am referring to here, which need to be managed and to have integrity, are Customer communications. They must be pushed into real time and they must make sense to the Customer and be fully cognisant of the Customer's current status and history. They must equally be in tune with the nature and style of the relationship. It follows logically, therefore, that control over such communications must be placed as near the front line as possible, preferably right at it.

- *The Prioritisation Issue* – Customer service standards should be corporately consistent. However, Customer perceptions of service levels vary and (this is an important realisation), they vary broadly in line with the Customer's value to the company. Customer priorities should be set along a 'cost to serve' rationale which develops the only permissible hierarchies in modern times – hierarchies of Customer service levels aligned with Customer values.

- *The Experimentation Issue* – one of the greatest accelerators of modern business learning is the recognition that an increased number of Customer sales and service units or teams is an opportunity to provide a certain amount less uniformity. In other words, there is a greater opportunity for problem solving, a valuable base for, and source of, experimentation. Sadly, I have experienced that, even where the need to experiment is accepted, methods are inhibited by fear of risk or an adverse attitude to it. What we are considering here is an attitude to risk. And we need to take more risks, otherwise no gains. Yet, even where managers are able to come to terms with accepting, even welcoming, the gain from taking risks, employees have an innate distrust and dislike of it – their experience over the years has demonstrated that what old attitudes define as failure is career limiting! The learning from both positive and negative outcomes must therefore be extracted and enshrined into new and successful business practice so that the benefits are seen and felt. The visibility of the gains neutralises the guilt and encourages the experimentation process. Above all, ensure the cross-fertilisation of shared experiences and shared successes.

Failure is a negative word and, when applied, so often precludes the adventurous and the innovative from the courage of taking initiative. To categorise people or events as failures denies that any learning has taken place, that experience has been gained and that some value, at least, can be achieved.

- *The Motivation Issue* – promotion and money, as motivators of employees, are now of increasingly dubious value. Managers have to find ways to replace them with personal growth and fulfilment and increased involvement in 'important' issues.

Forget what politicians tell you about 'full employment'. I get angry when I hear politicians of any persuasion, in almost any country, using those words. The hard fact of life in the new millennium is that unemployment is here to stay. Technology is causing unemployment faster than any improvement in a country's economy can create it. This will never slow down, it will only speed up. While, in human terms, this may give many of us reason to reflect on what we call progress and its toll – and what we think about politicians for that matter! – it is causing those who remain in work to re-evaluate what they deem to be career success.

With no hierarchy to climb, for the enlightened, greed is being driven out and it is being replaced by the creation of increasing value to the business. As time passes, this will also – to the delight of most shareholders – probably bring to an end what the popular press are inclined to call 'fat cat' salaries for the 'captains of industry'. Apart from a rich and talented bunch of genuine entrepreneurs, there are a talentless bunch of grey people at the front of many corporations right now. They are being paid as if they had built the empire rather than just found themselves at the top of it. This will shake out and settle back to the right money for the right people as shareholders and employees assert their views.

- *The Reward Issue* – I talked earlier about integrating different disciplines to construct and align multi-discipline teams with Customers. Often these teams have been motivated by different reward systems. Groups with common goals must flourish when they have common motivations and common reward criteria. It is my experience that, for example, bonus funds may be built from sales activity but distributed for the whole of the Customer aligned team against service, satisfaction or loyalty achievement. It can be 'paid' out as cash, but often much more imaginatively when reinvested in the individuals or for the team.

- *The Resource Issue* – corporations should only embark upon Customer-driven or quality marketing initiatives from the basis of strength, success and profitability. I have already demonstrated that the changeover from quantity to quality has many strands and thus it is very demanding of

■ Customer-Driven Marketing

time, energy and money. It therefore follows that the next issue is...
- *The Reason Issue* – businesses have to go into such complex and risky ventures for the right reasons. They have to believe in what they are doing; they have to commit to the long-term strategy. There is no quick fix here: the switch to quality drivers will not turn round or rescue an ailing business; it is little or no good for anything other than stress and increased work loads in the short term. The 'right' reason is generally a Customer reason such as developing continuously increasing levels of Customer loyalty by becoming expert beyond competitors at developing and managing successful long-term relationships with Customers – no less.
- *The Project Issue* – I remember sitting with a Client in Europe where we were having a project definition meeting to examine the necessary projects to establish 'state of the art' integrated marketing. We broke it down into no fewer than 40 major projects. With another Client, a Customer focus initiative comprised 84 separate but interconnected projects. Even when key staff are lifted out to dedicate themselves to major project work, I constantly observe other team members suffering stress and over-work through trying to achieve their normal day-to-day goals alongside all that 'vital' project work. This problem is now so widely present that I call it the 'Project Overload Syndrome'. Senior managers will need to watch this conflict carefully, recognising that the day-to-day work is the lifeline of the business for corporate survival in the short term, just as successful change programmes are their lifeline for the medium- and long-term.
- *The People Issue* – this has to do with making sure that those who are on-side move forward and those who are undecided or 'anti' move out. You have to be uncompromising about this. Change will only happen successfully if everybody wants it to: the moment you start carrying those who are undecided, or who will 'wait to see', then you slow the process down and dilute the team commitment. That being said, it is also vitally important that the right people are put into the right jobs. Sympathetic replacement of existing staff because they are existing staff rather than because they are right for the job is a dreadful inhibitor – often for them as well as for the business. If people are not happy with the change, they will not be happy with the outcome. Letting them move on in their life, to have the chance of working somewhere else where they can be happy and fulfilled, is the right answer. My advice, even if it is contentious, is to bite the bullet and do it, but do it sensitively and fairly.
- *The CEO Issue* – this has two manifestations: the first to do with gaining support, the second to do with personal power and leadership skills:
    - *Gaining support* – the support which must be gained is that of the often increasingly institutional – shareholders. CEOs who fail to

## Checklists for success ■

gain and maintain such support, find themselves exposed and vulnerable. There is no way major corporate change programmes, such as a shift from quantity driven to quality and Customer-driven marketing, can be undertaken without the understanding and support of this vital group. After all, as we have heard, things can get worse before they get better. The shareholders of successful businesses often do not see the need for major investments and risk-attached ventures. Things are going OK, aren't they? They have the dividends and the capital growth to prove it. 'Suddenly you want to retain some of it; suddenly you want to take huge sums to do things you haven't done before which may not pay back for five years? Why should I support you? And what do you mean you only have sketchy numbers to back up your case? What do you mean it *feels* like the right thing to do?'

CEOs need visibly to plan this element meticulously, to stay in constant touch with shareholders, keeping them fully informed. They must be clear about the long-term nature of the task at hand, the competitive advantage at stake and the costs involved. It is a constant reminder to CEOs that, just as the pressure is now on marketing directors or VPs to supply long-term loyal Customers, someone has to have the task of making sure that the business also has long-term loyal shareholders.

— *Personal power and leadership skills* – the new management style and culture required by the transformation to a Customer-driven quality marketing process needs actual demonstration from the top and huge amounts of powerful leadership. However, the leader in such a culture firmly believes in the old Chinese saying that 'the sign of a good leader is that the people believe they did it themselves'. The kind of leader who can usually fill this role is psychologically secure, confident, enjoys justifiably high self-esteem and has obvious charisma and personal power – not to mention is good at the work! These people have realised that leadership of a managerially democratic organisation is in itself a different skill which has to do with motivation through inspiration. I further contend that many leaders of today's Customer-driven businesses will agree with my belief that they have fundamentally to learn to make themselves totally unnecessary to the business but, at the same time, absolutely vital.

It is true that there are many – and some quite difficult – issues on that list which must be managed. However, the scale of each of the benefits they offer remains huge and indeed miraculous. The idea of sharing them with you was to highlight them for you: to prepare you. But you can be absolutely clear about which of these issues has the most devastating potential if not managed – it is the last on my list, the CEO Issue. To attempt a quality transformation without the heart, mind, body and soul commitment from a capable leader is almost a guaranteed, if not always

■ Customer-Driven Marketing

total, failure – particularly if he or she was not the original source of the initiative.

### Finally, a thought or two about solutions

I am learning more and more that solutions cannot be shared for the purpose of others using the same ones. More and more it becomes evident that experiences can be shared, but that shared solutions have less and less validity. Tailor-made solutions are the only ones which stick. They are harder to evolve, but much more robust when reached. I suspect that is why I am seeing increasing Client disillusionment with the larger management consultancies, many of whom seem to hawk round fixed ideas and fixed solutions; a number of them, it could be said, seeming to have been arrived at by pirating ideas from academics who are often either notoriously ahead of their time or notoriously 'head in the clouds'!

Don't be fooled. Where the action is happening is in *your business*, where the hands are dirty, where the sleeves are rolled up, where the souls are exposed, where the wounded lie screaming and where the heroes are constantly out there making a difference.

### So what of the future?

If you meet someone who can convince you they know the answer to this question, as much as you might want or need to, don't believe them. They can only be lying. The great business paradox of the new millennium is that consultants like myself are all telling you that you should be striving to get back to long-term values while experiencing that the long-term is a less and less predictable place to be. Despite this puzzling paradox, personally, I remain utterly convinced that the movement is right. How can I be so sure? Because to a lot of people like you, I am a Customer. And so, to a lot of other people, are you. As Customers our time has come. As marketers our time is up.

In this chapter we have covered much ground and many vital issues: – they can be summarised as follows:

- These major benefits accrue from a quality led approach to marketing
  — improved customer service
  — increased customer satisfaction
  — increased customer loyalty
  — increased marketing effectiveness
  — increased corporate stability
  — increased profitability
  — decreased or stabilised sales and marketing costs.

- There are certain inhibitors of a change programme designed to deliver quality into the marketing process and to become a Customer-driven corporation:
  — Command and control cultures which create contradictory dynamics with the change.
  — Centralised marketing decision making which blocks the move of Customer communications, and therefore the relationship, from moving into real time. The marketing department's task for the future is to become a centre of excellence, the guardian of brand and marketing standards, and a hyperactive training resource. Marketing should, however, retain responsibility for development and implementation of strategy.
  — Lack of desire and fully corporate commitment to the re-engineering of the sales and marketing process and organisation.
  — Separate sales, marketing and service teams which defy the delivery of seamless Customer attention because they perpetuate the seams.
- Finally, there are some enhancing and enabling issues which must be carefully controlled and managed in order to support and facilitate the change programme and process. These include:
  — cultivation, education and acceptance of the new management culture
  — plumbing the database from 'core to Customer'
  — having sufficient vision and courage to speed the shaping and planning stages of the programme so they do not detract in time from the implementation or delay its start
  — accepting that communications should adhere to the four-way marketing model and that, whereas all four dimensions are important, Customer communications must have integrity from the Customer's viewpoint, not just should they be in real time, but they should reflect the nature, style and state of the relationship
  — establishing the right priorities for Customer service levels per Customer. Levels can vary according to values. Standards should always be consistent
  — encouraging experimentation by turning the fear of failure into the joy of learning by enshrining the lessons into best practice as speedily and visibly as possible
  — understanding that human and team motivations are different in flatter more democratic organisations and that of decreasing significance are money and promotion; often increasing significance are involvement, personal growth and development and 'being able to make a difference'
  — groups with common goals and purposes flourish best when rewarded with common motivation and reward criteria. These in turn have to reflect the achievement of Customer objectives

## ■ Customer-Driven Marketing

- —corporations have the optimum possibility of success when embarking on quality marketing transformations from a healthy state and with sufficient resources
- —change programmes of this nature succeed best when they are initiated for the 'right' reasons. This means they are not a quick fix or a trendy gimmick, but a genuine long-term commitment to Customers and to quality thinking and activity. Strong conviction and desire build commitment and energy. The 'right' reason is generally a Customer reason
- —project overload is an increasingly frequent occurrence and the balance between investing people in the short term and taking them off-line for dedicated project work needs thought and monitoring
- —the vessel of change has no spare places on board. Uncompromising but sensitively handled action is recommended to make sure that the whole team are fully committed, passionate and obsessed by the desire to succeed. 'Don't knows' and 'maybes' dilute, damage and delay change and are a burden to their business
- —by far the greatest enhancement and enablement of Customer-driven change comes from the business leader: CEOs need to gain support from shareholders as well as from their teams. The long-term nature of the change must be accepted and value placed on the ethical and philosophical benefits to the business practices as well the huge profits and sales and marketing productivity benefits. A leader who is personally psychologically 'together' with high confidence and self-esteem will prove the most effective sponsor of change and will facilitate the progress democratically, believing that 'the sign of a good leader is that people believe they did it themselves'. Such a CEO will require that they become unnecessary to the business, but absolutely vital.
- Business solutions are becoming less valid and reliable for sharing and cloning for others. Tailor-made solutions are increasingly the only ones that stick.

# 27

# The should you, shouldn't you bit?

The road to Customer-driven marketing, as has been adequately demonstrated, is long, hard and paved with hazards and conundrums. However, as you have seen by now, it's a good road, a worthwhile road and, most of all, an exquisitely profitable road in the long term. All you have to do is get it right.

Well, maybe it's a tightrope, not a road. We're as far as we can go down the quantity end and we've got to get back along the quality end. Whichever way you picture it, the questions that must be in our minds now are: should we do it? Indeed why should we do it? How much of it should we do? What's in it for us if we do or don't? Let's consider the answers.

## Should we do it?

There seems little doubt that the business world, indeed the world at large, accelerated by the usual charming forces of human nature – greed, envy, lust and fear, etc! – seems set to continue along its precarious path, only faster. When you look at the power balance and the spread of material resources – the quantity and geography of who has and who hasn't – there is little short-term good news, globally speaking. So, as it always has been and always will be, life is full of spice, interest and intrigue. That's why, while freedom came to the Eastern Bloc on the one hand, the world was plunged into crisis in the Gulf or on the African continent on the other. History stands as relentless testimony to such trials and tribulations. OK, but life goes on. We marketers must get on with the job. So we must: but increasingly our jobs will have to do with the provision of safety and security. That's why it's important we understand that we can only deliver quality to our Customers if it keeps us healthy and provides for our own welfare and well-being at the same time. Quality is not a philanthropic issue; nor even at this stage a moral issue. In this context, it's a commercial survival and success issue.

The concept of four-way marketing lashed to the objective of relationship building is the practical formula which provides the vehicle I have unearthed for survival, stability and success. Thus we must look next at what is needed to build and nurture our all important relationships.

I maintain that there is little difference between the needs of a Customer relationship and those of personal ones. They're both fun, rewarding, satisfying, fulfilling and damned hard work to get right. Perhaps that's why, corporately, so many people are busy screwing each other – in the quality world, we make corporate love!

So what qualities must we supply to our Customers, along with our products and services, to build the relationships we need? The answer is trust, respect, integrity and affection. These are the nature of the ingredients which build relationships. Why should corporate relationships be any different? In my view, the more number-crunching, data processing and electronic transfers that go on, the more these human values will move into focus. The more robots, computers, machines and systems we devise, the more those things which win the business will revolve around the people. The electronics and the technology after all only breed short-term distinctions or competitive edges. In the long term they are levellers. Ultimately success and prosperity remain people issues. Importantly, it must be understood that quality is entirely a people issue. Quantity only builds immediate sales. Quality builds friends for your business. Friends yield greater quantities and for longer – arguably the biggest potential marketing miracle we can make.

## Reading the signs

You can see this already happening. Businesses, drowning under the expectations placed upon them by their Customers and pushed relentlessly forward by their competitors, are looking for friends, for people to help, partners and people to share and commit to each other. Customers appreciate those who get closer and more intimate as the service standards reach levels of excellence and customisation never before achieved.

Intimacy, getting close, even making corporate love, were not words or notions used in business a great deal in the decades of quantity. In those decades they called me an expert. Now they tell me I'm a guru. So is all this guruspeak idealistic lunacy or is it what's going to happen?

On that issue, I will leave you to make up your mind. After all, by now you know most of mine! All my marketing and management experience and the years of research and work that have gone into this project convince me that Customer-driven marketing is not a movement you can stop. It is a movement which will, over the coming years, obsess all honest, professional and ethical businesses. You can make your mind up about the rest, just as their Customers will.

## A compelling business issue

When I put myself in the place of a prospect considering two competitors, I ask questions. Of course! But I don't just ask questions about the product or services or back-up or country of origin ... I ask increasingly probing questions. After all, I want to be able to trust and respect these people. Finally, I ask myself this fascinating question:

Do I want to do business with ...

### A COMPANY THAT PAYS ITS PEOPLE TO EXPLOIT ME?

Or do I want to do business with ...

### A COMPANY THAT PAYS ITS PEOPLE TO SATISFY ME?

This is one of those questions to which you know the answer before you ask. It comes as a simultaneous bolt of lightening. It is a question Customers will ask in droves. They already are. That's why financial services people in Britain and other countries now have to reveal their commission levels with certain contracts. That's why, as an old-fashioned, commission driven quantity sales person, I would pray I didn't come up against anyone from Rank Xerox. You will recall from Chapter 21 that they pay commission to sales people but based on the levels of Customer satisfaction and loyalty they stimulate rather than on how much kit they can offload on to them. How would their competitors fare in answer to the two questions which preceded this paragraph?

You have no real choice about whether you accept Customer-driven marketing. The world will force it upon you. The questions are: when and to what extent? For as well as considering what accepting the Customer and quality ethics in relation to your marketing says about you, you must also consider what ignoring it says about you.

## Is a quality commitment and Customer-driven marketing good for you?

Perhaps this is the more interesting issue. Since we can see Customer-driven marketing is what must come next for selling, advertising and marketing, is it actually good for us – the marketers – or is the Customer the only winner?

■ Customer-Driven Marketing

I believe the answer is yes; emphatically yes. This is just another pressure to push us all down an inevitable channel. At the end both sides win. The Customer wins. But they were supposed to anyway. And the marketers win. At least the ones who get there first do.

I talked earlier of the 'quality lock'. It locks Customers to you. It locks competitors out. For that is the nature of marketing through relationships, not transactions; that is the result of satisfaction marketing, not exploitation selling.

## It gets worse before it gets better

We looked at three qualities that would be necessary to make the switch to Customer-driven marketing: time, courage and money. You need the money to invest in the reintroduction of quality standards, ethics and thinking; you need time to plan and implement all the changes that need to be made; and you need courage to do it and to stick it out.

The fact is that as you make the transition, things could get worse before they get better. This is why the ideal time to make the switch is from a position of strength and when things are going well, rather than as a corrective or panic measure in the hope of a boost to business. It doesn't, it can't, happen like that. Indeed, this is why the companies that have adopted the quality ethic in relation to their production or service base, and many have seen the benefits in productivity and performance, will find Customer-driven marketing such a natural follow on to Total Quality Management. What more natural way to take your quality product to market than through quality marketing methods! In fact it's a great shame there is such a wide gap between current marketing methods and quality marketing methods, since it pays no compliment at all to the valuable and valued efforts which companies all over the world are making to strive, first for quality and then onwards to perfection. It's such a noble ultimate goal. Why should marketing get left behind, or worse, left out?

However, this apparently simple change of process, concentrating on what we do *for* Customers rather than what we do *to* them, needs careful thought. For the managers planning change – Step 1, know where you are; Step 2, know where you want to be; and Step 3, understand the gap – quantifying the curve of 'decline-plateau-recovery' will be all important. Success will depend on critical analysis and control of these factors: if business will, as most typically, drop, how far will it drop, how long is the plateau, how high will it climb and at what rate or angle of ascent?

My experience suggests that there are other scenarios. Business does not always go down before it goes up. I have had a case where we managed a complex change process and kept business at the same level. And very proud of ourselves we all were! And, in one rare case, the solution included pumping up the old quantity way first, before instigating the change, since it was the only way we could sustain the momentum and keep the business in business while we got the miracles in place.

While the numbers and monetary values should be calculated and included in the case put to any board in support of Customer-driven marketing, it is important that the benefits are fully considered. That is not just the profits or ROCE (Return on Capital Employed) figures or whatever your yardstick, but the fact in these hard times ahead, that you will be keeping yours while all about are losing theirs!

I also have worked with one courageous business that decided to go ahead with the change programme I had proposed without any real end numbers to go on. They proceeded with a £39 million set of projects because 'We know it is the right thing to do. It brings our activity in line with our promise. It means we will live our mission statement'. I wish I could tell you that the business was flourishing. At the moment it is struggling hard. But its conviction is still right there.

## What will be the engines of the Customer-driven marketing movement?

I shall certainly be one! And so, no doubt, will Pip Mosscrop and his team at Collinson Grant and the many others who are acknowledged as contributing to my work. But what will be the key mechanisms that enable the changeover? I see them as follows:

- harnessing technology, the development of hybrids and the welcoming of IT people to marketing
- the acceptance of the need for, and provision of, Total Communications Management and moving communications control and decision making to the front line and as near as possible in real time
- the integration of marketing into a fused strategic process, the focus on marketing productivity, and the understanding of how and why marketing is a different mentality to selling
- the realisation of their absolute power by the Customer and their experiments with that power
- the overwhelming evidence that in the business climate of the immediate decade at least, quantity goals will do more harm than good.

## The need to make fast, urgent decisions

We started out together thinking about the information that the forthcoming years are years of chaotic change and with relentless rapidity. Certainty is a diminishing value. There is no such thing as safe, they say.

I disagree.

■ Customer-Driven Marketing

Safe is achievable, but it has to be worked at. Customer-driven marketing is the work.

Those companies that survive, let alone succeed, will have taken, as many of them can be seen to be doing right now, far-reaching steps to be sure they can weather the storms. In this context you can predict the factors which will build resilience and durability. They are as follows:

1. *Flexibility* – Can you reshape, regroup, replan, respond and react with intelligence and alacrity?
2. *Team spirit* – Do you encourage and reward commitment and effectiveness of both the corporate and Client serving team?
3. *Understanding* – Listening is not enough. Seeing, hearing, and caring are vital too. Is your company ready to go for share of market achieved by share of mind?
4. *Obsession* – This goes beyond dedication, commitment and service. Because the obsession is with perfection.

Also it is possible to single out the key elements for the survival of your business, those things which will unlock the Customer-driven marketing door for you.

1. Cultural – Can you transform your market and your ethics to the know-how and information based era?
2. Method – How soon can you restructure, re-educate and realign towards multi-discipline marketing?
3. Style – How fast can you successfully adopt a 'relationship orientation' complete with the prerequisite database capability?

Don't doubt the urgency or the critical nature of these, nor question the validity. Those who already know, who already understand, who already accept, are way ahead of you.

## Come on! It's miracle time!

Finding the marketing miracles is relatively easy. It's making them happen which stretches us. But when they do happen the effects are miraculous, not just for the Customer, but for everyone. Inside the business morale leaps; happiness, fulfilment and satisfaction soar; and commitment, energy and drive reach new peaks. These are businesses where it is difficult to get the people to go home at night as opposed to the kind most people work for. That transformation is a miracle too!

Over the years, we have already seen miracles happen in companies throughout the world. We have seen some of those companies thrive. And some years later, they went back to being also-rans. Just look at the

## The should you, shouldn't you bit?

helter-skelter ride of IBM since 1985. Brought to its feet by CEO John Akers 'taking his eye off the ball', it was reorganised and restructured into seven so-called autonomous business units (when it should have been 70!). Billed as the 'largest customerization in the world', costing $2420 million or $2.58 dollars per share, the initiative also knocked $1billion off IBM's expense rate and reduced the payroll by 50,000 staff. It further retrained and reassigned 60,000 people of whom about half were moved to positions directly involved with developing, making, marketing or servicing Customer solutions. I told the story more fully in the previous edition of this book, yet by the time the manuscript had gone through the publishing process and hit the bookshop shelves, 'Big Blue' was back in trouble again – global business pundits talking dramatically but earnestly as if it was about to sink without trace! Just for the record, at the time of writing this, IBM still exist and seem to be surviving. I expect they will still be around for a while! But whether they are on the way up or on the way down is what remains to be seen and probably depends on when you look!

So what does this tell us? IBM put themselves through the hoop, cost their shareholders a bucket of money and performed a miracle, only to find that they needed another one. This was partly because their initiative had some fundamental flaws and partly because, while they had their heads down getting on with this change programme for five years or so, some rat had snuck out, tippy-toed over to the goalposts and moved the damned things. Life had moved on.

Here's the point. Here's what the IBM story tells us. For me there are two real lessons: the first is that in business today, if you want to stay ahead of your competitors, you need one miracle after another. The old days where you could make a miracle and live off it for the next five or more years are gone, disappeared with the proverbial sands of time. In almost every area of an organisation, miracles – some big ones, some not so big ones – have been popping out of the bag for a while. If you are going to go prospecting for miracles, my advice is to ignore the old miracle fields which have been mined for so long and start looking for them where we know they're just sitting there waiting to be found; and where nobody has yet stumbled on any. It's still relatively virgin territory with rich pickings. It's marketing and sales.

The second lesson we can take out of the IBM story is that you cannot rely on the goalposts being in the same place when your change process matures. Just in the same way as you use your car headlight on dip for the short and medium view, every now and then we need to flip up to 'main beam' to check the validity of our long-term outcome. Otherwise the same goalpost-moving rodent might have tippy-toed out to confound you too!

■ Customer-Driven Marketing

## I've decided. This quality stuff is not for me!

Abandon hope all ye who feel this way. I beg you to take it as read that marketing must join the rest of the business world and embrace quality, not only as our approach to work, but more importantly as how we think about Customers.

The fact is that most organisations spend too much money on advertising and marketing. They shower money on prospecting which everyone who is honest knows is wasteful. It is as calamitous as it is ironic that it remains the conquest business and the prospecting which dominates spending and strategy, while returning the lowest possible value that can be obtained from the marketing unit of currency.

During the last 30 years, as a result of misguided and greedy thinking, marketing has become a high speed, high cost business. It is technologically backward and in many ways a decidedly inferior corporate investment. It will get worse unless you and I do something about it.

For many people involved in marketing, either in small businesses or at the other end of the scale in large, FMCG businesses, it is so easy, too easy, to lean back and say, 'Yes. OK. But it's not really for us.' To the smaller business I say this: we talked at the very beginning of this book about the craftsman, a one-man business that cannot see any difference between their craft and the Customer's need. Ask yourself why so many big businesses are trying so hard to break themselves down to become a network of organisations just like yours! It's because you are the perfect organisation to be able to get close to Customers, to work with them, to understand their needs and respond quickly. One of the greatest accelerators of the Customer-driven marketing concept is the envy so many people have of the effectiveness of the small business in these respects.

To the FMCG fraternity, I urge you to stay in control of your margin, listen to the real Customer, make your brand a (no!), *the* quality brand.

But, lastly, may I say something to you; whatever the size of your business, whoever your Customer is, however you feel about quality issues. I'd like to say thank you for taking the time to make friends with these ideas. I hope they'll serve you as well as the statement at the beginning of this book has served me. It has been my personal approach to business since I was grown up enough to have one.

Thank you for joining me on this wonderful, challenging and, I hope for you, provocative and stimulating journey into the minds of tomorrow's Customers. On that note perhaps I can leave you with one final thought. It's overleaf...

*THE CUSTOMER IS A HOLY COW.
YOU DON'T MILK A HOLY COW.
YOU WORSHIP IT.*

# Bibliography

Alder, Dr Harry (1995) *Think Like a Leader,* Judy Piatkus (Publishers) Ltd, London.
Barham, Kevin and Rassan, Clive (1989) *Shaping the Corporate Future,* Unwin Hyman Ltd, London.
Boot, Richard, Jean Lawrence and John Morris (1994) *Managing the Unknown,* McGraw-Hill Book Company Ltd, Maidenhead.
Champy, James (1995) *Reengineering Management,* HarperCollins Inc, New York.
DunnHumby Associates 'Use and attitudes to computers in marketing' (research document), DunnHumby Associates, London.
Forrest, Philip (1987) *Sold on Service,* Carlson Marketing Group International, Northampton.
Frazer-Robinson, John (1989) *The Secrets of Effective Direct Mail,* McGraw-Hill Book Company Ltd, Maidenhead.
FrazerRobinson, John (1991) *Total Quality Marketing,* Kogan Page Ltd, London.
Frazer-Robinson, John (1995) *Your Move – The Secrets of High Performance Sales Management,* L & M Group plc, Exeter.
Gray, John (1993) *Men are from Mars, Women are fom Venus,* Thorsons, London.
Hallberg, Garth (1995) *All Consumers Are Not Created Equal,* John Wiley & Sons Inc, New York.
Harman, Willis (1988) *Global Mind Change,* Knowledge Systems Inc, Indianapolis.
Harman, Willis and John Hormann, (1990) *Creative Work,* Knowledge Systems Inc, Indianapolis.

Harrison and Theaker (1989) *Dealing with Conflict,* Guild House Press, Whalley.
Heider, John (1986) *The Tao of Leadership,* Wildwood House Ltd, Aldershot.
Jaques, Elliot (1989) *The Requisite Organisation. The CEO's Guide to Creative Structure and Leadership,* Cason Hall, Gower Press, Aldershot.
Keenan, William Jnr (1994) *Commissions, Bonuses and Beyond,* Probus Publishing Company, Chicago.
Levitt, Theodore (1986) *The Marketing Imagination,* The Free Press, a division of Macmillan Inc, New York.
Lynch, Richard (1990) *European Business Strategies,* Kogan Page Ltd, London.
Naisbitt, John and Aburdene, Patricia (1990) *Megatrends 2000,* Sidgwick & Jackson Ltd, London.
Oakland, John S (1989) *Total Quality Management,* Heinemann Professional Publishing Ltd, Oxford.
Ohmae, Kenichi (1990) *The Borderless World: Power and Strategy in the Interlinked Economy,* Collins, London.
Penzias, Arno (1995) *Harmony,* HarperCollins Publishers Inc, New York.
Peters, Thomas J and Austin, Nancy (1986) *A Passion for Excellence,* Fontana, London.
Peters, Thomas J and Waterman, Robert H (1982) *In Search of Excellence,* Harper & Row Inc, New York.
Peters, Thomas J (1988) *Thriving on Chaos,* Macmillan Ltd, London.
Pettigrew, Andrew M (1988) *The Management of Strategic Change,* Basil Blackwell, Oxford.
Reichheld, Frederick F (1996) *The Loyalty Effect,* Harvard Business School Press, Boston.
Sveiby, Karl Eril and Lloyd, Tom (1987) *Managing Knowhow,* Bloomsbury Publishing Ltd, London.

# Index

ABB 54, 154, 156
above-the-line 42
accountability 269
added-value, notion of 223–4
advertising 20, 216–17
  above or below the line 42
  different nationalities approaches 64
  interactive 44, 85
  revolution 37
  versus word of mouth 146
advertising agencies 74–6, 191, 198, 199, 245–6
  choice criteria 203
  selection 217
  specialists 200
advertising power 45
Age of Quality 31
agencies 163–4
air traffic controllers (ATCs) 166
Akers, John 170
analysis based marketing 240
Argos 295
artificial intelligence 31, 45
asset valuation 291
AT&T 81, 109
attitudes 271–3
audio compression technology 109
automatic teller machines (ATMs) 76–7
automation 90–1
automobile industry 88

balance of power 291
banking service 77, 90–1
below-the-line 42, 103, 107
Bereza, Andy 44
BMW 44, 157, 162
board decision in organisational restructuring 291–2
board involvement in quality 34
*Borderless World: Power and Strategy in the Interlinked Economy, The* 60
Boston Consulting Group 81, 137
brainstorming 55
brand-building 63
brand equity 238
brand issues 203
brand loyalty 139–40
brand objectives 113

brand ownership 131–3, 136, 235, 236
brand understanding 64
brand zone 332
Branson, Richard 140
breakthroughs 17–18
  creating 19–20
  potential 18
bribery 33, 54
  and loyalty programmes 312–13
British Airways 154, 157, 320
British Broadcasting Corporation (BBC) 108
British Computer Society 158
British standards 182–3
British Telecom 46, 170
broadside array 296
Broker Brand 133
BS5750 31
business process re-engineering (BPR) 83
business revolution 337
business skills 156
buying behaviour and loyalty measurement 319–20

cable networks 107
cable television 88, 106, 114
cancer charity, case history 103–5
car insurance, case history 27–30
career risk and pay and rewards 288
case histories 18
CD-ROM 44, 45, 110
  market growth 45
centralised marketing decision making 340
centres of empathy 257
centres of excellence 257
CEO
  role in change 262
  role in organisational restructuring 290
  support role 344–5
change
  and prediction 41
  assessing the gap 264–5
  CEO role 262
  challenge of 261–2
  continuous 166

361

creating a vision for 264
creating means for 263
discontinuous 166, 167
getting organised for 273–4
implementation 35–6, 261–75
in marketing 50–1
key factors in managing 266–9
monitoring 269
new methods, new directions 36–7
openness in 266
origins of 155
planning for 154–69
present position 264
pressures for 155–6
programme failure 342
reason for 327
self-measurement regime in 265–6
steps involved 262–3
styles of 267–8
successes 268
support systems 268
versus status quo 51–3
Churchill, Sir Winston 103
classic marketing 42
client service team 246
CMT Direct 146
Coca-Cola 132
code of conduct 116
Cohen, Jack 33
Coke 66
Collinson Grant Consultants Ltd 261, 353
command and control cultures 340
commercial relationships 312–13
commission 32, 33
communication skills 73
communications 51, 250, 294–5, 306, 307–8, 342
  co-ordinated 129–30
  decision making 249
  equipment 163
  functionaries 246
  management 51
  present state 47
  revolution 51
  systems 293
  targeted 129–30
  techniques 85
  technology 87–97
  traffic jam prospect 96–7
company size 66–7
competitive edge 19, 53
compliance 32

computer disks 43
Computer Integrated Manufacturing (CIM) 80
computers 186, 246
conference technique 294
conflicts 271
consumer households, European Union 99
co-ordinated business functions 130–1
cooling-off period 116
corporate coronary 34
corporate culture 35
corporate deaths 20
corporate delivery levels 304, 305
corporate image 137–9, 181
corporate infrastructures 244–5
corporate issues 332
corporate positioning 181
corporate promise 313
corporate restructuring 35, 173
corporate stability 339
corporate strategies 125, 197
corporate structure 276
corporate survival, risk assessment 16–17
corporate values 271–3
cost effectiveness 180, 199
  and value 111–15
courage 182, 326
creativity 217–18
culture issue 65–6, 341
Customer care 85, 143, 151, 181, 230, 236
Customer Carelines 234, 236
Customer/competitor/channel orientation 127
Customer complaint handling 320
Customer delight 32, 35
Customer demands 231–7
Customer-driven marketing 141, 151, 155, 201, 203, 213, 219, 239
  benefits 351–2
  decision-making in 349–56
  implementing 200
  key elements 354
  key mechanisms 353
  model 314–16
  organisational restructuring 292
  preparation for 274–5
  prerequisite of 124
  qualities required for 352
Customer dynamics 126
Customer equity 238

Customer expectations  140, 141,
    149–50, 226, 231–7, 303, 304, 305,
    338
Customer-facing staff, grading process
    301–2
Customer fidelity programme  33
Customer-first decisions  27
Customer focus  27, 37, 50, 120
Customer gap  36
Customer information  175–6, 307
Customer involvement  234–7
Customer loyalty  33, 36, 55, 219, 283,
    310–25
  creating  311–12
  key benefits  338–40
  significance of  341
  step-by-step guide  316–19
Customer opinions  89
Customer participation  234–7
Customer perceived values  195
Customer profiles  48
Customer relationships  31, 35, 42, 51,
    55, 137, 150, 177, 200, 215–16, 229,
    233, 248–9, 279, 291, 300, 307,
    337–8, 350
Customer requirements, changing
    nature of  17
Customer response  27
Customer satisfaction  32, 53, 90, 282,
    338
  as loyalty measure  322
  creating  311–12
  measuring  338
Customer service  20, 87, 90, 128, 132,
    151, 181, 224, 230, 236, 338
  grading and integrated marketing
    304–6
  mini-hierarchies  245
  past  186
  versus number of Customers  91–2
Customer service units  245, 247
Customer Superformance  32, 36,
    149–50, 243
Customer value  303
Customer visiting card  148–9
Customer welfare  239
Customers
  existing  204
  feelings  31
  lapsed or past  204
  prospective  204
  representative  78
  versus system  30–1

customisation  248
customised marketing  126

data processing (DP)  75, 172
data storage  43
data transmission speeds  44, 115
databases/database marketing  44, 48, 50,
    51, 64, 74, 75, 141, 149, 175–6, 181,
    186, 213, 246, 249, 341
demassification  170, 173–4
design  128
Deutsche Bank  59
digital compression  108
Digital Postcards  44
digital programming  108
DIN9000  31
direct broadcast satellite (DBS)  107
direct mai  48, 85, 89, 90
direct marketing  43–4, 47, 50, 68, 74,
    88–9
  agencies  198
  global  51
DirecTV  107–8
disclosure  32, 238, 239
discounts  33, 313
Domino's  81
double glazing  32
Drucker, Peter  170–2
Duell, Charles  57
Duerden, Peter  137
Dunn, Edwina  71, 75, 85
DunnHumby Consultancy  71, 75, 85,
    156
DVI (Digital Video Interactive)
    technology  79

Eastern Europe  61, 62
economic forecasting  58
educational standards  182–4
electronic media  102
electronic publishers  100
electronic systems  57
e-mail  46
Esso  157
ethnic spreads  61
Eureka types  36
Euro-brand  63, 66
Euro-consumer  63
Euro-economy  64
EuroClient  63
EuroConsumers  64–5
Europe, cable television  107
*European Business Strategies*  63

363

European Community 63
European marketing 65-6
European Union, consumer households 99
Europeanisation 67, 181
excellence 25-37
experimentation 18, 51, 52, 342
external marketing 152

failures 143
feedback 272
fidelity bonuses 55
financial services 32, 95, 135, 137, 158, 238
First Direct 77
Fletcher, Frank 228
flexibility 60, 67, 250, 262, 354
flow charts
 marketing process 156
 sales 134-5
FMCG (fast moving consumer goods) 129, 235, 356
Focus Game 328-30
Forrest, Phillip 151
Frazer-Robinson Partnership 27
fringe benefits 287
future
 changing shape for 84-5
 global economy 58
 predictions 50-3
 shocks 33-4

Gates, Bill 79
gearing factors 279-80, 284
gender values 177
General Electric 81
global direct marketing 51
global economy 60
 future 58
global issues 151-3
global marketing 127-8
global village 32
global warming 59, 166, 167
globalisation 67
Golden Circles 65
granular marketing
 banking process 253
 culture 250-7
granular structures 243-57
 broadside 255, 256
 network 256
Gray, John 177, 178
Green movement 105

Grey Integrated 202
gross domestic product (GDP) 43

Harrison and Theaker 267
Heinz 235
Hewlett-Packard 81
hierarchies
 case for maintaining 174-5
 danger points 174-5
high activity marketers 218-19
home working 163
horizontal slicing 204-6
house-to-house distribution 47
Hughes Communications Inc 107
Humby, Clive 71, 75
hybrid managers 157-60

IBM 79, 81, 130, 154, 170, 174, 214, 232, 355
ICI 138-9
*In Search of Absolute Bloody Perfection* 130
*In Search of Excellence* 25
independent planning 201
individual behaviour 271-3
individualisation 34, 49-52, 226
individualised marketing 51
InfoBank 254
information systems 293, 295-6
information technology 57, 155-60, 175-6
 and marketing transformation 78-9
 research exercise 71-5
 skills 156, 157
innovation 52
insurance industry 27-30, 32, 35, 135
integrated agency 202-3
integrated marketing 103, 200, 202, 203, 298-309, 335
 and Customer service grading 306
 definitions 299
 'welding' process 307
integrated sales, marketing and service (ISMS) 298-9
 definition 298
 implementation activities 298-9
intelligence 213
interactive advertising 44, 85
interactive media 44, 110
interactive TV 102
internal marketing 53, 152
internationalisation 59-60, 181
Internet 44, 45, 65, 67, 79, 101, 108-11, 113, 115

Internet Providers (IP) 111, 114
Intranets 79
ISDN subscribers 46

Jacques, Elliot 174, 175
Japan 61–2
job description 286
job specifications 284–5
junk communications 96
junk mail 88–9, 92
Just In Time 82

Kaiser Associates 80
know-how 67, 232, 291
  as product 227
Know-how Bank 253, 254
knowledge workers 232
Kotler, Philip 117–19, 122–4, 126, 131, 194, 195

language problem 65–6
laptop computers 157–8
laser printer 48
leadership 173, 225–6
  development 294
  roles 164–5
  skills 345
Levett, Ted 122
life insurance businesses 158
local marketing 127–8
logical product/service line extension 95
loyalty
  suppliers 323
  see also Customer loyalty
Loyalty Effect, The 323
loyalty measures 319–22
  Customer satisfaction as 322
loyalty programmes 324–5
  and bribery 312–13
loyalty value bonus 148
L&R Group 234
Lynch, Richard 63

McDonald's 62
Magnin, Roland 281
mail order 44, 89, 96
mailing and mailing lists 47–8
mailing enclosing machinery 48
management
  integration 294
  re-engineering 19
Management Centre Europe 336
management styles 35, 160–2, 248

and culture 173
and structures 155
and values 272
Manila Bankers Life 89
margins, pressures on 180–1
Marie Curie Cancer Care 103, 329
Marie Curie Memorial Foundation 103
Marketing 2000 6, 70, 123, 146
marketing
  analysis of 123–4
  and sales 42
  and selling 117
  changes in 123
  effectiveness 339
  environment 57–69
  four-dimensional process 35
  four-way process 52–5
  future 123–4, 180
  new millennium 55–6
  object of 122
  optimised 173
  revolution 37
marketing budget 326
marketing department 67–8, 75, 159, 200, 290, 340
marketing miracles 20, 148
  creating 19–20
  implementing 354–5
  'instant' 326–32
  potential 314–16
marketing mix 125, 137, 196
marketing spend 67–8
Marlboro 66
Marriott Hotels 154
mass media, future role 102–3
mass production 67
media explosion 98–115
media growth 109–10
media networks 151
Men are from Mars, Women are from Venus 177
micro-agencies 164
micro-businesses 254–5
micro-hierarchies 245
Microsoft 43
middle manager, death of 171–3
monolith organisation 140
Moore's Law 43
Moscow 62
Mosscrop, Pip 83, 261, 353
motivation 271–3, 276, 279, 285, 343
motor insurance market 146
Motorola 81, 83

■ Customer-Driven Marketing

multi-disciplined teams 164, 341, 343
multi-national corporations 26
'My Businesses' 144–6

national branding 66
National Westminster Bank 77
NATO 165
Nescafé 66
Netcast 108–9
networks 79–80, 296
new marketing 122–42, 155
new markets 61
new millennium 55–6
new product launches 88
new technology 85
  equipment 48–9
newspapers 98, 99, 101
niche marketing 126, 240–2
  and retailing 228–30
Nielsen 107
NLP (neuro-linguistic programming) 327
Norsk Data 157

objectives 238
obsession 354
office equipment 32
Ohmae, Kenichi 60
one-man bands 26–7
one-to-one process 34, 103, 248, 300–1, 307
organisational design 270
organisational framework 269
organisational restructuring 290–7
  board decision in 291–2
  CEO role 290
  elegance of form 292–3
  impact of 293–5
organisational structure 243
outsourcing 68

partnerships 35, 54, 79, 165–6, 232
patron organisation 140
pay and rewards and career risk 288
pay per view (PPV) 102, 107
pay reform 279
Payless 143–4
performance monitoring 270
performance related pay 287
personal banking 90, 91
personal computers (PCs) 43, 45, 79, 110–13
personal power 345
personal relationships 176–7, 312–13

personalisation 48
personnel selection 214
perspectives, seller/buyer 36
Peters, T J and Waterman, R H 130
planned profit development 239–40
prediction 57
  and change 41
  and unpredictability 67
  for unpredictability 60
press 105–6
price sensitivity 180
pricing based on Customer perceived value 128–9
printed media 98, 102
prioritisation 342
problem recovery 321
problem solving 55
process diagram 156
process re-engineering 19
Procter & Gamble 183
product development 132, 180
product life cycles 53
product line rationalisation 127
product/market strategies 124, 196
product positioning 126
product supremacy through quality 25
professionalism 213
profitability 339
profits 353
Promotional Brand 133
purchase patterns 149

quality 25–37, 128
  board involvement in 34
  product supremacy through 25
  versus quantity 25, 26, 32–3, 37, 52–3, 350
quality businesses 26
quality commitment, benefits 351–2
quality culture 141
quality dedication 181
quality driven marketing 337
quality implementation 181
quality improvement 130, 213
quality influence 243–4
quality objectives 53, 238
quality standards 182, 184
quantity and quality see quality versus quantity

radio 105–6, 108–9
Rainbow Programming 108
Rank Xerox 182, 281–4, 351

# Index

Raphel, Murray  139
Ratner, Gerald  183
ready-made solutions  20
recruitment  214
re-engineering  19, 35, 83–4, 129, 157, 340–1
refrigerators as entertainment centres  49
Reichheld, Frederick  323
relationship marketing  103, 176–8, 202, 300, 335
remote control channel changer  87
remuneration
  changing systems  285
  politics of  278
  putting the package together  287–9
  strategy, key factors  285
Remuneration Map  278
Request Television  107
*Requisite Organisation: The CEO's Guide to Creative Structure and Leadership*  174
research industry  240
response rates  216
retailing  132
  and niche marketing  228–30
  growth in  228
reverse external marketing  53
rewards  343
  and corporate mission  277
Right First Time  82
ripple marketing  235
Robinson, Thomas Bernard  103
ROCE (Return on Capital Employed)  353
Royal Insurance  137–8
Royal Mail  70
Rubicam, Raymond  218

Sainsbury  133
salary increases  282–3
sales
  and marketing  42
  flow charts  134–5
  future methods  35–6
  quality driven  32
  revolution  37
  *see also* selling
sales managers  225
sales promotion  216
sales/selling, changes in style  221–30
Sapan, Josh  108
satellite broadcast media  65
schedule commitment  82–3

selective market coverage  127
self-managed unit (SMU)  295
self-measurement regime in change  265–6
seller/buyer perspectives  36
selling
  act of  32, 134–7
  and marketing  117
  as manipulative process  118
  changes in  116–21
  future  119–21
  mentality  118
  new culture  119–21
  preparing for new age  224–5
  three generations  222–7, 244
  *see also* sales
senior management
  energy flow from  37
  opposition from  37
shareholders' involvement  34–5, 53, 55
shopping  146–7
Silent TV Ad  87
six-sigma standards  141
small office/home office (SoHo) market  101
small to medium size companies  66–7, 79
socio-economic groupings  42
SoftAd Corporation  43
software market  48
*Sold on Service*  151
solutions  346
'spamming'  96
specialists  156, 232
speciality retailing  229
speed
  as management technique  80–1
  failure  341
  technique  81–3
staff loyalty  324–5
Stern, Louis W  66, 122–4, 126, 129, 131, 140, 141, 194, 195, 234
strategic alliances  130
strategic counsel  201
strategic mission for each product  127
strategic thinking  201–2
stress  234
success, checklists  335–48
Sun Alliance  137
Sunter, Clem  57, 176
supermarkets  33, 88, 146, 147
supplier relations  55
suppliers, loyalty building  323

367

suppliers/distributors as partners 129
supply chain management (SCM) 295
support marketing 53, 55

targeting and targeting criteria 65
Taylor, Stafford 162
team spirit 354
team work 163–4
  performance related pay 287
technologically advanced homes 87
technology
  and marketing 70–86
  Customer purpose 77–8
  development 52
  influence on future marketing 85–6
Technology Holocaust 70
telecommunications 46
telemarketing 85, 96
telephone banking 77
telephone charges 112
telephone marketing 109
tele-shopping 93
television 45, 98, 100, 102, 105–7
  future 107–8
television advertising 87
teleworking 46
Tesco 33, 132, 149
Thompson, Peter 202
time constraints 181–2
Time Tested Time Test 331
timeshare 32
Total Communications Management (TCM) 93–7, 129–30, 249–50

Total Quality Management 25, 27, 165, 281, 352
*Total Quality Marketing* 25, 34, 36, 53, 71, 80
traditional marketing 42
training and education 215
transaction marketing 192

umbrella organisation 140
understanding 213, 354
United Nations 165
United Nations Environment Programme 167

value and cost effectiveness 111–15
vertical slicing 204–6
video-conferencing 46
video mail order catalogues 93
Virgin Cola 132
virtual shopping 93
voice technology 46

Windows 95 43
women in marketing 176–9
word of mouth versus advertising 146
World Wide Web 79

Young, John 81
*Your Move – The Secrets of High Performance Sales Management* 288